THE ACCOMMODATED ANIMAL

THE ACCOMMODATED ANIMAL

Cosmopolity in
Shakespearean Locales

LAURIE SHANNON

THE UNIVERSITY OF CHICAGO PRESS

CHICAGO AND LONDON

LAURIE SHANNON is professor of English at Northwestern University and the author of *Sovereign Amity: Figures of Friendship in Shakespearean Contexts.*

The University of Chicago Press, Chicago 60637
The University of Chicago Press, Ltd., London
© 2013 by The University of Chicago
All rights reserved. Published 2013.
Printed in the United States of America

22 21 20 19 18 17 16 15 14 13 1 2 3 4 5

ISBN-13: 978-0-226-92416-8 (cloth)
ISBN-13: 978-0-226-92417-5 (paper)
ISBN-13: 978-0-226-92418-2 (e-book)
ISBN-10: 0-226-92416-5 (cloth)
ISBN-10: 0-226-92417-3 (paper)
ISBN-10: 0-226-92418-1 (e-book)

The University of Chicago Press gratefully acknowledges the generous support of Northwestern University toward the publication of this book.

Library of Congress Cataloging-in-Publication Data

Shannon, Laurie.
   The accommodated animal : cosmopolity in Shakespearean locales / Laurie Shannon.
      pages. cm.
   Includes index.
   ISBN-13: 978-0-226-92416-8 (cloth: alk. paper)
   ISBN-10: 0-226-92416-5 (cloth: alk. paper)
   ISBN-13: 978-0-226-92417-5 (pbk.: alk. paper)
   ISBN-10: 0-226-92417-3 (pbk.: alk. paper)
   [etc.]
   1. Shakespeare, William, 1564–1616—Criticism and interpretation.   2. Animals in literature.   3. Human-animal relationships in literature.   I. Title.
   PR3044.S48 2013
   822.3'3—dc23
                                                                      2012019392

When you are borne . . . you begyn to fele th[e] incomodities of the place, where you come to inhabite, the whiche . . . as it is to all other beastes accommodate, it is to you onelye, almost contrarye, and therefore wepinge is geven onely to you by nature.

—The Mole to Ulysses, Giovanni Battista Gelli, *La Circe*

If we impartially enter into judgement with our selves, we shall finde we are excelled in comeliness by many living creatures: Yea, of terrestriall creatures, that live with us. For, concerning those of the Sea, in colour, in neatnesse, in smoothnesse, and in disposition, we must give place unto them: which in all qualities we must likewise doe to the ayrie ones. . . . And that prerogative, which Poets yeeld unto our upright stature, looking towards heaven whence her beginning is, is meerely poeticall, for what beasts have not their face aloft and before, and looke not directly opposite, as we; and in their naturall posture descrie not as much of heaven and earth, as man doth?

—Michel de Montaigne, "The Apologie for Raymond Sebond"

Bowgh-wawgh! (*Burthen dispersedly*).

—William Shakespeare, *The Tempest*

CONTENTS

ILLUSTRATIONS

Color plates follow page 24

ACKNOWLEDGMENTS

I'm not sure whether this book has taken dog years or donkey's ears to write, but I do know it takes a pack to figure the reinforcements I've needed. I gratefully acknowledge the major support of the Guggenheim Foundation for a pivotal year of critical thinking. Northwestern University and Duke University provided me precious time for research and writing. For opportunities to test the legs of these ideas over the years and for helpful prompts and prods on diverse occasions, I thank Rebecca Ann Bach, Amanda Bailey, Bruce Boehrer, Russ Bodi, Joseph Campana, William Carroll, Lena Cowen Orlin, Julie Crawford, Tyler Curtain, Tony Dawson, Marianne DeKoven, Hillary Eklund, Kasey Evans, Jean Feerick, Erica Fudge, Kenneth Gouwens, Heidi Brayman Hackel, Jonathan Gil Harris, Bonnie Honig, Heather James, Coppélia Kahn, Shannon Kelley, Russ Leo, Michael Lundblad, Julia Reinhard Lupton, Madhavi Menon, Mary Janell Metzger, Barbara Newman, Wendy Olmstead, Frank Palmeri, Susan Pearson, Donald Pease, Susie Phillips, Peter Platt, Laurie Postlewate, Jessica Rosenberg, Manuela Rossini, Michael Schoenfeldt, Debora Shuger, Elizabeth Spiller, Joseph Sullivan, Mihoko Suzuki, Ramie Targoff, Henry Turner, Tom Tyler, Mary Weismantel, Will West, Cary Wolfe, Jessica Wolfe, Paul Yachnin, Patsy Yaeger and Julian Yates. At Northwestern, students in "Animal Letters," "Society and Species," and "The Early/Modern Animal" helped me think about how the history of creatures matters now.

For their kind shepherding through steeper passes, I remain indebted to David Bevington, Jonathan Crewe, Margreta de Grazia, Christopher Herbert, Cynthia Herrup, Karla Holloway, Karen Newman, Gail Kern Paster, Maureen Quilligan, Peter Stallybrass, and—many times over—Wendy Wall. I owe a special debt to my editor, Alan Thomas, for the patient encouragements he afforded me and for understanding why I wrote this book.

I thank the book's readers at the University of Chicago Press for their keen attentions and Randy Petilos, Mark Reschke, and Kathy Swain for their help in bringing the book into being. I'm also grateful to Daniel Garrison (Classics Department, Northwestern) for his collegial guidance in locating images from Vesalius. Help from Rebecca Oviedos (Folger Shakespeare Library), Joyce Edwards (Amsterdams Historisch Museum), Natalie Strasser (Collection Jean Bonna, Geneva), and Kathleen Daniels (English Department, Northwestern) proved essential. For permitting me to include haunting images of his *strandbeesten,* I thank artist Theo Jansen and photographer Loek van der Klis. And for their very kind permission to grace the book with Hans Hoffmann's irrepressible "Wild Boar Piglet" (1578), I stand forever grateful to collector Jean Bonna and photographer Patrick Goetelen.

Superanimate friends have swept me along my course with their creaturely splendor and hours of rangy talk. I won't pin a tail on the animists and theriophiles among them; they know who they are. Accompanied by loud, enthusiastic barking, I thank Sandra Alsante, David Baker, Lauren Berlant, Lara Bovilsky, Jim Chandler, Herrick Chapman, Liz Cohen, Mary DeAngelis, Leigh DeNeef, Drew Faust, Harold Gabel, Isabel Gabel, Steve Gabel, Jonathan Goldberg, Avery Gordon, Cynthia Herrup (again), Leny Jansen, the late Elmer Johnson, Mary Kelley, Patricia Leighten, Wahneema Lubiano, Vin Nardizzi, Alice Neiley, Christopher Newfield, Sharon O'Brien, Scott Radway, Charles Rosenberg, Marc Schachter, Irene Silverblatt, Maurine Stein, Marianna Torgovnick, Kate Torrey, Valerie Traub, Wendy Wall (again), and Gary Zickel. For their frolicking analysis and the ferocity of their humor, I especially thank Jay Grossman, Jeffrey Masten, Kathryn Schwarz, Julia Stern, and Robyn Wiegman. Nabil Abu-Assal remains my yoke-fellow in thought, as always. I thank Kurt and Judy Feuerherm: the property line between us was always obscure, but even blindfolded on a moonless night we could pick out that sure path through the Wellfleet woods to savor their peerless companionship. I will try to carry on the exacting eye and the imaginative arc of the late Maryla Nienhuis. Janel Mueller's erudition and counsel, her timely encouragements, and her lasting friendship have been an absolute tonic for me. I'm grateful to Kate Radway for the gift of her lightning perception and ready camaraderie. Susan McCreadie, my sister and cosmic ally, has always helped me keep my eye on the big picture and supplied unfailingly apt words, and I've been lucky to lean on her trusted arm. Brian McCreadie has "been there," for all of us. Pearl Shannon taught me to see that every creature has its own perspective and that it's not at all impossible to imagine what the view from there might look like. William Shannon showed me that it's only necessary to study a puzzle with sufficient patience and a workable solution will reveal itself. I hope my beloved parents see some fruits of their teaching—and how vital their backing has been—in these pages. I thank Jan Radway last and most. Her keen interest in questions of "kind," the gift of her thought and rousing queries over many years, and her patience with this book/my "beast"—along with a fine nose for what lies beyond it—have sustained the "wild braid" of my world.

To wag the tail of this accounting, I acknowledge (here, to humans) that animals have taught me some of the best things I ever understood. Reversing the sequence and denying the hypothetical of Derrida's musing, "And Say the Animal Responded," this book responds in part to the creatures who've addressed me. But, to them, a book presents itself mainly as a scent vessel—notes of wood fiber, tantalizing glue (apparently), mildew, smoke perhaps, or, in an ideal case, something illegible to us: the trace of a reader's hands. And so of course a book is a fecklessly human response to them. It recalls a scene Eve Sedgwick once explored: one creature points at the distant moon, and the other, with profound and studious goodwill, sniffs at the tip of the indexing finger instead. (To address this likely mismatch of attentions across species, Alan Thomas and the University of Chicago Press have had this book infused with a delectable scent that more traditional readers might not detect.) Though she scorned book reading as human folly, issuing colossal sighs of boredom as she waited for us to set the things aside, this book remembers Rosie most of all: a high-tailed Airedale who met the world with an open mouth; a creature of comic wit and alternative science; a riveting study in the leaps and arcs of *anima*, untied.

A section of my introduction appeared in *PMLA* 124, no. 2 (March 2009): 472–79. Parts of chapter 3 appeared in earlier form in *Shakespeare Quarterly* 60, no. 2 (Summer 2009): 168–96. The final paragraphs of my "Invisible Parts: Animals and the Renaissance Anatomies of Human Exceptionalism," *Animal Encounters*, ed. Manuela Rossini and Tom Tyler (Leiden, Netherlands: Brill, 2008), reappear at the end of chapter 5. I thank the Modern Language Association of America, *Shakespeare Quarterly*/Johns Hopkins University Press, and Brill Publishers for allowing me to air these ideas first in their publications.

NOTE ON TEXTS AND TERMS

Shakespeare's writings appear in their modern garb; throughout, I cite *The Complete Works of Shakespeare*, 5th ed., ed. David Bevington (New York: Pearson Longman, 2004), except where the First Folio is noted.

With other material, original spelling has been retained where applicable (with silent modernizations of u/v and i/j and expansions of orthographic contractions). Scriptural quotations are to *The Bible and Holy Scriptures Conteyned in the Olde and Newe Testament* (Geneva, Switzerland: Rowland Hall, 1560), except where the King James Version is noted.

When referring to humans I follow Montaigne, sometimes saying "them" and sometimes "us" in order to indicate the possibilities of an incomplete identification with traditional claims made in humanity's favor. I also sometimes use "man" to refer to the species as a kind. Figures of the human generally presupposed a masculine form, and I have not invariably adjusted this toward gender inclusivity. After all, the human status of women and their proximity to animals present ongoing questions of vast consequence for arrangements *among humans* (not my present subject). On the other hand, I often use the modern words "human" and "animal" in their current sense, even though this book hopes to set historical limits to a certain reckoning of "the human/animal divide." I agree with Erica Fudge's note in *Brutal Reasoning* to the effect that while "nonhuman animal" has a distancing and scientist quality, "animal" (however homogenizing) has the force of an appeal.

Creatures and Cosmopolitans:
Before "the Animal"

At least one human being was pleased when Charles Darwin laid out his case for a "community of descent" between humans and nonhumans in 1871. Noting how the philosophers had reckoned animals "nothing better than machines," author and alpinist Sir Leslie Stephen declared himself "glad to see the poor beasts getting their revenge."[1] Stephen refers, of course, to the beast-machine doctrine, forged in an account of humankind that generated one of the most recirculated lines of the seventeenth century: "I think, therefore I am."[2] Granting the free agency of thought to all humans and classifying the entire balance of creatures, from the oyster to the ape, as uniformly hardwired, René Descartes extracted people and animals alike from a longer cosmic inventory to face them off in an either/or metric of just two categories, or kinds. One was autonomous, a pure mind for which embodiment was beside the point and even unnecessary; the other was a mindless automaton for whom the material constraints of the body set an absolute limit on existence. While our perennial efforts to specify what is human show how hard it is to settle the question,

1. Charles Darwin, *The Descent of Man, and Selection in Relation to Sex* (London: Penguin Classics, 2004 [1871]), 43; Leslie Stephen, "Darwin and Divinity," *Popular Science Monthly*, June 1872, 191.

2. René Descartes, *The Discourse on Method*, trans. Donald Cress (Indianapolis: Hackett, 1998 [1637]), 19 (subsequent page references appear in the text and refer to this edition). Descartes's handling of species in the *Discourse* is detailed below. For a theoretical account of the consequences of the *bête-machine* doctrine, see Jacques Derrida, *The Animal That Therefore I Am*, trans. David Wills (New York: Fordham University Press, 2002); for a more historicist account, see Erica Fudge, *Brutal Reasoning: Animals, Rationality, and Humanity in Early Modern England* (Ithaca, NY: Cornell University Press, 2006).

Descartes's indelible formula tied the pair in a lasting knot of adverse definition. Few contemporary humanists or philosophers, for example, would deny evolution as natural history. But our continuing invocations of "the human/animal divide" and its more theoretical variant, "the question of the animal"—not to mention the nominalizations "the human" and "the animal" themselves—perpetuate an absolute sense of "the" difference (even when we are arguing that the alleged boundary is "blurred"). We keep relapsing to a categorical alterity at odds with the genealogical commons established in evolutionary theory. As vestigial traces of a Cartesian scheme, our habits of phrase still treat humans and animals as if they had sprung up on different planets by different laws instead of having evolved together in one cosmos.

Querying the retrospective horizons of our thought and expression, this book charts the creaturely dispensation into which seventeenth-century mechanism so decisively intervened. Two major resources converged to shape that dispensation: the rangy, encyclopedic archive of classical natural history and Genesis's spare but driving narrative of the six days of creation (the Hexameron). Like Darwinism, these traditions proposed joint origins in a common process that unfolded on a grand scale, while the staggering diversity that evidenced this unity was considered a marvel in its own right. Both traditions incorporate the major premise that animals are supposed to be here. A workable equivocation closed the theological gap between classical natural history and Christian doctrine, since either nature or God could name what one early modern historian of animals called "our common parent."[3] Well versed in natural-historical and hexameral traditions alike, early modern thinkers routinely understood a condition of membership and mutual participation to hold across species instead of simply stressing the "divide" our vocabularies reenact so reflexively. A bond of a very particular sort comes into view in this larger vision of belonging, and it offers a counterpoint to more familiar practices of boundary maintenance, whether biologically or ontologically conceived. For despite what contract-based definitions of politics still accustom us to

3. Edward Topsell, epistle dedicatory, *The Historie of Foure-Footed Beastes* (London: William Jaggard, 1607), iii (pagination added). (Subsequent references are to this edition unless otherwise noted.) Though he characterizes the conjunction as "awkward," Robert N. Watson describes how this convergence "made nature both the world God first created and a code-word for the elusive essences of things, and hedged on whether nature is a manifestation of the divine consciousness or a collection of entities with their own inherent properties" (*Back to Nature: The Green and the Real in the Late Renaissance* [Philadelphia: University of Pennsylvania Press, 2006], 325).

presume, a wide array of commentators invoked a fundamentally *political* idiom to characterize instead the state of relationship thought to hold among the world's creatures.

In calling this idiom "political," I do not refer to a general acknowledgment of power between humans and animals, but to a constitutionalist sense of legitimated capacities, authorities, and rights that set animals within the scope of justice and the span of political imagination. As the ensuing chapters detail, when early moderns describe relations between humans and nonhumans, they readily frame them in terms of polity. The polity they envision is sometimes well ordered and sometimes in disarray. They refer to rule and tyranny, liberty and bondage, obedience and rebellion, contingency and negotiation, and transgression and entitlement; they refer to citizenship. This unabashedly political vocabulary embeds within it the notion that animals possess their own subjective investments in the world, a point with its own kinetic ramifications and distinct from considerations of animal reason (a debate joined widely and with verve, on both sides, across sixteenth-century literature). Animal interests were almost never ranked as equal. But neither were they reduced to nothing, that categorical abyss from which Jeremy Bentham's comparatively minimal plea—"The question is not, can they reason? nor, can they talk? but, can they suffer?"—would later measure a hobbled advance.[4]

Setting animals within the reach of politics runs directly against the grain of traditional political thought from Aristotle to Agamben. It pays no heed to Aristotle's proposition that man alone is a "political animal" with an exclusive relation to justice, and it contradicts Agamben's gloss of "animal nature" as a form of being "without *any* relation to law and the city."[5] But the traditional relays excluding animals from politics (serviceable enough, perhaps, for most human conveniences) do not reflect the fullest sweep of our political ingenuity. Indeed, the political exclusion of animals and the phantasms of actual consent among humans that it supports obscure the way that political forms must entail some fictive leap of imagination.[6] Montaigne's language in "The Apologie for Raymond Sebond"

4. Jeremy Bentham, *An Introduction to the Principles of Morals and Legislation* (Oxford: Clarendon Press, 1781), 311.

5. Aristotle, *The Politics*, bk. 1, 1253a, in *The Politics and The Constitution of Athens*, ed. Stephen Everson (Cambridge: Cambridge University Press, 1996), 13; Giorgio Agamben, *Homo Sacer: Sovereign Power and Bare Life*, trans. Daniel Heller-Roazen (Stanford, CA: Stanford University Press, 1998), 105 (italics added).

6. As philosopher Thomas Nagel puts it in a game-changing footnote to his classic essay ("What Is It Like to Be a Bat?"), in contexts where evolutionary models of related-

(written in 1576 and published in the *Essais* in 1580, and a key text throughout this book) pulls no punches when he describes humans and animals as "fellow-brethren and compeers" (*confreres et compaignons*).[7] Shakespeare contemplates the claims and tenure of Arden's deer as the "native burghers of this desert city" (*As You Like It*, 2.1.22). Physician John Rowland's preface to the second printing of Edward Topsell's 1607 natural history, *The Historie of Foure-Footed Beastes*, calls on the strength of the hexameral tradition to assert that "next unto Man are these Creatures rankt in dignity, and they were ordained by God to live upon the same earth, and to be *Fellow-commoners* with Man." Rowland carries this claim for animal dignity to a strikingly unorthodox conclusion when he disregards the immortality claimed for the human soul: "Even one thing befals them both, as the one dyeth, so dyeth the other; so that *Man hath no preeminence above the Beasts*. All go unto one place, all are of dust, and all return to dust again."[8] One feature of this earlier dispensation, then, is its stipulation of cognizable forms of animal stakeholdership. Another, following fast on the heels of the first, gives cultural traction to a zoographically comparative measure of man, unleashing a skeptical spirit against his claims for "preeminence." Thus Montaigne wryly observes in the final paragraph of

---

ness are being acknowledged, imperfect knowledge across species cannot cancel its inevitable partial success. Imagination has its necessary place: "The distance between oneself and other persons and other species can fall anywhere on a continuum. Even for other persons the understanding of what it is like to be them is only partial, and when one moves to species very different from oneself, a lesser degree of partial understanding may still be available. The imagination is remarkably flexible." *Philosophical Review* 83, no. 4 (October 1974): 442n8.

7. Michel de Montaigne, "The Apologie for Raymond Sebond," in *The Essayes of Montaigne: John Florio's Translation*, ed. J. I. M. Stewart (New York: Modern Library, 1933 [French, 1580, 1588, and 1595; English translation, 1603]), 399; "Apologie de Raimond Sebond," in *Les essais de Michel de Montaigne: Édition conforme au texte de l'exemplaire de Bordeaux*, ed. Pierre Villey (Lausanne, Switzerland: Guilde du Livre, 1965 [1924]). Subsequent page references to both editions appear in the text. Montaigne's "Apologie" was begun in 1576 and first published as chapter 12 of book 2 in the first edition of the *Essais*; it is by far the longest "chapter" in the volume. It nominally defends a text from the 1420s or 1430s, Raymond Sebond's *Theologia naturalis; sive liber creaturarum magistri Raimondi de Sebonda* [Natural theology; or the book of creatures]. Montaigne had translated this important instance in the history of creatures at his father's request.

8. John Rowland, epistle dedicatory, in Edward Topsell and Thomas Muffet, *The History of Four-footed Beasts and Serpents [and] The Theater of Insects, or Lesser Living Creatures* (London: Elizabeth Cotes, 1658), A4r (italics added).

the last entry in his *Essayes* that even though we place ourselves "upon the highest throne of the World, yet sit we upon our own taile."[9] Steeped in the value accorded to creaturely variety in natural history and hexameral writing (and sometimes gracing it with the name of fellowship), early modern cosmopolity has room for beasts themselves, as well as a capacity to launch the species-based critique of an otherwise vaunted humanity.

To pursue the terms and conditions of this dispensation, *The Accommodated Animal* turns tail on the methodology implicit in Lévi-Strauss's unrebuttable proposition that "animals are good to think [with]."[10] (Given their primacy in category formation, it might have been even truer to call it impossible to think without them.) To read animals as tools for thought is to interpret what humans do, symbolically, when they use animals "to think with," and so it not only necessarily makes primary reference to arrangements among humans. It also replicates methodologically the appropriations and instrumentalities of the symbolic practices under study. This book asks, instead, what it has been possible to think *about* animals. As Donna Haraway firmly puts this threshold point for ethics and epistemology, animals are not just "an alibi for other themes" or "surrogates for theory; they are not just here to think with."[11] Thus this archive has occasionally required the odd defense of literal reading as a proper part of the critical repertoire: not all textual animals labor equally under the yoke of human symbolic service. Indeed, to assert the power of language to transmogrify everything into a common denominator of anthro-determination presumes the security of "the human" in the first place—even as that halting and defrocked figure haunts domains ranging from evolutionary theory to the cyborg landscapes of posthumanism. Haraway's neat gloss on Bruno Latour's *We Have Never Been Modern* proposes further (on biological, coevolutionary, and cultural evidence) that "we have never been human."[12] If *we* have never been human in the sense promulgated from the Enlightenment through neoliberalism, our language cannot have achieved some more impermeable and rigorous humanity. But for early moderns, who entertained the possibility that animals speak among themselves

9. Michel de Montaigne, "Of Experience," in *Essayes*, 1013.

10. Claude Lévi-Strauss, *Totemism*, trans. Rodney Needham (Boston: Beacon, 1963), 89.

11. Donna Haraway, *The Companion Species Manifesto: Dogs, People, and Significant Otherness* (Chicago: Prickly Paradigm Press, 2003), 5.

12. Donna Haraway, *When Species Meet: Adventures in Dogland* (Minneapolis: University of Minnesota Press, 2007); Bruno Latour, *We Have Never Been Modern* (Cambridge, MA: Harvard University Press, 1993).

with curiosity and interest, the nonhumanity of a power to signify would have been held obvious.

From the same cosmic vantage that sees "Fellow-commoners" when it looks at animals, the "Word" indexes divinity more than it suggests something exclusive to humans, whose Babel of confused languages were taken as vivid evidence of the Fall. At the same time, the natural world enjoyed its due claim to significance and signification. Romans 1:20 ("For the invisible things of him, that is, his eternal power and Godhead, are seene by the creation of the worlde, being considered in his workes") gave impetus to a "two books" tradition in which the Book of Creatures (or of Nature) and the Book of Scripture conveyed consistent messages. Indeed, the Book of Creatures made scriptural content accessible in a form better adjusted to the limited capacities of human readers and nonreaders alike. Topsell's *Historie of Foure-Footed Beastes* presses the point that "this History is to be preferred before the Chronicles and records of al ages made by men, because the events & accidents of the time past [may] never againe come in use"; the Book of Creatures reveals instead "that Chronicle which was made by God him selfe, every living beast being a word, every kind being a sentence, and *al of them togither a large history* . . . which shall continue (if not for ever) yet to the world's end."[13] Human beings, by these lights, could claim no monopoly on signification. And so this book has almost nothing to do with "animal imagery," a notion in which animals are successfully assimilated to human rhetorical, poetic, or literary control. Instead, it turns to discourses of natural history and creaturely embodiment; to theological accounts; to legal, constitutional, and quasi-legal models of language and its performative power; and to idioms emerging in the transition from the arts of *scientia* to the methods of technoscience, all in order to consider what one text distinguishes as "natural" animals and what— or what *else*—could be thought about them.[14]

The Eight Animals in Shakespeare

A foundational question presents itself, though in fact I did not discover it until my research was long under way. It suddenly dawned on me just how

13. Topsell, *Historie*, v–vi (italics added).

14. William Baldwin, *Beware the Cat: The First English Novel*, ed. William Ringler and Michael Flachmann (San Marino, CA: Huntington Library, 1988 [1570]), 20. I consider this caterwauling account of feline nightlife on the rooftops of London in chapter 4.

infrequently the word "animal" could be spotted in texts of the period and how critical that fact must be to any history of our thinking "about animals." The unusual term—automatic for us now and axiomatic for modern constructions (and deconstructions) of "the human/animal divide"— rarely appears in English vernacular usage before the 1590s.[15] Thus while *The Accommodated Animal* proffers certain defined critical frameworks for reading (zootopian constitution, human negative exceptionalism, zoographic critique, and disanimation), these conceptions are straightforward compared to that exotic creature-concept, "animal" itself. Between 1500 and 1800, we see the displacement of "animal's" closest cousin, "beast," and a meteoric rise in usage for "animal," their charted courses crossing in about 1675.[16]

The rarity of the term contrasts the ubiquity of those we conventionally shepherd into the enclosure of "animals" in Shakespearean material and early modern texts generally. The footprints all over this archive reflect the frequency with which early moderns encountered living and recognizably butchered animals in their daily routines. In 1542 Martin Luther's household in Wittenburg included, in addition to horses, "eight pigs, five cows, nine calves, besides chickens, pigeons, geese, and of course the immortal dog Tölpel, whom Luther . . . expected to meet in heaven"; John Calvin had dogs set on him by his opponents in Geneva and sometimes had trouble managing his horse; Shakespeare records his familiarity with the bursting energy of "youthful steers unyoked"; and Montaigne marveled at the "terrestriall creatures *that live with us*" (430; italics added).[17] As Keith Thomas describes, "In the towns of the early modern period animals were everywhere, and the efforts of municipal authorities to prevent inhabitants from keeping pigs or milking their cows in the street proved largely ineffective. The London poulterers kept thousands of live birds in their attics. . . . For centuries, wandering pigs were a notorious hazard of urban

15. *Oxford English Dictionary*, 2nd ed., s.v. "animal": "as n[oun] hardly in Eng[lish] bef[ore] end of 16th c[entury]."

16. "Animal" and "beast" searched in Google Labs Ngram Viewer, http://ngrams .googlelabs.com/ (23 April 2011). I am grateful to Alan Thomas for directing me to this resource.

17. Roland Bainton, *Women of the Reformation in Germany and Italy* (Boston: Beacon Press, 1971), 33 (for "the immortal Tölpel," see chapter 1); Peter Huff, "Calvin and the Beasts: Animals in John Calvin's Theological Discourse," *Journal of the Evangelical Theological Society* 42, no. 1 (March 1999): 71; William Shakespeare, *King Henry the Fourth, Part 2* (4.2.103).

life."[18] Humans and animals rubbed shoulders as "Fellow-commoners" in public spaces, with rich consequences for representation and the political imagination.

Beyond a daily engagement with domestic animals and "vermin," a host of textual resources appeared. The lively bestiary tradition, with its inventory of attributes (the elephant's memory, the peacock's pride, the dog's loyalty, the rabbit's fearfulness, the fox's cunning, and so on) and classical natural histories such as Pliny's *Historia naturalis* (ca. 77 AD) (read in Latin and new vernacular translations and universally tapped for animal lore) offered a rich archive, making even exotic animals familiar. So did the explosion in husbandry and hunting manuals (often translated from medieval and contemporary European texts) and a wave of natural history writing (fueled by colonialism and the concatenated rise of a "science of description").[19] Both ordinary observation and diverse forms of reading, then, made the repertoire of early modern representation "zoo-topian"—not (or not necessarily) a utopia for animals, but a place well populated with them and marked by a more pervasive cognizance of their presence than modern Western culture largely affords.

As a result, period idioms are also more broadly zoographic than ours. By "zoography," I refer to the way early modern writing insists on animal reference and cross-species comparison, while at the same time it proceeds from a cosmological framework in which the sheer diversity of creaturely life is so finely articulated, whether as a "great chain" of being or as an indication of nature's virtuosity. In other words, early modern culture is less provincially human than ours. Among Shakespeare's casts, we find Crab, the shaggy cur in *Two Gentlemen of Verona*; the notorious stage direction in *The Winter's Tale* ("Exit, pursued by a bear" [3.3.57]); and the dogs in *The Tempest*, sounding their "bow-wow" as a "burden, dispersedly" to Ariel's song (1.2.385). And if we tried to number all of the animal kinds Shakespeare mentions—the winter lion, Hyrcanian tiger, and baited bear; the little shrew and the necessary cat; bottled spiders and horned toads; brave harts and gentle hinds; the forward horse and preposterous ass; the temple-haunting martlet, morning lark, nightly owl, and winging crow; the nibbling sheep and hunger-starved

18. Keith Thomas, *Man and the Natural World: Changing Attitudes in England, 1500–1800* (Oxford: Oxford University Press, 1996 [1983]), 95. Most recently, see also Andreas Höfele, *Stage, Stake, and Scaffold: Humans and Animals in Shakespear's Theatre* (New York: Oxford University Press, 2011).

19. Brian Ogilvie, *The Science of Describing: Natural History in Renaissance Europe* (Chicago: University of Chicago Press, 2006).

wolves; the chafed boar, princely palfrey, fat oxen, and spotted leopards; stranger curs, mastiffs, hellhounds, and so on—we would be, as the saying goes, herding cats. But the word "animal" itself appears only eight times across the entire landscape of Shakespeare's works.

Shakespeare's practice on this point of nomenclature tilts overwhelmingly against "animal." By contrast, he recorded the terms "beast" 141 times and "creature" 127 times.[20] How does the early modern scarcity of this generic, collective noun shed light on present ways of framing the forms of life, idioms depending so heavily on a dualistic logic of human and animal? Also at stake is when and why it became conventional to speak using the radically departicularizing and inevitably grandiose nominalized adjectives "*the* human" and "*the* animal," where humanity refers to some positive attribute, however slippery (language, a soul, existential possibility, tool use, shame, and so forth) and animality to some corresponding deficit or privation that sets its signature feature. The category of "the animal"—a gross homogenization or "general singular" whose "bêtise" Derrida derides with wit and force—and the particularly binary "human/ animal divide" it serves are creatures of a later modernity and the lingering philosophical stagecraft of its Enlightenment inheritance.[21]

To put it in the broadest terms: before the *cogito*, there was nothing exactly comparable to "*the* animal" or, to borrow a rich phrase from Bar-

20. Martin Spevack, *The Harvard Concordance to Shakespeare* (Cambridge, MA: Belknap Press, 1973), 96–97, 250–51. I am grateful to Eric Wirth and Sara Seten Berhausen for their help with this accounting. "Creature" is the broadest term; "beast" is the narrowest. And, by all three, Shakespeare sometimes denotes humans and sometimes nonhuman animals. In comparison, the 1653 English translation of William Harvey's 1628 *Exercitatio anatomica de motu cordis et sanguinis in animalibus* [An anatomical exercise on the motion of the heart and blood in living beings] renders the *animalibus* of the title—as well as about half of the iterations of "animal" in the text—as "Living Beings," living creatures, or some variation on that phrase. For Harvey's anonymous translator, the English word "animal" did not necessarily serve for the *animalia* of Harvey's Latin. For a discussion, see Laurie Shannon, "Invisible Parts: Renaissance Anatomies of Human Exceptionalism," in *Animal Encounters*, ed. Manuela Rossini and Tom Tyler (Leiden, Netherlands: Brill, 2008), 149–50. For Montaigne, *bête* far outstrips both "animal" and "creature." See Roy Leake, *Concordance des essais de Montaigne*, 2 vols. (Geneva, Switzerland: Droz, 1981), 1:61, 156–57, 297. I am grateful to Marc Schachter for helping me with this data.

21. "This agreement concerning philosophical sense and common sense that allows one to speak blithely of the Animal in the general singular is perhaps one of the greatest and most symptomatic asinanities of those who call themselves humans." Derrida, *The Animal That Therefore I Am*, 41.

bara Herrnstein Smith, *"the ontological thrill* of the animal" that would develop in and for modernity.[22] There were creatures. There were brutes, and there were beasts. There were fish and fowl. There were living things. There were humans, who participated in "animal nature" and experienced the same material and humoral conditions of life as animals did. As Gail Kern Paster demonstrates, this understanding made "identification across the species barrier" routine for early moderns; because of a substrate of substantial likeness, such an identification cannot be described as anthropomorphism.[23] These humans were measured as much in contradistinction to angels as to animals, taking their place within a larger cosmography, constitution, or even "world picture" (scaled from the stars and the heavens down to elements and atoms). None of these classifications lines up with the fundamentally modern sense of *"the* animal" or even "animals" as humanity's persistently ontological foil.

In early modern English, the commonest phrasings take a more elaborate census. When one subcategory of what we call animals was intended, "beast" often serves, as Shakespeare's data shows. But "beast" offers no synonym for the modern "animal," because "beast" intends neither fish nor fowl, but a quadruped (often livestock). A list appears, instead of a single collective word, to denote more than one subcategory of animals. To give a Shakespearean instance: "We cannot live on grass, on berries, water, / As beasts and birdes and fishes" (*Timon*, 4.3.427–28). This litany of kinds draws its rhythms, of course, from Scripture; in English translations of Genesis we find "the fish of the sea," "the foule of the heaven," and "the beast of the fielde" (Gen. 1:26–30, 2:19–20). These hexameral phrasings further incorporate a sense of quasi-proprietary domains or proper spheres of action for diverse kinds (putting special pressure on relations between humans and quadrupeds, as we will see in chapters 2 and 4, because their assigned domains overlap). Then there is the consequential grant made to

22. Barbara Herrnstein Smith, "Animal Relatives, Difficult Relations," *differences* 15, no. 1 (2004): 5 (italics in original).

23. Gail Kern Paster, *Humoring the Body: Emotions and the Shakespearean Stage* (Chicago: University of Chicago Press, 2004), 150, 145n30. Although he analyzes randomness in Lucretius's theory of an "aleatory swerve" rather than the more piloted locomotion I consider in chapter 2, Jonathan Goldberg's treatment of early modern atomism likewise stresses a bedrock sameness for material things (composed of like atomic "stuff"); he also reads period theorizations of nonhuman activity as philosophically consequential. Jonathan Goldberg, *The Seeds of Things: Theorizing Sexuality and Materiality in Renaissance Representations* (New York: Fordham University Press, 2009), 5–6, 125.

animals in Genesis concerning their sustenance, a provision whose period effects have been largely unattended: "Likewise to every beast of the earth, and to every foule of the heaven, and to every thing that moveth upon the earth, which hath life in it selfe, every greene herbe shall be for meate" (Gen. 1:30) (chapters 1 and 5 detail the historical force of this provision). Creaturely inventories in the vernacular bibles and homilies of the Reformation reinforced a traditionally expansive cosmic census: they attentively noted the presence of other creatures by listing them.

When a higher level of generality is sought, scripture again plays a role. As Julia Reinhard Lupton has shown, the overarching category of the creature had profound philosophical and theological implications.[24] Early modern Genesis makes countless collective references of this kind, supplying terms such as "creatures," "living things," or "living beings."[25] For example: "God spake . . . to Noah . . . saying, Behold . . . I establish my covenant with you, and with your seede after you, And with *every living creature* that is with you, with the foule, with the cattell, and with every beast of the earth with you, from all that goe out of the Arke" (Gen. 9:8–10; italics added). This passage uses the general "creatures" nomenclature *plus* the enumerative approach to representing animals, a form of legalistic variation that suits the quasi contract being made. With characteristic period emphasis, when "creature" appears in these influential texts, it is commonly intensified by "every," as here. The word "animal," however, never appears in the benchmark English of the Great Bible (1539), the Geneva Bible (1560), or the King James Version (1611). And so the noun in my title springs from a modern idiom. But its odd bird of an adjective, "accommodated," speaks a more obsolete language to pick up the thread from this eclipsed dispensation that I most hope to restore to our archives of creaturely life and the histories we tell of it.

Trials of Membership: Montaigne versus Descartes

What does it mean to be "accommodated"? The natural-historical and hexameral traditions both speak directly to this condition. The overarching

---

24. Julia Reinhard Lupton, "Creature Caliban," *Shakespeare Quarterly* 51 (2000): 1–23.

25. This shows its relative precision compared with modern translations. The original Hebrew *nefesh chaya* means "living *souls*" (despite a tradition of reserving those words for Adam and using "living *creatures* or *things*" for nonhumans). See J. R. Hyland, *God's Covenant with Animals: A Biblical Basis for the Humane Treatment of All Creatures* (New York: Lantern Books, 2000), 73.

sense of accommodation derives from the widely evident bias in favor of animal earthly tenure and cosmic citizenship; it is an attested point of divine intention, according to no less an authority than Genesis 1. A more particular sense draws on the emphasis that classical natural histories place on how well outfitted or equipped animals seem to be for survival in the world. Chapter 3, "Poor, Bare, Forked," details the stakes of a perception that animals have been better provisioned by nature. It also explores a nagging anxiety about weaknesses of the human species that could only be remedied by prolonged nursing, arduous education, and prosthetic bodily aids. As Montaigne articulates this comparatist sentiment, "Of all creatures man is the most miserable and fraile" (398). Though reading the human body as a disadvantaged point of weakness, in itself, offers a powerful critique of human exceptionalism, the lament rarely concerns embodiment alone. It also rises to a question—spectacularly posed by *King Lear*'s "unaccommodated man"—of cosmic belonging. By these lights, as my epigraph from Giovanni Gelli's *La Circe* (1548–49) puts it, the world "is to all other beasts accommodate," while to wretched humans alone it is "almost contrary."[26]

It is this cosmic measure of animal accommodation that frames an extended controversy between Montaigne's "Apologie" and Descartes's *Discourse*, a controversy I must sketch briefly here as a preface to questions at stake throughout this book. Both address epistemological certitude about the world, putting the terms and conditions of human knowledge in question (and both carefully skirted heresy charges).[27] Calculations of kind are so fundamental that neither text can be imagined without its animal examples. Montaigne and Descartes maintain perfectly adverse positions on the epistemological implications of contingencies of species and embodiment. For Montaigne, beasts reveal man's epistemological presumption by making visible how sensory capacities vary and how knowledge is contingent on bodily specifics. For Descartes, animals appear only in an attempt

26. Giovanni Battista Gelli, "The fyrste Dyalogue. Ulysses and Circes, Oister and Mole," in *Circes of John Baptista Gello, Florentine* [*La Circe*], trans. Henry Iden (London, 1557–58), unpaginated. This volume is discussed in more detail in chapter 3.

27. The prologue to Sebond's book had been placed on the Index of Forbidden Books in 1558–59 (because its emphasis on reading the Book of Nature could be seen as insufficiently deferential to scripture and faith), but Montaigne artfully translated it without facing any formal accusation of heresy himself. Nevertheless, the translation still needed defending. For background on Sebond and the theological prudence of Montaigne's translation, see M. A. Screech, ed. and trans., *An Apology for Raymond Sebond* (New York: Penguin, 1987), xi–xvi. On Descartes and heresy, see *Discourse*, viii.

to guarantee that knowledge and mind are uniquely human. I address the epistemological and cognitive problems this presents in chapter 4, but the aspect of the controversy of concern here centers on the ethical and cosmopolitical effects when species is accepted or denied as a contingency on being and belonging. Montaigne and Descartes, *pro et contra*, stage a historically pivotal debate in which animal stakeholdership is being adjudicated—not just as the trial of mind in which Descartes's position is so well known, but more specifically as a trial of membership or accommodation.

Montaigne takes up traditional arguments about the vanity of human knowledge to announce that his "purpose is to crush, and trample . . . this humane pride and fiercenesse under foot, to make them feele the emptinesse, vacuitie, and no worth of . . . the silly weapons of their reason; to make them stoope" or bow down from the upright posture they claimed as a distinction (395). Speaking of this mankind in the third person, as if he were not fully or necessarily assimilated to it, Montaigne excoriates man's "impudency" when he "selecteth and separateth himselfe from out the ranke of other creatures" and replaces him instead "among the generall throng" (399, 406). Issuing his verdict directly on human exceptionalist thought itself, he concludes that it proceeds from "a foolish-hardiness, and self-presuming obstinacie" when we "prefer ourselves before other creatures, and sequester ourselves from their condition and societie" (432). He offers a sweeping glimpse of a "societie" that stretches beyond single kinds (and their self-satisfactions too).

Elevating animals as he tramples humankind "under foot" and makes it "stoope," Montaigne argues that "it is not said, that the essence of things, hath reference to man alone." When he continues that "hardnesse, whitenesse, depth and sharpnesse, touch the service and concern the knowledge of beasts as well as ours: Nature hath given the use of them to them, as well as to us," he limns a cosmos of diverse participation and stakeholdership, setting the widest horizon for subjective investments in the world (541). He ridicules presumptions otherwise. Concerning "the privilege" man repeatedly claims as "the onely absolute creature in the huge worlds-frame, perfectly able to know the absolute beautie and severall parts thereof," he asks, "Who hath sealed him this patent? Let him shew us his letters of privilege." When he ascribes the idea that the world pertains to man alone to mere "impudency," he defrocks humankind from its claimed right to talk alone about truth. He also sets a limited scope on the "rule" established in Genesis 1:26 and 1:28 when he demands to see the human "patent" for a usurped "privilege" (396).

Instead of policing human overreach on this front, Descartes outlines

a method for seeking and ratifying truths. As is so well known, he establishes a beachhead on truth by experimentally choosing to doubt the existence of everything (including the body or any need for one) and then noticing, in the course of that experiment, one truth that cannot be doubted:
cogito ergo sum. In a certain tension with the mind/body dualism generally credited to Descartes's account, he argues that for humans, "even if
there were no body at all," the soul or thinking faculty the *cogito* represents "would not cease to be all that it is" (19). Proposing the conjunction of a needless body and an undoubtable mind in humans, Descartes's
imaginary scientific trial proceeds to its notorious equation between bodies and machines or automatons and absorbs the entire being of animals
within machinic embodiment. Conjuring the image of "machines having
the organs and shape of a monkey or of some other animal that lacked
reason," Descartes claims that "we would have no way of recognizing that
they were not entirely of the same nature as these animals" (31). If such
a machine simulated a human being, however, it would be easy to identify the travesty because a language test will readily ascertain the real
presence of a human soul beneath. But a logical glitch or dilemma arises
here. Descartes specifies the use of words to "declare [one's] thoughts to
others"—an externalization of authority notably absent from the proofs
of mental existence in the *cogito ergo sum* sequence—as a separate and
additional criterion exclusively *for others* (32). Only expressed symbolic
language, which he believes no beast-machine can accomplish, indexes
mind.[28]

The thingifying attribution of linguistic incapacity to animals is familiar enough (although Montaigne contrarily uses the existence of animal language to assert that the natural language of humans is not speech
but body language, a language "common and publike to all" [401]). In
Descartes's hands, however, the language charge unfolds with unexpected
interest and irony, for the idiom of a virtual experiment or scientific trial
slides over into the language of a legal trial. This modulation, in turn, lets
slip the ethical and political implications of a double standard regarding
burdens of proof among trial parties. While the Cartesian "I" proved itself
to itself just by thinking, the animal "you" is denied, *in itself*, for a failure
to prove itself to another by speaking that other's unforeseeable dialect
or language. While "even the insane" among humans are capable of com-
posing "a discourse by means of which they might make their thoughts

---

28. For Descartes, it is "impossible for there to be enough organs in a machine to
make it act in all the contingencies of life . . . as our reason makes us act" (32).

understood," he argues, no animal, however perfect in its kind, "does the like" (32). Apparently not in Latin, and not in French either!

Extending the vocabularies of a legal trial, Descartes proposes that animals fail to "*testify* . . . to the fact that they are thinking about what they are saying; . . . and this *attests* not merely to the fact that beasts have less reason than men but that they have none at all" (32; italics added). Animal soul/mind is at stake in this trial, but no form of testimony exists by which it might be affirmed. It is a controversy in which animals are both required to speak and precluded from testifying. Or, worse, they are summoned to appear only to testify against themselves—in a trial procedure designed to deny their capacity to testify.[29] Cartesian method, then, makes no offer of a method concerning other minds. Because that knowledge can only proceed by mediated analogy to the certitude originally precipitated from the *cogito*, itself observed inside the closed sphere of a self testifying only to itself idiolectically, it can never meet the preset standards for certitude. In any case, no further questions about subjective investments or cross-species concatenations of knowledge can be entertained in this literally unaccommodating protocol.

Rather than abandoning the challenge of cross-species conversation, though, Montaigne had offered Plato as precedent. In what he calls "the golden age under Saturne," man had communication with animals, "of whom enquiring and taking instruction, he knew the true qualities, and differences of every one of them: by and from whome he got an absolute understanding and perfect wisdome" (399). Posing a question Descartes forecloses us from asking, Montaigne queries, "That defect which hindreth the communication betweene them and us, why may it not as well be in us, as in them?" (399). Descartes condemns the suggestion that beasts might speak and that we might fail to understand them. Yet his indictment, perhaps inadvertently, seems to admit that animals observably communicate with each other. Animals cannot speak, Descartes asserts, "for if that were true, . . . they could make themselves as well understood by us as they are by their fellow creatures" (33). The acknowledgment of apparent "understanding" and animal communication among themselves—in the course of affirming their failure to testify to us as proof they have nothing to say—makes the dilemma clear. Speaking only counts if it means speaking to us and in our language. Just being is good enough to certify

29. Jean François Lyotard defines this trial dilemma as a *différend* in *The Differend: Phrases in Dispute*, trans. Georges Van Den Abbeele (Minneapolis: University of Minnesota Press, 1988).

a singular human self, but animal others face the further hurdle of *being understood*.

Instead of removing beasts from the perspectival question about knowledge or its collaborative production, Montaigne makes the range of capacities across species necessary to any ultimate claim. Emphasizing collaborative models by using terms such as consultation, concurrence, accord, consent, and contribution, he suggests that the diverse embodied perspectives would have to be assembled and conferred, in a pan-creaturely vision of a truth trial or investigative commission (534). "If the senses be our first Judges, it is not ours that must only be called to counsell: For, in this facultie, beasts have as much (or more) right than we" (540). In any counsel "to judge the senses operation," he writes, "it were . . . necessary we were first agreed with beasts" (542). The format of this trial fantasy differs wildly from the one later staged virtually by Descartes. Here there would be animal witnesses and counselors, and the "competent Judge" would be a "body . . . without any preoccupation of judgement" and who thus would be "no man" (544). For all of man's claims to omnicompetence as a paragon, in this cosmopolitical vision of a body or community of conferral, Montaigne's nonsufficient man must treat beasts as copartners and fellow stakeholders with "as much (or more) right than we" to lodge their perspectives. Pitching his discussion at the level of a "generall throng," he enacts not a trial of animal psychic existence, but what he calls instead a "triall of our ignorance" (531).

In a separate essay, Montaigne stresses the "neere resemblance betweene us and beasts" and the "likelyhood" with which "they are compared unto us" in order to bring stronger language to this question. In a phrase analyzed further in chapter 1, he charges humans with the usurpation of an "imaginarie sovereignty" (*royauté imaginaire*) over other creatures.[30] In a 1646 response to objections from the Marquess of Newcastle, Descartes makes explicit reference to Montaigne, perhaps reacting to this particular charge. He announces, "I cannot share the opinion of Montaigne and others who attribute understanding or thought to animals," emphasizing that he entertains no moral doubt on this point: he is not "worried that people say that men have an *absolute [empire]* over all the other animals."[31] When Cambridge neo-Platonist Henry More charged the *Dis-*

---

30. Michel de Montaigne, "On Cruelty," in *Essayes*, 384; *Essais*, 435.

31. Descartes, letter to the Marquess of Newcastle (23 November 1646), in *The Philosophical Writings of Descartes*, ed. John Cottingham et al. (Cambridge: Cambridge University Press, 1991), 302 (italics added). The original reads: "Un empire absolu sur

course with a "deadly and murderous sentiment," Descartes's reply points out the utility of his thought for human ethical convenience. "My opinion is not so much cruel to animals as indulgent to men—at least those of us not given to the superstitions of Pythagoras—since it absolves them from the suspicion of crime when they eat or kill animals."[32] Alongside the period chestnut of dismissing Pythagoras as a lunatic on the point of transmigration of souls, Descartes concedes the political questions at stake in this woolly debate: whether or not meat means murder and whether or not we need trouble ourselves about an accountability to animals as subjects.

Between Montaigne's exposé of human sovereignty as "imaginarie" and Descartes's endorsement of an *empire absolu*, a certain confidence emerges in which new claims on behalf of human knowledge supply the "patent" for the human privilege Montaigne had denied. And while Montaigne had so carefully navigated Counter-Reformation definitions of heresy, Descartes charges him retrospectively with a new kind of heresy for modernity: doubting the doctrine of a sovereign and self-sufficient humanity. The only thing worse than Montaigne's view is, of all things, *atheism*. "After the error of those who deny the existence of God," Descartes declaims, "there is none at all that puts weak minds at a greater distance from virtue than to imagine that the soul of beasts is of the same nature as ours, and that, as a consequence, we have nothing to fear or hope for after this life any more than do flies and ants" (33). Here we see how human-exceptionalist ideological ends trample ordinary logic "under foot." If animals "thought as we do, they would have an immortal soul like us. This is unlikely, because there is no reason to believe it of some animals without believing it of all, and many of them such as oysters and sponges are too imperfect for this to be credible."[33] Leveraging a modern determination of the word "animal"—on the narrow back of the oyster—to encompass the entire sweep of nonhuman creatures within one category, Descartes enunciates a modern prohibition on what it is possible to think about "them." He likens an insufficiently human bias to religious heresy.

---

tous les autres animaux." Descartes, *Oeuvres et lettres*, ed. André Bridoux (Paris: La Pléiade, 1953), 1254. Here Descartes considers humans to be "animals" too, with power over "les autres"; when considering distributions of soul (below), he consolidates animals as "them."

32. Descartes, letter to Henry More (5 February 1649), in *Philosophical Writings*, 366. For More's letter (11 December 1648), see Leonora D. Cohen, "Descartes and Henry More on the Beast-machine: A Translation of their Correspondence Pertaining to Animal Automatism," *Annals of Science* 1, no. 1 (1936): 50.

33. Descartes, letter to Newcastle, 304.

Range of Chapters

Before the dissemination of Cartesianism, then, what was it possible to
think about animals? Then, as now, a vast tangle appears. Thomas's landmark *Man and the Natural World: Changing Attitudes in England, 1500–
1800* offered a comprehensive account of the contradictions at large in
English culture.[34] In groundbreaking studies of these contradictions, Erica
Fudge and Bruce Boehrer have each brought questions of history keenly
to bear on the more contemporary focus of animal studies, and this book
follows their lead in that pursuit. By detailing the heightened way that
the mutually erosive interpenetrations characteristic of binaries apply in
human/animal matters in early modernity, Fudge and Boehrer decisively
capture the performative dimension of this boundary and insist on the re-
petitive *work* required to draw and police a border between humans and
animals, because the line will not hold on its own.[35] As Thomas puts the
case overall, while "official attitudes" largely showed an "uncompromisingly aggressive view of man's place in the natural world," reflective accounts and actual practices alike widely and readily belied them.[36] Foraging among these contradictions, *The Accommodated Animal* tracks
a particular tradition that accommodates the presence of animals and
conceives them as actors and stakeholders endowed by their creator with
certain subjective interests. Its cosmopolitical vision enlists terms of political relation *across* species rather than inevitably stressing a divide between them, and it is this reckoning that Descartes particularly targets in
offering *la bête-machine* as a countermeasure, as we have seen. The "zoo-
topianism" of this arrangement concerns the way it acknowledges animal
populations, as opposed to a dispensation that ignores, discounts, or exter-
minates them or one that firmly confines them from view.[37]

34. Thomas, *Man and the Natural World*, 17–50.
35. Erica Fudge, *Perceiving Animals: Humans and Beasts in Early Modern Culture*
(Houndmills, UK: Palgrave, 1999), and Fudge, *Brutal Reasoning*; Bruce Boehrer, *Shakespeare among the Animals: Nature and Society in the Drama of Early Modern England*
(Houndmills, UK: Palgrave, 2002).
36. Thomas, *Man and the Natural World*, 50.
37. Without implying that early modern animals experienced utopian conditions,
we can readily contrast their situation with the radical elimination of wild habitats
and the staggeringly dystopic circumstances of modern livestock (see below, especially
notes 40–43). And while the cruelty of historical entertainments such as bear baiting is
extreme, it matches the similarly spectacular public cruelties then enacted on human
bodies.

While, then as now, many assumed a license for the unregulated in-strumentalization of animal life (with or without reference to Genesis), close readers—both Protestant and Catholic alike—paused more carefully over the Hexameron with unpredicted effects. My foundational chapter, "The Law's First Subjects," makes the case for a zootopian constitution by reading Genesis as a constitutional lawyer would read it: as a char-ter with operational and performative force. It shows that early modern theologians, political theorists, and literary writers demonstrably grasped Genesis in this constitutional way. Thinkers as diverse as Calvin, Lu-ther, Etienne de la Boétie, Philip Sidney, Montaigne, George Gascoigne, and Shakespeare—to our modern surprise—find animal entitlements to be specified in Genesis. Most of these writers then draw on its provisions to forge a quasi-legal discourse of "animal complaint" that gives the rela-tionship between humans and animals the worst available name in the sixteenth century. Voicing an epithet that reflects the ethical moorings of period political thought and names the extremest case of justice denied, they call it *tyranny*.

The next brace of chapters explores how the terms of embodiment af-fect claims to freedom and sovereignty. One traces the cross-purposes of human upright posture and the vectors of quadruped locomotion; the other assembles texts engaging in a comparative question about human naked-ness and animals' natural provisioning (born, as they are, with sufficient coats on their backs). More particularly, chapter 2, "A Cat May Look upon A King," traces the struggles between would-be ruling bipeds and unruly quadrupeds, citing a waggish proverb that conveys animal resistance, dis-obedience, and prerogative against the hopes of a panoptical model of man. Human uprightness, so often rehearsed as the basis for authority over other creatures and celebrated as a physical emblem of the divine spark in man, faces nothing but flaunts from the quadruped's signature locomotion, and the flourish of a beast's tail adds insult to injury. As natural law expresses itself in an unfolding of "the course of kind," quadruped directionality and movement collide with human ambitions for control. Animal mobil-ity cannot be effectively distinguished from will or intentional action, so the power of beasts to run, bite, stay, balk, or go expresses a constantly mobilizable freedom.

Chapter 3, "Poor, Bare, Forked," finds humankind in a worse predica-ment, but here too the problem is related to the body. Delving into natural-historical traditions conveyed to the Renaissance by Pliny and Plutarch and sixteenth-century responses in Gelli's *La Circe* and Montaigne's "Apologie," the chapter argues that we should read the discourses now known as "the happy beast tradition" with an eye to the actual rationales they give for animal happiness. These discourses compose a critical perspective on humankind, a zoographic critique that ranks animal perfections as superior to the uniquely human traits of misery, folly, and nakedness. Pliny's resonant phrase for the human condition, *nudus in nuda terra* (naked on the bare earth), asserts man's cosmic orphanage in contrast to the bodily preparedness a benevolent nature grants to the diverse animal estates. If mankind is exceptional, here he appears as creation's *negative* exception. Natural history and the happy beast tradition converge to fuel this human negative exceptionalism, despite our general association of an aggrandizement of human capacities with Renaissance culture. In this context, Shakespeare's *King Lear* extensively engages not only Pliny but Gelli in particular. Deploying one of Shakespeare's eight "animals," Lear anatomizes man as a "poor, bare, forked animal," and these natural-historical specifications ground the larger, cosmic claim that man's signature feature is the insufficiency that his "unaccommodated" condition makes painfully evident (3.4.105–6).

The final chapters juxtapose two further cross-species visions, one in which human authority over other creatures is qualified as intermittent and episodic at best, the other in which new extremes of human violence over creatures are invented, as if to overcome the disappointments of an incomplete power with ever more gruesome displays of animal abuse. Chapter 4, "Night-Rule," reads nighttime as a nonhuman jurisdiction. It proceeds from the ubiquitous early modern fear of the dark and of the blinded incapacity night brings for vision-dependent human beings as compared to nocturnal creatures. It returns to Montaigne's "Apologie" and Descartes's *Discourse* on a more epistemological front. What does the question of species have to do with the history of skepticism—and why? How do the palpably different (and often superior) sensory capacities of animals affect our measure of human perceptual skills or effectiveness? "Night-Rule" considers the handicapping effect of night blindness and sensory dependence on human claims to panoptical or sovereign earthly rule. In close considerations of nighttime as an empire where nonhumans rule instead, William Baldwin's *Beware the Cat* (1570) and Shakespeare's *A Midsummer Night's Dream* (ca. 1595) set species-defined limits on human authority instead of celebrating it or exaggerating its extent.

The last chapter, "Hang-Dog Looks," begins with the detailed account of an extraordinary phenomenon in Continental legal history: the criminal and civil trials of animal defendants. Commentators often shift the scholarly venue for animal cases to the domain of anthropological reading (making them symbolic rituals that use animals "to think with") rather than analyzing them jurisprudentially. But if we attend to the precedential force accorded to the Hexameron in these practices, a new horizon for "literal" reading appears for these cases. With the premises of the legal trials as a backdrop, the emphasis given, for example, to Venetian law's accommodation of "strangers" in *The Merchant of Venice* (where Shakespeare makes his most explicit reference to the legal trials of animals) takes on interspecies dimensions. The chapter then plots the decline of the legal trials against the rise of technoscientific or experimental trials of animals. In the first trial regime, animals appear as subjects of law; in the second, they are disanimated as objects of science. The "hang-dog look" (an expression derived from the judicial and quasi-judicial hanging of bad dogs) migrates from domains of law to those of science. In a larger process I call "disanimation," the traumas of vivisection and the vacuum tube take place as theatrical spectacles with routinized scripts. Enactments of the sovereignty human beings already considered themselves to have consumed numberless seventeenth-century animals, who were cut open while sustained temporarily alive or suffocated in the casual brinksmanship of "experiments" with the evacuated cylinder. In the strange new context of public science and animal trauma, divergent reactions arise among observers. Some recoil at cruelty; others see instead a confirmation of animals as the machines Descartes described. The split opening between spectators in this early iteration of a public forum would eventually lead to the anticruelty movements of modernity, on the one hand, and the retreat of technoscientific experimentation into the proprietary spaces of institutional and corporate secrecy, on the other.

A tailpiece titled "Raleigh's Ark" returns us to the Noah story. While the vexed cosmopolitics of the ark's landing (described in chapter 1) suggest a collapse of community and an exilic trajectory for all creatures after Eden, embarkation tended instead to stress the incredible variety of earthly kinds, whether as testimony to divine omnicompetence or a natural-historical "veneration" for nature's generativity. For painters, the scene of boarding occasioned *tour de force* interpretations of the prodigal riches thought to characterize nature's repertoire of forms, textures, colors, and kinds. To conjure this scene was to accord significance to natural diversity as such. In an instance from the school of Jacopo Bassano (ca. 1575), this traditional preoccupation yields a grand promenade of creatures lining up to board the ark (plate 2). In this lush painting, neither the painter nor Noah himself seems to be counting strictly "by the book." Exotic animals (elephants, giraffes, and camels) linger a little hazily in the distance, as the painter bravely takes on the diversity of this bodily scene, flexing his technique as he renders the coats, feathers, and other tactile accoutrements of animal estate and marking the human participants with painterly flourishes of bright silk cloth. This is not even to mention the coy surplus of dogs scattered throughout the scene, quite free of the "two-by-two" constraints of the original narrative. As if the painter were doting instead on the kaleidoscopic variety, the implied passenger list seems not to end, but rather to extend itself with a tail-wagging et cetera. Alongside this traditional cosmic vision of marvelous plenty, however, another approach to the ark arose, one with an altogether different arithmetic. It drew on a new empirical mathematics of (ac)counting, doctrines of technoscientific mastery, and the colonial impulse as well—not only to abridge the raw numbers of creaturely kinds on the ark but to reduce to finitude the wonder-inducing variety that had once seemed infinite.

Looking Back

For all that this book is a historical meditation on the imaginative capacities of literature, law, theology, political thought, and science to accommodate animals, it also acknowledges a cruder kind of intervening change: the statistically overwhelming confinement of animals and the resulting apartheid of modern animal life. Analyzing this historic shift, John Berger argues that animals confined for display in modern zoos "constitute the living monument to their own disappearance," whereas "before this rupture, animals . . . were with man at the centre of his world."[38] And indeed, for early modernity, hardly an urban, rural, or domestic scene could be drawn without them. Jan van der Heyden's grand cityscape of Amsterdam's main square (1668) dramatizes the public visibility of dogs and horses in particular as they make their way alongside humans, threading the central civic monuments of the town hall and the New Church (plate 1). The painting muddies any distinction between beasts of burden and creatures of leisure: one man totes a heavy load in a visual echo of the horse's labors; a dog plays with a man who is rolling a hoop; diverse creatures rest, forage, or wander in the square—living creatures pursuing life, ensemble, beneath a vast and overarching early modern sky. Humans then simply had more contact with more animals than most of us generally

38. John Berger, "Why Look at Animals?" in *About Looking* (London: Writers and Readers, 1980), 24, 1.

now do. And for a species like ours, with its weak ears and terrible nose, out of sight really does mean out of mind.

In a prescient intimation of the future, Thomas More's 1517 *Utopia* imagined a noncitizen class of butchers performing a hidden form of slave labor, a labor deemed too brutal for its citizens even to witness. More's Utopians designate places "outside the city" for this and "do not allow their citizens to accustom themselves to the butchering of animals, by the practice of which they think that mercy, the finest feeling of our human nature, is gradually killed off."[39] Other scholars and advocates have documented the degree to which More's fantasy has become our reality. One website hosts an animated graphic charting slaughter rates in the United States (287 chickens per second, 3.68 pigs per second, and 1.12 cows per second), visibly displaying the number of animals slaughtered in the duration of one's web visit; virtually all of this slaughtering is screened from public view.[40] While educational signposting, for example, in the Lincoln Park Zoo's "Farm-in-the-Zoo Presented by John Deere" in Chicago makes much of the way modern agribusiness "provide[s] us with the food we need to live," its simulacrum of a quaint red barn substitutes pastoral farm imagery for Orwellian reality, suppressing how the system actually works. The massive industrialization of livestock production depends on the near total invisibility of its animals.

The focused argumentation of Peter Singer's landmark *Animal Liberation* (1975) and his continuing advocacy have played a major role in disseminating actual facts about the shrouded lives of both experimental subjects and ordinary livestock. As Singer sees it, "It is ignorance, rather than indifference to animals, that keeps massive, institutional cruelty to animals in place."[41] J. M. Coetzee's *The Lives of Animals* (1999), however, relentlessly

39. Thomas More, *Utopia*, ed. Edward Surtz (New Haven, CT: Yale University Press, 1964 [Latin, 1517]), 77–78.

40. These official figures from the U.S. Department of Agriculture are for 2008. Animation available at http://www.animalvisuals.org/data/slaughter/?y=2008 (accessed 1 May 2011).

41. Peter Singer, *Animal Liberation* (New York: HarperCollins, 2009), x. The outcome of California Proposition 2 (2008), Standards for Confining Farm Animals, confirms Singer's insight to a significant degree. After a media blitz by the Humane Society of the United States that simply showed images of "normal" current conditions, the proposition passed, with 63.5 percent of the vote (an extraordinary margin). The law prohibits "the confinement of farm animals in a manner that does not allow them to turn around freely, lie down, stand up, and fully extend their limbs." "California Proposi-

attacks the way acknowledgment of the open secret of these facts is cen-
sored and suppressed at every juncture, from the intimately social level of
the dinner party to the unimaginable scale of industrial commerce.[42] Taking up this question of scale, Derrida affirms that a "war" has been waged:
"Traditional forms of treatment of the animal have been turned upside
down by the joint developments of zoological, ethological, biological, and
genetic forms of *knowledge*, which remain inseparable from *techniques* of
intervention into their object . . . namely, the living animal." He insists on
the significance of scale in the modern economy of meat production: "No
one can today deny this event—that is, the unprecedented *proportions* of
this subjection of the animal."[43] While Derrida emphasizes the undeni-
ability of "subjection," a gargantuan repression remains operative. Animal
advocates have to break laws against trespassing if they are to convey the
hidden conditions of animal life and the clandestine practices of animal
management into public knowledge. The same measures once used to
breach the proprietary enclosures of scientific experimentation are now
required to enable us simply to *see* these animals. Commentators over
many years have unfolded the moral calamity of the forms of confinement
in which an extraordinary percentage of the planet's live animals now find
themselves as livestock. Exploring an earlier arrangement framed on other

---

tion 2 (2008)," http://www.voterguide.sos.ca.gov/past/2008/general/title-sum/prop2
-title-sum.htm, and http://ballotpedia.org/wiki/index.php/California_Proposition_2_
%282008%29.

42. J. M. Coetzee, *The Lives of Animals* (Princeton, NJ: Princeton University Press,
1999).

43. Derrida, *The Animal That Therefore I Am*, 31, 25 (italics in original). Derrida
compares humans and animals to evoke the scope of carnage: it is "as if, for example,
instead of throwing a people into ovens and gas chambers (let's say Nazi) doctors and
geneticists had decided to organize the overproduction and overgeneration of Jews, gyp-
sies, and homosexuals by means of artificial insemination, so that, being continually
more numerous and better fed, they could be destined in always increasing numbers
for the same hell" (26). Overgeneration is no metaphor: businesses producing hens
from breeds developed for egg laying, for example, massively overgenerate male chicks.
Because these males can neither lay eggs nor grow quickly enough to become meat
efficiently, and because there is "unfortunately, no way to breed eggs that only produce
female hens," two hundred million of these male chicks a year in the United States
are culled from a conveyor belt in the first days of life and tossed alive into a grinder in
what one company calls "instantaneous euthanasia." See http://www.msnbc.msn.com/
id/32647389/ns/business-consumer_news/from/toolbar (Associated Press, 1 September
2009; accessed 1 May 2011).

Plate 1. Jan van der Heyden, *Dam Square* (1668). Image courtesy of the
Amsterdams Historisch Museum, Amsterdam.

Plate 2. School of Jacopo Bassano, *The Animals Guided onto Noah's Ark* (1570s).
© ADP—Management Fratelli Alinari. Photograph by Vito e Michele Rotondo. Galleria Doria
Pamphilj, Rome, Italy. Photograph: Alinari / Art Resource, New York.

Plate 3. Theo Jansen, *Animaris Umerus* (2010). Image courtesy of Theo Jansen;
photo courtesy of Loek van der Klis. www.strandbeest.com and www.kliski.com.

Plate 4. Theo Jansen, *Animaris Percipiere* (herd) (2008). Image courtesy of Theo Jansen;
photo courtesy of Loek van der Klis. www.strandbeest.com and www.kliski.com.

imperatives, *The Accommodated Animal* demonstrates the consequential increment of difference that animal cultural visibility makes.

In Latour's pivotal account of the divisions instituting "the modern constitution," he concisely describes how "the scientific power [is] charged with representing things and the political power charged with representing subjects."[44] This seventeenth-century division, to an extent, corresponds to the more persistent idea Robert N. Watson anatomizes with such elegance and poignancy in *Back to Nature: The Green and the Real in the Late Renaissance* when he describes the perennial human conceit "that humanity was structurally opposed to nature."[45] The early modern archive shows just how much animals trouble this opposition; they are not placed reliably outside the pale that protects those properties designated human. As undeniable agents in our interactions with them, as vectors of intention in motion, they often seem to people to be more like people than an unambivalent part of that nature that is set apart from human being. Documenting the incomplete assimilation of animals to an idea of "nature," this book thus concerns resistances to the category reassignment the Latourian division entails for them, a shift from second- or third-class subjects to objects. Despite an apparently human tendency to convert questions of kind into more abstracted matters of ontology, politics durably refers to embodiment. Because embodiment keeps refusing to comply with the erasure prescribed for it, embodiment keeps returning us to a political frame.

As detailed in chapters 2 and 5, the quadrupeds condemned to live with us have legs and can "vote with their feet" if they are not caged or tied. They look back in ways that are not sufficiently unreadable to deny; they sometimes fail or refuse to be docile. Indeed, as the opening line of no less a document than John Ponet's 1556 *Shorte Treatise of Politike Power* (with its landmark justification of tyrannicide) shows, animals hold a privileged place in the long human history of conceiving obedience and disobedience. Offering in the first chapter to define "wherof politike power groweth, werfore it was ordayned, and the right use and duetie of the same," Ponet grounds the entire project on an analogy: "As oxen, shepe, goates, and suche other unreasonable creatures cannot for lacke of reason rule them selves, but must be ruled by a more excellent creature, that is man: so man, albeit he have reason, yet bicause through the fall of the furst man,

44. Latour, *We Have Never Been Modern*, 27–29.
45. Watson, *Back to Nature*, 336.

this reason is wonderfully corrupt . . . is not hable by him self to rule him self, but must have a more excellent governour."[46] As a result of this likeness in governability, the division excluding animals from political representation that Latour describes requires extra enforcement measures to be taken. Bodily restraints and confinement rein in the locomotion that had defined animal character since Aristotle, and internment makes their immured gazes impossible to engage.[47] Contemporary Dutch artist Theo Jansen's magical *strandbeesten* contemplate these dilemmas of anima (breath, spirit, soul, life—and the root of the adjective "animal") as they step, prance, and stroll, wind powered across the wide open beaches of the North Sea (plates 3 and 4). Proposing the narrative of a new creation complete with its own evolutionary processes, Jansen provocatively describes these ghostlike, skeletal creatures as "new forms of life," built not from "pollen or seeds but plastic yellow tubes."[48] As jaw-dropping invocations of the enigma of locomotion, Jansen's animated creatures take our breath away. From our present perspective—a perspective aware, as sixteenth-century thinkers were not, of a horizon called extinction—the arresting experience of watching the *strandbeesten* "walk on the wind" echoes with an uncanny note of elegy.

In seventeenth-century attempts to implement the "modern constitution," though, we still see the marks of negotiation with lingering forms of animal prerogative. Despite the rising imperative to limit politics to representations of (human) subjects, political terminologies persist to describe the human imperial project and its attempt to render "imaginarie sovereignty" real. Descartes, calling for an *empire absolu*, equivocates between the dominion over subjects (mastery) and the control of objects (possession) when he celebrates a "practical philosophy, by means of which . . . we might be able . . . to . . . render ourselves, as it were, masters and possessors of nature" (35). For Robert Hooke (the first Curator of Experiments

46. John Ponet, *A Shorte Treatise of Politike Power* (Strasbourg, Germany: W. Köpfel, 1556), Aii.

47. Berger anatomizes the industrial eradication of the returned glance of animals. See also Una Chaudhuri, "(De)Facing the Animals: Zooësis and Performance," *Drama Review* 51, no. 1 (Spring 2007): 8–20, especially discussion of the PETA initiative, "Did your food have a face?"

48. Theo Jansen, http://www.strandbeest.com (accessed 8 May 2011); Jansen posts films of his *strandbeesten* in full career. An audience at the 2007 TED conference burst into reflexive murmur and applause at the beautiful, startling motion of these "creatures." http://www.ted.com/talks/theo_jansen_creates_new_creatures.html (accessed 8 May 2011).

for the Royal Society), the microscope and other "Mechanical helps for the Senses" enable "us, *with the great Conqueror*, to be affected that we have not yet overcome one World when there are so many others to be discovered," and every "improvement of Telescopes or Microscopes" yields "new Worlds and Terra-Incognita's to our view."[49] Robert Boyle (a cofounder of the "Invisible College" that was formed to pursue natural philosophy in the 1640s and was eventually chartered as the Royal Society in 1660) laments that "the veneration wherewith men are imbued for what they call nature has been a discouraging impediment to the empire of man over the inferior creatures of God."[50] The articulated goal remains one of unimpeded human empire over creatures who keep eluding it.

Stephen Toulmin has indexed an error that we tend to make concerning the course of historical change, an error that is even more common than nostalgia. He points to the tacit orthodoxy that a progress narrative inevitably describes history's course. As I hope this book begins to show, that orthodoxy represents a provincially human perspective. Among the casualties of what Toulmin calls "the hidden agenda of modernity," the zoographic critique of man and the impediment to *empire absolu* that it posed were brought, at the very least, to the verge of extinction.[51] But as Virginia Woolf once proposed, "There is a spot the size of a shilling at the back of the head which one can never see for oneself. It is one of the good offices that sex can discharge for sex—to describe that spot the size of a shilling at the back of the head. . . . A true picture of man as a whole can never be painted until a woman has described that spot the size of

49. Robert Hooke, *Micrographia, or Some Physiological Descriptions of Minute Bodies Made by Magnifying Glasses* (London: John Martin and James Allestry, Printers to the Royal Society, 1665), xvii–xviii (pagination and italics added).

50. Robert Boyle, *A Free Enquiry into the Vulgarly Received Notion of Nature*, ed. Edward Davis and Michael Hunter (Cambridge: Cambridge University Press, 1996 [1686]), 15.

51. Stephen Toulmin, *Cosmopolis: The Hidden Agenda of Modernity* (Chicago: University of Chicago Press, 1992). Though I use "cosmopoly" to refer to a nonmodern dispensation rather than to modernity, Toulmin's larger argument about a "retreat from the Renaissance" finds support in the animal archive considered here (30). In a related way, Margreta de Grazia emphasizes the broad ethical importance of attending to discontinuity, as opposed to the teleological assumption that "the relevant history [is] a prior version of what we already are and live." See "The Ideology of Superfluous Things: *King Lear* as Period Piece," in *Subject and Object in Renaissance Culture*, ed. Margreta de Grazia, Maureen Quilligan, and Peter Stallybrass (Philadelphia: University of Pennsylvania Press, 1996), 21.

a shilling. Mr. Woodhouse and Mr. Casaubon are spots of that size and nature."[52] Early modern writing shows a substantial capacity to imagine and accommodate animal viewpoints as critical ones and to describe such a "spot . . . at the back of the head" in species terms. Having, as Haraway puts it, "never been human," diverse writers take up a vantage that is incompletely human—a practice that Cartesianism would successfully shame as heretical for modernity. Obviously my own view is that animals and their claims pertain in their own right. Regardless of that, it has surely been well established how much animal labor goes into building the edifice known as "the human." What *The Accommodated Animal* contributes further is an account in which attention to animals teaches us less about "what it means to be human" than about what it does not mean, and when. Tracing early modern frameworks for cosmopolity across species, it opens historical horizons for imagining a quadruped's perspective—even as it, in turn, eyes the concept of humanity from its unvaunted dorsal side.

52. Virginia Woolf, *A Room of One's Own*, ed. Susan Gubar (New York: Houghton Mifflin Harcourt, 2005 [1929]), 89.

CHAPTER ONE

The Law's First Subjects:
Animal Stakeholders, Human Tyranny, and
the Political Life of Early Modern Genesis

Puffing about his own acting skills in *A Midsummer Night's Dream*, Bottom declares that his "chief humor is for a tyrant"—a role he glosses as "a part to tear a cat in" (1.2.24–25). TYRANT; TEAR-CAT. With this "queer jingle," the Athenian who will become an ass associates the ranter with the render of flesh and casts the political figure of the tyrant as a monstrous butcher.[1] In annotating the line, Shakespeare's early editor George Steevens lists several examples of this striking phrase, including to "rend and tear a cat" (from 1610).[2] The redundancy of "rend" and "tear" makes it difficult to gloss over the reference to dismemberment. Attributions of a "beastly" ferocity or an animalistic taste for blood to tyrants were, of course, a rhetorical commonplace in the period. John Ponet, for example, calls the tyrant a "monstre and a cruell beast covered with the shape of a man"; another tract itemized him as "a Tigar, a fearse Lion, a ravening wolfe, a publique enimy, and a bloody murtherer."[3] But Bottom's

---

1. Virginia Woolf dubs such Shakespearean echoes "queer jingles" in *"Twelfth Night at the Old Vic,"* in *The Death of the Moth and Other Essays*, ed. Leonard Woolf (London: Hogarth Press, 1942), 34.

2. *The Plays of William Shakespeare in Ten Volumes*, ed. Samuel Johnson, George Steevens, and Isaac Reed (London: C. Bathurst, etc., 1778), 3:19.

3. John Ponet, *A Short Treatise of Politike Power* (Strasbourg, Germany: W. Köpfel, 1556), chap. 6, Giiir; Robert Parsons et al., *A Conference about the Next Succession to the Crowne of Ingland* (Antwerp[?], 1594), pt. 2, 61. Rebecca Bushnell details how persistent this association was; she also discusses Machiavelli's bold proposal that the sovereign *should* be half man, half beast. See Bushnell, *Tragedies of Tyrants: Political Thought and Theater in the English Renaissance* (Ithaca, NY: Cornell University Press, 1990), 50–56. The ancient aphorism calling the tyrant the most dangerous animal among the wild beasts (and the flatterer the most dangerous among the tame)

phrase maps tyranny across species in the reverse direction. A cat, ripped
apart by human hands, indexes the tyrant's perversity and violence.
One early editor of Shakespeare's play, however, asserted that we
would be "wholly mistaken" to imagine it is "the domestic animal, the
cat, which is spoken of" by Bottom here. Another claimed that, instead,
"we should read, *A part to tear a* CAP *in*. For as a ranting whore is called a
tear-sheet, . . . so a ranting bully is called a *tear-cap*."[4] These early efforts
and others like them have intervened to prevent our taking "cat" literally, and modern editors tend to glide past literal meaning to classify the
phrase simply as a metaphorical or proverbial expression for "rant."[5] As
one Victorian commentator asserted, "It is difficult to believe that such a
brutal and disgusting action, taking the words in their literal Saxon sense,
could ever have happened."[6] Brutal, indeed. But as Derrida puts the point

---

was widely cited. See, for example, Erasmus, *Education of a Christian Prince*, ed. Lisa
Jardine (Cambridge: Cambridge University Press, 1997), 55, and Ben Jonson, *Sejanus*, ed.
Jonas Barish (New Haven, CT: Yale University Press, 1965), 1.2.437–38; the main classi-
cal source is Plato's *Republic*, bk. 8, 565–66.

    4. Andrew Becket, *Shakespeare's Himself Again: or, the Language of the Poet
Asserted* (London: A. J. Valpy, 1815), 267 (italics in original). Becket suggests "a part to
tear: à catin," glossing "tear" as "rant," converting the English "cat" to a French term
for "a drab, a low and vulgar woman," and proposing "à" to function for "like" (267).
He likewise "corrects" two other violated cats, one blinded and the other probably
castrated: *The Taming of the Shrew*'s "she shall have no more eyes to see withal than a
cat" (1.2.114–15) ("it is not the well known domestic animal that is here spoken of") and
"gib cat" (*King Henry IV, Part 1*, 1.2.77). For tear-cap, see Johnson, Steevens, and Reed,
Plays of William Shakespeare, citing William Warburton (1747), 19.

    5. For further readers finding no cat in the line, see *A New Variorum Edition of
Shakespeare: A Midsommer Nights Dreame*, ed. H. H. Furness et al. (Philadelphia:
J. B. Lippincott, 1895), 36. Among modern editors, David Bevington and G. Blakemore
Evans gloss the phrase "i.e., rant" (Bevington, ed., *The Complete Works of Shakespeare*,
5th ed. [New York: Pearson Longman, 2004], 154); Evans, ed., *The Riverside Shakespeare*, 2nd ed. [Boston: Houghton Mifflin, 1996], 259); Stephen Orgel calls it a "common expression . . . for stage ranting" (Orgel, ed., *The Complete Pelican Shakespeare*,
2nd rev. ed. [New York: Penguin Classics, 2002], 153); and Stephen Greenblatt's edition
glosses it directly as "rant" (Greenblatt, ed., *The Norton Shakespeare*, 2nd ed. [New
York: Norton, 2008], 820).

    6. Charles Mackay, *A Glossary of Obscure Words and Phrases in the Writings of
Shakespeare and His Contemporaries* (London: Sampson Low, 1887), 407. In a virtuoso
avoidance of literal reading, Mackay gives a Gaelic alternative for tear-cat (*duire-cath*,
or "obstinate combat"). For a bracing account of the "regular persecution" of cats in
early modernity, see Bruce Boehrer, "*Gammer Gurton's* Cat of Sorrows," *English Literary Renaissance* 39, no. 2 (2009): 268.

in a different context, at the bottom of everything else we might say about this, there "is a real cat, . . . *a little cat*[;] it isn't the *figure* of a cat."[7] The line's dramatic utility and poetic force depend on its literal sense.

To make vivid what he means by the tyrant's part, Bottom in this line conjures the murderous dismemberment of a semi-domesticated household creature, one whose state of being Shylock (himself "a stranger cur" in Venice) would amplify as "a harmless necessary cat."[8] As we will see, to be both harmless and necessary is to be an innocent presence and an integral part. No "out-law," the harmless, necessary cat is neither a threat nor an alien. Bottom's association of questions of justice and political malfeasance with the little, liminal, literal cat suggests the stakes of thinking historically about the species dimensions of membership, not to mention the definitions of harmlessness and murder that depend on it. It asks us to hesitate before construing every textual animal as an overwhelmingly figurative artifact of human imaginative authority—as though everything we represent were *wholly* humanized thereby (through projection, anthropomorphism, allegory, and so on) and as though "the human" had sufficient categorical integrity and inevitability to achieve a total conversion of all things to itself. It requires us to resist any reflexive confinement of animal significance within the minor literary category of "animal imagery."

This chapter unearths the broader intellectual foundations for Bottom's passing suggestion that, in their relations with humans, early modern animals could be understood as the subjects of *tyranny*—the most abiding concern across sixteenth- and early seventeenth-century political thought (alongside obedience, to which animals have a special relation, as we will see). It also explores what this understanding might teach us generally about the evolving terms and conditions of membership or belonging within a domain of governance as those criteria expand and contract

7. Jacques Derrida, *The Animal That Therefore I Am*, ed. Marie-Louise Mallet, trans. David Wills (New York: Fordham University Press, 2008), 6 (italics in original). With rich irony, he later indicates our freedom to see this as a reference to *Through the Looking Glass*, if we "insist . . . on suspecting [him] of perversity" in stressing the facticity of this cat (7).

8. *The Merchant of Venice*, 1.3.116, 4.1.55. On partial membership, justice, and animal belonging in *Merchant*, see chapter 5. On the continuing moral force of "harmlessness," see Harper Lee: "Mockingbirds don't do one thing but make music for us to enjoy. They don't eat up people's gardens, don't nest in corncribs, they don't do one thing but sing their hearts out for us. That's why it's a sin to kill a mockingbird." *To Kill A Mockingbird* (New York: HarperCollins, 2010 [1960]), 148.

in Western discourses.[9] I am not (or at least not necessarily) conceiving of membership as a group of beings consciously committed to the shared principles of a voluntary social order. Such an Enlightenment ideal of consensual or contractarian democracy now seems a point of nostalgia just considering humans among themselves. Consent, externalized in transparent verbal expression, remains a critical forensic standard among humans. But because we no longer understand it as actually descriptive of an origin for human political life, our horizons for thought are ill served by continuing to wield the litmus of consent against determinations of animal stakeholdership—while a great deal we might say about relatings across species is occluded by its vestigial bar against animal participation.

Instead of invoking (and then discovering!) an ontological "divide" between human and animal or even demonstrating that divide to be a blurry, shifting, or unsustainable one, this chapter pursues the ways living creatures before Descartes were held to be *related* within a shared regime of order or laws that governed them commonly. This is not to say that the terms and conditions of this order were equalizing but that profound ambivalence about humanness left room for greater cognizance of nonhuman claims than has become customary for us. While now "animal rights" struggle against the grain of presumptions about consciousness and language that inform modern liberal thought and the species-inflected notion of "human" rights it cultivated, these particular presumptions do not widely pertain in premodernity. At its very heart, this earlier dispensation incorporated cross-species relationships, and it named them in the firmly political terms of sovereignty and subjection. The political dimension then attributed to human/animal relations, as suggested in the introduction, refers not to the obvious fact that those relations involve power ("brute" or otherwise) but to legal and constitutional concerns such as the legitimacy of authority and the justifiability of its acts, the terms of subjection and obedience, and thus the setting up of parties, membership, and rights. Elucidating this perspective depends in part on historicizing inherited circumscriptions of what might be counted as "language" or "signification,"

9. For a powerful proactive account of species and belonging, see Martha Nussbaum, *Frontiers of Justice: Disability, Nationality, Species Membership* (Cambridge, MA: Belknap Press, 2006). Nussbaum addresses the incapacity of social contract theory to account for social justice among unequal parties, suggesting an approach to political cooperation based instead on "capabilities." As indicated in chapter 2, early modernity attributes sovereign "properties" to each creature, offering a historical cognate for capability and showing that "thinking otherwise," as Nussbaum proposes we should begin to do, also has precedents.

even as we displace language-based ideas of social contract from their lingering monopoly on definitions of politics. Setting to one side later developments in philosophy, technoscience, and political theory (most obviously, Descartes and Hobbes), we can attend to the more natural-historical and theologically inclined sixteenth-century arrangements against which they proceeded.

Conrad Gesner, the Swiss compiler of the most important animal encyclopedia of the sixteenth century, introduces his magisterial, multivolume *Historiae Animalium* in the 1550s by distinguishing "living creatures, . . . Fishes, Foules, Cattell, and creeping things," from the whole balance of creation in precisely these terms of political participation. They alone, he writes, are "expressely . . . submitted and vassalaged to [human] Empire, authority, and government."[10] Being *ruled* puts them inside a certain pale, rather than simply outside the city walls. They are "vassals" of human government. Human sovereignty is not unconditional, just as animal subjection entails its due measure of participation or "voluntary servitude." In 1578 Guillaume du Bartas confirms the fundamentally political cast of these conceptions. Addressing readers, he proposes that

> soone as ever [God] had framed thee,
> Into thy Hands he put this Monarchie:
> Made all the Creatures know thee for their Lord,
> And come before thee of their owne accord.

On the basis of their "knowing" man to be a duly established monarch, a ruler by right, animals by "their owne accord" acknowledge the sovereignty of man, whom Du Bartas calls the "King of Creatures."[11] We find this rendering of cross-species relations in the idiom of politics in more

10. Conrad Gesner, "The First Epistle of Doct. Conradus Gesnerus," in Edward Topsell, *The Historie of Foure-Footed Beastes* (London: William Jaggard, 1607). References to Gesner and Topsell are to this edition. Gesner's Latin volumes were published during the period 1551–58 by Christopher Froschauer in Zurich.

11. Guillaume du Bartas, *Bartas: His Devine Weekes and Workes*, trans. Joshua Sylvester (London: Humphrey Lownes, 1605), 224, 225. Sylvester's translation includes Du Bartas's epic account of creation's first week, *La Sepmaine, ou Création du Monde* (1578), and his *La Seconde Sepmaine, ou Enfance du Monde* (1584). Sidney's translation of *La Sepmaine* is lost (see Alan Sinfield, "Sidney and Du Bartas," *Comparative Literature* 27, no. 1 [Winter, 1975]: 8–20). Du Bartas's work was a key precedent for Milton's *Paradise Lost*, which uses the same political vocabularies: "All the Earth / To thee and to thy Race I give; as Lords / Possess it. . . . Each Bird and Beast behold / After their kinds; I bring

practical contexts too. For example, the training manual *An Hipponomie or The Vineyard of Horsemanship* (1618) argues that although man was originally given "Soveraignty & rule" over animals, his fall made "all other Creatures which before were loving and obedient to Man" turn instead "to Rebellion."[12] At the broadest level, this habit of explicitly reckoning animals and people as (sometimes even willing) parties in political relation figures a "zootopian constitution," or cosmopolity, terms I will be using throughout this book.[13]

Political and fiduciary nomenclatures for relatings across species register nowhere in the human-exceptionalist, sovereign politics of the nation-state after the seventeenth century, a paradigm in which intensifying controversies about citizenship and human title center on clashes among humans. For this regime, animals have been fully objectified (as clocks or robots, in Descartes's account) and relocated to the emerging disciplines of technoscience. In Bruno Latour's account of this separation of the human ("culture") from all things nonhuman ("nature"), animals become undifferentiated within humanity's remainder, a nature now recalibrated as inarticulate.[14] This historical homogenization revises the former status and particular distinction of animals. Astonishingly, yet partly for this reason, theories of biopolitics arising from a critique of the dynamics of the modern nation-state have virtually nothing to say about nonhuman living creatures. "The biological," instead, addresses a torsion *within* the human. Because they both analyze the modern state, Foucault's biopolitics and Agamben's "bare life" remain essentially human in reach. Foucault describes "the set of mechanisms through which the basic biological features of the human species became the object of a political strategy,"

them to receive / From thee their Names, and pay thee fealty / With low subjection" (John Milton, *Paradise Lost*, ed. David Kastan [Indianapolis: Hackett, 2005], 8.338–45).

12. Michael Baret, *An Hipponomie or The Vineyard of Horsemanship* (London: George Eld, 1618), 1–2.

13. Another apt term is Latour's "nature-culture," although he seeks by it to make visible the underlying "hybrids" that are fractured and *denied* by what he terms "the modern constitution." Bruno Latour, *We Have Never Been Modern*, trans. Catharine Porter (Cambridge, MA: Harvard University Press, 1993), 2, 7. In comparison, I stress the political quality of premodern discourses used to affirm continuities and relations that we call "hybrids" only in retrospect.

14. On these vast seventeenth-century separations, see also Steven Shapin and Simon Schaffer, *Leviathan and the Air-Pump: Hobbes, Boyle, and the Experimental Life* (Princeton, NJ: Princeton University Press, 1985), and Latour's discussion of it (*We Have Never Been Modern*, 15–29).

and Agamben distinguishes human "bare life" from "animal nature," which lacks "any relation to law or to the city."[15] The phenomenon they address, however, an erosion of "civic" or stakeholding politics in the name of technologized (bio)management of human "life," repeats with a vengeance what a previous transition had already accomplished for non-humans. Among the backfired colonizations of late modernity, in other words, humans, too, enter the categorical abyss of "livestock" first created for quadrupeds. But *before* these two recalibrations—one ending any glimmer of animal stakeholdership, the other commodifying human citizens as "docile bodies"—the language of explicit political relation suffused a frame that was at once larger and smaller than the modern state: the more intimate cosmos of early modernity.

Into the beginning of the seventeenth century, as for centuries before, this constitutional frame derives overwhelmingly from the establishments described in the first chapters of Genesis, as the passages from Gesner and Du Bartas so clearly show. The broad "multidisciplinary" impact of its hexameral verses in particular (accounting for the six days of creation) cannot be overstated. Enjoying overwhelming currency as the account that begins "in the beginning"—and that in a culture that saw itself in a custodial or genealogical relation to that beginning—Genesis touched all spheres of learning. The Hexameron also specifically instanced natural history writing because it explained the diversity of creaturely life while setting forth the legitimate relations among natural kinds. Because early modern animals were understood to have their genealogical progenitors listed in its charter (just as early modern humans saw their ances-

---

15. Michel Foucault, *Security, Territory, Population: Lectures at the College de France, 1977—1978*, ed. Michael Senellart, trans. Graham Burchell (New York: Palgrave Macmillan, 2007), 1; Giorgio Agamben, *Homo Sacer: Sovereign Power and Bare Life*, trans. Daniel Heller-Roazen (Stanford, CA: Stanford University Press, 1998), 103. Agamben relates "bare life" to the "simple natural life" within the human that was excluded from the polis and located instead, in Athenian contexts, within the *oikos* as "reproductive life," not noting the gendered nature of that seclusion as political (2). In this respect (too vast to give due attention here), the likeness between women and animals as foundational exclusions appears. Discussing the wolf-man, Agamben asserts that the fact that "such a man is *defined as a wolf-man and not simply as a wolf* . . . is decisive here. The life of the bandit . . . is not of a piece with animal nature [which is] without any relation to law and the city" (103; italics added). These instances suggest how, despite deeply cogent analyses of *human* circumstances within the nation-state, biopolitical critique has not traced questions across species as much as it might have been reasonable to expect.

tors there), the creatures of Genesis 1 represent animals *as animals* for
the purpose of reflecting on their divine origin and our due relations with
them. In other words, classifying them as "imagery" entirely misses their
import as natural-historical—here, literal—animals. With effects that
were integral to its theological traction, then, early modern Genesis also
represented a founding document in the political sense and an origin story
in the natural-historical sense.

Stemming mainly from intellectual traditions of book learning (rather
than empiricism), classically derived natural history in early modern
contexts operated less as a narrative about origins and more as a catch-
all of recorded knowledge, ancient and modern. In Latin and in vernacular translations, Pliny's encyclopedic *Historia naturalis* dominated the
natural-historical scene, and writers harvested some of their most memorable animal notions from its treasury. Pliny relayed the popular idea that
"bievers . . . gueld themselves, when they see . . . they are . . . in danger
of the hunters: as knowing full well, that chased they bee for their genet-
oires." He also conveys the conceit that bears lick their cubs into shape: at
"first, they seeme to be a lump of white flesh without all form, little bigger than rattons, without eies, & wanting haire; only there is some shew
and apparance of claws that put forth. This rude lumpe, with licking they
fashion by little & little into some shape" (a proposition perhaps due to the
relative nearsightedness typical of humans).[16] Along with astronomy and
geography, the *Historia* treated "the wonderfull shapes of men in diverse
countries"; it catalogued "land creatures, and their kinds," "all fishes, and
creatures of the water," "flying fouls and birds," and "insects" (each a section), and also pharmacology, mining and minerals, and painting, sculp-
ture, and architecture. Pliny and his imitators swept from the stars to the
elements with a comprehensive eclecticism governed more by attention
to scale than by chronology or plot. Nicholas Jardine and Emma Spary describe natural history as a kind of "universal discipline," one that shared
with "civil and sacred history in the revelation of the workings of divine
providence."[17] More particularly, its bursting storehouse of information

16. Pliny, *The Historie of the World, Commonly called, the naturall Historie
of C. Plinius Secundus*, trans. Philemon Holland (London: Adam Islip, 1601), bk. 8,
chap. 30, p. 212, and chap. 36, pp. 215–16. Reactions to the comparative weakness of human vision are discussed in chapter 4 below.

17. Nicholas Jardine and Emma Spary, "The Natures of Cultural History," in
Cultures of Natural History, ed. N. Jardine, J. A. Secord, and E. C. Spary (Cambridge:
Cambridge University Press, 1996), 5.

perfectly complemented the Hexameron's extreme economy of detail, and so it proved readily assimilable to the powerful narrative structure Genesis provided.

The very scope of natural-historical concern (whether we call its holism uni- or multidisciplinary) infused and amplified divine and hexameral writing in early modernity. Du Bartas's 1578 blockbuster verse epic, *La Sepmaine, ou Création du monde* (translated by Joshua Sylvester as *Bartas: His Devine Weekes and Workes* in 1605), and Walter Raleigh's *History of the World* (1614) exemplify painstaking assimilations of natural history's encyclopedic lore to the sequence laid out in the Genesis story.[18] Following Pliny, for example, Du Bartas gives priority among creation's beasts to the elephant, thus inserting a creature not mentioned in scripture but privileged as Pliny's first entry among the land animals:

Of all the Beasts which thou this day did'st build,

. . .

I see (as vice-Roy of their brutish Band)
The Elephant, the Vaunt-guard doth commaund:
Worthie that Office.

Illustrating his awareness of sixteenth-century "news" in natural history as well, Du Bartas records two notorious discoveries at sea:

The Mytred Bishop, and the Cowled Fryer:
Whereof, Examples but a few yeeres since,
Were shown the Norwayes and the Polonian Prince.

For Du Bartas, all of natural history's accumulating detail belongs in this divine story of creation: "Thear's not any part / In this great Frame" he will omit.[19] In a sermon preached before Charles I in 1629, John Donne highlights just such a constitutional, natural-historical Genesis: "Never such a frame . . . set up as this . . . for . . . it is the whole world."[20]

18. Milton's later *Paradise Lost* continued this practice of synthesizing hexameral and natural-historical/scientific material. See Karen L. Edwards, *Milton and the Natural World: Science and Poetry in Paradise Lost* (Cambridge: Cambridge University Press, 1999).

19. Du Bartas, *Devine Weekes*, 192, 147.

20. John Donne, "Sermon Preached before King Charles I," in John Donne, *The Major Works*, ed. John Carey (Oxford: Oxford University Press, 2000), 391.

Across the domains of early modern knowledge, the "great Frame" of Genesis provided a common discourse about how things were ruled. The "whole world" ranged from elements to angels. But for animals in particular, one consequence of this hexameral approach was that a political conception of animal membership and even entitlement presented no insurmountable logical conundrum (as debates about animal rights now seem to do, deriving awkwardly from "*human* rights"). For in addition to the political language of sovereigns and subjects, animals are repeatedly reckoned in terms that sound more ethnographic than taxonomic. The trio of original locales so central to Genesis's account of creation and so important in itemizing the plenary set of living creatures—the seas/waters, the heavens/air, and the field/earth—engendered a sense of proper domains or rightfully assigned spaces specific to different creaturely kinds.

The way Genesis refers to birds, fishes, and beasts each being "of" one of these domains yields a set of subjurisdictions arrayed beneath the monarchy of man. Indeed, the repeated phrasings about animals multiplying "in their kind" suggest not only that there would be a reproductive "keeping to kind" but also that each "race" of creatures would multiply in the sympathetic element proper to its body. Considering why creatures were formed from specific domains, Du Bartas opines that this served so that "each creature might . . . / Part-sympathize with his owne Element."[21] This domain right is, in the language of constitutional analysis, implicit or penumbral in Genesis 1, but it pervades hexamerally inflected literature. For example, Du Bartas narrates how God

> rang[ed] beneath [man's] rule the scaly Nation
> That in the Ocean have their habitation:
> Those that in horror of the Desarts lurke;
> And those that cap'ring in the welkin worke.

He likewise refers to "the skalie Legions / That dumbly dwell in stormie water-Regions" (fishes), the "fethered fingers . . . that haunt the Desarts," and the land creatures, or "stubborn droves" who inhabit "shadie Groves."[22] Repeatedly the locale or domain of the three major kinds appears as proper to them. Indeed, Philip Sidney's translation of Psalm 8:6–9 ("Thou hast made him to have dominion in the workes of thine hands. . . . All sheepe and oxen: yea, and the beastes of the fielde: The foules of the

21. Du Bartas, *Devine Weekes*, 208.
22. Ibid., 273, 334.

ayre, and the fish of the sea, and that which passeth through the paths
of the seas") markedly registers this sense of animal subjurisdictional
claims. He writes,

Thou under [man's] dominion placed
    Both sheep and oxen wholly hast;
    And all the beasts for ever breeding,
    Which in the fertile fields be feeding.

The bird, free-burgess of the air;
    The fish, of sea the native heir;
    And what things else of waters traceth
    The unworn paths, his rule embraceth.[23]

The bird's status as a "free-burgess of the air" and the fish as the sea's "native heir" suggest autonomies and inheritance rights in tension with an unlimited principle ("wholly") of human dominion, a tension with vivid paral-
lels in English constitutional monarchy. Sidney's further stretch—asserting
man's rule over *whatever else* may trace "unworn paths"—reveals the special hubris of a claim to actual rule over things known to be unknown.

By these lights, here I read the early chapters of Genesis broadly in
the mode of constitutional analysis. For early moderns, the constitution it
established cast "everie thing that crepeth and moveth" as a party in interest (Gen. 1:26). In Montaigne's terms, "It is not said, that the essence of
things, hath reference to man alone."[24] Instead, "living creatures" figured
an assemblage of mobile, willing actors with a political order appointed
to them. This zootopian dispensation was enormously cognizant of the
presence of creatures within it, but it was no utopia. As Rebecca Bushnell explains, the earliest legal distinction between a tyrant and a king
proposed that "the king rules willing men, according to the laws; the tyrant rules unwilling men and not according to the laws."[25] Following a
fairly straightforward reading of Genesis, one demonstrably available to
Renaissance and Reformation readers, animals undergo just this historical

23. Quoted in David Norton, *A History of the English Bible as Literature* (Cambridge: Cambridge University Press, 2000), 130.
24. Michel de Montaigne, "The Apologie for Raymond Sebond," in *The Essayes of
Montaigne: John Florio's Translation*, ed. J. I. M. Stewart (New York: Modern Library,
1934), 541.
25. Bushnell, *Tragedies of Tyrants*, 11 (citing Xenophon, *Memorabilia*, 4.6.12).

passage from proper monarchy to endured tyranny, complete with the vexing dilemma of what is to be done with, or to, a tyrant. Animal rebellion,
however, seems more openly endorsable than human rebellion. In Du Bartas's vivid account, "Rebellious *Adam*, from his God revolting, / Findes
his yerst-subjects 'gainst himselfe insulting"; when Adam breaks the order
of law, his "yerst-subjects" resist—with cause—the tyrant's turn. Even domestic animals demonstrate this resistance:

> The Masty[ff] fierce in force,
> Th' untamed Bull, the hot courageous Horse,
> With teeth, w[i]th horns, and hooffes besiege us round,
> As griev'd to see such tyrants tread the ground:
> And there's no Flie so small but now dares bring
> Her little wrath against her *quondam* King.[26]

Here, anyway, the one-time king and now tyrant feels, as justice, the political consequences of his own ethico-legal collapse.

A Zootopian Constitution

The biblical account of the "set[ting] up" of "such a frame" describes the
first arrivals of those living creatures whose habitat—and stage—the world
would become. While the "rule" (Gen. 1:26) granted to man is the best-
known detail of human/animal relations in this story, Genesis's early
chapters do not distinguish man and animal for every purpose.[27] In the
Hebrew text, the recurring phrase *nefesh chayah*, "living soul," characterizes both humans and animals (though in the traditions of its translation,
"living soul" accrues to humans, and "living things" names the balance
of other beings).[28] The overarching conceptual category of "creatures" had
enormous philosophical and ethical significance, as Julia Reinhard Lupton has shown in an important account of *The Tempest*'s Caliban. "Above

---

26. Du Bartas, *Devine Weekes*, 334–35 (italics added).

27. Here and in Genesis 1:28, the King James Version uses "have dominion" instead
of "rule." See *The Holy Bible conteyning the Old Testament, and the New: newly
translated out of the originall tongues: . . . by his Majesties speciall co[m]mandement*
(London: Robert Barker, 1611), A1v. For a religious critique of dominion, see Matthew
Scully, *Dominion: The Power of Man, the Suffering of Animals, and the Call to Mercy*
(New York: St. Martin's, 2002).

28. J. R. Hyland, *God's Covenant with the Animals: A Biblical Basis for the Humane Treatment of All Creatures* (Brooklyn, NY: Lantern Books, 2000), 73.

all a theological conceptualization of natural phenomena," Lupton writes, the term "creature" "indicates a made or fashioned thing but with a sense of continued or potential process, action, or emergence"; "in the discourse of the creaturely, the image of the cosmos . . . is never distant."[29] Creatureliness, then, unifies the living artifacts of Creation in a shared status that is, at once, both contingent and stakeholding—the classic ambivalence inherent in the structure of the political subject as such.

Genesis 1 not only blesses all creatures by exhorting them to be fruitful and multiply. It also explicitly accords all created beings a common entitlement to plants as food. In the words of the Geneva Bible (1560), "God said, Behold, I have given unto you every herbe bearing sede . . . & everie tre, wherein is the frute of a tre bearing sede: that shall be to you for meat." Immediately on the heels of this grant to humans, the grant to other creatures is described as the same: "Likewise to everie beast of the earth, and everie foule of the heaven, & to everie thing that crepeth and moveth upon the earth which hathe life in it selfe, everie grene herbe shalbe for meat."[30] One grant is made to mankind as addressee and the other in the third person, but the speech act the text claims to record characterizes "everie thing that moveth" as *likewise* entitled. If we consider vulnerability to being devoured as "meat," a more primal divide than the one separating man from beast distinguishes "everie thing that moveth" from plants. Chapter 2 will detail how animal locomotion persistently disturbs their corralling inside the fixed category of either fodder or objects. But while an observer such as Martin Luther could pose the question, "Whereunto serve the raven and crows, but to call upon the Lord who nourishes them?" and thus accord animals their part in the service of God, as we have seen in the introduction the Cartesian paradigm will deprive animals of any residual claim to stakeholdership by revising Genesis and reclassifying animals as unentitled things, whether as "meat" or "machines."[31]

Genesis's first charter thus fashions plants as commodity-like con-

29. Julia Reinhard Lupton, "Creature Caliban," *Shakespeare Quarterly* 51, no. 1 (2000): 1, 3. Eric Santner explores "creaturely life," though (as we have seen in Foucault and Agamben) for the modern writers he addresses, "creaturely life is a dimension of human existence" rather than a name for that life that is not exclusive to humans. *On Creaturely Life: Rilke, Benjamin, Sebald* (Chicago: University of Chicago Press, 2006), xv.

30. Gen. 1:29–30. For discussion of this verse's legal force, see chapter 5.

31. Martin Luther, *The Table Talk of Martin Luther*, ed. William Hazlitt (London: Bohn, 1857), 58. A posthumous compilation of sayings, the first German edition, *Tischreden oder Colloquia Doctor Martin Luthers*, was published in Eisleben in 1566

sumable *things* for human and animal use, but animals are placed in a
political relation with humans as the herb-entitled subjects of human
"rule." Indeed, when he dubs animals our "Fellow-commoners" in his introduction to Edward Topsell's *The Historie of Foure-footed Beastes*, John
Rowland reflects this sense of a specifically scriptural entitlement and
measures its consequences in political terms: "Next unto Man are these
Creatures rankt in dignity, and they were ordained by God to live upon
the same earth, and to be Fellow-commoners with Man; having all the
Plants and Vegetables appointed them for their food as well as Man had."[32]
The mutual right to plants established in Genesis casts animals and people as "Fellow-commoners" as an inclusive matter of rank and dignity, the
very terms used to calibrate authorities among people. The opening line
of Genesis's second chapter, which begins the seventh day, retrospectively
gathers these grass-fed creatures as a "hoste": "Thus the heavens and the
earth were finished, & all the hoste of them" (Gen. 2:1). The Geneva Bible,
with its prolific annotations, glosses this host as "the innumerable abun-
dance of creatures in heave[n] & earth."

Referencing the arrangement of kinds that Genesis initially records,
this chapter assesses the dynamics within its "hoste" to argue that early
moderns read Genesis historically—not just in terms of human history
but also in terms of natural history. They conceived cross-species relations
by scriptural lights and as a result understood those relations in much
more political and constitutional terms than we now conventionally do.
As is evident in Latour's elucidation of "the modern constitution" (in
which "the scientific power [is] charged with representing things and the
political power charged with representing subjects," as we have seen) or
even in the exclusively human idea familiar in British studies as "the un-
written constitution," constitutional analysis is not limited to narrowly
contractual arrangements.[33] Constitutions are not always on paper. At the
same time, we need not be especially metaphorical or abstract regarding
the constitutional and even legal valences of early modern Genesis. Ani-

---

under the editorship of Johannes Aurifaber, who studied with Luther and was serving as
his private secretary at the time of Luther's death.

32. Edward Topsell and Thomas Muffet, *The History of Four-footed Beasts and
Serpents [and] The Theater of Insects, or Lesser Living Creatures*, ed. John Rowland
(London: Ellen Cotes, 1658 [1607]), A4v. Subsequent references to Rowland's introduc-
tion to his republication of Topsell appear as Rowland (1658).

33. Latour, *We Have Never Been Modern*, 27–29.

mated by its dispensations, commentators endorsed a zootopian constitution, that is, a multikinded domain whose diverse parties are governed
by shared rules. What Donne calls "the whole world" is a realm where
nature has not yet been made a distinct sphere dictated by the separate
mechanical principles of what would become modern science, as Latour
has indelibly described. A broader discourse of the arts of governance, instead, underwrites a largely continuous domain of natural and theological knowledge. Each creature is incorporated and enfranchised to act by
a kind of enabling legislation, a law of its nature. In Du Bartas's rhyme,
"Forming this mighty Frame, [God] every Kind / With divers and peculiar
Signet sign'd."[34] These inscribed principles of governance enshrine a far
more textual and legal sense of the world as an unfolding of "divers and
peculiar" but connate nature(s) inscribed in bodies by a lawgiver.

The life and motions of the world were described not by physics or
numerical principles, but instead by a profoundly textualist sense of law
as written in things and continually emerging through their actions.
Animals presented a unique situation among the rest of creation. Inter-
action with them, however "unreasonable" they were officially said to
be, had led the observant to note their tendencies to recalcitrance, will,
resistance, and prerogative. Their mobility and normal physical freedom
highlighted this. Although elsewhere he defends a human power over the
inclinations set within things themselves, in construing the suggestion in
Romans 8:19–22 that creatures, too, await deliverance with hope, John
Calvin calls on this sense of natural law. "Since there is no reason in
[mute] creatures, their will is to be taken . . . for their natural inclination,
according to which the whole nature of things tends to its own preservation and perfection," he writes, adding that "in the sad disorder which followed the fall of Adam, the whole machinery of the world would have in-
stantly become deranged, and all its parts would have failed had not some
hidden strength supported them."[35] Listing each item of the cosmos, the
Edwardine *Homily on Obedience* (1547) likewise describes how creatures
jointly and severally "kepe their ordre," "keepe them in their ordre," and
"kepe their comely course and ordre," configuring natural law as a disper-

---

34. Du Bartas, *Devine Weekes*, 148. For a discussion of "signatures," see Michel
Foucault, *The Order of Things: An Archeology of the Human Sciences* (New York:
Vintage Books, 1970), 24–29.

35. John Calvin, *Commentaries on the Epistle of Paul to the Romans*, trans. John
Owen (Whitefish, MT: Kessinger Publishing, 2006 [1849]), 304–5.

sal of agency and autonomy.[36] In the same vein, Richard Hooker's magisterial *Of the Laws of Ecclesiastical Polity* (1593) asserts that God's "commanding those things to be which are, and to be in such sort as they are, to keep that tenure and course which they do, importeth the establishment of nature's law."[37] There are scattered microsovereignties and dispersed capacities in the lawful cosmic framework of the sixteenth century. Echoing Lupton's description of creaturely "emergence," each has its own proper law (the law of its nature), which is a "course" it is said to "keep" by its own inclination. The meaningfulness of "following" or "obeying" a law, of course, incorporates not only the power of not following but the sense of "accord" Du Bartas indexed.

Usage in these contexts shows how "law" indicated a less anthropocentric and much vaster phenomenon than that plenary set of enactments in a human jurisdiction that the term now usually denotes. Meanwhile, human-enacted laws suggested a compensatory adaptation to humanity's fallen state and a limping imitation of the divine model. Vigorous debates about the relations among natural, civil, and canon law, of course, would concern thinkers of all stripes throughout this period. More broadly, however, for the purpose of considering the interface between law and species, two key attributes of natural law stand out. Its priority in time and its unlimited applicability or global reach both highlight the local and transient quality of laws that are (merely) the "inventions" of a humbler humanity. Reflecting the premodern importance of the three creaturely domains, for example, Justinian's *Institutes* described natural law in Roman contexts this way: "The law of nature is that which nature teaches all animals. For that law *is not proper to the human race, but it is common to all animals* which are born on the earth and in the sea, and to the birds also."[38] We see this proposition relayed by the early English theorist of equity, Christo-

36. "On Good Order, and Obedience to Rulers," in *Certain sermons or homilies (1547)* and *A homily against disobedience and wilful rebellion (1570)*, ed. Ronald B. Bond (Toronto: University of Toronto Press, 1987), 161. This homily is attributed to Thomas Cranmer.

37. Richard Hooker, *Of the Laws of Ecclesiastical Polity*, ed. Arthur Stephen McGrade (Cambridge: Cambridge University Press, 1989), 60. Hooker distinguishes between "natural" and voluntary" agency; nonhumans exercise both kinds, though in a different balance than humans (59, 68, 77, 124). On the dispersal of powers suggested by diverse natures and their laws, see chapter 2; on intermittency, see chapter 4.

38. Justinian, *Institutes*, bk. 1, 1.2, quoted in Jean Porter, *Nature as Reason: A Thomistic Theory of Natural Law* (Grand Rapids, MI: William B. Eerdman, 2005), 346 (italics added).

pher St. German, who accords "unreasonable creatures" their own proper
relation to law: "The lawe of nature maye be consydered in two maners,
that is to say generally & specially . . . considered generally, then it is referred to all creatures, as well reasonable as unreasonable: for all unreasonable creatures lyve under a certayne reule to them gyven by nature[;] . . .
the law of nature specially considered . . . also called the lawe of reason[,]
pertayneth onely to creatures reasonable[,] that is[,] Man."[39] This sense of
law as "not proper to the human race," but as both divine and commonly
operative among creatures "unreasonable" (who nevertheless manage to
live "under . . . reule") indicates how natural history and theology alike
drew on legally inflected notions of dispersed or delegated governance, of
things *keeping themselves* in order—in Du Bartas's sense, by "their owne
accord."

The canonist Gratian's twelfth-century assimilation of Roman law to
Christian doctrines had also emphasized a law prior to human law and
ranked above it, asserting that "all ordinances are either divine or human"
and that "Divine ordinances are determined by nature, human ordinances
by usages; and thus the latter vary since different things please different people" (here we see why human law is variable and therefore inferior in kind); the glossator of Gratian's *Decretum* indicates, further, that
natural law thus defined "possesses the greatest antiquity and dignity."[40]
St. German evidences the same confidence in a law before and apart from
the human. Defining the "Law Eternal," he avows that "it is well called
the first, for it was before all other laws and *all other laws be derived of
it.*"[41] Human laws, then, were held to be weaker derivatives of something
larger that was dispersed among creatures and persistently named as the
law's original. As Cynthia Herrup puts this comparative circumspection
about human government, the need for it was considered "a consequence
of humanity's fall from grace," because "Christian theorists had for centuries agreed that a holy commonwealth would have no need of externally
imposed discipline[;] [k]ingship was the best form of government because

39. Christopher St. German, *The Dialogues in Englysshe, bytwene a Doctour of
Dyvynyte and a Student in the lawes of Englande* (London: Wyllyam Myddylton, 1543),
fol. 4 (chap. 2). This is believed to be St. German's own translation of his *Dialogus de
fundamentis legum Angliae and de conscientia* (1528).

40. Gratian, *The Treatise on Laws (Decretum DD 1–20)*, trans. Augustine Thomp-
son, with *The Ordinary Gloss*, trans. James Gordley (Washington, DC: Catholic University of America Press, 1993), 3–4.

41. St. German, *Dialogues in Englysshe*, fol. 2 (chap. 1) (italics added).

it was the simplest, but monarchy was still only the best of a bad lot."[42] James I, in *Basilikon Doron* (1599), sharply distinguishes "betwixt the expresse commandement and will of God in his word, and the invention or ordinance of man," cautioning his heir against the overgeneration of new laws.[43] Because statutory enactments and positive law were "human inventions" that only imitated prior, more durable, and more sweeping cosmic laws, their human authorship positioned human laws as the lowest-ranked iteration of lawfulness. A human origin, in other words, was no special virtue in a law.

Its consideration of lawfulness as not exclusively human but as a characteristic of animals too marks the zootopian quality of the premodern constitution; it sets law apart from a narrowly human sense of language and into the wills, bodies, and actions of all "creatures." Beyond distributed lawfulness of this sort, creaturely capacities for signification in general associate animals, law, and legibility in perhaps a more familiar way. From a broad historical standpoint concerning the alleged humanness of language and signifying capability, the highly durable "two books" tradition aligned the earlier Book of Creatures with the subsequent Book of Scripture, making "the Word" an attribute of God, *not an index of humanity*. Shakespeare's much-cited phrase gives the densest compression of this tradition: there are "tongues in trees, books in the running brooks" (*As You Like It*, 2.1.16). For Renaissance commentators, as for their predecessors, the scriptural locus for this line of thought is Romans 1:20: "For the invisible things of him, that is, his eternal power and Godhead, are seene by the creation of the worlde, being considered in his workes." The passage generated controversy when an interpretation of it might seem to erode the supremacy to be accorded to scripture, and it held serious potential for unorthodox claims on behalf of natural evidence and lay readership (as evident in Montaigne's translation of and apology for Raymond Sebond's *Liber naturae sive creaturarum*). It was also very widely cited by scientific observers as justification for what otherwise might seem their transgressions against divine secrets.

When Raleigh analyzes Paul's verse in *The History of the World* ("the invisible thinges of God [saith S. Paul] are seene by creation of the world,

42. Cynthia Herrup, "The King's Two Genders," *Journal of British Studies* 45 (July 2006): 497.

43. King James VI and I, *Basilikon Doron*, in *Political Writings*, ed. Johann Sommerville (Cambridge: Cambridge University Press, 1994), 19. See also Erasmus, *Education of a Christian Prince*, 79–80.

being considered in his Creatures"), he describes the world as the "understood language of the Almightie, vouchsafed to all his Creatures, whose Hieroglyphicall Characters [are] . . . written . . . on the Earth and the Seas, by the letters of all those living Creatures, and plants, which . . . reside therein."[44] Topsell's book on quadrupeds even claims that this living textual material should be "preferred before the Chronicles and records of al ages made by men." With no experience of extinction, he distinguishes creaturely life as permanently relevant compared to the merely accidental nature of human history: "This History . . . sheweth that Chronicle which was made by God himselfe, every living beast being a word, every kind being a sentence, and all of them together a large history . . . which was, which is, which shall continue . . . yet to the world's end."[45] Indeed, for Topsell, a clergyman himself, natural history had such a divine pedigree that "no man ought rather to publish this unto the World, then a Divine or Preacher."[46] Literalized in the biblical injunction to "aske now the beasts, and they shall teach thee, and the foules of the heaven, and they shall tell thee" (Job 12:7), the scriptural fabric of natural thought generally accorded signifying power to all parts of creation and not uniquely to humans. For figures such as Topsell, the study of nature would even take the human race forward in a project where "confused Babels tongues are againe reduced to their significant Dialects."[47] Brutish human gibberish could be improved by the study of a coherence evident in animals. Meaning, then, was no monopoly of human speech; it certainly did not depend on the Babel of our fallen languages.

As Peter Harrison has described, the lingering "hieroglyphic conception of nature" marking the "two books" tradition locates sixteenth and early seventeenth-century natural history largely within the sphere of "humane learning," where "the elucidation of the natural world . . . called for an interpretive, rather than a classificatory or mathematical, science" and where interpretation led away from "naked words to the infinitely more eloquent things of nature" to which human language referred.[48] This

---

44. Walter Raleigh, *The History of the World* (London: Walter Burre, 1614), 2.

45. Topsell, epistle dedicatory, *Foure-Footed Beastes.*

46. Ibid., A3v.

47. Ibid. A3.

48. Peter Harrison, *The Bible, Protestantism, and the Rise of Natural Science* (Cambridge: Cambridge University Press, 1998), 2–4 (see esp. 3n5). Harrison's account provides comprehensive analysis of religion and science in the larger context of shifting interpretive practice, tracing the eclipse of textualism in the transition from *scientia* to technoscience.

textually framed, legible cosmos would be superseded in the seventeenth
century in a transition that James Bono has concisely termed a passage
"from symbolic exegesis to deinscriptive hermeneutics" (emphasizing, for
example, Galileo's "advocacy of mathematics as the proper language of nature").[49] Against this conceived eloquence of nature, according to the eye-
witness account of Nicholas Fontaine (1625–1709), the Cartesians at Port
Royal "administered beatings to dogs with perfect indifference, and made
fun of those who pitied the creatures as if they felt pain. They said the animals were clocks; that the cries they emitted when struck were only the
noise of a little spring that had been touched, but that the whole body was
without feeling."[50] Indeed, the Cartesian Nicolas de Malebranche vividly
compressed the claim that animals "eat without pleasure, cry without
pain, grow without knowing it; they desire nothing, fear nothing, know
nothing."[51] Fueled by such renderings of the cries of animals being "rent
and torn" under vivisection as nonsignifying, the seventeenth-century
collapse of this hermeneutic approach to nature would consequentially
deny "the capacity of things to act as signs."[52] Writers such as Gesner had
been persistently motivated to include all of the animals mentioned in
scripture in their collections, and the colophon to his *Historiae Animalium* shows an Edenic scene (fig. 1.1). Rowland introduces Topsell's translation with sweeping biblical comparisons: "This History seems . . . to be
like another Ark of Noah, wherein the several kinds of beasts are . . . met
together for their better preservation in the understanding of man," and it
is also "like to another Paradise, where the Beasts, as they were brought to
Adam, are again described by their natures."[53] Topsell's own epistle dedicatory defends the divinity of the subject with passion. Indeed, in praising
Gesner's colossal research (achieved by coordinating a far-flung network of
contributors, as Aristotle's had been), Topsell imagines a scene in which

49. James J. Bono, *The Word of God and the Languages of Man: Interpreting Nature
in Early Modern Science and Medicine* (Madison: University of Wisconsin Press, 1995),
167–68.

50. Nicholas Fontaine, *Memoirs pour servir à l'histoire de Port-Royal* (Cologne,
Germany, 1738), quoted in Alan Carter, "Animals, Pain, and Morality," *Journal of
Applied Philosophy* 22, no. 1 (2005): 17. See also Richard Ryder, *Animal Revolution:
Changing Attitudes toward Speciesism* (Oxford: Berg, 2000), 53.

51. Cited in Steven Nadler, ed., *The Cambridge Companion to Malebranche* (Cambridge: Cambridge University Press, 2000), 42.

52. Harrison, *Bible, Protestantism*, 4.

53. Rowland, epistle dedicatory (1658), A4r–v.

Figure 1.1. Conrad Gesner, colophon, *Historiae Animalium, Liber 1*
(de Quadrupedibus) (Zurich, 1551). Image courtesy of the Charles Deering
McCormick Library of Special Collections, Northwestern University Library.

"all living creatures shall witnesse for him at the last day."[54] No creaking
hinges or squeaky gears, these creatures participate in the cosmos, taking
the part of articulate witnesses.

Due to the convergence of natural-historical material and the Christian theology by which it was read, to treat creation's animals and their
descendants as emblems, allegories, animal imagery, or *topoi*—that is,
literary/poetic projections of exclusively human meanings—would be to
miss the preoccupations of early modern thought. As we have seen in the
introduction, Haraway challenges Lévi-Strauss's anthropological notion
that "animals are good to think with" for its investigative and intellectual
limitedness. Arguing against the species myopia that would make animals
no more than "an alibi" for human themes, she insists on a less exclusively
human account. Animals "are not just here [for us] to think with," but have
an earthly tenure glaringly similar to our own, a tenure that was especially

54. Topsell, epistle dedicatory, *Foure-Footed Beastes.*

vivid for writers steeped in a hexameral narrative.[55] John Berger, analyzing a historic break in cross-species relations, argued that "before this rupture, animals constituted the first circle of what surrounded man. Perhaps that already suggests too great a distance. They were with man at the centre of his world."[56] Topsell's language literally verifies Berger's observation: "It is most cleare in Gen[esis] how the Holy ghost remembreth the creation of al living creatures, and the Four-footed next before the creation of man, as thogh they alone were apointed the Ushers, going immediately before the race of men."[57] From this perspective, animal proximity and participation signified as much as their categorical difference (let alone binary opposition); a "hoste" of creatures partake in a remembered creation.

Reading by the lights of Genesis, animals—obviously—were there at the beginning. They were even "here first," as we say in human contexts of imperial and colonial conquest. Although priority in time can be trumped by other rationales, it ranks as one of the most powerful principles in ethico-legal debates that weigh competing interests. Rowland stresses it in his introduction to Topsell: "Next unto man in dignity," he notes, animals "have obtained one priviledge beyond us, in that they were created before man was."[58] As the close readers of the Renaissance and Reformation well knew, Genesis unveils an articulated procession of animal kinds, each given form from the elements that had just been separated into earth and water, which themselves were fashioned from a world that was "without forme & voyde" (Gen. 1:1). Man comes last in the series. First of all the creatures, from the waters on the fifth day, "everie creping thing" arises (the Geneva Bible glosses them marginally as "fish and wormes whiche slide, swimme, or crepe"); then come "the great whales"; and then "everie fethered fowle." On the sixth day, "the beast[s] of the earth" are created, "the cattel," and "everie creping thing of the earth," and then "[f]urthermore . . . man" (Gen. 1:20–26; italics added). Genesis then places all preceding creatures under the newcomer's responsibility and governance, allowing humans to "rule over the fish of the sea, and over the foule of the heaven, and over the beastes, & and over all the earth, and over everie thing that crepeth & moveth on the earth" (Gen. 1:26).

55. Donna Haraway, *The Companion Species Manifesto: Dogs, People, and Significant Otherness* (Chicago: Prickly Paradigm Press, 2003), 5.

56. John Berger, "Why Look at Animals?" *About Looking* (London: Writers and Readers, 1980), 1.

57. Topsell, epistle dedicatory.

58. Rowland, epistle dedicatory (1658).

Once installed in Eden, Adam is tasked to "dresse it and kepe it." The Geneva gloss explains this charge as a prevention of idleness, "thogh as yet there was no nede to labour" (Gen. 2:15, k). This represents the sole textual elaboration of what prelapsarian human "rule" entails.

The Fall "of man" affects everybody, including animal bystanders to human sin. For animals, the great change manifests itself as a transformation in the kind of dominion they endure. We could read this broad impact as some commentators do: as proof that animals (and indeed the entire material world) are mere stage properties for an exclusively human moral drama. Calvin, for example, anticipates certain objections to such a reading. Commenting on Hosea 4:3 and instancing again the tripartite realms of creaturely life, he argues that "the Prophet here enlarges on the greatness of God's wrath; for he includes even the innocent beasts and the birds of heaven, yea, the fishes of the sea. . . . But some one may . . . object . . . that it is unworthy of God to be angry with miserable creatures, which deserve no such treatment: for why should God be angry with fishes and beasts?" He counters this objection by answering that because "beasts, and birds, and fishes, and, in a word, all other things, have been created for the use of men, it is no wonder that God should extend the tokens of his curse to all creatures, above and below, when his purpose is to punish men."[59] Despite the ready availability of rationales like this, by some equitable logic or nagging doubt, a lingering sense of the mismatch between human transgression and the wider sweep of its consequences leaves open for many writers what we can only call *a justice problem*.

For these thinkers, Genesis suggests a political narrative of dispossession and unjust servitude. If, as Donne muses, "only perchance beasts sin not," and "both beasts and plants [were] cursed in the curse of man," why does their innocence bear the burden of punishments proper to Adam and Eve?[60] As a result of this lingering justice problem, for Protestant reformers, resistance theorists, and writers including Du Bartas, Montaigne, Sidney, Gascoigne, and Shakespeare, postlapsarian animals languish under conditions they readily name tyrannical. What effect does the possibility that animals might be subject to something called "tyranny" have on our ideas of human/animal arrangements before Descartes? Or on the cross-

59. John Calvin, *Commentaries on the Twelve Minor Prophets*, trans. John Owen (Edinburgh: Calvin Translation Society, 1846), 1:143–44.
60. John Donne, "To Sir Henry Wotton," in *The Complete English Poems*, ed. A. J. Smith (London: Penguin, 1986), 215, line 41, and John Donne, "Anatomy of the World," in ibid., 275, line 200.

species identificatory potential that shared vulnerability to tyrannical oppression suggests? Or, for that matter, on the species limits we routinely
place on a term such as "politics"? The question of tyranny, after all, cen-
trally organized the collective sixteenth-century rumination on the nature of monarchical power. If animals were legible as *tyrannized subjects*,
in other words, something properly belonging to them, some sovereignty
they retained, was understood to have been abused or denied. Though such
animal entitlements may seem unenforceable, a verdict of constitutional
abuse still holds: their apparently remediless situation echoes sixteenth-
century human subjects' own general lack of a clearly *licit* remedy against
tyrannical kings. In most accounts of human politics, modern contractual
or language-based mythologies of threshold consent did not yet apply in an
operative way; thus political resistance stood in such need of theorists.[61]

At stake in reading the political valences of the Christian doctrine of
Creation is the fact that—against emerging seventeenth-century technoscience and the grain of most discourses of politics—pre-Cartesian thought
very commonly accorded certain forms of stakeholdership to animals.
Throughout *The Devine Weekes*, for example, Du Bartas calls animals
citizens, burghers, and people: God "peopled this large Theater / With living Creatures," with "Sea-Citizens" or "the people of the water" and with
the earthy "slimie Burgers of this Earthly ball."[62] This is not to say that
early moderns ranked animals as equals. They were constantly dubbed
"unreasonable creatures."[63] But, in certain tallies, the creatureliness mat-
tered more than the alleged unreasonableness. The scripturally influenced
reckoning I am tracing classifies animals as the law's first subjects and
the first plaintiff-victims of tyrannical oppression. Against this backdrop,
contemporary habits of abjecting animals as "outside the law" derive from

61. In fact the animal entitlements of Genesis were *not* wholly beyond judicial
cognizance (see chapter 5). Ponet's justification of tyrannicide must invoke an implicit
right: "Now forasmuche as ther is no expresse positive lawe for punishement of a
Tyranne among christen men, the question is, whether it be lawfull to kill" one (*Short
Treatise*, chap. 6, Giiir).
62. Du Bartas, *Devine Weekes*, 146, 145, 208.
63. As Erica Fudge and Karen L. Raber have carefully demonstrated, debates about
animal reason served to convey substantial evidence that they did, despite this moniker. See Fudge, *Brutal Reasoning: Animals, Rationality, and Humanity in Early Modern England* (Ithaca, NY: Cornell University Press, 2006), and Raber, "'Reasonable
Creatures': William Cavendish and the Art of Dressage in Early Modern England," in
Renaissance Culture and the Everyday, ed. Patricia Fumerton (Philadelphia: University
of Pennsylvania Press, 1998), 42–66.

a more recent human-exceptionalist model of symbolic language. This model cancels animal membership even as it romanticizes their so-called freedom from the law. A fundamentally modern sense of *"the* animal" as humanity's persistent, solitary, ontological opposite derives from a mode of thought whose trajectory may be said to end with a suggestion in Derrida's *The Animal That Therefore I Am.* To deconstruct the confinement of "the animal," he writes, would "be a matter . . . perhaps of acceding to a thinking, however fabulous and chimerical . . . that thinks the absence of the name and of the word . . . as something other than a privation."[64] That major sentence, however oblique its formulation, is the closest approach philosophy (postmodern or otherwise) makes to the premodern, natural-historical, and scripturally informed vision of a zootopian constitution, where the possession of animated and cognizable interests is not yet the monopolistic property of a more singularized humanity.

Instead—partly because humans have never so mastered meaning that they could exclude the nonhuman from their signifying acts, partly because the idea that signification is exclusively human depends on the rise of technoscience in the seventeenth century, and partly because at times we have aimed to speak of them—with the early modern descendants of Genesis we "really" are talking about those we now group under the collective English noun "animals." In the aftermath of technoscience and the Enlightenment, we have preferred our textual animals "fabulous and chimerical," as fables, symbols, "animal imagery," or any other confinement we can think of to dematerialize their stakeholdership or participation. But the broadly hexameral discourses of the long sixteenth century did not construct them that way. The balance of this chapter will trace the persistently political cast accorded to human/animal relations in early modern commentators on Genesis: biblical scholars, resistance theorists, Sidney's "On Ister Bank," Gascoigne's poems of animal complaint, Montaigne, and Shakespeare's *As You Like It,* a familiar text for which this analysis of historical animals provides, I hope, a new horizon of possibility.

The Political Terms of Cross-Species Relations

Introducing his discussion of sovereign power and "bare life," Agamben suggests that to speak of "a *zoë politikë* of the citizens of Athens would have made no sense."[65] Normal definitions of politics reject the (fabulous,

---

64. Derrida, *The Animal That Therefore I Am,* 48.
65. Agamben, *Homo Sacer,* 1–2.

chimerical) *non*-sense of animal membership and make animals their
first, often implicit, exclusion. They refer instead to relations within the
human or among a subset of humans, with occasional important considerations of humans-not-human-enough to partake in the polity, such as
women, slaves, prisoners, or immigrants. Consistent with his glossing of
man as the "political animal" (and less consistent with his voluminous
accounts of actual animals), Aristotle begins the long, Western philosophical characterization of nonhumans as *un*-political animals. He marshals
a now-familiar discourse of language-based association:

> Man is by nature . . . more of a political animal than bees or any other
> gregarious animals. . . . Man is the only animal who has the gift of
> speech. And whereas mere voice is but an indication of pleasure or
> pain, and is therefore found in other animals (for their nature attains to
> the perception of pleasure and pain and the intimation of them to one
> another, and no further), the power of speech is intended to set forth
> the expedient and inexpedient, and therefore likewise the just and the
> unjust. And it is a characteristic of man that he alone has any sense of
> good and evil, of just and unjust.[66]

Note how Aristotle's account of animal "voice" contravenes the framework
supporting the idea that they "cry without pain." Man's being relatively
"more" of a political animal than bees and "other gregarious animals"
might be seen to concede a measure of politicity to animals. The force of
Aristotle's argument here, however, continues in the opposite direction,
asserting the rhetorical "power of speech" over those mere voicings and
"intimations" of meaning relayed among animals. As Descartes would
do later, Aristotle works backward from the general comprehensibility of
human speech to other humans (i.e., communication within species), to

---

66. Aristotle, *The Politics*, bk. 1, 1253a, in *The Politics and The Constitution of
Athens*, ed. Stephen Everson (Cambridge: Cambridge University Press, 1996), 13. To opposite effect, Alice Kuzniar observes the powerful force of shame among pack animals,
contradicting the idea of an exclusively human sense of right and wrong. See Kuzniar,
Melancholia's Dog: Reflections on Our Animal Kinship (Chicago: University of Chicago Press, 2006), 71–72. As Foucault reflects, contemplating the rise of biopolitics and
an end of traditionally conceived politicity, "for millennia, man remained what he was
to Aristotle: a living animal with the additional capacity for political existence; modern
man is an animal whose politics place his existence as a living being in question."
Foucault, *The History of Sexuality*, vol. 1, *An Introduction*, trans. Robert Hurley (New
York: Vintage Books, 1990 [1976]), 143.

the assertion of political capacity in humans, to a denial of it in animals. Animals have no language, the disjointed argument goes, because we fail to understand them. The animal political potential that is denied in this mode of analysis, of course, could never be demonstrated *across species* in the absence of a shared denominator of translation or comprehensibility (the unavailability of which Montaigne blamed as much on us as on them).[67]

Thomas Aquinas further bolts the door: "When we hear it said, 'Thou shalt not kill,' we do not take it as referring to trees, for they have no sense, nor to irrational animals, because they have no fellowship with us."[68] Animals lack rational fellowship with us, so it follows that the obligations of the Ten Commandments cannot pertain. Hobbes, too, invokes his considerable expertise on contract to explain that "to make Covenant with bruit Beasts, is impossible; because not understanding our speech, they understand not, nor accept of any translation of Right, nor can translate any Right to another: and without mutuall acceptation, there is no Covenant."[69] Levinas, despite his astonishingly suggestive account of animal testimony in "The Name of the Dog," likewise excludes animals from ethical participation.[70] In *The Animal That Therefore I Am*, as we have seen, Derrida gestures toward grave philosophical questions concerning this exclusion of animals, but the premise of *The Beast and the Sovereign* unites beast and sovereign in their nonsubjection to the law.[71] This prem-

67. Montaigne, "Apologie," 399. For an account of this epistemological dilemma second only to Montaigne's, see Thomas Nagel, "What Is It Like to Be a Bat?" *Philosophical Review* 83, no. 4 (October 1974): 435–50.

68. Thomas Aquinas, *Summa Theologica*, question 64, article 1, cited in Andrew Linzey, *Animal Theology* (Urbana: University of Illinois Press, 1995), 14. Christian thought often holds cruelty to animals disrespectful of their divine origins, but the obligation is to God, not animals. See Keith Thomas, *Man and the Natural World: Changing Attitudes in England, 1500–1800* (Oxford: Oxford University Press, 1996 [1983]), 155–58, and Erica Fudge, *Perceiving Animals: Humans and Beasts in Early Modern English Culture* (Urbana: University of Illinois Press, 2002 [1999]), 143–66.

69. Thomas Hobbes, *Leviathan*, ed. Richard Flathman and David Johnston (New York: Norton, 1996), 77.

70. Emmanuel Levinas, "The Name of a Dog," in *Difficult Freedom* (Baltimore: Johns Hopkins University Press, 1990), 151–53, and Levinas, interview, *Animal Philosophy: Essential Readings in Continental Thought*, ed. Matthew Calarco and Peter Atterton (London: Continuum, 2004), 49–50. For more detailed analysis of this paradox in Levinas, see chapter 5 below.

71. Jacques Derrida, *The Beast and the Sovereign*, trans. Geoffrey Bennington (Chicago: University of Chicago Press, 2009).

ise pertains more to a secular and post-seventeenth-century narrowing of what law (and language too) can mean. To propose that the sovereign was above or outside the law was an insurgent conservative idea in early modernity, advocated, for example, by James I in *The Trew Law of Free Monarchy* (1598); the idea that beasts were outside the law had no force at the cosmographic level from which ideas of human "law" derived, as we have seen.

From Aristotle to Aquinas, to Hobbes, to Agamben, and even to Levinas, we see an echo of the popular *human* opinion, philosophical and exceptionalist in nature, that there is a capacity possessed exclusively by humans called politicity and that is manifested directly through the consent mechanism of a functioning symbolic language that animals can be said to lack—although few contemporary commentators sustain a faith in the efficacy or transparency of language when considering it for other purposes. As Keith Thomas has observed, "Official attitudes" normally express an "uncompromisingly aggressive view of man's place in the natural world," while actual practices were more ambiguous and scatter in several directions.[72] Even within human acts of representation, diverse signifying imperatives persistently undermine more direct, "official" proclamations. This, in part, is why a literary-historical inquiry yields a different account of human and animal relations than the philosophical tradition.

Against the official chorus of human denials both philosophical and mundane, Genesis establishes a sequence of fundamentally political relations between humans and animals: good governance or stewardship, obedience, and then a new adversity triggered by human transgression of divine law. The asymmetrical degeneration of human/animal relations stems from human sin. As Calvin reflects, "It is indeed meet for us to consider what a dreadful curse we have deserved, since all created things, in themselves blameless, undergo punishment for our sins; for it has not happened through their own fault that they are liable to corruption. Thus the condemnation of mankind is imprinted . . . on all creatures."[73] Those clearly blameless, Calvin emphasizes, incur liability without fault; in another context, as we have seen, he stresses their guiltless condition as "innocent beasts." Because this handling of "punishment" contradicts the fundamental logic of justice, for a host of writers human-exceptionalist

72. Thomas, *Man and the Natural World*, 50. Thomas gives an extensive sample of "official attitudes" in early modernity into the eighteenth century (17–25). See also Fudge, *Perceiving Animals*, especially the discussion of the bear garden (11–33).

73. Calvin, *Commentaries on the Epistle of Paul to the Romans*, 305.

theological rationales are insufficient to put this justice problem to rest. This context shows how notions of "animal innocence" derive not just from some rising sense of wild freedom from culture or law that develops with industrialization or from their infantilization in the Disney World of contemporary commodity culture. Instead, "animal innocence" derives from its legal and biblical sense at this pivotal moment in biblical mythography. As Calvin points out here (and as Donne later echoes), when it comes to sin, animals must be found *not guilty*—yet they still bear the burden of its penalties. As we will see, this problem is recognized as a political one, with the dramatic result that Renaissance assessments of human/animal relations readily turn to rich period vocabularies for the critique of political tyranny.

The first stage of these relations—humankind's duly established, benevolent government—is brief. Calvin says of the "authority" first granted to man that God "appointed man, it is true, lord of the world; but he *expressly* subjects the animals to him, because they *having an inclination or instinct of their own, seem to be less under authority from without.*"[74] As we have already seen, Gesner likewise registered this particular distinction for animal estate as uniquely "vassalaged" in the domain of human governance. Genesis's second chapter records an alternative temporal sequence. Adam appears for the first time. Contradicting the earlier affirmation that "he created them male and female" (Gen. 1:27), God muses, "It is not good that the man shulde be him selfe alone: I wil make him an helpe mete," and so he proceeds to form "of the earth everie beast of the field, and everie foule of the heaven, & broght them unto the ma[n] to se[e] how he wolde call the[m]: for howsoever the man named the living creature, so was the name thereof" (Gen. 2:18–19).[75] The Geneva gloss

74. John Calvin, *Commentaries on the Book of Genesis*, trans. John King (Edinburgh: Calvin Translation Society, 1847), 1:96 (italics added). See also *A Commentarie of John Calvine, upon the first booke of Moses called Genesis*, trans. Thomas Tymme (London: John Harison and George Bishop, 1578): "For he made him Lorde of the world, and made the beasts expressely subject unto him: who bicause they have their proper obedience assigned them, seeme not to be under the rule and becke of others" (45).

75. The hoped-for helpmeet does not materialize, and God proceeds on that bumpier course we know so much more about: Plan B, the creation Eve, not of earth, but from Adam's rib (Gen. 2:21–23). We may see the inadequacy of animals in this or the proximity of Eve to animals, whose anticipated role she fills here as a second try. Theologically, a recurrent if not fully mainstream question was posed about the humanity of women. See Ian Maclean, *The Renaissance Notion of Woman* (Cambridge: Cambridge University Press, 1980), 12–14. Much of this debate centered on whether Adam and Eve were

affirms that this scene of nomenclature entails a voluntary servitude—
itself such a resonant political concept in the period. God "mov[ed] them to
come & submit the[m]selves to Adam (italics added)," it instructs, and we
hear in this an echo of the Pauline dictum, so central to human doctrines
of political obedience (from Tyndale's *Obedience of a Christian Man* to
the homilies), that Protestants should submit themselves to "the higher
powers."[76] Du Bartas stressed that the animals obeyed, bowing "their self-
obedient neck," by "their owne accord" and so described Edenic politics in
terms of model rule:

> Then happy we did rule . . .
>
> . . .
>
> At every word they trembled then for awe,
> And every winke then serv'd them as a lawe,
> And alwaies bent all dutie to observe-us,
> Without command, stood readie still to serve us.[77]

These two variant accounts in Genesis, despite certain discrepancies,
make up a first stage, one in which animals are subject to the benign and
duly authorized power/knowledge of man, exercised in a nonviolent vegetarian domain with visions of companionate "helpe" across species.

The second stage is all too familiar, though a few notes will complicate
it, species-wise. Of that speaking snake, we learn that "the Serpent was
more subtil than anie beast of the field," (Gen. 3:1). But ambiguity enters
immediately, and the Geneva glosses suggest that the snake did not act
independently, but as an instrument. "As Satan ca[n] change him selfe into

---

equally formed in the image of God. In 1558 John Knox (citing Augustine) answers this
tricky dilemma by reference to species difference: "Woman (saith he) compared to other
creatures is the image of God, for she beareth dominion over them; but compared unto
man, she may not be called the image of God, for she beareth not rule . . . over man, but
ought to obey him." Knox, *The First Blast of the Trumpet against the Monstrous Regi-
ment of Women* in *On Rebellion*, ed. Roger Mason (Cambridge: Cambridge University
Press, 1994), 17. Interestingly, at the mid-seventeenth century, Milton justifies the
failure of an animal helpmeet by having Adam challenge God: "Among unequals what
society / Can sort, what harmony or true delight?" and he instructs God that "of fellowship I speak / Such as I seek, fit to participate / All rational delight, wherein the brute /
Cannot be human consort" (*Paradise Lost*, 8.383–84, 8.389–92).

76. "Let every soule be subject unto the higher powers" (Rom. 13:1).

77. Du Bartas, *Devine Weekes*, 168, 224, 334.

an Angel of light, so did he *abuse the wisdome of the serpent* to deceave man," and "God suffered Satan to make the serpent his instrument and to speake in him" (Gen. 3:1, a, b; italics added). The serpent possesses a "wisdome" that is capable of being abused, but his speech, though Eve seems unsurprised by it, is attributed to Satan. Godly interrogation quickly exposes Adam and Eve's misstep. But the first subject cursed is the serpent, and in this we also hear the included curse of all creatures: "Because thou hast done this, thou art cursed above all cattel, and above everie beast of the field"; the Geneva gloss further proposes that God gives Adam and Eve a chance to repent, but "not the serpe[n]t, because he wolde shewe him no mercie" (Gen. 3:14, m).

The entire scenario, read from a species perspective, leaves unresolved a number of justice problems, given the primal scene of retributive justice recorded in the expulsion from Eden. If Satan was the agent, what guilt pertains to the snake, as snake? If the snake was guilty, why do other animals receive a curse along with him? God curses "the earth for [Adam and Eve's] sake," but the gloss simply reasserts—rather than offer an interpretation— that "bothe mankinde and all other creatures were subject to the curse" (Gen. 3:17, s). Eden's cursed exiles remain vegetarian, though in restating they will "eat the herbe of the field," God also announces that the earth will yield them thorns and thistles, despite all their new labors tilling it (Gen. 3:18–19). Some animals, in the commentary tradition, now become venomous and are no longer invariably tame. Calvin describes beasts as "endued with a new ferocity," and Du Bartas refers to "cruel'st Creatures, which for Maisterie, / Have vowed against us endles Enmitie."[78] Until the Noah story, animals play a more secondary role. Most notably Abel's keeping of sheep entails making offerings of them to God, who finds this acceptable (Gen. 4:2–5). Abel's use of sacrificial animals, clearly no Edenic practice, points toward the even deeper ambivalence of the aftermath of Noah's ark.

The ark reunites the "hoste" of "living creatures" under completely non-Edenic conditions. In the Geneva translation, the repeating phrases "all flesh," "everie living thing," and even "everie thing in whose nostrels the spirit of life did breathe" unify the class of beings—human and animal alike—to be "destroyed" by drowning in the waters of the Deluge

78. Calvin, *Commentaries on the Book of Genesis*, 1:290. The 1578 English version reads: "Beastes, after the fall of man, became more fierce and cruell" (217); Du Bartas, *Devine Weekes*, 167.

(Gen. 6–8 passim; 7:22). Again, an unresolved question about the application of justice appears: if the Flood revenges widespread *human* corruption, why eradicate all the host of creatures? The Geneva gloss addresses
this obviously persistent question of the scope of punishment—again, in a
gloss without gloss. It simply marvels that here "God declareth how much
he detesteth sinne, seeing the punishment thereof exte[n]deth to the brute
beasts" (Gen. 6:7, h). This annotation implicitly acknowledges that the justice delivered seems out of measure.

While some celebrate the preservation of species representatives in the
ark as evidence of an equal concern for mankind and animals, how then
do we evaluate the new regime for which they are saved? For while Noah's
people go on to reconquer the world, the estate of animal survivors of the
Deluge appreciably worsens. First, a "feare" and "dread" of humans is
placed on them: "The feare of you, and the dread of you shalbe upon everie
beast of the earth, and upon everie foule of the heaven . . . & upon all the
fishes of the sea: into your hand are thei delivered." Next, in a literal conversion of animals to fodder, God licenses human carnivorousness for the
first time: "Everie thing that moveth & liveth, shalbe meat for you: *as the
grene herbe*, have I given you all things" (Gen. 9:2–3; italics added). This
extreme alteration seems justly to reflect Shakespeare's poetic measure (in
The Tempest) of suffering a "sea change" (1.2.404).

In the original dispensation, mankind was granted rule over animals—
with the express mandate of a vegetarian diet for all.[79] First, all creatures

79. At a practical level, the early modern diet was unabashedly carnivorous.
Constraints on it were normally due either to economics or to various food asceticisms
(whether heretical or orthodox). As references to Pythagoras (i.e., the doctrine of the
transmigration of souls and the diet it suggested) commonly indicate, vegetarianism
was shorthand for lunacy. See Ken Albala, *Eating Right in the Renaissance* (Berkeley:
University of California Press, 2002), 16. For humanist readers (such as Montaigne),
however, Plutarch's vivid essay against meat eating surely provoked reflection, if not
changed habits: "But you demand of mee, for what cause Pythagoras abstained from
eating flesh? And I againe do marvell, what affection, . . . or what motive or reason had
that man, who first approched [sic] his mouth unto a slaine creature, who durst with
his lips once touch the flesh of a beast either killed or dead; or how he could finde in
his heart to be served at his table with dead bodies . . . which a little before did blea,
low, bellow, walke, and see." Plutarch, *The Philosophie, commonlie called, The Morals*,
trans. Philemon Holland (London: Arnold Hatfield, 1603), 572. Making a larger argument about how meat eating both establishes and erodes human status, Erica Fudge
clarifies the reasons that scriptural support for vegetarianism was largely ignored in
the Reformation. She shows that carnivorousness was handled as a memento mori and
index of human corruption. "The eating of meat held a more powerful position in theo-

were witnesses and messengers of God's glory, subject to Adam as Adam was subject to God; after the Deluge, their flesh, not just their fealty, is conscripted to relatively weaker or nondoctrinal rationales such as human convenience, comfort, or necessity. Calvin argues that "men may render animals subservient to their own convenience, and may apply them to various uses, according to their wishes and necessities."[80] The Geneva gloss alleges likewise that "by this permission man may with a good conscience use the creatures of God for his necessitie" (Gen. 9:3, c). These rationales track precisely with the way a tyrant tramples his subjects' rights and subordinates them to private desires. Thomas Smith's 1583 treatise on government is typical when it asserts that the tyrant "hath no regard to the wealth of his people, but seeketh onely . . . to satisfie his vicious and cruell appetite."[81] How does the situation deteriorate so that the consumption of animals enters the arrangement? The shift Genesis narrates follows the politically familiar course of benign rule turned to enmity, of stewardship or care converted to predation—paradigmatically indexing the perversions of tyranny. Martin Luther's commentary on this pivotal transition uses staggeringly political vocabulary. After the flood, animals endure what he calls "a more oppressive form of bondage," and humans exercise "a more extensive and oppressive dominion" because "animals are subjected to man as to a tyrant who has absolute power over life and death."[82] Indeed, construing Romans 8:18–22, Luther ascribes a firm power of legitimate complaint to all creatures, affirming that "on the last day all creatures will utter an accusing cry against the ungodly who have shown

logical terms than any attempt to regain the vegetarian innocence of Eden. A return to purity—a refusal of meat—would take away a point of humiliation for humans that was vital to their understanding of their place in the universe." See Erica Fudge, "Saying Nothing concerning the Same: On Dominion, Purity, and Meat in Early Modern England," in Fudge, ed., *Renaissance Beasts: Of Animals, Humans, and Other Wonderful Creatures* (Urbana: University of Illinois Press, 2004), 75.

80. Calvin, *Commentaries on the Book of Genesis*, 1:291. The 1578 text reads: "Men may enjoy the beastes to their owne commoditie, and may applie them to divers uses for their necessitie" (218).

81. Thomas Smith, *De republica Anglorum*, ed. Mary Dewar (Cambridge: Cambridge University Press, 1982), 55.

82. Martin Luther, *Lectures on Genesis 6–14*, trans. George Schick, in *Luther's Works*, ed. Jaroslav Pelikan (St. Louis: Concordia Publishing, 1960), 2:132; see also discussion in Scott Ickert, "Luther and Animals: Subject to Adam's Fall?" in *Animals on the Agenda*, ed. Andrew Linzey and Dorothy Yamamoto (Urbana: University of Illinois Press, 1998).

them abuse here on earth, and will call them tyrants to whom they were unjustly subjected."[83] Oppression, bondage, dominion, unjust subjection, and tyranny: without necessarily suggesting an earthly remedy for this sorry state of affairs, words such as these rate the animal condition in the sharpest available terms of human political evaluation.

The new dispensation after the Flood thus becomes a flashpoint for puzzling or rationalization. Luther observes, "Until now the animals did not have to die . . . to provide food for man," for until then "man was a gentle master of the beasts rather than their slayer or consumer."[84] As Calvin points out, the infusions of animal "feare" and "dread" after the Deluge assure that "sovereignty over the rest of animals might remain with men"; in setting up an order of things after the Flood, only a new godly endowment can ensure "that the same dominion shall continue."[85] As Luther stresses, however, that original benevolent dominion involved no hunting, killing, or taming, and we have no continuous dominion with Adam's: in "that first dominion . . . there was no need of skill or cunning. . . . Therefore we retain the name and word 'dominion' *as a bare title*, but the substance itself has been almost entirely lost."[86] In Du Bartas's formulation, animals were politically obedient "without command" in that "first dominion." Effectively acknowledging the shakiness of this transition in human sovereignty, even Calvin wonders, "Since we perversely exalt ourselves against God, why should not the beasts rise up against us?"[87] We have already seen Du Bartas warn how "Rebellious *Adam*, from his God revolting, / Findes his yerst-subjects 'gainst himselfe insulting," and Donne likewise would ask, directing his apostrophe to the horse, the bull, and the boar in Holy Sonnet 12, "Why brook'st thou . . . subjection?"[88] Among the Reformers, Luther appears attuned to animal claims, and Calvin is more invested in a freer scope for human dominion. But for both,

83. Martin Luther, "The Fourth Sunday after Trinity," in *Luther's Epistle Sermons: Trinity Sunday to Advent*, trans. John Nicholas Lenker (Minneapolis: Luther Press, 1909), 3:105.

84. Luther, *Lectures on Genesis 6–14*, 132.

85. Calvin, *Commentaries on Genesis*, 1:290.

86. Martin Luther, *Lectures on Genesis 1–5*, in *Luther's Works*, ed. Jaroslav Pelikan (St. Louis: Concordia Publishing House, 1958), 1:67 (italics added).

87. Calvin, *Commentaries on the Book of Genesis*, 1:290. The 1578 text reads: "And no marvell: for seeing we are disobedient unto God, why should not the beastes rebell against us?" (218).

88. Du Bartas, *Devine Weekes*, 334 (italics in original); John Donne, "Holy Sonnet 12," in *Complete English Poems*, 313–14, lines 5–6.

the Reformation's own complex relation to political authority fuels the commentary around this ominous biblical conversion. The discourse of tyranny makes the tyrant a devourer: he "bloodieth his handes with the slaughter of innocents," and their blood he "devoureth up with his unclean mouth."[89] According to the chronology of Genesis, in just this way animals literally become *meat for their sovereign*.

Calvin dwells on the biblical temporalities of this problem of meat eating. Even when annotating God's provision of plants "for meat" in Genesis 1:29–30, Calvin disregards the textual fact that what he calls human "rights" in relation to animals are readily limited by the shared right to plants as "meat." Instead, he suggests that those who infer Edenic vegetarianism from the passage have insufficient reasons, questioning whether humans were really vegetarian until the Deluge. "Since the first men offered sacrifices from their flocks" and "were clothed in skins," he concludes— against those who might say flesh eating was then "unlawful"—that "it will be better for us to assert nothing of this matter."[90] He resumes the debate more assertively, though, in connection with the express permission to eat meat granted in Genesis 9:3 on the ark's return to land. Rejecting the simplest inference that licit meat eating begins when scripture makes it licit, he claims not to "see what obligation should prevent . . . the eating of flesh," which he then repeatedly refers to as a "liberty" that "we must firmly retain."[91] Calvin is challenging Catholic ideas about fasting here, but he so firmly defends this "liberty" to eat meat that he, like the traditional practices he indicts, must leave textual warrant behind to do so.

While Calvin overreaches on this point, Luther entertains a different possibility. Using blunt language in the *Lectures on Genesis 6–14* about

89. Johan Ferrarius, *A Woorke of Joannes Ferrarius Montanus, touchying the good orderynge of a commonweale*, trans. William Bavande (London: John Kingston, 1559), fol. 169, quoted in Bushnell, *Tragedies of Tyrants*, 50.

90. Calvin, *Commentaries on the Book of Genesis*, 1:99. Passages from the 1578 text read: "He had possession of his right" and "lawfull," and "Therefore I thinke it shall be better if we say nothing concerning the same" (48).

91. Ibid., 291–92. The 1578 text reads: "Seeing they killed before beastes to offer sacrifice unto God, & seeing it was lawfull for them so to do, and of their skins, to make them garments & tentes: I see not what should debarre them from the eating of flesh" (219), and "Nowe we must holde fast that libertie, whiche the LORD hath given unto us" (220). Luther agrees substantially with Calvin: although "for Adam it would have been an abomination to kill a little bird for food," the dispensation after the Flood "make[s] up, as it were, for the great sorrow that pious Noah experienced" and is a sign of God's compassion (for people). Luther, *Lectures on Genesis 6–14*, 133–34.

God ("in this passage God sets himself up as a butcher"), he stresses elsewhere the superiority of the original dispensation: "I am sure Adam, before his fall, never wanted to eat a partridge; but the deluge spoiled all.
It follows not, that because God created all things, we must eat of all
things. Fruits were created chiefly as food for people and for beasts; the
latter were created to the end we should laud and praise God."[92] Indeed,
Luther appears especially cognizant of the possibilities inhering in animals' intended worldly presence. With a dateline of "Wittenberg, 1534," he
composed a quasi-legal document titled "Complaint of the Birds to Luther
against Wolfgang." Drafted in the voice of songbirds ("we thrushes, black-
birds, finches, linnets, goldfinches, and all other pious, honorable birds")
who faced capture by one of Luther's servants, the letter protests how one
Wolfgang violates the domain rights entailed in Genesis and "undertakes
to rob us of the freedom God gave us to fly through the air." As we have
already seen, Sidney would call the bird a "free-burgess of the air." The
"pious, honorable" birds of Wittenberg go on to point out that a more just
approach would direct Wolfgang's "wrath and industry agains sparrows,
swallows, crows, ravens, mice, and rats . . . [who] do you much harm, rob
and steal corn, oats, and barley."[93] Echoing in words the exquisite animal
portraits of his contemporary, Albrecht Dürer (fig. 1.2), Luther further declares in his *Lectures on Genesis 1–5* that "the mouse, too, is a divine creature. . . . It has a very beautiful form—such pretty feet and such delicate
hair that it is clear that it was created by the word of God with a definite
plan in view. Therefore here, too, we admire God's creation and workman-
ship. The same thing may be said about flies."[94] The here-and-now facticity of observed animals grounds their privilege and divine appointment,
and their presence as such warrants a spiritual attention.

When it came to the eschaton, Calvin argued (presumably without
irony and applying his favored metaphors of animal control to human inquiry) that "some subtle men, but hardly sober-minded, inquire whether

92. Luther, *Lectures on Genesis 6–14*, 133; Luther, *Table Talk*, 58.
93. Preserved Smith, *The Life and Letters of Martin Luther* (Boston: Houghton
Mifflin, 1914), 360–61. (The birds' argument prefigures the precise moral of *To Kill a
Mockingbird*.) Nevertheless, Luther surely savored his meats: in one letter concerning a
banquet for the doctoral achievement of one of his students, he urges, "Buy us all sorts
of birds and fowls of the air, and whatever elese is subject to man's dominion and lawful
to eat in the aerial kingdom of feathers—but not crows. . . . Moreover, if you can buy
or catch . . . any hares . . . send 'em on, for we are minded to satisfy your stomachs for
once, especially if it can be done with malt liquor" (357).
94. Luther, *Lectures on Genesis 1–5*, 52.

Figure 1.2. Albrecht Dürer, *Hare* (1502). Image courtesy of the Graphische Sammlung Albertina, Vienna, Austria. Photograph: Erich Lessing / Art Resource, New York.

all kinds of animals will be immortal; but *if reins be given to specula-tions where will they at length lead us?*" Luther's *Lectures on Genesis*, likewise, affirm the official view that "animals . . . live only their animal life, without hope of eternal life."[95] But at other points, his perspective is more expansive: indeed, at moments not so closely bound up with the

95. Calvin, *Commentaries on the Epistle of Paul to the Romans*, 305 (italics added); on the typicality of the metaphor in Calvin, see Peter A. Huff, "Calvin and the Beasts: Animals in John Calvin's Theological Discourse," *JETS* 42, no. 1 (March 1999): 67–75; Luther, *Lectures on Genesis 1–5*, 117.

discipline of scriptural commentary, especially those recorded in Luther's
Table Talk, his vision is expansively hospitable. Speaking of the household
dog, Tölpel (translated variously as Clownie or Blockhead), Luther con-
jured a zootopian scene not just of "the beginning" or the now but of eternity. Asked whether Tölpel would participate in eternal life, he replied (in
Roland Bainton's translation), "Certainly. . . . Peter said that the last day
would be the restitution of all things. God will create a new heaven and a
new earth and new Tölpels with hide of gold and fur of silver. . . . Snakes,
now poisonous because of original sin, will then be so harmless that we
shall be able to play with them."[96] Even the curse on the serpent will be
reversed when venom is no more. Luther's moral gauge of "harmlessness"
stands out as he figures the eschaton as a place of reestablished animal
participation, undoing their worldly disenfranchisement under the tyrannical regime of fallen man. Not just witnesses at the "last day" (though
that in itself affirms a politically significant capacity to testify), they also
inhabit his vision of restored life.

Bestiae contra Tyrannos: Sidney's "Ister Bank"

For early moderns thinking about political relations gone wrong, "butchering" and "devouring" those for whom one has an affirmative duty of care
were persistent hallmarks of tyranny. Christopher Marlowe's Edward II is
called "a tyrant" and "a butcher . . . / Unnatural king, to slaughter noble-
men and cherish flatterers"; Shakespeare's Macbeth likewise is dubbed "an
untitled tyrant, bloody scepter'd," whom poetic justice reduces to a "dead
butcher" by play's end.[97] Tyrannized human subjects have been "turned
into beasts" or placed "under the yoke" of tyranny. Yokes, bits, collars,
reins, whips, traps, nets, and so on—the instruments of animal control—
appear throughout the metaphorics of tyranny. In an extended elaboration,
Ponet's *Short Treatise* (1556) blisteringly compares the tyrant's behavior
toward his subjects to human behavior toward animals:

> As an huntour maketh wilde beastes his praie, and useth toiles, nettes,
> snares, trappes, dogges, firrettes, mynyng and digging the grounde,

---

96. Roland H. Bainton, "Luther on Birds, Dogs, and Babies," in Bainton, *Studies in
the Reformation* (Boston: Beacon Press, 1963), 71–72. See also Luther, *Table Talk*, 322.

97. Christopher Marlowe, *Edward II*, in *The Complete Works of Christopher
Marlowe*, ed. Fredson Bowers (Cambridge: Cambridge University Press, 2008), 4.1.4–8;
Shakespeare, *Macbeth*, 4.3.105, 5.8.70.

gunnes, bowes, speares, and all other instrumentes, engynes, devises, subtilties and means, . . . so dothe a wicked governour make the people his game and praye, and useth all kindes of subtleties, deceates, craftes, policies, force, violence, crueltie, and suche like devillishe wayes, to spoyle and destroyethe the people, that be committed to his charge. . . . [He fains] uniust causes to cast them in to prison, wher like as the bearewardes mosell the beares, and tye them to the stakes, . . . so he keepeth them in chaines, whilest the bishoppes and his other tormentours . . . doo *teare and devoure* them.⁹⁸

More economically, but in the same spirit, the monarchomach *Vinidicae contra tyrannos* (circulating in the 1570s and an important Huguenot influence on Sidney) asserts that tyrants "suck the blood of the people."⁹⁹ Etienne de la Boétie's *Servitude volontaire* (printed five times in the 1570s and famously referred to by Montaigne) condemns being "under the yoke," lamenting how, under tyranny, "you bring up your children . . . to be delivered into butchery."¹⁰⁰ For La Boétie, animals play a bold part in the critical resistance to tyranny. He puts

brute beasts in the pulpit to throw light on their nature and condition. . . . *The very beasts, God help me! if men are not too deaf, cry out to them, "Long live Liberty!"* Many among them die as soon as captured. . . . Others, from the largest to the smallest . . . put up such a strong resistance by means of claws, horns, beak, and paws, that they show clearly enough how they cling to what they are losing; afterwards in captivity they manifest by so many evident signs their awareness of their misfortune, that it is easy to see they are languishing rather than living,

98. Ponet, *Short Treatise*, chap. 6, Giiv (italics added). For a comprehensive account of how hunting enacted human dominion at a practical and ritual level, see Edward Berry, *Shakespeare and the Hunt: A Cultural and Social Study* (Cambridge: Cambridge University Press, 2001). For an attentive exploration of the ranging cultural symbolics of bear baiting, see Rebecca Ann Bach, "Bearbaiting, Dominion, and Colonialism," in *Race, Ethnicity, and Power in the Renaissance*, ed. Joyce Green Macdonald (Madison, NJ: Fairleigh Dickinson University Press, 1997), 19–35.

99. Hubert Languet (more likely Philippe Duplessis-Mornay), *Vinidicae, contra tyrannos*, trans. George Garnett (Cambridge: Cambridge University Press, 1994), 146. *Contra tyrannos* was published in Basel in 1579 but circulated earlier.

100. Etienne de la Boétie, *Servitude volontaire* (1548 manuscript), published as *The Politics of Obedience: The Discourse of Voluntary Servitude*, trans. Harry Kurz (Auburn, AL: Ludwig van Mises Institute, 2008), 52.

and continue their existence—-more in lamentation of their lost freedom than in enjoyment of their servitude.[101]

Animals "in the pulpit" literalize the exhortation in Job 12:7 urging humans to get good teaching from the beasts. They demonstrate their knowledge of freedom. There is rich ambiguity as to how much the animals cry
out "Long live Liberty!" to inspire tyrannized human subjects by their
example and how much they do it to defy tyrannical humans in their own
acts of politically disobedient resistance.

Calvin had suggested that human dominion manifests itself in "the
fact that oxen become accustomed to bear the yoke," that "the wildness of
horses" can be subdued, "that cows give milk," and that "sheep are mute
under the hands of the shearer."[102] But referring to horses, Erasmus's Folly
registers an entirely different view, stressing "the sharp-toothed bit, prick-
ing spurs, prison-like stable, whips, bridle, rider, the whole tragedy of the
voluntary servitude the horse chose to undergo."[103] Likewise, the republican La Boétie invokes natural history to claim that the elephant breaks
off its own tusks "as a ransom for his liberty," and he stresses how much
work is required to subdue a horse: "He is tamed with such difficulty that
when we begin to break him in he bites the bit, he rears at the touch of the
spur, as if to show . . . that, if he obeys, he does so not of his own free will
but under constraint." La Boétie even offers his own verse to conclude the
passage: "The oxen under the weight of the yoke complain, / And the birds
in their cage lament."[104] At stake here is the vitality of animals as political subjects in themselves and not just didactic fables for humans. Across
a range of writings inflected by Genesis as a natural-historical and legal-
theological precedent, the terms and conditions of human sovereignty
over real animals operate as an example of tyranny—not just an emblem
for it.

After a European sojourn among such Protestant advocates in the

101. Ibid., 57 (italics added) (here La Boétie draws from Plutarch, as discussed in
chapter 3 below.

102. Calvin, *Commentaries on the Book of Genesis*, 1:291.

103. Erasmus, *Praise of Folly*, ed. and trans. Betty Radice (New York: Penguin
Books, 1993), 53 (italics added).

104. La Boétie, *Servitude volontaire*, 57–58. Animal training manuals understood
the Genesis story to define their challenge. Of the horse, Michael Baret explained:
"Although God gave unto Horses such excellent qualities at their Creation, now are
they changed in their use and are become disobedient to man, and therefore must be
subjected by Art." Baret, *Hipponomie*, 7.

1570s, when his celebrated association with the Huguenot Hubert Languet arose, Philip Sidney wrote his prose romance, the *Arcadia* (written by 1580 and published in 1590). The *Arcadia* is steeped in the commitments of Sidney's political vision, and at its center, in the only instance where it refers to an actual person, Sidney placed a verse naming Languet as its source.[105] The poem, "On Ister Bank," is sung by the shepherd Philisides, a figure for Sidney. Philisides, a kind of cousin to the melancholy Jacques in *As You Like It*, begins "upon the ground at the foote of a cypresse tree, in so deep a melancholy" that the others try to rouse him. "Ister Bank" has been repeatedly called a "beast fable" by commentators concerned with Sidney's political investments, a fable warning of the tyrannical potential inherent in the monarchical form of government.[106] But, as we'll see, Sidney's original reworking of the creation story in conjunction with another key Bible passage politically and intellectually goes beyond his more fabulous sources.

In the poem's archaic diction, the verse opens "on Ister bank," the ancient name of the Danube, suggesting the Viennese locales where Sidney and Languet associated.[107] Philisides situates himself and his flock at nightfall, which prompts him to rehearse his fiduciary care for them and sing "lest stray they should" (line 21). But his song, he says, was Languet's. Three stanzas name "old Languet / . . . the shepherd best swift Ister knew" as Sidney's teacher:

With old true tales he wont mine ears to fill:
     How shepherds did of yore, how now, they thrive,
     Spoiling their flock, or while twixt them they strive.
(lines 22–23, 33–35)

Here Sidney's pastoral suggests the predations of tyrants and their subjection of the people's good to selfish strife among potentates (a key detail in

---

105. See Blair Worden, *The Sound of Virtue: Philip Sidney's Arcadia and Elizabethan Politics* (New Haven, CT: Yale University Press, 1996), 267; see also Andrew Hadfield, *Shakespeare and Republicanism* (Cambridge: Cambridge University Press, 2005), 87.

106. See Hadfield, *Shakespeare and Republicanism*, 87–89; Worden, *Sound of Virtue*, 266–80; and Annabel Patterson, *Fables of Power: Aesopian Writing and Political History* (Durham, NC: Duke University Press, 1991), 67–75.

107. Philip Sidney, *The Countess of Pembroke's Arcadia (The Old Arcadia)*, ed. Katherine Duncan Jones (Oxford: Oxford University Press, 1999), 221–25; line numbers for "Ister Bank" shown above refer to this edition.

Erasmus's *Education of a Christian Prince*). Philisides moves to the tale itself by concluding, "Thus in oak's true shade recounted he / Which now in night's deep shade sheep heard of me." Philisides's woolly auditors attend an animal creation story that borrows its nostalgia from Ovid's account of the Golden Age in *The Metamorphoses* (book 1, lines 113–43), but its crisis comes most immediately from the Bible. Describing a world free of humans and one in which beasts "might freely roam or rest" (line 48), the verse takes the peaceable kingdom—envisioned in Isaiah 11:6–9 for some future day—and puts it resolutely in the past. Philisides insists on the meaningful orderliness of this animal-only world:

> The beasts had sure some beastly policy;
> For nothing can endure where order nis.
> For once the lion by the lamb did lie;
> The fearful hind the leopard did kiss;
> Hurtless was the tiger's paw and serpent's hiss.
>   This think I well: the beasts with courage clad
>   Like senators a harmless empire had.
>   (lines 50–56)

Pivoting on the moral force of harmlessness, Sidney presents a "harmless empire" among animals and before humans—a functioning beastly polity—that presents a noninjurious, working order. No human sin had engendered animal venom in this "hurtless" world. Sidney's aristocratic perspective, we may suppose, leads him to suggest that those "beasts with courage clad" governed, operating like no less a body than the senate of republican Rome.

Wavering about the causes of ensuing political change in the animal world—perhaps the animals without "courage" envied those who had the power courage accrued, or perhaps "they *all* to changing did incline"—Philisides reports that

>   the multitude to Jove a suit imparts,
>   With neighing, bleating [*sic*], braying, and barking,
>   Roaring, and howling, for to have a king.
>   (lines 57–63)

(As the poem clarifies later, this line does not mock a lack of speech.) The owl warns against this request and flees "to deserts" when he sees where things are heading (line 70). Jove, too, warns them against kings:

O beasts, take heed what you of me desire.
Rulers will think all things made them to please,
And soon forget the swink [toil] due to their hire.
(lines 72–74)

The idea that subjects serve the convenience, pleasure, and comfort of the
sovereign, of course, reflects a tyrant's presumption (and also rationales
supporting meat eating). Those familiar with political debates about the
legitimacy of resistance to kings will immediately recognize the source
of this story and its unfolding details from chapter 8 of the first book of
Samuel (to which we will return momentarily). There, the Israelites ask
Samuel to "make us nowe a King to judge us like all nations." Samuel and
God read this desire as a rejection of right rule. There follows a rushing
inventory of harms and predations; the king will take everything his subjects have and make them his servants (1 Sam. 8:11–17).

Sidney's poem next reverses the Prometheus myth, in which all available attributes were given to animals, leading Prometheus to give humans
practical wisdom and fire instead.[108] In acquiescing to the animals' request, Sidney's Jove asks each to contribute something to this new creature, man. Reading "Ister Bank" deconstructively as a "fable not about politics but about being human," Erica Fudge underscores the fact that all of
man's attributes are animal contributions to suggest how much "Sidney's
man is . . . more animal than the animals themselves."[109] Philisides lists
twenty-nine such gifts explicitly and gestures to more. The animals offer
a range of qualities, positive and negative. The lion, the elephant, the fox,
the eagle, the wolf, the ant, and the chameleon donate just what we still
know to expect from them. But other, less familiar gifts also appear: from
the mole, "a working thought"; from the monkey, "sweet breath"; from
the cow, "fair eyes"; and from the cat, melancholy. The crocodile gives its
tears, the ape its hand (lines 78–97). Last, in a revision of Aristotle on animal speech, their passion to be ruled (a voluntary servitude gone wrong)
leads the animals foolishly to agree "that from henceforth to all eternity, /
No beast should freely speak, but only" man (lines 104–5).

In telling what happens next, Sidney inventories the injuries typi-
fying any slide into tyrannical government, just as they had been item-

108. Plato, *Protagoras*, trans. Stanley Lombardo and Karen Bell (Indianapolis: Hackett,
1992), 321a–321c.
109. Fudge, *Perceiving Animals*, 79, 80.

ized in Samuel. At first, wily man, "fellow-like, let[s] his dominion slide" (line 110). Once he sees that the animals depend on him, "then 'gan he factions in the beasts to breed," tricking them into violent behavior for which he conveniently executes them in sham actions of justice, as Ponet envisioned (line 120). After man suborns the services of a few and controls them with bits and collars, the transition from kingship to tyranny reaches its inevitable, bloody, and carnivorous conclusion—man's choice to play "a part to tear a cat in":

> Worst fell to smallest birds, and meanest herd,
> Who now his own, full like his own he used.
> Yet first but wool, or feathers, off he teared;
> And then when they were well used to be abused,
> For hungry throat their flesh with teeth he bruised;
> At length for glutton taste he did them kill;
> At last for bloody sport their silly lives did spill.
> (lines 141–47)

In this evocation of human meat-eating as tearing and bruising, Sidney exploits the opening provided by the relatively weak rationales licensing carnivorousness after the Flood, likening those rationales to the frivolity widely associated with "bloody sport" in the period and linking postlapsarian, carnivorous human dominion to moral certainties about the predations of a tyrant as a cynical butcher and devourer of his people.

The penultimate stanza addresses the two parties to this sad story, the tyrant and his victims, gluttonous man and "poor beasts." "O man," the verse instructs,

> rage not beyond thy need;
> Deem it no gloire to swell in tyranny.
> Thou art of blood; joy not to make things bleed.
> Thou fearest death; think they are loathe to die.
> A plaint of guiltless hurt doth pierce the sky.
> (lines 148–52)

"Guiltless hurt" sounds the note of paradox at the heart of the justice problem Genesis encodes; man's innocent subjects are despoiled by human tyranny's incapacity for restraint. The poem ends when morning comes, and contention breaks out among Philisides's auditors over what was meant by the song. The oldest shepherd condemns its engagement with political topics as a breach of pastoral decorum, saying that "he never saw thing worse proportioned than to bring in a tale of he knew not what beasts at such a banquet when rather some song of love, or matter of joyful melody, was to be brought forth," and he quickly changes the subject from those who may be on the table.

What Sidney has crafted here is no beast fable—if by "beast fable" we mean an allegory of speaking animals who personate human moral failings and so indict the follies of humans as such or among themselves. What we find here does something more. Sidney's story of human/animal relations offers a political account in which beasts, as beasts, play an essential role in the generation of meaning, just as "man" stands for man; they do not simply stand in for something else with their animal capacities suspended or subdued. "Ister Bank" certainly invokes Aesop's Samuel-like story of the naïve frogs who beg Jove to give them a king. In that classic beast fable, Jove first casts down a log for them (which they discover is not a "real" king). When they insist on a real one, Jove sends them a large stork who proceeds to devour them (figs. 1.3. and 1.4). "Ister Bank," however, relates

Figure 1.3. Aesop, *The Fables of Aesop as First Printed By William Caxton in 1484*, ed. Joseph Jacobs (London: David Nutt, 1889). Image by permission of the Folger Shakespeare Library, Washington, DC.

Figure 1.4. Bernard Salomon, *Les Fables d'Esope Phrygien* (Lyon, 1547).
Image courtesy of Houghton Library, Harvard University (Typ 515.47.123).

beast and man in a political narrative of their mutual history, ranging into
biblical pastures for its measure of tyrannical degeneration. It veers from
the beast fable tradition insofar as the poem's viability (even as an allegory
for political rebellion among humans) depends on the prior legibility of
human/animal relations as an instance of tyranny—following the biblical
narrative of a degeneration from cross-species stewardship into savagery.
Sidney's animals look like the animals of Genesis rather than those of
Aesop; they are more natural-historical than emblematic; they are parties
to the story. After all, if man's dominion over "real" animals were morally
neutral, this entire "fable" would, as they say, lack teeth.

The thrust of the passage in Samuel, of course, is to deny any right of
proceeding against a tyrant. An admonition warns the Israelites, "Ye shall
crie out at that day, because of your King, whom ye have chosen you, and
the Lord will not heare you at that day" (1 Sam. 8:18). The passage proved
a flashpoint for debates about the legitimacy of resistance to tyranny. But
the last lines of Sidney's verse contravene Samuel's message that, once acquired, a king cannot be escaped. They intimate, instead, an animal up-
rising, as we have already seen in Calvin, Du Bartas, and Donne. Warn-

ing man against swelling tyranny, Sidney addresses "poor beasts" to urge them to either "in patience bide your hell" or "know your strengths, and then you shall do well" (lines 153–54). Sidney evokes the human fear that animals might quit their tame obedience and resist immoral dominion.[110] Mobilizing the morally stained incursions on animal entitlement that Genesis records against Samuel's denial of appeals for tyrannized (human) subjects, Sidney's "Ister Bank"—like La Boétie's *Servitude volontaire*— endorses a creaturely rebellion against human tyranny to *derive* human rights against their wayward kings.

Desert Citizens: Edenic Species-Memory in Shakespeare's Arden

The persistent idea that a tyrant declines from a civil humanity into savage animality contradicts a rival observation about species and violence. In Erasmus's version,

> If you are looking for what corresponds to the tyrant, think of the lion, the bear, the wolf, or the eagle, who live by mutilation and plundering . . . except that the tyrant outdoes even these creatures . . . who are condemned for savage cruelty [but] at least refrain from attacking their own species. . . . But the tyrant, a man, directs his animal ferocity against men, and, although a citizen himself, against citizens.[111]

Here Erasmus conventionally imagines the human/animal divide as a question of citizenship and murder, but his initial likening of the tyrant to a beast falters when he then turns the comparison against humankind *as a kind* by pointing out the tyrant is "a man." Likewise, Luther saw a moral lawfulness in animals that he doubted in humans

> Wild beasts and irrational animals keep this law. When a pig is slaughtered or captured and other pigs see this, we observe that the other pigs clamor and grunt as if in compassion. Chickens and geese and all wild animals do the same thing; when they see one of their own kind in trouble, they quite naturally grieve with it and are sad, and if they can,

110. For a contemporary version, see Margaret Atwood, "The Animals Reject Their Names and Things Return to Their Origins," in *The Tent* (New York: Anchor Books, 2006), 77–84.

111. Erasmus, *Education of a Christian Prince*, 30.

they help it. Only man, who after all is rational, does not spring to the aid of his suffering neighbor in time of need and has no pity on him. What a shame and scandal!¹¹²

If we were to conjure the absent entry for humans in the encyclope-dia of animals, or compose an early modern profile in kind following natural-historical models, such testimonies to irrational cruelty would ri-val claims for rationality as humanity's signature. Calling man "the great-est tyrant in the world" in his *Divine Considerations of the Soule* (1608), Nicholas Breton presses the point: "What Butcher can more cruelly teare in peeces the limmes of a beast, then one man in his malice will the very heart of another?"¹¹³ A tendency to moral catastrophe indelibly marks hu-man beings as such, not just the tyrants among them.

And sixteenth-century animals seem to know all about it. Among the several animal complaint poems added by George Gascoigne to his trans-lation of *The Noble Arte of Venerie or Hunting* (1576), one in particular— "The Otter's Oration"—concentrates on the species politics of meat and the morality of "devouring" it.¹¹⁴ The otter was long the target of campaigns for elimination as a rival hunter of fish stocks in rivers; Isaak Walton's *The Compleat Angler* (1653), for example, claims that "the Otter devours much fish, and kills and spoils much more than he eats."¹¹⁵ Topsell calls otters "dogs of the water" and "very biting Beast[s]"; he marvels how they can smell "fishes in the waters a mile or two off," but notes how many drown in fishnets for their "greediness of fishes."¹¹⁶ Topsell's portrait, following Gesner's, shows an otter "very bitingly" eating a fish; Gascoigne's does the same (fig. 1.5). But Gascoigne's otter rebuts these "slandrous" charges of excessive consumption "for which we Beastes be slayne" and reverses it against "all Adams seede"—returning to the benchmark of Genesis for leverage. The otter precludes human recourse to any reading of Genesis to argue for unlimited human use or dominion. "Yet mee thinkes, I heare

112. Luther, *Sermons 1*, trans. John Doberstein, in *Luther's Works*, ed. Helmut Lehmann (Philadelphia: Muhlenberg Press, 1959), 51:10.

113. Nicholas Breton, *The Works in Verse and Prose of Nicholas Breton*, ed. Alexan-der Grosart (Lancashire, UK: Chertsey Worthies Library, 1879), 2:22.

114. George Gascoigne, *The Noble Arte of Venerie or Hunting* (London: Henry Bynneman for Christopher Barker, 1576), 359–61. Poems in the voice of the hart, hare, otter, and fox stand out for figuring an animal perspective on man; chapter 3 below discusses the "happy beast tradition" on which they draw.

115. Isaak Walton, *The Compleat Angler* (New York: Dover, 2003 [1653]), 32.

116. Topsell, *Foure-Footed Beastes*, 444–46.

Figure 1.5. George Gascoigne, *Otter*, in *The Noble Arte of Venerie or Hunting* (London, 1576). Image by permission of the Folger Shakespeare Library, Washington, DC.

him preache this Texte, / *Howe all that is, was made for use of man"*; this preaching, the otter argues, reads out of context and without regard to

> this heavie place, expounde it who so can:
> *The very scourge and Plague of God his Ban,*
> Will lyght on suche as queyntly can devise
> To eate more meate than may their mouthes suffice.
> (italics in original)

While "men crye out that fishe I do devoure," he argues tauntingly, "master Man" indiscriminately "feedes his fill on every fleshe and fishe." Asserting that no otter ever ate "more meate at once, than served for his share" or "more than may do them good," the otter, with his colorful itemization of human gluttonies, turns the tables on name-calling humans to indict instead "beastly man." Though man "us seely Beastes, devouring Beastes do call," the otter propounds, "he himselfe [is] moste bloudie beaste of all."[117]

While Gascoigne's otter stresses the bloody-mindedness of man as a devourer, his other animal complainants press the justice-oriented terms of harmlessness and murder with which we began. The hare refers to itself as "a harmelesse thing" and a "silly harmelesse Hare," chastising at the same time the "bloudie minde of Man" and characterizing humans as "murdrying men" who have a taste for "murder."[118] The "harmelesse hart" complains of "nets and instruments," suggesting a perverse human plea-

117. Gascoigne, *Noble Arte*, 359–61.
118. Ibid., 176–77.

sure in animal suffering. While the hart accepts both "fear" and "dread" as the political terms of the dispensation after the Flood, it questions why "play[ing] the man" means "killyng harmelesse Deare." Instead, the hart interprets Genesis to require only such sacrifices as are naturally cast from its body: "Such hornes, such heare, suche teares as I have tolde, / I mew and cast for man's avayle." Considering man's "murdryng cruell minde," the hart asks, "Canst thou in death take suche delight? breedes pleasure so in paynes?" An assessment of disproportionate greed and insatiate appetite leads the hart to pray that man's tyrannical cruelty will rebound on itself:

> Lo here I crave of mightie Gods, whiche are bothe good and just:
> That Mars may reygne with Man, that stryfe and cruell warre,
> May set mans murdrying minde on worke, with many a bloudy Jarre.[119]

Violence and strife within kind appear to be mankind's most singular property.

In the sixteenth century, two elements define tyranny. The tyrant either displays a cruel violence that violates his fiduciary charge, or he usurps another's place (quite often we find both).[120] Like Erasmus, Luther, Gascoigne, and Breton, Montaigne too charges humanity, *as a species*, with both aspects of this crime. In "Of Cruelty" he writes that those who are "bloodie-minded towards harmlesse beasts, witnesse a naturall propension unto crueltie," which he glosses paradoxically as nothing less than a human "instinct to inhumanitie." He notes how "no man taketh delight to see wild beasts . . . make much one of another: Yet all are pleased to see them tugge, mangle, and enteteare one another."[121] Referencing the justice problem of "harmless beasts" that figured in readings of Genesis and specifically according meaning to our shared hexameral origin, Montaigne continues that "considering that one selfe-same master (I mean that incomprehensible worlds-framer) hath placed all creatures in this his wondrous palace for his service, and that they, as well as we, are of his household: I say it hath some reason to injoyne us to shew some respect

119. Ibid., 136–40.
120. Early modern notions refer variously to questions of character or cruelty in holding an office and unlawful methods of obtaining it. See Smith, *De republica Anglorum*, chaps. 7–9. See also Bushnell's account of Greek psychological versus legal models (*Tragedies of Tyrants*, 10–11).
121. Michel de Montaigne, "Of Cruelty," in *Essayes*, 383.

and affection towards them." Indeed, he confesses that when one considers the "neere resemblance betweene us and beasts, and what share they have in our greatest privileges, and with how much likely-hood they are compared unto us," one can no longer assert "that imaginary soveraigntie that some give and ascribe unto us above all other creatures."[122] Recalling Luther's sense of postlapsarian human dominion as reduced in moral stature to a "bare title" and Sidney's hubristic mankind claiming dominion over even the unknown, Montaigne's "imaginary soveraigntie" brings mankind lower, as a fraud.

We have seen that in those locales of reading where the resources supplied by Genesis are in play, animals appear as the subjects of the law who then become the abjects of tyrannical man and his greedy seizure of "imaginary soveraigntie." A wide range of thinkers call mankind a tyrant in relation to nonhumans. Early modern political logic invokes these animals not exclusively as metaphors for human folly, suffering, and political oppression by means of the techniques of the beast fable or prosopoetic talking animals. Instead—under the auspices of Genesis as the governing account of first foundations and as typological history—these animals signify as political subjects. They are conceived to be capable of meaningful (i.e., willing) obedience and vulnerable to wrongful dispossession and likely to rise in a legitimate rebellion that La Boétie and Sidney cast as exemplary.

My conclusion returns to Shakespeare. Numerous passages reflect the interconnected issues of harmlessness, animal entitlement or liberty, and human violence at stake in this reading of Genesis. In *Titus Andronicus*, for example, when young Marcus kills a "poor, harmless fly" who "with his pretty buzzing melody / Came here to make us merry," Titus cries, "Out on thee, murderer! thou kill'st my heart." Amplifying the murder charge, he describes his eyes as "cloyed with view of tyranny," which he glosses in turn as "a deed of death done on the innocent" (3.2.63–65, 54–56). There is Don Pedro's dark reflection in *Much Ado about Nothing*—invoking human restraints made on a number of species all at once—that "I am trusted with a muzzle and enfranchised with a clog; therefore I have decreed not to sing in my cage. If I had my mouth, I would bite; if I had my liberty, I would do my liking" (1.3.30–33). There is also Ross's report to Macduff about what the "bloody tyrant" and "butcher" Macbeth has done to his family:

Your wife and babes
Savagely slaughter'd. To relate the manner

122. Ibid., 384.

Were, on the quarry of these murder'd deer,
To add the death of you.
(4.3.205–8)

"Murder" applies outside of kind, and acts of human tyranny take place across species.

We have already explored the significance of the fact that the word "animal" appears only 8 times in Shakespeare, whereas together the words "beast" and "creature" occur 268 times. Three of these eight "animals" inhabit the woods of *As You Like It*, with two of them in a single scene. In act 2, the exiled duke contemplates the woods to imagine a reversal of the Genesis narrative we have been considering: "Here feel we not the penalty of Adam" (a proposition undermined immediately by his reference to the "sweet" uses of adversity) (2.1.5). When he then proposes "shall we go and kill us venison?" he immediately indexes a concern:

And yet it irks me the poor dappled fools,
Being native burghers of this desert city,
Should, in their own confines with forkèd heads
Have their round haunches gored.
(2.1.21–25)

These "native burghers" echo other creaturely reckonings of citizenship: Du Bartas's "Sea-Citizens" and "Burgers of this Earthly ball" and Sidney's "free-burgess of the air." The duke's interlocutor in the scene, a lord, reports that one of their companions—the melancholy Jacques—

grieves at that,
And in that kind swears you do more usurp
Than doth your brother that hath banished you.
(2.1.26–28)

The lord recounts Jacques's response to a wounded deer, a "poor sequestered stag" described as a

wretched animal [who] heaved forth such groans
That their discharge did stretch his leathern coat
Almost to bursting, and [whose] big round tears
Coursed one another down his innocent nose.
(2.1.33, 36–39)

The death of an "innocent" sounds the note of tyranny already. Deer hold title to their domain as citizens of "this desert city," and the animal's betrayed innocence recalls Calvin's sense of liability without fault or what Sidney called the "plaint of guiltless hurt." Here we see the specific dilemma Genesis bequeaths to quadrupeds: despite the notion of distinct and assigned animal domains in the sea, in the air, and in the field, those of four-footed estate must share a land-based life with us, to their particular harm. Hexameral writing in the Renaissance handles this glitch in domains largely by dividing land-living creatures into humans and those populating spaces where humans are absent, hence the repeated references to "deserts" in Du Bartas and Sidney. The seeming oxymoron, then, of Shakespeare's "desert city" captures the way that animals are not so easily and simply understood as outside of polity or as unpolitical.

As the woodland dialogue continues, we hear more about Jacques's musings. He has called the duke's party

> *usurpers, tyrants, and what's worse,*
> To fright the animals and to kill them up
> In their assigned and native dwelling place.
> (2.1.61–63; italics added)

Assignment refers to the domain rights we have seen Genesis establish, and the sense of heirship and inheritance in Shakespeare's repetition of "native" compounds the rightfulness of the deer's claim. Jacques's tears and moralizing on the spectacle of the deer surely serve as fodder for wordplay in the scene, but in fact they only extend the duke's own first remark that something uncomfortable, or irksome, inheres in the thought of killing deer—here called "fat and greasy citizens" (2.1.55)—in a domain that is legitimately "theirs." There is something "bloodie-minded" about it. Here, we are not in Agamben's Athens, where it makes "no sense" to speak of a *zoë politikë*. We are in Arden, a place populated by citizen-creatures whose unhonored entitlements persist in forms sufficient to irk or trouble interloping bipeds. In terms of Renaissance political theory, it would be very hard to say *"what's worse"* than a usurper or tyrant. It appears it must be "man." Arden is not Athens; neither is it Eden. Even so, the literally melancholic trace of Edenic arrangements across kinds lingers as a sort of species memory in Arden, where the bloody tyrant—perhaps to our surprise—is *us*.

CHAPTER TWO

A Cat May Look upon a King:
Four-Footed Estate, Locomotion, and
the Prerogative of Free Animals

This chapter starts preposterously—with the tail. An anatomical tail adorns only nonhuman animals (and nearly all of them at that); unless trimmed out as demons or monsters, humans lack its final signature.[1] By the natural tail's retrospective measure, the persistent early modern borrowing of the term to signify metaphorically in humans (as an unornamented rear "end" or as genitalia) tracks the more literal animal debts King Lear will tote up as the needful accessories of "unaccommodated man."[2] Even to say the upright human body "ends" there, rather than at the head or foot, requires some bowing down toward the horizontal extension of the quadruped's spine and tail. A mongrel psychoanalytic method lurks in this, one pinning the "lack" so central to modern conceptions of animality on humankind instead and perhaps suggesting psychic motives for a gratuitous practice such as tail docking. But the upending metric of "human *negative* exceptionalism"—a discourse that calibrates human-

1. Aristotle accounts for human taillessness by suggesting that "man is the only animal that stands upright" and that "to make the upper parts light and easy to carry," nature reduced the upper body "to make the buttocks and the thighs and the calves of the legs fleshy" (which also made the buttocks "useful for resting the body"). This redirection of substance consumes nourishment "before it can get as far as the place for the tail." *The Progression of Animals,* in *Parts of Animals, Movement of Animals, Progression of Animals,* trans. A. L. Peck and E. S. Forster (Cambridge, MA: Harvard University Press, 1937), bk. 4, sec. 10, pp. 385–87.

2. To give just one instance, in *The Taming of the Shrew,* Kate and Petrucchio debate whether a wasp stings with his tail or his tongue. When Kate dismisses Petrucchio, he balks, suggesting he cannot leave "with [his] tongue in [her] tail" (2.1.128). For a rich account of the unruly "tail" of the letter Q, see Jeffrey Masten, "Spelling Shakespeare, and Other Essays in Queer Philology" (manuscript in progress).

82

ness through lack and judges animals integral and complete (in period terms, "perfect")—is detailed in the next chapter. This one concerns early modern reckonings of tails and feet.

If we return now to that flourish that is notoriously absent in humans, we find that the tail also has a way of leaving us behind when beasts "turn tail" and "show us their backs." In Thomas Wyatt's lyric, "Whoso list to hunt," the matter of who leads and who follows does not always confirm human authority or dignity:

> The vain travail hath wearied me so sore,
> I am of them that farthest come behind.
> Yet may I by no means my wearied mind
> Draw from the deer, but as she fleeth afore
> Fainting I follow.[3]

Following the deer and failing to catch her: the human subject (over-freighted with capacities as hunter, lover, royal subject, and pursuer of knowledge) keeps running, but falls increasingly far behind a forest citizen who "hightails it" out of reach. This chapter discusses the way that wagging, flicking, trailing tail punctuates an entire logic of course, direction, and forward motion for the quadruped's body, a logic that accords a rival form of sovereignty to uncaptured early modern beasts.

As we will see, a tight link between locomotion and logic grounds rangy principles of right proceeding: sequential "steps" that progress (step forward) or procede (go forward) in a "due" or "natural course." Indeed, the thrust of bodily motion structures the very idea of "discourse" itself, from the Latin *discurrere*, to run about. At the same time, vectors of quadruped locomotion establish a plane that cross-cuts the more fixed, perpendicular line of human "uprightness" as well as the upward gaze constantly associated with it in early modernity. This much-celebrated erectness crowns humanity with governance over other creatures, but an odd side effect casts the human body in relatively stationary terms. While we are anchored, looking up to contemplate the heavens, they run around, ignoring boundaries and escaping our grip. Free, uncaged animal locomotion like that we have seen La Boétie call up and name "liberty"—with its autonomy, unpredictability, and deadly accuracies—makes no acknowledgment of what we have seen Montaigne call the "imaginary soveraigntie" of man.

3. Thomas Wyatt, "Whoso list to hunt, I know where is an hind," in *The Complete Poems*, ed. R. A. Rebholz (New Haven, CT: Yale University Press, 1981), 77.

On this front, the diverse terms and conditions of creaturely embodiment
(especially evident in tails and feet) hobble human claims of unfettered authority or control across species. Free animal prerogative, instead, mocks
human sovereignty, sometimes by "turning tail" and sometimes by looking back defiantly.

Our notions of order and sequence still borrow logic from embodiment.
That something is amiss if "the tail wags the dog" still holds rhetorical
traction and commonsense appeal. But it also figured in the taxonomic
procedures laid out in Aristotle's discussion of the animal gait. He proposes that the "dimensions by which animals are naturally bounded are
six in number[:] superior and inferior, front and back, and also right and
left. . . . Things which not only live but are also animals have both a front
and a back" (and "nothing possesses a natural movement backwards").[4]
The horizontal backbone of the average quadruped runs parallel to the
ground. Head and tail, before and behind, create an arrow of frontally directed motion. By one measure of the mechanics of locomotion, the tail
helps a "prone" creature move efficiently; the quadruped's forward gait
and its ability to turn at speed are said to utilize the tail for balance.[5] Thus
Aristotle proposed that human uprightness "takes away the need and necessity of a tail."[6] Although contemporary docking and other practices of
animal mutilation make entirely self-serving claims about hygiene, industrial efficiency, or "breed standards," the early modern curtailed (or curtal)
dog was "the dog of a person not qualified to course, which, by the forest
laws, must have its tail cut short, partly as a mark, and partly from a notion that the tail is necessary to a dog in running."[7] Renaissance regula-
tors aimed to cur-tail illicit pursuits by cutting short the pursuer; amputa-
tion of the tail notionally disabled a dog from chasing game as it visibly
marked its station.

On this point, in the "Apologie" Montaigne describes watching a sight
hound dream, and he conjures the "Hare, which a grey-hound imagineth
in his dreame, after whom as he sleepeth we see him bay, quest, yelp, and

4. Aristotle, *Progression of Animals*, 491, 499 (secs. 4 and 6). On footedness, dorsal-
ity, and the different spacializations they engender, see Barbara Herrnstein Smith,
"Animal Relatives, Difficult Relations," *differences: A Journal of Feminist Cultural
Studies* 15, no. 1 (2004): 4.

5. Aristotle considers this in greatest detail for birds, comparing the tail to "the
rudder in a ship." *Progression of Animals*, 517 (sec. 10).

6. Aristotle, *Parts of Animals*, 387 (sec. 10).

7. Robert Nares, *A Glossary, or Collection, of Words, Phrase, Names* (London: Robert Triphook, 1822), s.v. "cur-tail dog," 115.

snort, stretch out his taile . . . and perfectly represent the motions of his course."[8] Catching a dream hare involves the real tail; without the tail's extension, the dog, and his representation too, are imperfect. The grey-hound's course entails flat-out running, the tail stretched out in a line behind. The trajectory of this course demonstrates a sequential process of before and behind, with properties not unlike reason. The quadruped moves neither preposterously (putting what is behind, before) nor precipi-tously (flying improperly headlong—a figure for stumbling logic based on the human body), but instead proceeds in *due course*.[9] Good order unfolds in its embodied motion. Setting cross-species standards for young men, Castiglione's *Book of the Courtier* finds judgment and reason legible in these motions of "brute beastes." The young man is ideally of "a certayne sagenesse . . . and few woordes, and . . . wythoute . . . busye gestures and unquyete manners," and the *Courtier* celebrates how "mylde beehavyour conteyneth in it a . . . syghtelye fiersenesse, because it appeereth to bee *sturred, not of wrathe but of judgemente*, and rather governed by reason then [*sic*] appetyte." Castiglione invokes animal motion to illustrate this virtue. "We see it lykewyse in brute beastes . . . as the Lion and the Egle, [and] neither is it voide of reason, forsomuche as that violente and sodeyne mocyon withoute woordes or other token of coler whyche wyth all force bursteth oute together at once" stems from a "quietnesse, whyche is con-trary to it."[10] Animal motion is not only free of the deformations of passion but also full of the shaping force of quiet "judgemente." In Montaigne's rich compression, "their motions discourse" (400).

The logical quality attributed to coursing or tracking played a star-ring role in an ancient account of a deliberative dog, one who—in Topsell's version—"cast[s] about for the game, as a disputant doth for the truth, as if [he] should say either the Hare is gone on the left hand, or on the right

8. Michel de Montaigne, "The Apologie for Raymond Sebond," in *The Essayes of Montaigne: John Florio's Translation*, ed. J. I. M. Stewart (New York: Modern Library, 1934), 428. Subsequent page references appear in the text.

9. Patricia Parker shows how early modern preposterousness "links something represented as sexual inversion with the whole range of recto and verso, front and back, before and behind." *Shakespeare from the Margins: Language, Culture, Context* (Chi-cago: University of Chicago Press, 1996), 27.

10. Baldessare Castiglione, *The Book of the Courtier*, trans. Thomas Hoby (London: D. Nutt, 1900 [1528; English trans. 1561]), bk. 2, 121–22 (italics added). Likewise, Henry on St. Crispin's Day: "In peace there's nothing so becomes a man / As modest stillness and humility: / But when the blast of war blows in our ears, / Then imitate the action of the tiger" (*Henry V*, 3.1.2–5).

hand, or straightforward, but not on the left or right hand[,] and therefore
straight forward. Whereupon he runneth foorth right after the true and in-
fallible footesteps of the Hare."[11] The four-footed dog thinks in "handed"
alternatives, a narrative mixing up hands and feet in the inevitable border-
lands between two- and four-leggedness, but he solidly demonstrates the
correct logical sequence of before and behind when he "runneth forth right
after." As Lucian Floridi has amply detailed, the figure of the dog pursuing
a scent has a durable role in representations of intellectual investigation.[12]
In *The Advancement of Learning*, for example, Bacon's darkly prophetic
image defined the new sciences as a "following, and as it were hound-
ing nature in her wanderings."[13] The particular trope of the deliberating
dog was attributed to Chrysippus and relayed by an array of commentators (including Aelian, Sextus Empiricus, Ambrose, and Montaigne)—and
the case *pro et contra* was actually tried in a Cambridge debate under the
auspices of a visit by James I in 1615. "The question was tempered and fit-
ted to his content: *whether dogs could make syllogismes.*"[14] The respondent and the opponent in this performance took the respective positions
of no and yes. *Pace* Descartes's impending assertion in the *Discourse on
Method* that "none of our external actions can show anyone who examines them that our body is not just a self-moving machine but contains a
soul with thoughts, with the exception of words," Chrysippus's example
offers a "method" for affirming the existence of other minds by reading

11. Edward Topsell, *The Historie of the Foure-Footed Beastes* (London: William
Jaggard, 1607), 141. John Caius's account of hunting dogs (discussed below) presumes
canine sagacity without debate, naming one type of hunting dog *Sagax. Of Englishe
Dogges, the diversities, the names, the natures, and the properties*, trans. Abraham
Fleming (London: Richard Johnes, 1576), 3.

12. Lucian Floridi, "Scepticism and Animal Rationality: The Fortune of Chrysippus' Dog in the History of Western Thought," *Archiv für Geschichte der Philosophie*
79, no. 1 (1997): 27–57. Floridi details the impact of Sextus Empiricus (touching nicely
on Sherlock Holmes as well). For strong and helpful analysis of the human/animal paradoxes concerning reason in the episode, see Erica Fudge, *Brutal Reasoning: Animals,
Rationality, and Humanity in Early Modern England* (Ithaca, NY: Cornell University
Press, 2006), 101–4.

13. Francis Bacon, *The Advancement of Learning* (New York: Modern Library, 2001
[1605]), bk. 2, 75.

14. John Mayor, "King James I on the Reasoning Faculty in Dogs," *Classical
Review* 12, no. 2 (March 1898): 93 (italics in original). Mayor reprints a 1628 account
(written by Thomas Ball, a student of the opponent, John Preston) and surveys classical
and early Christian sources, giving original language passages.

the sequence of bodily motions as no weaker evidence of rationality than words.[15]

Or so the king (an avid huntsman himself) interpreted it. The report has him entering the fray to side with the opponent and claim that "a hound had more in him than was imagined," giving the example of one of his own dogs that he observed stray from the pack to pursue a scent, then forgo that trail to fetch "his fellows" and to "prevayle" on them— "by such yelling arguments as they best understand"—to follow him back to the quarry. Recounting this vision of canine rational self-rule, James suggested that the moderator should "thinke better of his dogs or not so highly of himselfe." The report ends with an admirably deft, partial concession by the nay-saying respondent, who yields that "His Majesties dogs were always to be excepted, who hunted not by common law, *but by prerogative.*"[16] The royal hounds doubtless got their prerogative by association with James, with whom it was so much associated as a strategy of royal power. But the resonant term is apt, for dogs traditionally serve as decisional agents and proxy judges in domains where human judgment fails, detecting scent evidence invisible to humans and keeping watch when human senses falter in the dark.[17] With this modulation to *prerogative,* we have edged from a question of abstract reason (difficult to resolve even in humans) toward the more political question of a contingent range of interactive agencies concerning not only will and choice as such but also whose decisional authority will be acknowledged by others, and when.

The dog's "prerogative" leads us back to questions about the authority over animals said to belong to humans, a conception in which certain agentive attributes of generic kingship provision each individual specimen of humankind. Ideological confabulations about a human perpendicular sovereignty over coursing animal subjects, however, run afoul of an implicit grid orienting these kinds of bodies in space. The true north of the

---

15. René Descartes, "Letter to the Marquess of Newcastle (23 November 1646)," in *The Philosophical Writings of Descartes,* ed. John Cottingham et al. (Cambridge: Cambridge University Press, 1991), 303.

16. Mayor, "King James I," 94 (italics added).

17. The dog's nose continues to find new applications. Michael McCulloch et al., "Diagnostic Accuracy of Canine Scent Detection in Early- and Late-Stage Lung and Breast Cancers," *Integrative Cancer Therapies* 5, no. 1 (March 2006): 30–39; Hideto Sonoda et al., "Colorectal Cancer Screening by Canine Scent Detection," *Gut: An International Journal of Gastroenterology and Hepatology, Online First* (31 January 2011), doi:10.1136/gut.2010.218305. Sonoda et al. refer to "canine scent judgment."

animal body is graphed horizontally and related to reason, while the human body's true north sets a contrary axis but is also associated with reason. These divergences make the line between the highest two forms of soul in the Aristotelian scheme, the locomotive and the rational, difficult to fix in one place.[18] Instead, incommensurate vectors mark two forms of being less as ontologies than as courses or routes of unfolding action. Running at right angles, so to speak, and perhaps on a collision course too, the dispersed bodily motion of animals locates a countersovereign autonomy in the life of moving creatures, suggesting just how propositional full human dominion—Descartes's *empire absolu sur tous les autres animaux*—still remained.[19]

Biped Fantasies: Mah-ah-ah-ah-ah-narch of All I Survey!

In the archive of comparative considerations, the upright, biped posture of the human body is repeatedly claimed as unique and used to justify political authority over other creatures. As C. A. Patrides puts it, "Few commonplaces of thought have been so enthusiastically supported by authorities of the first magnitude and, in close pursuit, by a legion of lesser talents."[20] Patrides reviews the endorsements of Plato, Aristotle, Cicero, and Ovid; of Christian commentators including Justin, Augustine, Basil, Gregory, Ambrose, Boethius, and Calvin; and of a host of Renaissance English and Continental writers. Arthur Golding's translation of Ovid's formulation in the *Metamorphoses* (1567) reckoned quadrupeds as groveling and particularly colored later iterations:

> Where all other beasts behold the ground with groveling eie,
> [God] gave to Man a stately looke replete with majestie.
> And willde him to behold the Heaven wyth countenance cast on hie.[21]

18. Though often only three are listed, Aristotle gives five ascending faculties or powers of soul: vegetative or nutritive, sensitive, appetitive, locomotive, and rational or intellectual. See *On the Soul, Parva Naturalia, On Breath*, trans. W. S. Hett (Cambridge, MA: Loeb Classical Library / Harvard University Press, 1957), 81, 414a29–32.

19. Descartes, "Letter to the Marquess of Newcastle," 302; *Oeuvres et lettres*, ed. André Bridoux (Paris: Gallimard/La Pléiade, 1937), 1254.

20. C. A. Patrides, "'With His Face towards Heaven': The Upright Form of Man," in *Premises and Motifs in Renaissance Thought and Literature* (Princeton, NJ: Princeton University Press, 1982), 85.

21. Ovid, *Ovid's Metamorphoses: The Arthur Golding Translation of 1567*, ed. John Nims (New York: Paul Dry Books, 2000), bk. 1 (lines 97–99), 6.

This "stately looke," majesty, and privilege all resound in Milton's version, perhaps the best-known instance of the conceit. He describes man as

> a creature who not prone
> And brute as other creatures, but indued
> With sanctity of reason, might erect
> His stature, and upright with front serene
> Govern the rest, self-knowing, . . .
> . . . with heart and voice and eyes
> Directed in devotion, to adore
> And worship God supreme.[22]

By contrast, in an instance from 1613, "the brutish Beasts . . . are crooked, bended, and looking downe upon the earth."[23] To be crooked and bent with a downcast look is to have bowing submission spelled out in one's body.

Helkiah Crooke ("Doctor of Physicke, Physitian to his Majestie, and his Highnesse Professor in Anatomy and Chyrurgerie") offers extensive commentary on crookedness and uprightness in his 1615 *Microcosmographia: A Description of the Body of Man*. Echoing the claim that "man onely is of an upright frame and proportion," he attributes this mainly to the vector of the soul "being infused into the body from heaven" and the mandate that man "might behold and meditate on heavenly things." In a uniquely focused celebration of the human hand ("hee alone amongst all Creatures had the Hand given him by God"), the surgeon Crooke poses a series of rhetorical questions inspired by the characterization of four-footedness as a kind of groveling:

> Now, if the figure of man had been made with his face downward, that
> Divine Creature should have gone groveling upon his handes, as well
> as upon his feete, and those noble and worthy actions of his Hand, had
> been forfeited, or at least disparaged. For, who can write, ride, live in a
> civill and sociable life, erect Altars unto God, builde shippes for warre
> or trafficke, throwe all manner of Darts, and practise other infinite
> sorts of excellent Artes; eyther groveling with his face downward, or
> sprawling on his backe with his face upward?

22. John Milton, *Paradise Lost*, ed. William Kerrigan (New York: Modern Library, 2008), 7.506–15).
23. Quoted in Patrides, "With His Face towards Heaven," 84.

With this comic vision of the human body gone awry from its proper axes, Crooke's human panic over groveling leads him to contradict Aristotle's account of the six "dimensions by which [all] animals are naturally bounded." Crooke claims instead that "onely man amongst all other creatures . . . hath his parts distinct, the upper, the neather, the fore, the backe parts, those on the right hand, and those on the left hand; the rest of the Creatures either have them not at al, or very confused." It is as if the appalling image of human groveling requires a repudiation so strong that it equates uprightness with bodily order itself and proneness with monstrous confusion.[24]

Donne likewise echoes Ovid's "groveling" language in *Devotions on Emergent Occasions, and severall steps in my Sickness* (1624), but with a difference. In the meditation titled "The Patient Takes His Bed," he begins: "Wee attribute but one priviledge and advantage to Mans body, above other moving creatures, that he is not as others, groveling, but of an erect, of an upright form, naturally . . . disposed to the contemplation of Heaven." While "other creatures look to the earth," man, unlike them, "is not to stay there. . . . Man in his naturall forme, is carried to the contemplation of that place which is his home." Complicating these measures, however, Donne cautions against a Miltonic overconfidence in this privilege, reminding readers that "when God came to breath[e] into Man the breath of life, he found him flat upon the ground." Attacking spiritual complacency, he asks, "This is Mans *prerogative*; but what state hath he in this dignitie? A fever can fillip him downe, a fever can *depose* him; a fever can bring that head, which yesterday caried a *crown of gold* . . . as low as his own foot, today." Donne's searing attention to man's precarious "state" and its inherent structural risk of collapsing to the proneness of the sickbed shows human presumption to be his main concern, rather than the "crookedness" of beasts or the cross-species authority uprightness normally mandated. Yet even within the terms of salvific analysis of humanity as such, Du Bartas's "*quondam* King" of creatures resonates in Donne's brilliant play on the toppled "crown" of the man who *would be king*.[25]

Despite this chorus of agreement about a prerogative over prone crea-

24. Helkiah Crooke, *Microcosmographia: A Description of the Body of Man* (London: William Jaggard, 1615), 4–5.

25. John Donne, *Devotions upon Emergent Occasions* (London: Thomas Jones, 1624), 40–42 (italics added); Guillaume du Bartas, *Bartas: His Devine Weekes and Workes*, trans. Joshua Sylvester (London: Humphrey Lownes, 1605), 335 (italics added).

tures attaching to upright estate, a less pious countertradition of equal du-
rability dogs its heels. Aristophanes's cartwheeling double being in Plato's
Symposium acquires upright posture through a punishing act of divine
vengeance. In this account, primeval men freely "moved around . . . in
either direction as they wanted. . . . When they set off to run fast, they supported themselves on all their eight limbs, and moved quickly round and
round, like tumblers who do cartwheels," but a retributive Zeus hobbles
them, resolving, "I shall now cut each of them into two; . . . They will
walk around upright on two legs. . . . If . . . they don't settle down, I'll cut
them in half again so that they move around hopping on one leg."[26] These
gaits prefigure Aristotle's detailed classifications by locomotive style, but
here standing on "only" two legs—and any concomitant measure of man
that bipedalism would imply—registers as diminution, not privilege.

Another classical example, however, serves as the moral center of a tradition resisting human authoritative privilege, whether based on uprightness or reason. Diogenes of Sinope delivered a notorious scorched-earth
mockery of Plato's definition of man as a "featherless biped." Diogenes
showed up dramatically at Plato's Academy, brandishing a plucked capon
to embarrass the exceptionalist and academic claim. The report of the
scene is wry: "Plato had defined Man as an animal, biped and featherless, and was applauded. Diogenes plucked a fowl and brought it into the
lecture-room with the words, 'Here is Plato's man.' In consequence of
which was added to the definition, 'having broad nails.'"[27] For good reasons like this, Diogenes, as a Cynic philosopher (from the Greek *kynikos*,
doglike, and *kyôn*, dog) earned his moniker, "the Dog." This Dog's readi-
ness to show his fangs in pithy sarcasm and scandalous public behavior
captivated early modern writers.[28]

As Diogenes's staged entrance makes vivid, the footedness categories
carried with them inevitable difficulties. The natural historians, for example, had only awkwardly fit apes in the quadruped column, with some-

26. Plato, *The Symposium*, ed. Christopher Gill (New York: Penguin, 2003), 22–23.

27. Diogenes Laertius, *Lives of Eminent Philosophers*, vol. 2, trans. R. D. Hicks
(Cambridge, MA: Harvard University Press, 1925), bk. 6, 41–43.

28. Diogenes mobilized his nickname in good currish style: "Other dogs bite their
enemies, but I bite my friends to save them." Diogenes of Sinope, in John Stobaeus, *Anthology* (*Johannes Stobaei Anthologium*), ed. Curt Wachmuth and Otto Hense [Berlin:
Weidmannos, 1884], 3:13.44). Diogenes appears in John Lyly's *Campaspe* (1584) and as
"Apemantus" in Shakespeare's *Timon of Athens*. See John Leon Lievsay, "Some Renaissance Views of Diogenes the Cynic," in *Joseph Quincy Adams Memorial Studies*, ed.
James McManaway (Washington, DC: Folger Shakespeare Library, 1948), 447–55.

times heady consequences for a reckoning of hands and feet. Topsell writes (following Gesner, who had tracked Aristotle closely on the ape), "Their hands . . . are like a mans, . . . their feet are . . . not like mans . . . for they are like great handes [and] . . . they use their feete both for going and handling." And assessing the ape's troublesome difference from "other Quadrupeds," Topsell says that they *"grow out of kinde*[:] . . . They live more downward than upward, like other foure footed Beasts, [yet] . . . they have no taile, like 2-legged creatures."[29] By Topsell's accounting, it is hard to say what apes are: four-handed, four-footed, or neither. To be more downward than upward, yet have no tail (an otherwise reliable index), troubles the usual consequences of being upright or prone.[30]

In Shakespearean contexts, we also see confidence wobble on the ostensibly obvious point of human two-leggedness. In *The Tempest*, when Stephano discovers Caliban and Trinculo hiding under Caliban's cloak, he defies fear and garbles a proverb: "I have not scaped drowning to be afeard now of your four legs. For it hath been said, 'As proper a man as ever went on four legs cannot make him give ground'" (2.2.59–62). (Fluellen in *Henry V* uses the proverb less elaborately: thanking the king for his glove, he says, "I would fain see the man that has but two legs that shall find himself aggriefed at this glove" [4.7.159–61]). Once Caliban and Trinculo start speaking, Stephano reconnoiters before and behind and concludes, "Four legs and two voices—a most delicate monster! His forward voice now is to speak well of his friend; his backward voice is to utter foul speeches and to detract" (2.2.90–93). In *Henry IV, Part 1*, Falstaff swears on the fuzzy math of his encounter with men he thought were robbers: "If I fought not with fifty of them, I am a bunch of radish. If there were not two- or three-and-fifty upon poor old Jack, then am I no two-legged creature" (2.4.183–86). We will return to the vegetable comparison shortly, but here, because the audience knows Falstaff is lying, for us he denies his own two-legged condition. If we factor in period zeal for jokes about riding backward (and possibly prone) on the back of an ass, skimmington style, or being laid low by drink or sleep, or falling down on all fours in exhaustion, the consensus on human prerogative in official commentaries begins to

29. Topsell, *History of the Foure-Footed Beastes*, 4 (italics added); Aristotle, *History of Animals, Books 1–3*, trans. A. L. Peck (Cambridge, MA: Loeb Classical Library / Harvard University Press, 1984), bk. 2, pt. 8, pp. 103, 105.

30. For an excellent account of the cultural work of the ape in Renaissance humanism, see Kenneth Gouwens, "Human Exceptionalism," in *The Renaissance World*, ed. John Jeffries Martin (London: Routledge, 2007), 415–34.

sound like whistling in the dark.[31] Two-leggedness is a high-maintenance proposition: it figures precarity as much as it projects authority.

In this now heavily cross-hatched grid of body mapping, two commentators make a frontal assault on upright status and its associated claims: Montaigne and Thomas Browne. Thwarting the orthodoxies of anthrocentric physio-theology, Montaigne's "Apologie" brings down the species presumption of reading vertical posture as a divinely indexed ontology of man and names it ideological. Basing his claims on natural-historical reading and direct observation, Montaigne accuses Plato of raising "his flight aloft in . . . cloudy Poesies" and "gibbrish," asking "what dreamed or doted he on when he defined man to be a creature with two feet, and without feathers?" and he quotes Ovid's Latin verses on this point to call their bias to account (489).[32] Urging that if, instead, "we impartially enter into judgement with our selves," we find that

> that *prerogative*, which Poets yeeld unto our upright stature, looking towards heaven whence her beginning is . . . is *meerely poeticall*, for, there are many little beasts that have their sight directly fixed towards heaven: I finde the Camels and the Estridges necke much more raised and upright, than ours. What beasts have not their face aloft and before, and looke not directly opposite, as we; and in their naturall posture descrie not as much of heaven and earth as man doth? (430; italics added)

Echoing the charge of "imaginary soveraigntie" we saw him make in "Of Cruelty," Montaigne rejects convenient substitutions of the "meerely poeticall" for the fairly observable. Instead, he calls upright "prerogative" a mere invention. This converts the customary privilege accorded to human vertical orientation into a losing question of impartial reason and indicates at the same time another human failure to measure up to another of its claimed marks of distinction: orderly judgment.

31. On gender and the orders of before and behind, on top and beneath, see Natalie Davis, "Women on Top," in *Society and Culture in Early Modern France: Eight Essays by Natalie Zemon Davis* (Stanford, CA: Stanford University Press, 1975), and Ruth Melinkoff, "Riding Backwards: Theme of Humiliation and Symbol of Evil," *Viator* 4 (1973): 153–76. On crawling on all fours (in the dark), see discussion of *A Midsummer Night's Dream* in chapter 4.

32. Montaigne quotes Ovid's Latin verses follows: "Pronaque cum spectent animalia catera terram, / Os homini sublime dedit, calumque videre / Iussit, et erectos ad sidera tollere vultus" (430); Arthur Golding's English translation of the passage is discussed above in the text.

When Browne enters the fray in *Pseudodoxia Epidemica* (1646), he too
cites Ovid's lines. In a *tour de force* of bloodless anatomization, he first defends uprightness in a "strict" and medical sense (in the style of Aristotelian biomechanics), but then debunks any privileging of the human body's
erect status and its associated gaze as a "vulgar error." Browne's modern
intervention would make uprightness a mere true fact, devoid of any particular meaning (exemplifying the move "from symbolic exegesis to deinscriptive hermeneutics" James Bono described[33]). Browne first points out
that to say "that onely Man hath an Erect figure, and [that] for to behold
and look up toward heaven . . . is a double assertion."[34] He addresses them
one at a time (in due course). The first he allows to be true under stated
conditions:

> If we take Erectness strictly, and so as Galen hath defined it; for they
> onely, saith he, have an erect figure, whose spine and thigh-bone are
> carried in right lines; . . . so indeed of any we yet know Man only is
> erect. For the thighs of other animals do stand at angles with their
> spine, and have rectangular positions in birds, and perfect Quadrupeds.
> Nor doth the Frog, though stretched out, or swimming, attaine the rec-
> titude of Man, or carry its thigh without all angularity. (155)

The surprising appearance of the frog as a challenger grimly derives in part
from its "stretched" posture on a vivisection board. The erectness of man
as formulated here depends on the strict measure of a "right line" that nevertheless must break into an angle the moment man begins to move; the
man "without all angularity" is a stationary man.[35] Crooke had likewise

33. James Bono, *The Word of God and the Languages of Man: Interpreting Nature
in Early Modern Science and Medicine* (Madison: University of Wisconsin Press, 1995),
167–68.

34. Thomas Browne, *Pseudodoxia Epidemica; or, Enquiries into very many Received Tenents and Commonly Presumed Truths*, 3rd ed. (London, 1658), bk. 4, ch. 1,
155. Subsequent page references appear in the text.

35. Aristotelian motion results from leverage through the flexing angles of joints:
"It is clear . . . that movement is impossible if there is nothing in a state of rest, and
above all in the animals themselves. For if any one of their parts moves, another part
must necessarily be at rest; and it is on this account that animals have joints. For they
use their joints as a centre, and the whole part in which the joint is situated is both one
and two, both straight and bent, changing potentially and actually because of the joint"
(Aristotle, *Parts of Animals*, 441–43 [sec. 1]).

stressed an unbending leg: "Onely Man by the straitnese of his legges goes exactly upright."[36] Browne continues that, on the other hand, "if Erectness be popularly taken, and as it is largely opposed unto proneness, or the posture of animals looking downwards, . . . it may admit of question" (156). Leaving aside whether the "proneness" of quadrupeds positions them "face down," Browne calculates proneness in an array of creatures with detailed attention: "Though in Serpents and Lizards we may truly allow a proneness, yet Galen acknowledgeth that perfect Quadrupeds, as Horses, Oxen, and Camels, are but partly prone, and have some part of erectness. And birds or flying animals, are so far from this kind of proneness, that they are almost erect; advancing the head and breast in their progression, and only prone in the Act of volitation" (156). Rectitude or angularity, perpendicularity or proneness: these are the fundamental angles in this clinical dissection of the human conceit. Flying, however spectacular an ability, lowers birds' heads to proneness. Imperfect quadrupeds go on their bellies (they might as well all be snakes). Perfect quadrupeds, to use Topsell's terms, "grow out of kinde," and they seem hybrids rather than the true exemplars of a properly prone axis. And despite the caveat that "*of any we yet know* Man only is Erect," Browne next gives two counterexamples that drolly undermine a human monopoly on uprightness:

> If that be true which is delivered of the Pengin or *Anser Magellanicus* often described in Maps about those Straits, that they goe erect like men, and with their breast and belly do make one line perpendicular unto the axis of the earth; it will almost make up the exact erectness of man. Nor will that insect come very short which we have often beheld . . . which stands not prone, or a little inclining upward, but in a large erectness, elevating alwaies the two fore legs, and sustaining it self in the middle of the other four; by Zoographers called *Mantis* . . . as being generally found in the posture of supplication, or such as resembleth ours, when we lift up our hands to heaven. (156; italics in original)

The penguin comes by hearsay from the Straits of Magellan, but the praying mantis is cited as a familiar insect. Not only do the penguin (walking in "one line," without angles) and the mantis achieve virtually human perpendicularity—measured by the surface of the earth; even more pointedly, in the (six-legged!) insect's case Browne stresses the very attitude of

36. Crooke, *Microcosmographia*, 12.

prayer so sacrosanct to advocates of a prerogative in human uprightness. The gaze of many animals, he concludes, "makes an higher arch of altitude then [sic] our own" (157).

From Diogenes to Browne, this countertradition registers several disturbances in the conceit of uprightness on which humanness makes its stand. First of all, as Montaigne makes so plain, any eyes that look can see that other creatures manifest uprightness: camels and ostriches, penguins and mantises, the problematic ape, and "many little beasts" make their appearances. Second, the erectness of man, especially if measured in the terms Browne uses, lends to the human body a certain fixity or rootedness. So despite claims of godlike power, the human form seems as much an anchored plant as a free animal. A host of punning references enact this comparison in the period—the body as a trunk or stock, affiliations (familial or not) as grafting or as rooting and branching, references to growth itself—but in this context to be plantlike is to be stuck or rooted in one place, without the ability to change geographic location by implementing a willing decision to traverse space.[37] Even Shakespeare's notorious quasi-confutation of plant fixity—Macbeth's scoff, "Who can impress the forest, bid the tree / Unfix his earth-bound root?" (4.1.95–96), and the improbable march of Birnam Wood that follows—depends on classic riddling logic. The trees do not "unfix" their roots, but marching soldiers camouflage their numbers with felled branches. In these lights, the durable trope of uprightness on which man has been resting his case may be something of a red herring.

If we review the language used to advocate upright prerogative, we see that it tracks dynamics of vision and regard; it really makes a claim about sightlines. Insofar as sight so thoroughly dominates the human sensorium (compared to other animals), this failure of imagination—mistaking vision for mastery while forgetting or deriding other capacities—is perhaps

---

37. On plant thinking, see Rebecca Bushnell, *Green Desire: Imagining Early Modern English Gardens* (Ithaca, NY: Cornell University Press, 2003). See also Jeen Feerick, *Strangers in Blood: Relocating Race in the Renaissance* (Toronto: University of Toronto Press, 2010); Feerick, "Botanical Shakespeares: The Racial Logic of Plant Life in *Titus Andronicus*," *South Central Review* 26, no. 1 (2009): 82–102; Vin Nardizzi, "Shakespeare's Penknife: Grafting and Seedless Generation in the Procreation Sonnets," *Renaissance and Reformation* 32, no. 1 (2009): 83–106; and Nardizzi, "The Wooden Matter of Human Bodies: Prosthesis and Stump in *A Larum for London*," in *The Indistinct Human in Renaissance Literature*, ed. Vin Nardizzi and Jean Feerick (Basingstroke, UK: Palgrave, 2012), 119–36.

to be expected (challenges to this proposition about human vision are laid out in chapter 4).[38] Uprightness enables, or so the proposition ventures, a special kind of gaze. Montaigne undercuts this scheme, showing that bipedal erectness does not even entail an "upward" look but a horizontal one and that it is simply not unique: "What beasts have not their face aloft and before, and looke not directly opposite, as we; and in their naturall posture descrie not as much of heaven and earth as man doth?" We might posit something typically human in the conceit that surveillance or regard establishes ownership or dominion, making man the so-called monarch of all he surveys.

William Cowper's 1782 poem on this theme comes later, as a complex response to imperial projections of limitless agency over the New World:

> I am monarch of all I survey,
> My right there is none to dispute;
> From the centre all round to the sea,
> I am lord of the fowl and the brute.[39]

Contemporary familiarity with Cowper's line depends, ironically, on the Cowardly Lion in *The Wizard of Oz*, who sings a stammering fantasy of the power over other animals that the lion was always said to have. The lion sings,

> I'd command each thing
> Be it fish or fowl
> With a woof and a woof
> And a royal growl . . .
>
> . . .

38. Vicki Hearne describes how "for us seeing is believing. Aristotle opens the *Metaphysics* with a small warning about this. . . . The other senses are mostly ancillary." *Adam's Task: Calling Animals by Name* (New York: Skyhorse Publishing, 2007 [1986]), 79. For the psychoanalytic coordinates of the comparative sensorium—in which "devaluation of olfactory stimuli" leads to an (upright) condition where shame is operative and "visual stimuli are paramount"—see Sigmund Freud, *Civilization and Its Discontents*, ed. James Strachey (New York: Norton, 2005), 87n1 (discussed below).

39. William Cowper, *Selected Poems*, ed. Nick Rhodes (Sussex, UK: Taylor and Francis, 2003), 38. Mary Louise Pratt proposes a "monarch-of-all-I-survey genre" that has the New World in view and empire in mind. See *Imperial Eyes: Travel Writing and Transculturation* (London: Routledge, 1992).

Each rabbit would show respect to me
The chipmunks genuflect to me.
. . .
Monarch of all I survey
Mah-ah-ah-ah-ah-ah-ah-ah-ah-narch!
Of all I survey![40]

But the "stately looke" paradigm stems from a long tradition of reading
the erect human body in a way that advances a *panoptical man*, a man
who is master of all he can see. By the time of its new deployments in
European geopolitical colonization, this chestnut had been well worked
in the environs of human/animal relations, supplying a zoographic fable
about political consequences for the coordinates of embodiment. Panoptical man would be king not only by the establishments of Genesis but also
by bodily design. Framings of human rule as monarchy also suggest how
theorizations of a singular *absolute* (perfect, unfettered) monarch provided
certain genetic material to the *liberal* (free, unrestrained) subject.[41] And
insofar as human eyes, however conveniently situated, are not comparatively strong, the microscope and telescope (both developed in Zeeland by
eyeglass makers at the turn of the seventeenth century) would serve pros-
thetically to enhance imperial sightlines for human vision. The figure of a
panopticon described by Foucault as a later surveillance mechanism over
(human) political subjects thus makes a prior appearance, one in which a
panoptical model of man defines the species as a surveilling agency over
"prone" creaturely subjects within the sweep of his "stately looke."
     With uprightness "meerely poeticall" and panoptical humanity still
fairly propositional in the preindustrial domains of early modernity, the
border skirmish that "uprightness" tends to obscure concerns the distinction between creatures that move and plants that do not, one of the two
categorical divides so central to the Hexameron. As noted in chapter 1,
Genesis 1:30 granted to *"everie thing that moveth* upon the earth which
hathe life in it selfe" a right to "everie grene herbe . . . for meat."[42] Donne

40. Harold Arlen and Yip Harberg, "If I Were King of the Forest," in Noel Langley
et al., *The Wizard of Oz: The Screenplay* (Brooklyn, NY: Delta Publishing, 1989), 96.
     41. The optics of authority surrounding the king as singular "spectator" of court
masques dramatized this. Stephen Orgel, *The Illusion of Power: Political Theater in the
English Renaissance* (Berkeley: University of California Press, 1975), 10–11.
     42. Gen. 1:30 (italics added). For "everie thing that moveth," see also, for example,
Gen. 1:26, 7:22, and 9:3.

labeled this group *"moving* creatures," a category that asserts a critical likeness between humans and animals. Chapter 1 explored how the constitutional dimensions of this dispensation entitled nonhuman creatures to a cognizable stakeholdership (now largely foreign to our thought) and framed them politically, as tyrannized subjects, in early modernity. Nowhere do we find plants accorded anything like this status; plants are on board the ark as fodder, not passengers, and plants are not imagined as "witnesses" who serve. The capacity to move and all the implications of prerogative and intentionality that attend it fuel this primal plant/animal divide, and the Aristotelian concepts of locomotive and rational soul prove to overlap.

Aristotle well knew that there were fixed animals and moving plants. In *The Parts of Animals* he writes that the sponge "is in all respects like a plant: it lives only while growing on something, and when it is pulled off it dies"; at the same time, creatures he calls "Sea-lungs" float freely "unattached," but they otherwise live "just as if they were plants."[43] Nevertheless, attachment and free movement remain a crux of practical evaluation, even for an analyst of Aristotle's subtlety. In his treatise on comparative locomotion, Aristotle elaborates on the "dimensions" or orientations of moving creatures, claiming that "bipeds have their superior part . . . corresponding to the superior position of the universe[,] polypods and footless animals in a position corresponding to the middle region, and plants . . . to the inferior. The reason is that plants lack [locomotion], and the superior part is situated with a view to nutriment, and their nutriment comes from the earth."[44] Locomotion—movement in respect to place, as opposed to growth—unites nonplant life. Before a Cartesian regime would demote organisms who were alleged to lack a soul as *mere* automatons (that is, beings who move without volition), this power of locomotion in itself worked as a more positively remarkable criterion. Descartes thus reverses the significance of "automaton," which otherwise distinguished things that were "self-acting" (from the Greek *autos,* "self," and *matos,* "thinking, animated, willing") and therefore also autonomous, or self-ruling and mobile. Traditionally this distinction had elevated animals. As we will see, the very concept of "proneness" contained both horizontality and a likeliness to be active in a certain way—an "inclination" or prerogative to move.

Disparagers of Darwin would focus their derision on primates in order

43. Aristotle, *Parts of Animals,* 335 (sec. 5).
44. Aristotle, *Progression of Animals,* 497 (sec. 5).

to attack the way evolutionary theory put humans in proximate relations
with animals; in a related strategy, Descartes highlighted those creatures
he thought most embarrassed animal estate, the lowest or simplest creatures to further undermine the importance of an ability to move. Using
"imperfect" oysters and sponges rhetorically to stand in for all the rest, he
associated animals with the immobile and vegetable nature of plants: "If
they thought as we do, they would have an immortal soul like us. This is
unlikely, because there is no reason to believe it of some animals without
believing it of all, and many of them such as oysters and sponges are too
imperfect for this to be credible."[45] Genesis 1 had constitutionally distinguished between plants (as commodities available to all) and "everie thing
that moveth," while among moving creatures nonhumans were cast as the
political subjects of proper (vegetarian and stewardlike) human monarchy.
Descartes seeks to undo the memory of this aspect of Genesis, converting animals to plantlike fodder to supply—not "serve" in—the precarious
modern monoculture of man as self-crowned king: *cogito ergo sum*.

The problem Descartes perceived a necessity to address was the consistent investment of cosmographic significance in creaturely movement
as such, a characteristic prioritized in Aristotelian biomechanics and Genesis alike. "Life," Topsell writes, offering to define it in an improvisation
on Aristotelian ensouledness, "is different and diverse, according to the
spirit wherein it is seated, and by which it is nourished *as with a current*."[46] "Current" derives from the Latin *currere*: to run or move quickly.
The balance of this chapter surveys the treasury of period formulations,
all indicating set inclinations for motion ("the course of kynde," "nature's
bias," "run the race," "against the grain," and "against the haire"), connecting them to ideas about natural "properties," quadruped biomechanics, and free animal locomotion. To intend or decide to move or "stay," as
we will see, expresses the *decision* fundamental to conceptions of political
capacity, whether in regard to obedience, acknowledgment of authority, or
resistance by fight or flight. To make an end to this inquiry, the chapter
considers certain early modern quadrupeds who look back, particularly attending to how they regard human would-be kings. If freedom lurks in an
ability to "vote with your feet," as the painter Hans Hoffmann registers in
his 1578 watercolor of a wild boar piglet (fig. 2.1), resistance flashes in the
eyes. As art historian Stijn Alsteens describes Hoffmann's lively studies of

45. Descartes, "To the Marquess of Newcastle," 304.
46. Topsell, epistle dedicatory, *History of the Foure-Footed Beastes* (italics added).

Figure 2.1. Hans Hoffmann, *Wild Boar Piglet* (1578). Image courtesy of the
Collection of Jean Bonna, Geneva; photo courtesy of Patrick Goetelen, Geneva.

animals, he "animated his works by slightly narrowing the eyes of the animal depicted," suggesting an "alertness absent from the nature studies by
Dürer, who tended to stress the objectivity of his observation" instead.[47]
The sparkle recorded in the eye of this young boar, doubtless modeled by
an adopted orphan of the hunt, records the painter's apt sense that the
creature is about to make his move.

The Course of Kind, "Unyoked"

The notion of diverse embodied charts of characteristic motion is repeatedly termed the "course of kynde" in period texts. In a lovely 1507 example
about the coming of winter,

> All strength and vertue of trees and herbes sote
> Dyscendynge be, from croppe in to the rote.

47. Stijn Alsteens, *A Wild Boar Piglet* (Sus Scrofa), in *Raphael to Renoir: Drawings
from the Collection of Jean Bonna*, ed. Stijn Alsteens et al. (New York: Metropolitan
Museum of Art, 2009), 92.

And every creature by course of kynde
For socoure draweth to that countre and place
Where for a tyme, they may purchace and fynde
Conforte and rest.[48]

Plant "vertue[s]" recede to the roots, and animals withdraw to their dens.
The course-of-kind trope finds continuing life in such contemporary expressions as "in due course," "in the ordinary course," "as a matter of
course," or "letting nature take its course." An idea of "course" still sets
parameters for the normal or usual, what is—"of course!"—true. As we
have seen in chapter 1, early modern laws of nature are particularizing
rather than homogenizing laws.[49] They disperse and dehumanize lawfulness, giving kind-ness a performative power that refers to the ways things
have of going about their business in their ordinary courses. Following
the familiar division of airy, earthly, and watery domains, the Edwardine
Homily on Obedience (1547) embarks on a poetry of lists to describe how
these things *keep themselves* in order:

> Almighty GOD hath created and appointed all things in heaven, earth,
> and waters, in a most excellent and perfect order. . . . The sunne, mone,
> sterres, rainbow, thunder, lightning, cloudes and al birdes of the aire,
> do kepe their ordre. The yearth, trees, seedes, plantes, herbes, corne,
> grasse, and all maner of beastes keepe them in their ordre. . . . All kyndes

---

48. Antoine de La Sale, *The Fyftene Joyes of Maryage*, trans. Robert Copeland[?]
(London: Wynken de Worde, 1509 [1507]), proheme, lines 6–11. The frequency of *"against*
the course of kind" attests to the prerogative inhering in things. See, for example, the
following: a denunciation of hierarchy among brothers as "against all course of kinde"
(Thomas Sackville and Thomas Norton, *The Tragedie of Gorboduc* [London: William
Griffith, 1565], 1.1.11); cannibalism as a "monstrous cruelty 'gainst course of kynde"
(Edmund Spenser, *The Faerie Queene*, ed. Thomas Roche [New York: Penguin, 1979],
6.8.36); a "flock of silly sheep" turn militant "'gainst course of kind" (*Thomas of Woodstock* [ca. 1591–95], from MS Egerton 1994, fols. 161–185b, in *Thomas of Woodstock*, ed.
Peter Corbin and Douglas Sedge [Manchester, UK: Manchester University Press, 2002],
142 [4.2.23–24]); and a reference to "comets and stars appearing contrary to the course
of kind" (Thomas Lodge, *The Divel Coniured* [1596], in *The Complete Works of Thomas
Lodge*, ed. Edmund Gosse [Glasgow: Robert Anderson, 1883], 3:63).
49. Human law, too, has courses: the duke in *The Merchant of Venice* "cannot deny
the course of law" (3.3.26); it is described as "meet" that Gloucester should "be condemned by course of law" (*Henry VI, Part 2*, 3.1.237); and to interfere with it is "to trip
the course of law" (*Henry IV, Part 2*, 5.2.87).

of fishes in the sea, rivers and waters, with all fountaynes, sprynges, yea, the seas themselfes, kepe their comely course and ordre.[50]

The refrain accords each party to the cosmic census—beasts among all the created forms—that sovereignty of keeping itself in its particular path, maintaining its own distinct tenure, and durably surviving in time. This natural law reflects a dispersal of agentive autonomy, expressed in "comely course[s]."

Richard Hooker's *Laws of Ecclesiastical Polity* (1593) similarly defines law as the expression of natural properties in routes of travel: "All things that are have some operation not violent or casual . . . for unto every end, every operation will not serve. That which doth assign unto each thing the kind, that which doth moderate the force and the power, that which doth appoint the form and the measure, the same we term a law." Such things or kinds, "in such sort as they are," trace out a "course" established by "nature's law." Considering how "it fareth in the natural course of the world," Hooker asks an extended rhetorical question about the result "if nature should intermit her course." To pose it, he itemizes nature into its many presentations, listing its many "wonted motions," "unwearied courses," and "beaten ways."[51] Ulysses offers the same vision in *Troilus and Cressida*, but the fixity of "degree" endorsed there reveals itself in movement:

> The heavens themselves, the planets, and this center
> Observe degree, priority, and place,
> Insisture, course, proportion, season, form,
> Office, and custom, in all line of order.
> (1.3.85–88)

While the homily likened bodies beyond the moon and creatures in their observance of courses, we also see distinctions made between the perfection of superlunary motion and the sublunary world.[52] Montaigne's

---

50. "On Good Order, and Obedience to Rulers," in *Certain sermons or homilies (1547) and A homily against disobedience and wilful rebellion (1570)*, ed. Ronald B. Bond (Toronto: University of Toronto Press, 1987), 161.

51. Richard Hooker, *Of the Laws of Ecclesiastical Polity*, ed. Arthur Stephen McGrade (Cambridge: Cambridge University Press, 1989), 54, 60.

52. I consider cosmic disjunction and questions of course in "Lear's Queer Cosmos," *Shakesqueer: A Queer Companion to the Complete Works of Shakespeare*, ed. Madhavi Menon (Durham, NC: Duke University Press, 2011), 171–78.

"Apologie," for example, refers to "the incorruptible life of the celestiall bodies, their beauty, [and] greatnesse, and agitation, continued with so just and regular a course" (396). Sublunary things, however, failing the celestial perfection of a circular orbit, are never exactly regular or perfectly predictable—even in their ordinary courses.

Thus other observers are less assured than Hooker or Ulysses about the geometric regularity of nature's courses. In the *Advancement of Learning* (1605), Bacon stresses diverse types of courses when he divides knowledge into three categories. The "history of nature," he writes, "is of three sorts; of nature in course, of nature erring or varying, and of nature altered or wrought." Nature in course he calls the "history of creatures," nature erring is the "history of marvels," and nature diverted is the "history of arts." Research in the latter two categories he proclaims deficient, especially regarding "the works of Nature which have a digression and deflexion from the ordinary course . . . the heteroclites or irregulars of Nature."[53] Nature, not bound to ordinariness, retains a power of errancy or wandering, a power of moving, whether in or out of a customary course. Following a "proper" course thus does not strictly mean one in line with juridical or decorous requirement, but rather the prerogative to move in one owned by or pertaining to the being in motion, as a kind of self-title or virtual copyright in one's own way of working.

These courses are not necessarily straight or regular, like those of heavenly objects. To head for a destination is commonly to "wend one's way" or to "bend one's course." Such a curving route was often indexed by reference to an inbuilt "bias" in the moving body, an image drawn from the off-center weight implanted in the balls rolled toward the jack in the game of bowls. In *Twelfth Night*, "nature to her bias drew" (5.1.263), and in *King Lear*, "The King falls from bias of nature" (1.2.108–9). In *The Taming of the Shrew*, Petrucchio exhorts, "Well, forward, forward. Thus the bowl should run, / And not unluckily against the bias" (4.6.25–26). Here natural forward motion is not rectilinear, but a swerving "bias." In "Of Experience" Montaigne claims that because "my health is to keepe my accustomed state . . . sicknesse dothe on the one side . . . divert me from it, and . . . Physitians, . . . on the other side will turne me from it: So that both by fortune and art, I am cleane out of my right bias."[54] In all these

53. Bacon, *Advancement of Learning*, bk. 2, 74.
54. Michel de Montaigne, "Of Experience," in *Essayes*, 977. See also my "Nature's Bias: Renaissance Homonormativity and Elizabethan Comic Likeness," *Modern Philology* 98, no. 2 (2000): 183–210.

instances, the notion of "the bias" establishes that the implanted weight sets the ball's peculiar arc as something proper to it.

This arc sometimes faces impediments or "rubs," but when left alone keeps its own course, according to the prerogatives of its "right bias," as Montaigne terms it. In *Richard II* the unfortunate queen shuns bowling, saying, "'Twill make me think the world is full of rubs / And that my fortune runs against the bias" (3.4.4–5). As in Petrucchio's example, the logic here makes clear that bad fortune runs *against* the autonomous course set by the weight or bias implanted within the ball; the curving trajectory of the bias neither occasions nor describes the straying of fortunes. Paradoxically, this means that to follow one's "bias," however curving or unpredictable, is not to swerve or deviate, but to follow a particular law of one's own. When interfering impediments are lifted, things quite vigorously revert to their customary courses.[55] One suggestive impediment is the yoke: in *King Henry IV, Part 2*, an army in disarray

> is dispersed . . .
> Like youthful steers unyoked, they take their courses,
> East, west, north, south.
> (4.2.340–42)

As soon as they are free of the imposed constraint of the yoke, the quadrupeds in the simile take up their own "courses"; their natural prerogative to go spins the compass dial.

The multivalent term "race" operates very similarly to "course," especially in mapping an individual life as a race to be run. So the Earl of Surrey remembered Wyatt, saying he "lived, and ran the race, that Nature set."[56] When George Gascoigne calls on the kinetic image of a headstrong horse to evoke the waywardness of his younger days, his way of life registers as both a course and a race—and as "unbridled" motion: "Unbridled youth had run his recklesse race, / And caried me with carelesse course, to many a great disgrace." Gascoigne describes looking back on his prodigal period: "With heavie cheare I caste my head aback, / To see the fountaine

---

55. See also Bacon's *New Atlantis*, where the "feast of the family" reproves members who "take ill courses" (*Three Early Modern Utopias*, ed. Susan Bruce [Oxford: Oxford University Press, 1999], 169), while *King Lear*'s Kent, on the other hand, promises to "shape his old course in a country new" (1.1.186).

56. Henry Howard, "W. Resteth Here," in *Renaissance Literature: An Anthology*, ed. Michael Payne and John Hunter (Oxford: Blackwell, 2003), 131 (line 31).

of my furious race."[57] "Furious race" and "carelesse course" describe the same thing, and Gascoigne turns his head "aback" to review them. While prodigal Gascoigne refers to the bridle, Thomas Dekker invokes another instrument of animal control, calling the contemplation of Christ's sacrifice "a spurre unto us whilst we are upon earth, to runne the race of blessedness" and asks for "grace to run wel without stumbling."[58] These usages for "runne the race" stem in part from ancient ideas about the longevity of the oak, the raven, and the stag, but the stag has particular authority shaping the language of the "race."[59] In George Whitney's 1586 *Choice of Emblemes*, for instance, the verse glossing *Tempus omnia terminat* moralizes how "the princelie stagge at length his race doth ronne[,] / And all must ende, that ever was begonne."[60] "Race" indicates a moving line, in time and in space; it encompasses the arc of a life span (from birth to death) and a course or "way" of life (reckless or blessed)—in addition to its transindividual significance as a genealogy or tribe, where familial and genetic lines extend through time in either human or animal contexts.

Alongside "the course of kind" and "running the race," we may add the colloquialisms "against the grain" (still in familiar use) and its obsolete, more evidently mammalian counterpart, "against the haire" (since evolved into the expression "rub the wrong way"). These phrasings likewise encode the directional arrow of an inbuilt compass, in Surrey's words, by "Nature set." "Grain" now tends to be associated with the orientation of wood fiber, but the "grain" of animal skin (whether shaved intact or tanned as leather) bears equal historical force. Florio's Montaigne points out how "towards goodnes, benignitie, or temperance" our human zeal "goeth but slowly, and against the haire" (391). The phrase appears in

57. George Gascoigne, "The complaint of the greene Knight" and "Sonnet 5" (in his corona on a theme given by Alexander Neville), in *The Posies*, ed. John Cunliffe (Cambridge: Cambridge University Press, 1907), 372, 68.

58. Thomas Dekker, "The Foure Birdes of Noah's Arke," in *The Non-Dramatic Works of Thomas Dekker*, ed. Alexander Grosart (Printed for private circulation, 1886), 5:98.

59. The idea of persistent longevity in some creatures relates to Old Testament suggestions of a reverse evolution: a decline in human stature and life span after the Fall. Michael Bath surveys the sources, beginning in Hesiod, for Donne's reference to the "Stag, and Raven, and the long-liv'd tree" in "Donne's 'Anatomy of the World' and the Legend of the Oldest Animals," *Review of English Studies* 32, no. 127 (1981): 302–8.

60. George Whitney, *A Choice of Emblemes and Other Devises* (Leiden, Netherlands: Christopher Plantijn, 1586), 230. The "princelie" stag underscores the rival sovereignty I am proposing for animals in this chapter (see below).

Romeo and Juliet ("Thou desirest me to stop in my tale against the hair" [2.4.91]), *The Merry Wives of Windsor* ("If you should fight, you go against the hair of your professions" [2.3.40–41]), and in *Troilus and Cressida* ("He is melancholy without cause, and merry against the hair" [1.2.26–27]), just to give Shakespearean instances.[61] But we may refer to Randle Cotgrave's 1611 *Dictionarie of the French and English tongues* by way of a grand finale on these early modern figures for dispersed sovereignties of motion among creatures. Cotgrave defines *rebours* and *rebourser* in a litany of reversals sufficient to qualify as an Aristotelian nightmare: "Arseward, backward, preposterously, oblikely, awry, overthwartly, quite contrary, full against the course, wooll, or haire" and to "set, or place the wrong way; turne inside outward, upside downeward; . . . take a course against all course."[62] This last, taking "a course against all course," suggests the ranging kinds of motion that "course" works to convey and the scope of a prerogative in things to determine such courses. Courses are charted by kind, but kinds, though they are by "Nature set," unfold in the open-ended creaturely discourse of continual emergence Julia Lupton has described, adapting the creation language of the Hexameron to a broader vision of the living arts of nature. Kinds are "set" (made), but not "set" (fixed).

The refrain in Genesis 1, each "according to his kinde," appears in no less than ten instances in verses 11 through 25. "Kind" is used of plants and animals both (humans constitute "one kind" and thus need not be so subspecified). Although the phrase tends now to be associated with reproduction within species, its force does not attach to the exhortation to "bring forthe frute and multiplie" (Gen. 1:22). Rather, what is envisioned as being performed "according to . . . kinde" is the *original* creation of different plants and animals, an act (and an inventory) of creative plenitude that is measured by many-kindedness. At God's word, the "earth broght forthe" plants and trees; the "waters broght forthe" fish and fowl; and again the earth "bring[s] forthe . . . the beast of the earth," each "according to his kinde" (Gen. 1:11–12, 20–21, 24–25). The phrase is ubiquitous in medieval and early modern English, serving less as a figure for control than as a gesture of multiplicity in a frame where order *is* variety. Ideas of "kynde" were considerably more flexible than a modern lay concept of "species," with its genetic and human-exceptionalist attentions trained

---

61. See also reference to France, "armed and reverted, making war against her heir" (*Comedy of Errors*, 3.2.124–25).

62. Randle Cotgrave, *A dictionarie of the French and English tongues* (London: Adam Islip, 1611), s.v. "rebours" and "rebourser."

to models of heterosexual (human) reproduction. The multiple criteria by which animals are said to vary in early modern classificatory thinking display an additive, cumulative, or inventorying sense of diversity. The "properties" of a kind, its qualities or features, express themselves in action, by working.

"Properties" had a special urgency in botanical contexts, where given plants were sought out and claims for their salubrious effects recorded in the archive of the materia medica. In critical commentary, the term "sovereignty" has come almost exclusively to signify the extremely singular state power Hobbes proposed in the mid-seventeenth century, likening it to the emblematic Leviathan of Job 41:21: "Non est potestas Super Terram quae Comparetur ei" (There is no power on earth that can be compared to him) as his 1651 frontispiece reads.[63] Before the evolving specialization of the term, "sovereignty" also familiarly referred to the diverse efficacies of a host of herbal medicines, or "sovereign remedies"—and thus to a plethora of operational "sovereignties" rather than "the one."[64] Thomas Wilson's *The Rule of Reason* (1551) offers a concise definition of the sense of "property" on which such sovereignties were based: a "property is a natural *proneness* and manner of doing, which agreeth to one kind, and to the same only."[65]

63. Thomas Hobbes, *Leviathan*, ed. Richard Flathman and David Johnston (New York: Norton, 1996).

64. Philemon Holland's translation of Pliny refers to "a certaine hearbe called Calaminth, most *soveraigne and singular* against the biting of Serpents" (a fact demonstrated to humans by lizards) and to "the root of a wild rose, called the sweet Brier or Eglantine" as the "*sure and soveraigne* remedie for them that are bitten with a mad dog." Pliny, *The Historie of the World, Commonly Called, the Naturall Historie of Plinius Secundus*, trans. Philemon Holland (London, 1601), bk. 8, chs. 27, 41 (pp. 210, 220) (italics added). What is sovereign is "singular," "sure," and "excellent," but there are many "sovereign" things. The same term describes animal parts used medicinally: the hare's "skynne burnt to pouder, is a soveraine medicine to stenche bloud" (George Gascoigne, trans., *The Noble Arte of Venerie* [London: Christopher Barker, 1576], 160). Shakespeare's Venus imagines the sweat of Adonis's palm as "earth's sovereign salve to do a goddess good" and also finds his hound licking its own wounds "'Gainst venom'd sores the only sovereign plaster" (*Venus and Adonis*, stanzas 4 and 151); Menenius refers to "the most sovereign prescription in Galen" (*Coriolanus*, 2.1.115). For an unnerving account of ingredients (crab's eyes, boy's urine, dried fox lungs, oil of scorpions, powdered swallows, bull's penis, bezoar stone, just-whelped puppies, and so forth), see William Brockbank, "Sovereign Remedies: A Critical Depreciation of the 17th-Century London Pharmacopoeia," *Medical History* 8 (1964): 3.

65. Thomas Wilson, *The Rule of Reason, conteyning the Arte of Logique* (London, 1551), sig. B7v (italics added), quoted in Rebecca Bushnell, *A Culture of Teaching: Early*

The formulation suggests not so much an inexorable or incorporative force, but rather the diversity of local effects. Given things are prone to express the individuating law of their (diverse) natures, to display severally their unique qualities and inclinations. In Thomas Elyot's *Book of the Governour* (1531), we hear this impulse to ramifying dispersal: "Every kynde of trees, herbes, birdes, beastis, and fisshes, besyde theyr diversitie of fourmes have . . . a peculier disposition appropered unto them."[66] The unusual term "appropered" goes further than the more predictable term, "appointed," to suggest that dispositions are held as property in an almost modern sense. Dispositions are not "peculier" in the sense that they are odd, but in that their particularity is conceived as irreducible.

Animal encyclopedias, particularly Gesner's volumes and their vernacular expansions, took up, with impressive tenacity, the huge task of recording the diverse properties of creatures. In a recent account, Brian Ogilvie persuasively characterizes early modern natural history as a "science of describing." Ogilvie's detailed analysis concerns plant sciences rather than zoography, and herbals vastly outnumbered histories of animals due to their practical role in pharmacology.[67] But his emphasis on description captures the commitments of sixteenth-century accountings for creatures as well. Beginning with the late fifteenth-century philological reconstruction of classical texts of natural description, Ogilvie stresses the sixteenth-century additive practice of cataloguing new plant species. Natural historical entries for animal kinds relatedly sought to collect every bit of information that could be acquired about already existing animals. As Ogilvie summarizes it, for each entry "Gessner included a picture, a learned account of its name in several languages, a physical description, an account of its habits, the medical use of its parts, its use in food, and a large section he called philology that summarized references to the animal in history, literature, and art."[68] Peter Harrison likewise underscores the role of accretion and gathering in the histories of creatures when he describes natural history as steeped in the intellectual culture of the book.

Modern Humanism in Theory and Practice (Ithaca, NY: Cornell University Press, 1996), 80.

66. Thomas Elyot, *The Book Named the Governour*, ed. Foster Watson (London: J. M. Dent, 1907 [1531]), 4.

67. Brian Ogilvie, *The Science of Describing: Natural History in Renaissance Europe* (Chicago: University of Chicago Press, 2006), 49–50. Animal encyclopedias, too, referred to medical applications, but practical zoology really expanded with the seventeenth-century rise of physiological investigation (ibid., 50, 51).

68. Ibid., 44.

The criterion for inclusion "was not whether it existed in the world, but whether it existed in books"; a failure to mention any creature appearing in the textual record "was failure of scholarship."[69] Animal encyclopedias never appealed to utility (medical or otherwise) to quite the degree that botanical texts did, and neither topic elicited much zeal for systematizing. As David Freedberg emphasizes, natural historians "began with a commitment to the local, and, never relinquishing that, ended by reaching across oceans and into the starry heavens"; their passion for accumulating data meant that their work "stopped short of all but the most perfunctory of theories" of a larger or systemic order.[70] In Ogilvie's account of the demise of natural history as a mode of knowledge, we see a shift away from particular description of enumerated kinds, toward systematic classification and modern taxonomies instead.[71] The title of Carl Linnaeus's pivotal *Systema naturae* (1735) encapsulates this shift.

Systematic classification requires as much likening of creatures as differentiations of them. Early modern zoography's comprehensiveness-by-particulars reveled instead in a woolier, more proliferative aesthetic. Topsell's *The Historie of Serpents* (1608), for example, refuses to "contend" whether the word "Crocodilus" refers to a "Genus or Species," leaving "the strife of words to them that spend their wits about tearmes and syllables only." Instead, Topsell opts to pursue each and every "particular kinde," a figure of maximal partitive and enumerative force.[72] In his short story "Funes the Memorious," Borges describes the title character as "incapable of general, platonic ideas."[73] It was, he continues, "not only difficult for him to understand that the generic term dog embraced so many unlike specimens of differing sizes and different forms; he was also disturbed . . . that a dog at three-fourteen (seen in profile) should have the same name as the dog at three-fifteen (seen from the front)." Funes's mind suggests a

69. Peter Harrison, *The Bible, Protestantism, and the Rise of Natural Science* (Cambridge: Cambridge University Press, 2001), 66, 74. Thus our amusement at the way natural history lists "real" and "fabulous" animals alike somewhat misconstrues their project. Harrison describes how Albertus Magnus and followers had already marked fabulous creatures as fabulous (65–66).

70. David Freedberg, *The Eye of the Lynx: Galileo, His Friends, and the Beginnings of Modern Natural History* (Chicago: University of Chicago Press, 2002), 10.

71. Ogilvie, *Science of Describing*, 271.

72. Edward Topsell, *The Historie of Serpents, or, the Second Booke of Living Creatures* (London: William Jaggard, 1608), 127.

73. Jorge Luis Borges, "Funes the Memorious," in *Ficciones*, ed. Anthony Kerrigan, trans. Anthony Bonner (New York: Grove Press, 1962), 114–15.

sixteenth-century one, affected (as we learn) by reading Pliny's *Historia naturalis.* English physician Dr. John Caius (a correspondent for Gesner in the compilation of the *Historia animalium*) was also a great reader of Pliny—and to similar effect. Caius published *De canibus britannicus* in 1570, and it was broadly translated by Abraham Fleming as *Of Englishe Dogges; the diuersities, the names, the natures, and the properties* (1576). The redundant emphasis of the subtitle underscores the investment in specific diversity expressed in properties that we have just explored. Though we may think of the dog as an exceptional case (its extreme diversity of form the result of centuries of human intervention that accelerated exponentially in the 1800s), for early moderns canine diversity made the natural variety understood to pertain in nature especially clear.

Caius's treatise offers to provide an "epitome" of "suche dogges as were ingendered within the borders of England."[74] Despite the sense of an abstract or abridgement that an epitome suggests, Caius's catalogue records a persistently open-ended variety. In the preface, the translator attests that "an ignoraunt man would never have been drawne into this opinion to thincke that there had bene in England such variety & choise of dogges, in all respectes . . . so divers and unlike." He announces that he will "expresse and declare [Englishe Dogges] in due order, . . . the difference of them, the use, the propertyes, and the diverse natures of the same," a reckoning that will follow a tripartite hierarchical (and clearly human) division of "gentle," "homely," and "currish kinds" (2). This quest for set kinds duly ordered, however, yields disorderly lateral difference. Rather than ordering beasts, Caius multiplies their unlikeness.

Breaking down, for example, the "whole estate" of hunting dogs into two headings, Caius separates those engaged in "chasing the beast" and those in "taking the byrde." He offers etymological background, too: "Both which kyndes are tearmed of the Latines by one common name, that is, *Canes Venatici,* hunting dogs" (2–3). But Englishmen, he continues, "make a difference" and "tearme the Dogges . . . [of] these sundry games by divers names" (3). This proliferation continues as Caius itemizes the "properties" of the game-dog types: "perfect smelling," "quicke spying," "swiftnesse and quicknesse," "smelling & nymblenesse," and, last, "subtiltie and deceitfulnesse" (3). These types are further varied by sub-

---

74. Caius, *Of Englishe Dogges,* "To the Reader," first paragraph. Subsequent page references appear in the text. Caius also wrote the well-known book on sweating sickness, *A boke or counseill against the disease called the sweate* (London, 1570) and in 1557 refounded Gonville College as Gonville and Caius.

specifications of the prey they follow; eleven kinds are listed, and the list
"ends" with an open-ended orthographic gesture to more, "&c"—et cetera
(4). Although we now understand breed varieties in dogs and other domestic animals as what Bacon called "nature altered or wrought" by human
"arts," early moderns did not necessarily hold this view of domestic animal kinds or of dogs in particular. As Caius explains regarding the dogs
defined by this open-ended list of their singular prey, "Every severall sort
is notable and excellent in his naturall qualitie and appointed practice."
However, introducing some invisible exponent, Caius notes that even

> among these sundry sortes, there be some . . . apt to hunt two divers
> beasts, as the Foxe otherwhiles, and other whiles the Hare, but they
> hunt not with such towardnes and good lucke after them, as they doe
> that whereunto nature hath formed and framed them, not onely in ex-
> ternall composition and making, but also inward faculties and condi-
> tions, for they swarve oftentimes, and doo otherwise then [sic] they
> should. (4)

Unlimited kinds ("&c") are appointed by nature to particular purposes, but
"oftentimes" they multiply these purposes and invoke their prerogative to
"swarve." This canine multiplication of more kinds within kind served
as a shorthand for natural variety in the period. For example, Ben Jonson
explained human variety by saying that "some dogs are for the deer, some
for the wild boar, some are fox-hounds, some otter-hounds"; in *The Compleat Angler*, likewise, Izaak Walton proposes that the various kinds of
bait "differ as much as dogs do: that is to say, as much as a very cur and a
greyhound do."[75] Nature "formed," "framed," and "appointed" them with
particular purposes—and also a creative power to "differ" and "swarve."

   To explain variety, as we have seen, Elyot referred to the "peculier disposition appropered" to each creaturely kind. Shakespeare refers to the
same thing as a "particular addition." In *Troilus and Cressida* (1601), a
beastly blazon of Ajax reverses the Prometheus story to rob animals of
"their particular additions." When Cressida responds to Alexander's assertion that Ajax is "a very man per se / And stands alone," she scoffs at the
claim as a meaningless universal (with a swipe at bipedal posture too): "So

75. Ben Jonson, *Timber; or, Discoveries Made upon Men and Matter*, ed. Felix
Schilling (Boston: Ginn, 1892), 29 (Jonson speaks of horses likewise in the extended pas-
sage); and Izaak Walton, *The Compleat Angler, or The Contemplative Man's Recreation*
(New York: Modern Library, 1998 [1653]), 221.

do all men, unless they are drunk, sick, or have no legs." Alexander then describes him further as a man who "hath robbed many beasts of their particular additions. / He is as valiant as the lion, churlish as the bear, slow as the elephant" (1.2.15–21). Suggesting gender's likeness to species as a form of kindedness, Shakespeare coyly uses just the same logic in "Sonnet 20" (where nature "by addition me of thee defeated, / By adding one thing to my purpose nothing" [lines 11–12]) to describe human sexual differentiation.

Shakespeare's fullest exploration of this phrasing, though, occurs in *Macbeth* (1605), and it relies directly on Caius's "catalogue." Caius had explained to Gesner that "as in your language Hunde is the common word, so in our naturall tounge dogge, is the universall, but Hunde is particuler and a speciall" (40). Parsing universals and particulars like Cressida and Caius, Macbeth, in his incitement of Banquo's murderers to their bloody task, challenges them as to whether they are really "men." When they avow that they are, Macbeth undermines this claim as an empty universal, and he uses dog-breed distinctions to do so:

> Ay, in the catalogue you go for men,
> As hounds and greyhounds, mongrels, spaniels, curs,
> Shoughs, water-rugs, and demi-wolves are clept
> All by the name of dogs.
> (3.1.93–96)

The idea that all canine kinds are "clept / All by the name of dogs" falsifies each of them somehow. What really matters instead are the differences among them; the most important categorization, what Shakespeare calls the "valued file," is one that

> distinguishes the swift, the slow, the subtle,
> The housekeeper, the hunter, every one
> According to the gift which bounteous nature
> Hath in him closed, whereby he does receive
> Particular addition, from the bill
> That writes them all alike.
> (3.1.97–102)

Because the more valued inventory is the one that "distinguishes," we see the same valorization of inventoried, yet proliferating difference as in Caius's catalogue. The free "gift" of the "particular addition" is that property that makes a thing what it is and makes it go how it goes. In *King Lear*, we see a similar itemizing approach. When Edgar offers to rid Lear of the doglike spirits that "bark at me" and haunt him in the fantasy trial, Edgar's incantatory expulsion ("Avaunt, you curs!") seems to need to touch every legalistic variation on the dog to take effect:

> Be thy mouth or black or white,
> Tooth that poisons if it bite,
> Mastiff, greyhound, mongrel grim,
> Hound or spaniel, brach [bitch] or lym [bloodhound],
> Or bobtail tike or trundle-tail—
> Tom will make him weep and wail;
> For, with throwing thus my head,
> Dogs leaped the hatch and all are fled.
> (3.6.62–72)

"Avaunt, you curs!" is too weakly general a speech act to work; Edgar's particularized list seems more up to the task.

The language in *Macbeth* and *Lear* celebrates the natural particularizations that Caius's classifications enshrine. Quibbling on deer kinds in *Love's Labors Lost* shows the same emphasis and the linguistic effort to specify all of them (closely associated with the play's zeal for overarticulation and legal variation). Here we see a quarrel whether the deer in question was "sanguis, in blood," "a buck of the first head," an old gray doe (i.e., misapprehending "haut credo"), a sore, a "pretty pleasing pricket," or a sorel (4.2.1–58).[76] Shakespeare's revelry in these plastic nomenclatures perfectly matches natural-historical habits of thought, imagining "Nature"—and especially her errant animals—to be governed less by a general law than by "peculiar" laws of irreducibly different naturedness. Referring even to the highest rank of canine being (hunting dogs), Caius advances the proposition that "they cannot all be reduced and brought under one sorte" and that he will have to explore "certaine specialties" in order to "apply to them their proper and peculier names" (3). Proper and peculiar: the conjunction and the context indicate these words mean the same thing, that the proper is (the) peculiar. Kinds have specific gravity or weighty particularity, and their courses, or biases, indicate prerogatives of

---

76. For an account of this quibble—and an actual glossary of English deer terminology—see Edward Berry, *Shakespeare and the Hunt: A Cultural and Social Study* (Cambridge: Cambridge University Press, 2001).

Figure 2.2. George Gascoigne, *Hare*, in *The Noble Arte of Venerie or Hunting* (London, 1576). Image by permission of the Folger Shakespeare Library, Washington, DC.

free locomotion or self-sovereignty. And because each specifiable property or difference engages in a sovereign performance, classifying dogs is no easier than herding cats.

Fight, Flight, or Stay and Obey: Animal Prerogatives

In Gascoigne's *The Noble Arte of Venerie* (1576), a chapter specifying "the properties of an Hare" alerts us to their signature feature: "subtleties and pollecies."[77] Lest I give excessive priority to coursers and trackers as emblems of a four-footed prerogative to decide, I turn to the harried hare, a prey animal and evolutionary specialist in defensive technique (fig. 2.2). Eons of predation led hares to devise a signature manner of moving: *the zigzag*. Gascoigne devotes several chapters to hunting the hare, claiming that "of all chases, the Hare maketh greatest pastime and pleasure" because of "the subtiltie of the little poore beaste and what shift she can make for hir selfe" (162). (The hare is gendered female here as much for

77. Gascoigne, *Noble Arte*, 160; see also p. 174. Subsequent page references appear in the text.

her wiles as her vulnerability.) One chapter, titled "Of the subtilties of an Hare, when she is runne and hunted," recounts "all hir crossings, doublings, &c," and how when first roused "they will doe (in manner) nothing else but turne, crosse, and double" (161–62). "Turning and winding in the bushes," the female "never maketh endwayes before the hounds," but the male "will leade them sometimes three or foure myles endwayes before he turn the heade" (161–62). The hare's swerving course frustrates the dogs mightily, who prefer to run "endwayes," or flat-out: "An Hare maketh sometimes so many doubles, crossings, &c that an hounde can not well tell where he is . . . nor will doe any thing else (in maner) but holde up their heades, and looke to the huntesmen for helpe and comfort," because "an hound will scarcely beleeve that the Hare were gone directly backwardes" (166, 163). But, *pace* Aristotle and the dogs, she has. As Caius used "&c" to indicate the surplus that eluded his list, the tail wagging "&c" Gascoigne adds to the hare's doublings and crossings seem to point to her reversings, a prerogative specially favored by the hare.

Shakespeare embeds an extensive account of the hare's run for its life in *Venus and Adonis* (lines 673–708), an account evincing a certain sympathy for the hare (even though Venus is attempting to persuade Adonis to pursue a safer course by hunting hare, not boar).[78] While the stanzas call

78. The hare's defensive art of swerving is attested to not only in hunting manuals and natural histories but also in anticruelty verses of animal complaint written in the hare's voice. Thomas More voices the plight of the hunted rabbit: "Mustelam obliquo dilapsa foramine fugi. / Sed feror humanos heu misera in laqueos" (I fled the weasel by turning sideways into a gap. / But, alas and misery, I am carried instead into human snares). Thomas More, "Cunicula loquitur" [A rabbit speaks], in *The Latin Epigrams of Thomas More*, ed. Leicester Bradner and Charles Lynch (Chicago: University of Chicago Press, 1953), 27 (my translation). Topsell glosses the existential dilemma thus: "When her ardent desire maketh her straine to fly from the dogges, she falleth into the nettes, for such is the state of the miserable, that while they runne from one perill, they fal into another; according to the saying of Scripture, Esay 24. *He that scapeth out of the snare, shall fall into the ditch.*" Topsell, *Historie of the Foure-Footed Beastes*, 268. Margaret Cavendish gives a hair-raising account of the hare's perspective: "To champian plains he went, / *Winding about for to deceive their scent,* / And while they snuffling were to find his track / Poor Wat, being weary, his swift pace did slack." Cavendish, "The Hunting of the Hare," in *Poems, and Fancies* (London, 1653), 110–13 (italics added). The hares' swerves in More and Cavendish—as well as in Gascoigne's own poem in the hare's voice—fail in the end, and they fall, in Gascoigne's terms, as "harmelesse" victims of "murdrying men" and their "bloudie minde[s]" (177). Cavendish wages adamant ethical opposition to this, reflecting the discourses analyzed in chapter 1, saying men make "their Stomacks, Graves which full they fill / With

the animal a "poor wretch," "Poor Wat," and a "dew-bedabbled wretch" and moralize on its condition by noting how "misery is trodden on by many, / And, being low, never relieved by any," they also detail with interest the martial strategies of the hare. Venus urges Adonis to contemplate how the hare,

> to overshoot his troubles
> . . . outruns the wind and with what care
> He cranks and crosses with a thousand doubles.

She calls the hare's zigzag "a labyrinth to amaze his foes." In addition to his ability to cover his scent by running "among a flock of sheep" or threading through "a herd of deer," Venus returns to the reverse-angle coursing at the end of the passage. She urges Adonis to mark Wat's "turn, and return, indenting with the way." The hare's indentings or jagged route, his crossings, and his "thousand doubles" enable him to craft a baffling "labyrinth" against "foes."

Topsell likewise confirms the craftsmanlike ingenuity of the zigzagging path run by the coursed hare: "In hir course she taketh not one way, but maketh heades like laborinthes to circumvent and trouble the dogs."[79] Her labyrinthine course initiates many "heades" or directions rather than "one way" in an elaborate strategy of self-defense by a "little poor beaste." Thus humankind, even with its engines, nets, dogs, and stratagems, can fail to catch the wily hare. In his entry on the "Cony," which he calls a "third rank" among hares, Topsell explains that it is called *Cuniculus* after the "Latin word for a hole or cave in the earth" and further reports how "the conies . . . had undermined a whole citty in Spain" and that the "proverbe *cuniculos agere* tooke his beginning, when one by secret undermining and not by open violence overthroweth a Towne or nation."[80] Varying this tradition on the martial rabbit's assault on human settlements, the experienced soldier Gascoigne proposes that animal prey are,

---

Murthe'd Bodies, that in sport they kill . . . / And that all Creatures for his sake alone, / Was made for him, to Tyrannize upon" (113).

79. Topsell, *Historie of the Foure-Footed Beastes*, 269. Comparing the hare's ears to the biomechanical functionality of the tail, Topsell says, "As it is said of the Lyons, that with their tailes they stirre up their strength and courage, so are the eares of this beast like Angels wings, ships sailes, and rowing Oares, to helpe her in her flight; for when she runneth, she bendeth them backward and useth them instead of sharpe spurs to prick forward her dulness" (269).

80. Ibid., 110.

like the hunter, engaged in elaborate, military stratagems (however defensive).[81] Suggesting that "Foxe and Badgerd both, make patterns (in their denne) / Of Plotforms, Loopes, and Casamats devisde by warlike men" ("casamat," literally "slaughterhouse," is an anglicized Spanish term for a certain military fortification), he turns his attention to the hare. He picks up the hare's signature swerve as a triumphant form of self-defense, asserting that "the nimble Hare, by turning in hir course, / Doth plainly prove that Pollicie sometime surpasseth force."[82] In an adverse negotiation and a condition of asymmetrical power, the hare does not lack the military and intellectual resources of policy, prerogative, and "turning."

Not all beasts "turn tail" to run, however, and few beasts fail to keep their eyes on what a nearby human is about to do. Thus another shortfall in a panoptical model of man, beyond its sleight of hand about uprightness, is the prospect that the human gaze has its animal counterpart. In *The Order of Things*, Foucault opens his examination of a shift in visual regimes of representation and sovereignty with a well-known discussion of Diego Velasquez's *Las Meninas* (1656), a painting of the Spanish royal family among their entourage of servants, dwarfs, and the painter (fig. 2.3). In the distant center of the painting, Velasquez placed a mirror palely reflecting the "models," King Phillip and his wife, in whose imagined "place" any viewer of the painting must be situated. If we read the painting by ordinary principles of composition, however, we see that the foregrounded "subject" of the painting is their daughter, the infanta. Foucault here gives an account of how visibility of representation (things shown in the painting) competes with the invisible things implied by the structures of vision (i.e., the model or sovereign and the viewer) to serve as a kind of allegory for the separation of paintings of things from this painting of representation "itself," what he calls "representation in its pure form."[83]

Especially because it goes on to consider natural history and the dynamics of subjects and objects under its auspices, what is arresting about Foucault's discussion for these purposes is something it does not address. The subject, or object, closest to the viewer and quite prominent in scale

81. For discussion of Gascoigne's ambivalence about human warfare and hunting (as an experienced soldier but a "woodsman" who shoots awry), see my "Ambivalent Aims: Gascoigne's 'Woodmanship' and Animal Complaint Poetry" (unpublished manuscript, 2012).
82. "George Gascoigne, in the commendation of the noble Arte of Venerie," *Noble Arte*, prefatory verses.
83. Michel Foucault, *The Order of Things: An Archaeology of the Human Sciences* (New York: Routledge, 2002 [1966]), 18. Subsequent page references appear in the text.

Figure 2.3. Diego Velasquez, *Las Meninas* (1656). Image courtesy of Museo del Prado, Madrid, Spain. Photograph: Erich Lessing / Art Resource, New York.

is a fairly large dog. It is a mountain dog or mastiff/guard-dog type with a richly detailed body and facial expression, and its coat is as vividly rendered as the silks and velvets of the assembled court. Even when Foucault is just counting, the dog disturbs the analysis: Foucault counts "eight characters" in the painting "if we include the painter" (but apparently not the dog) (13). He then refers to "eddies of courtiers, maids of honour, animals, and fools" (14) in the painting (*le tourbillon des courtisans, des suivantes, des animaux et des bouffons*), though the painting shows only one animal.[84] More to the point, when he does look at the dog, he dispatches it as "the only element in the picture that is neither looking at anything nor moving." Strikingly, Foucault's metric for countable presence seeks either mobility or the power of the gaze, the two vectors of political viability we have been charting. It is a complicated matter to say how the other figures in the painting could be said to be "moving." But if the dog is indeed "not looking," that immediately pertains to any regime of representation that is being laid out through acknowledging gazes and the invisible mechanisms of vision. Foucault broadly concludes that this dog "is not intended, with its deep reliefs and the light playing on its silky hair, to be anything but an object to be seen" (15). Given the way period cross-species arrangements have been so bound up with figures of monarchical authority, this disanimating reading of the dog as only "an object to be seen" in a portrait of sovereignty cannot possibly be correct.

The dog's impassivity affirms something; it notes a caveat to the orders of meaning being structured around the political apparatus of royal sovereignty and its pendant creature in Foucault's account, the "sovereign" viewer. In a regime of crosscut glances, the dog's eyes are closed, but he is not sleeping. This marks a limit to an order underwritten by acknowledging gazes. In the dog's "not regarding" the sovereign, a prerogative is expressed. One of the great commonplaces of Renaissance horse lore—the notion that horses do not flatter—stems from a report in Plutarch's *Moralia* celebrating just this kind of animal nonsubscription to regimes of order that are merely human. Writers pithily observe that horses only acknowledge good horsemanship—they are not moved by the fact that a rider is a king. In Ben Jonson's version, "They say princes learn no art truly but the art of horsemanship. The reason is the brave beast is no flatterer. He will throw a prince as soon as his groom."[85] Returning to Caius, we find similar considerations of mastiffs on this score. In Henry VII's time, he reports, when the "politique and warlike" king understood that the mastiff stood "in feare of no man" and could take on lions, he "commaunded all such dogges (how many soever they were in number) should be hanged, being deeply displeased . . . that an yll favored rascall curre should . . . assault the valiaunt Lyon king of all beastes" (26). As Ian MacInnes has shown,

84. For the French phrasing, see *Let mot et les choses* (Paris: Editions Gallimard, 1966), 28.

85. Jonson, *Timber*, 41. See also Elyot, *Book Named the Governour*, 163, and Erasmus, *Education of a Christian Prince*, ed. Lisa Jardine (Cambridge: Cambridge University Press, 1997), 56.

the mastiff in this period takes on increasing nationalist significance.[86] Here the mastiff makes visible a tension between a realm figured through singular royal sovereignty and a competing yeoman (or even rascally) version of popular nationhood. The "yll favored . . . curre" threatens a rival sovereignty, just as the dog puts brackets around fictions of human sovereignty in *Las Meninas*.

While Velasquez's dog declines to acknowledge the structures of sovereignty forming around him through the dynamics of human vision by refusing to look, an English text from the same decade takes the taunting proverbial expression "a cat may look upon a king" as its sword-rattling title. The expression first appears in print in John Heywood's 1562 collection of proverbs: "What, a cat may look on a king, ye know!"[87] Likewise, *Alice in Wonderland*'s Cheshire cat, when invited to kiss the king's hand, states, "I'd rather not," and Alice supports his prerogative to "be impertinent": "'A cat may look at a king,' said Alice. 'I've read that in some book, but I don't remember where.'"[88] Perhaps Alice had been reading Civil War tracts. With ferocious defiance, *A Cat May Look Upon A King* (1652) profiles English kings from William the Conqueror to Henry VIII (each one more terrible, depraved, or perverse than the last). It refuses comment on Edward VI, Mary, or Elizabeth (because one was a child and "I have nothing to do with women, and I wish I never had") and then proceeds with a scandalous account of his main target, James I.[89]

The text of *A Cat May Look* makes no rhetorical use of the lively saying used as its title, but the frontispiece and title page serve the argument in an extraordinarily graphic way (fig. 2.4). His motto, *beati pacifici* (blessed are the peacemakers), circles James's portrait, but his image is countercaptioned with a "prophecy" concerning the end of English kingship. The prophecy, alleged to have been made in the time of Henry VII, flourished in Civil War contexts. Listing monarchs since Henry VII, the prophecy ("Mars, Puer, Alecto, Virgo, VULPES, Leo, Nullus" [Mars, a boy, a fury, a virgin, a fox, a lion, none]) makes James a fox and suggests that the sequence of royal succession will end with "none." If that were not

86. Ian MacInnes, "Mastiffs and Spaniels: Gender and Nation in the English Dog," *Textual Practice* 17, no. 1 (2003): 21–40.

87. John Heywood, *The Proverbs, Epigrams, and Miscellanies*, ed. John Farmer (London: Early English Drama Society, 1906 [1562]), 70.

88. Lewis Carroll, *The Annotated Alice: Alice's Adventures in Wonderland and Through the Looking-Glass*, ed. Martin Gardner (New York: W. W. Norton, 2000), 87.

89. Anthony Weldon (possibly Marchamont Nedham), *A Cat May Look Upon A King* (London: William Roybould, 1652), 34.

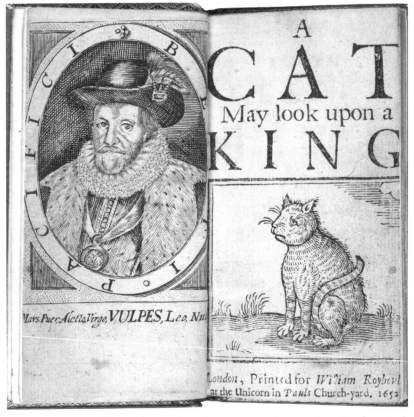

Figure 2.4. Anthony Weldon, frontispiece, *A Cat May Look upon a King* (London, 1652).
Image by permission of the Folger Shakespeare Library, Washington, DC.

vivid enough, the facing title page situates a large, roughly drawn cat staring very boldly across and back at James. This cat stares down the king,
refusing to lower its gaze to an Ovidian "groveling eie," and so takes an
old proverb about animals and subordinates into the midcentury terrain of
Republicanism and the justification of regicide.

The most storied cat in early modern letters, however, is Montaigne's.
Her brief appearance in the "Apologie" is the essay's best-known detail, a
marvel of simple attention that yields immense intellectual and ethical
consequences. Complaining that man baselessly "separateth himselfe from
out of the ranke of other creatures . . . his fellow-brethren and compeers,"
Montaigne asks the question whose ethical and epistemological hesitation
to deny thought to animals Descartes would disallow: "How knoweth he
by vertue of his understanding *the inward and secret motions of beasts?*"

(399; italics added). Here we see early modern ideas of movement converge explicitly with the inward and intentional grounds of prerogative. The sovereign apartness of animal inwardness from imperial human understanding evokes the controversial apparatus of "mental reservation" as that doctrine specifically developed for political subjects negotiating obedience in shifting contexts of religious orthodoxy and dissent.

Montaigne's query presses onward, though—without the extreme adversarialism of an inquisition and despite the paradigm of human/animal political authority we have been considering—to intimate the reality of a cat's prerogative. This prerogative is moored by "inward and secret motions," whatever they may be. "When I am playing with my Cat," Montaigne asks, "who knowes whether she have more sport in dallying with me, than I have in gaming with her?" And the 1595 edition of the *Essais* further embellishes this thought by answering: "We entertaine one another with mutuall apish trickes; *If I have my houre to begin or to refuse, so hath she hers*" (399; italics added). Apishness looks to another confounder of "kind" to locate a common denominator for mutuality, as Montaigne uses cross-species imitation to link a man and his cat in an exchange that testifies as strongly to another's prerogative as it may be possible to do. In the interstices of the domestic day, they meet. Perhaps he "gets down on all fours," or she rises up, or both, or neither—"mutuall apish trickes," as we have already seen, leave the business of footedness and uprightness wide open. Whatever scope of freedom the man has to propose or to decline, so the cat has. The grammatical balance and creaturely imbrication of Montaigne's proposition that "if I have, so hath she" likens man and cat in the precise domain of their decisional freedom to look or to leave, to engage or to remove, to stay/play or to go, to say yes or to say no. The cat's prerogative, because prerogative is prerogative, is no less than the man's.

The Flick of History's Tail

Four-hundred-odd years later, Derrida considers his own "real cat, truly, believe me, *a little cat*," one who likewise confronts him within domestic spaces (modernized as bedroom and bathroom).[90] Derrida stresses her irreducible particularity: she is not "an allegory for all the cats on the earth"

90. Jacques Derrida, *The Animal That Therefore I Am*, ed. Marie-Louise Mallet, trans. David Wills (New York: Fordham University Press, 2008), 6, 9. Subsequent page references appear in the text; all italics are Derrida's unless otherwise noted.

and not "the *figure* of a cat" (6). Then a new paragraph embarks, asserting
further that *this* little cat is not *that* one: "This cat . . . isn't Montaigne's
cat either" (6). In this disclaimer of identity between the two cats, though,
we must ask what metric of likeness and difference might apply between
the two men. Derrida refers to the "Apologie" as "one of the greatest pre-
or anti-Cartesian texts on the animal" (6). As I hope my introduction
began to illustrate, even this firm claim understates the case. In a long
footnote, Derrida attests not only to the way Montaigne richly enlivens
a tradition that "attributes much to the animal, beginning with a type of
language" but also to how he recognizes something more on the animal's
part, "namely, *a capacity to respond*," citing Montaigne's query, "In how
many ways do we not speak to our dogs? *And they answer us*" (6n8). Affirming that "the 'Apology' needs to be examined very closely," *The Animal That Therefore I Am* gives Montaigne's extraordinary contribution to
a critique of "the question of the animal" no further attention.

Montaigne's disappearance would (perhaps) be less striking if Derrida
were less straightforward in his next step. Reversing the early modern tax-
onomer's inability to put an end to his lists of kinds without the flourish of
an "&c," Derrida claims the world contains only "two grand forms of theoretical or philosophical treatise regarding the animal"—and immediately
takes one of them away by concluding it has no examples (13). The first
"are those texts signed by people . . . [whose] gaze has never intersected
with that of an animal directed at them." These thinkers, assured of the
ongoing force of uprightness in the categories of above and below, "neither
wanted nor had the capacity to draw any systematic consequence from
the fact that an animal could . . . address them . . . *from down there*" (italics added). This includes all philosophers and theoreticians "as such," and
Derrida names the names (13–14). With them, he writes, "we can do little
more than turn around this immense disavowal whose logic traverses the
whole history of humanity" (14) and decipher its legacy in symptoms.

Of the second type of discourse on the animal, however—"whose
signatories are . . . poets and prophets . . . those who admit taking upon
themselves the address of an animal that addresses them"—he claims to
know "of no statutory representative," though he alleges that "it is in that
very place that I find myself, here and now" (14). We *should* be able safely
to conclude that Montaigne has seen himself being seen by an animal:
he has set the animal prerogative made evident in this experience at the
heart of the most relentless treatise in the Western tradition arguing for
the consequential existence of animal points of view. Whether we cali-

brate Derrida's "here and now" as the end of philosophy or the beginning of poetry, then, his historiography of human modes of engaging animal claims raises what Bacon might call "barking questions."[91] In "that very place" where Derrida situates himself as unprecedented and alone (and naked, as we shall see), Montaigne was just standing (either on two legs or perhaps "all fours," but presumably not naked).

If Derrida's little cat is not Montaigne's, the two writers register a greater difference. The flick of history's tail yields two vastly different scenes of encounter. Most of what we are used to thinking of as the modern history of human subjectivity in the West separates them. Derrida sets a modern scene: "Finding oneself naked, one's sex exposed, stark naked before a cat that looks at you without moving, just to see," he especially focuses on how "the cat observes me frontally naked, face to face, and . . . I am naked faced with a cat's eyes looking at me as it were from head to toe, just to see, not hesitating to concentrate its vision . . . in the direction of my sex . . . without biting, though that threat remains on its lips" (4). The cat is not (yet) "moving," but in the parameters of its prerogative it might leap and bite. The durable and familiar problem of uprightness still shapes the question, but with the new twist of a modern conceptualization of nudity (as opposed to what we might call early modern nakedness). "Frontally naked," "face to face," and surveilled "from head to toe" in a "frontal exhibition" that confers vulnerability rather than authority (4, 11)—Derrida is upright, but he does not stand, in Milton's terms, "with front serene."

As we will see in chapter 4 (where an abused cat will fly with extended claws onto a chaotic tangle of naked people), even to approximate a scene like this in early modernity is to foreclose the possibility of its being *serious*. A characteristically modern mythography of human uprightness, however, holds Derrida's episode back from the brink of the inevitable ribaldry it would have incited in a different "here and now." As Freud articulates this modern narrative, upright prerogative is less a birthright written into bodily design than an achievement of organic repression. A diminution of scent awareness "seems . . . to be a consequence of man's raising himself from the ground, of his assumption of an upright gait; this made his genitals, which were previously concealed, visible and in need of protection, and so provoked feelings of shame in him. The fateful process of civilization would thus have set in with man's adoption of an

91. Bacon, *Advancement of Learning*, bk. 2, 29.

erect posture."[92] Male genital exposure, in this narrative, triggers a concept of shame and nakedness (and civilization too). Derrida reports being ashamed to be ashamed before the little cat, but he also imagines the cat specifically contemplating his genitals ("not hesitating to concentrate its vision . . . in the direction of my sex"). In his account of the problem, erect posture and the (male) frontal nudity it encodes return us to an ancient hypothesis about uprightness, now indelibly marked by a modern nudity centered on genitality, whether in terms of protection or shame. Here Derrida further discovers a "contre-temps between" the human and animal, between "two nudities without nudity" (15). Because the animal is naked without knowing it, it is not truly nude, and because man's shame about nudity leads him to cover it, he is conscious of nudity but not practicing it. By this logic, Derrida continues, picking up the traditional natural-historical vocabulary we have been considering, "clothing would be proper to man, one of the 'properties' of man" (5).

Clothing may be "proper" to humankind in the registers of decorum and possession or ownership, but it is not a "property" in the early modern sense of either a natural-historical endowment or way of working. In early modern terms, the problem of clothing suggests just the reverse: a supplement calibrated as a debt humans incur rather than a property owned or mobilized. Clothing must be borrowed, from mainly animal creditors at that. And early modern animals, in turn, do not fail to be naked for the modern reasons Derrida elucidates (that is, by lacking consciousness of a sociolinguistic, psychoanalytic, or religious concept of "nakedness"). Instead, because nature is understood to have equipped them fully by bestowing "particular additions," *they are fully clothed just as they are*. In other words, in the comparative integrity of their embodiment, animals are not naked because they are consistently conceived as the best-dressed creatures on the planet. They, not humankind, are the creatures whose "coats" are "proper" to them. This, as we will see in the next chapter, has even more drastic consequences for human dignity.

92. Freud, *Civilization and Its Discontents*, 87n1. Freud explains human ambivalence about dogs in this context, suggesting that the name of humankind's "most faithful friend in the animal world" would not have become "a term of abuse if that creature had not incurred . . . contempt through two characteristics: that it is an animal whose dominant sense is that of smell and one which has no horror of excrement, and that it is not ashamed of its sexual functions." This account echoes the very public transgressions of bodily decorum that made Diogenes so notorious in Renaissance perceptions of him (see Lievsay, "Some Renaissance Views of Diogenes").

CHAPTER THREE

Poor, Bare, Forked:
Animal Happiness and the Zoographic
Critique of Humanity

In an epiphany of mad reason, Lear considers the naked Edgar, who has stripped himself of clothes to put on the disguise of a madman. "Thou art the thing itself," Lear declaims; "unaccommodated man is no more but such a poor, bare, forked animal as thou art" (3.4.105–7). Each point of specification the old king offers in this familiar line assesses human estate by comparative reference to the bodily forms and natural capacities of nonhuman animals. It is worth reminding ourselves how sharply negative these comparisons are. Like Diogenes waving his plucked fowl as a corrosive gloss on Plato's "featherless biped," Lear unravels the species pretensions of humanity. Here, however, we find neither roaring comedy nor the bark of satiric correction. Lear's lament offers a natural-historical account of human estate, reflecting the enumerated technical "specs" found in the animal encyclopedias. But instead of inventorying abilities, properties, and bodily treasure, Lear's comparative zoographic description of man proceeds in an entirely privative mode, as a staccato of shortfalls. "Poor, bare, forked" responds to Plato's classification of man as a featherless biped by adopting it—*as critique.* Lear's inventory of subtractions interprets man as a helpless, radically exposed creature (and a "thing" at that), one who, with the aid of (only) two feet, walks on the ground. To fit himself out from misery to sufficiency, this creature needs borrowed robes, engendering a debt to animal bodies that Lear tries to cancel: "Off, off you lendings!" (3.4.107). No measure of all things, this man starts in a deficit position and runs up his debts from there. The king's "poor, bare, forked" verdict on man, in other words, makes an insufficient animal of him.

Lear's sense of human poorness refers to the frail and underprovisioned entrance humans make into the world and to a corresponding need for extended nursing and painstaking education, in contrast to then-current notions of animal self-sufficiency, moderation, and natural wisdom whose cultural traction this chapter will consider. The bareness of humans might seem to go without saying (and it is a point of some convergence among classical, natural-historical, and Christian traditions), but it provokes doubtful questions about whether any animal other than man may fairly be termed naked and whether the term names a material or an immaterial condition, a bodily circumstance or a cosmic embarrassment. By both Christian and classical precedents, the "lendings" that cover human nakedness are secondhand coats, commandeered from the more sufficiently furnished bodies of other creatures. In Pliny's pivotal phrasing, man is cast "nudus in nuda terra" (all naked on the bare earth).[1] "Poor" and "bare" are diminishing enough. But Lear's third term, "forked," introduces a more sinister gloss on the human body by evoking the useless "legs" of the mandrake root and the split tongue of devilish speech. To call man "forked" is to look askance at man, unpersuaded by claims about his bipedal uprightness or the ontological movement toward divinity it was alleged to index.

Traditional exaltations of humankind as an immortal, upright, and rational creature promote a unique privilege for it as the best "accommodated" animal. Human/animal binarism and human exceptionalism often overlap, but they are not identical. Human exceptionalist frameworks, regardless of period, assert human distinction by claiming exclusive possession of some critical attribute (an immortal soul, reason, language, uprightness, nakedness and shame, consciousness of death, tool use, the capacity to lie, political life, and so on); these considerations normally intensify around animals due to their visible and proximate challenge to such claims, but human exceptionalism juxtaposes the human with the entirety of "nature." In contexts after Descartes where a binary "human/animal divide" is posited (either before or despite Darwin's intervention), humanity's creaturely remainder is enclosed within perhaps the most extreme compression in our thought: "the animal." In binary logic, "animal-

1. Pliny (the Elder), *Natural History*, ed. and trans. Horace Rackham et al. (Cambridge, MA: Harvard University Press, 1942), vol. 2, bk. 7, 506; *The Historie of the World, Commonly called, The Naturall Historie of C. Plinius Secundus*, ed. and trans. Philemon Holland (London: Adam Islip, 1601), Proeme, bk. 7, 152. Subsequent page references for Latin or English appear in the text and refer to these editions. Pliny is not the first to articulate this idea, though his formulation is its main resource in Renaissance literature. See James Hutton, *Themes of Peace in Renaissance Poetry* (Ithaca, NY: Cornell University Press, 1984), 243–46.

ity" is generated by likening all animals in terms of their lack of whatever attribute singularizes humanity. Although Agamben, for example, calls for an end to such positive articulations of the human in favor of "the central emptiness, the hiatus that—within man—separates man and animal," he still asserts a singularizing human feature (a hiatus within) separating man from some signature animality.[2] By a lingering either/or calculus, there exists in all humans a signifying emptiness that all nonhumans lack. In modern binaristic or post-Cartesian human exceptionalism, the constitutive detail establishing the "animal" is a deficit (even if revised, as here, to name a lack that animals lack). Whatever is "animal" has been measured as missing that single variable. In a contrast that highlights the importance of history to these considerations, *King Lear* wields this stringently privative metric against humans instead.

The shapes of human exceptionalism vary over time, and thus we can distinguish pre-Cartesian instances from later developments of the more powerfully binary *cogito ergo sum* doctrine on which the post-Enlightenment concept of humankind has largely been based. Earlier dispensations invoke and police a very active border between man and beast, to be sure. Bruce Boehrer and Erica Fudge have richly deconstructed these period configurations, showing that man and beast display the blurred interdependency typical of opposed pairs with a special intensity; they have also exposed how much vituperation and performative reiteration are required to enact and maintain the boundary.[3] At the same time, early modernity asserts nothing truly equivalent to the homogenization effected by a post-Cartesian, modern philosophical nominalization like "the animal." As we have seen, it shows extensive investments in a contextualizing, articulated, ecosystemic frame in which man, beasts, birds, and fishes (and angels, stars, plants, bodies of water, and minerals too) find their due cosmic places.

Even a classically humanist and surely human-exceptionalist earlier source such as Pico della Mirandola's *On the Dignity of Man* (1486), for

2. Agamben's man shares some DNA with those rescued by Prometheus in the *Protagoras* (discussed below): he is an animal without properties. Unlike the *Protagoras* or *King Lear*, however, Agamben conglomerates "the animal" as deficiency. Giorgio Agamben, *The Open: Man and Animal*, trans. Kevin Attell (Stanford, CA: Stanford University Press, 2004), 27.

3. Bruce Boehrer, *Shakespeare among the Animals* (London: Palgrave, 2002); Erica Fudge, *Perceiving Animals: Humans and Beasts in Early Modern Culture* (Urbana: University of Illinois Press, 2002), and Fudge, *Brutal Reasoning: Animals, Rationality, and Humanity in Early Modern England* (Ithaca, NY: Cornell University Press, 2006).

example, emphasizes something less binary than the sheer "divide" that contemporary critical vocabularies tend to transpose on the pre-Cartesian archive. Extolling the "great and wonderful happiness of man," Pico specifies human uniqueness in terms of a plenary participation in everything else. According to Pico's Christianization of Aristotle's typology of souls, God placed in man "every sort of seed and sprouts of every kind of life. The seeds that each man cultivates will grow and bear their fruit in him. If he cultivates vegetable seeds, he will become a plant. If seeds of sensation, he will grow into a brute. If rational, he will become a heavenly animal. If intellectual, he will be an angel, and a son of God. . . . Who does not wonder at this chameleon which we are?"[4] The way this passage and many others like it are populated makes a menagerie of man. They confirm Donna Haraway's claim, made from the frontiers of technoscience, genetics, and feminist political criticism, that we have always been hybrids and "have never been human."[5] In more historical terms, Gail Kern Paster has shown that widespread understandings of the humors, as the shared stuff of human and animal embodiment, sufficiently undercut notions of human difference to make "identification across the species barrier" habitual in early modern representation.[6] Alongside the press of their adjacent position in a hierarchy of being, the sometimes cohabitational and widely collaborative proximity of animals certainly put enormous pressure on a border between us and them. But whether we consider the question philosophically or materially, early modern man—however exceptionalist in design—was not simply measured in the narrowest dualistic terms of a "human/animal divide." Rather, cultural attitudes toward man accorded him the "best" (sublunary) place in a much broader demographic array.

For Pico, human exceptionality is a positive source of wonder and celebration. He conceives of a providential exceptionalism, one where an omnicompetent man, alone among creatures, is endowed with the capacity to "self-fashion," as Stephen Greenblatt so concisely named it.[7] Only man is existentially free, while the being of all others unfolds within the terms

4. Pico della Mirandola, *On the Dignity of Man*, ed. Paul J. W. Miller, trans. Charles Wallis (Indianapolis: Hackett, 1998), 5.

5. Donna Haraway, *When Species Meet* (Minneapolis: University of Minnesota Press, 2008).

6. Gail Kern Paster, *Humoring the Body: Emotions and the Shakespearean Stage* (Chicago: University of Chicago Press, 2004), 150.

7. Stephen Greenblatt, *Renaissance Self-Fashioning from More to Shakespeare* (Chicago: University of Chicago Press, 1983).

of a naturally specified, hard-wired condition.[8] As Giovanni Battista Gelli extolled this privilege, "Man onely can chose of him selfe, a state and ende after his owne mynde, and . . . canne rather rule his lyfe freely accordinge to tharbitremente of his owne will, then to thinclination of nature."[9] But rather than standing opposite to beasts across the abyss of a "human/animal divide," Pico's sedimentary or cumulative man possesses attributes of each element of the cosmos in order to complete the self-fashioning task he alone is assigned—hence the delightfully ironic detail that it takes both plant fertility (seeds and sprouts) and a chameleon to represent his multiplex capacity. Shakespeare's variant of this menagerie man, Ajax in *Troilus and Cressida*, "hath robbed many beasts of their particular additions. He is as valiant as the lion, churlish as the bear, slow as the elephant" (1.2.19–21). Likewise, in *The Tempest* a dazzled Ferdinand applies the plenary image of "man" to praise Miranda across the otherwise strong barrier gender difference presents to the masculine, biological concept of perfection. "But you, O you," he exclaims. "So perfect and so peerless, are created / Of every creature's best!" (3.1.46–48). These notions instance human exceptionalism, to be sure, but it is an exceptionalism where man's "wonderful happiness" and peerless perfection cheerfully vocalize just how much in the way of animals is in man.

8. Agamben is ambiguous on this unique agentive power separating human and animal life. He considers how Linnaeus wittily recorded "no specific identifying characteristic next to the generic name, *Homo*, only the old philosophical adage: *nosce te ipsum* [know yourself]" and suggests that the eventual modifier, *sapiens*, may only be a "simplification of that adage." In this account of Linnaeus, Agamben writes that "to define the human not through any *nota characteristica*, but rather through his self-knowledge, means that man is the being which recognizes itself as such, that man is the animal that must recognize itself as human to be human," a conception quite similar to Pico's (*Open*, 25–26). But in calling for man to stop seeking "new . . . articulations" and instead to "show . . . the hiatus that—within man—separates man and animal," Agamben still invokes a special (self-risking) form of human moral agency (without, of course, Pico's celebratory tone). He calls for us to in some way choose to end "the machine that governs our conception of man" and for a "Shabbat of both animal and man" to let "both of them be outside of being" at one "messianic banquet of the righteous" (92).

9. Giovanni Battista Gelli, "To the moste myghtie and excellent Prince Cosimo de Medici," *Circes of John Baptista Gello, Florentine* (*La Circe*), trans. Henry Iden (London, 1557–58), unpaginated. Subsequent citations in the text refer to this edition. Gelli's *La Circe*, discussed in detail below, was originally published in 1548–49; the immensely popular volume saw five Italian editions before 1600 and was soon translated into Latin and vernacular editions.

Even so, if we take early modernity—in official terms, and on the whole—to subscribe to a less simply binary but still predominantly human exceptionalist view, we must stop to puzzle the implications of *King Lear*'s extraordinarily downbeat instance. Man normally appears as, at once, the condensed summation and the capping triumph of creation. The following are just two pertinent examples of this commonplace. In *De humani corporis fabrica* (1543), the sixteenth-century anatomist Andreas Vesalius justifies his research on the human body by referring to man as "the most perfectly constructed of all creatures," whose body "corresponds admirably to the universe and for that reason was called a little universe by the ancients"; in his *Historie of the World* (1614), Walter Raleigh describes man as "a little World . . . an abstract or modell, or briefe Storie of the Universall."[10] Shakespeare's *King Lear* diverges sharply from these more orthodox endorsements. It disassociates man from both perfection and plenitude; humankind is neither the paragon of creation nor its microcosmic "brief story." Man remains exceptional, indeed, but *King Lear* defrocks, downgrades, and reclassifies him instead as creation's *negative* exception.

By what logic can "human negative exceptionality" be articulated in the play and in the period? From what standpoint could writers understand humanness as not only a precarious advantage but an achieved calamity (instead of draping it in the warm light of a "great and wonderful happiness," as Pico puts the privilege)?[11] To what extent do animal comparisons, marshaled from the rich storehouse of natural history, suggest that humanity occupies the "woorse estate," as one early modern commentator called it?[12] And how might stipulating the existence of nonhuman points of view enhance this more quarrelsome perspective on man,

10. Andreas Vesalius, "Preface to Charles V" (1542), in Charles Donald O'Malley, *Andreas Vesalius of Brussels, 1514–1564* (Berkeley: University of California Press, 1964), 324; Walter Raleigh, *The History of the World* (London: Walter Burre, 1614), 30. On microcosmic man, see Leonard Barkan, *Nature's Work of Art: The Human Body as Image of the World* (New Haven, CT: Yale University Press, 1975).

11. For a discussion of *King Lear*'s sense of humanity as a negotiation between beastly and angelic conditions, where man's occupation of "the privileged but precarious middle ground between animals and angels" makes him vulnerable to animalization, see Andreas Höfele, "*Bestiarium Humanum*: Lear's Animal Kingdom," in *German Shakespeare Studies at the Turn of the Twenty-First Century*, ed. Christa Jansohn (Newark: University of Delaware Press, 2006), 88.

12. Plutarch, *The Philosophie, commonlie called, The Morals*, ed. and trans. Philemon Holland (London: Arnold Hatfield, 1603), 561. Subsequent citations to Plutarch in

despite that creature's apparently unsatisfiable desire to hear his virtues rehearsed and advocated? These inquiries and the texts that pursue them can be called "zoographic" in that they employ modes of discourse and writing undergirded by broadly comparative structures of reference across species. Zoographic writing endorses the scheme of "gift[s]" and "particular addition[s]" (to recall Shakespeare's terms in *Macbeth*, discussed in chapter 2), like jewels scattered prodigally by nature across a fabulous array of creatures. In this context, natural-historical practices enshrining the far-flung particulars of creaturely kinds supply both argumentative material and a point of leverage from which to look askance at humankind itself. They arm and fortify a zoographic critique of humanity.

The Insufficient Animal

This chapter takes the zoographic bearings of Lear's speech seriously, tracking the animal resources for this searing play's most searing statement on human estate. Linking the scheme of cross-species reference in *King Lear* to its intellectual contexts, it reads the play as part of a larger zoographic critique of man—a discourse whose leverage will be largely extinguished in the course of the seventeenth century, as we will see in chapter 5.[13] In a superb recent analysis of *King Lear*, Valerie Traub reads the play by looking ahead to the development of a new "conceptual logic of the grid" (based on cartography and anatomy), a grid that creates "a serviceable ratio" in "the creation of an abstract, common humanity"; this logic enshrines "the concept of a universal human nature by which one can compare 'humanity' *to itself.*"[14] The production of this humanly self-referential grid entails the historical eclipse of the very cross-species logic on which zoographic critique depends. By engaging in species-comparative discourses at the heart of the Renaissance "invention of the human" and before the emergent, abstracted human norms that will ground the politics and sciences of the

the text refer to this edition. The phrase "worse estate" appears in Holland's editorial headnote to "That Brute Beastes Have Use of Reason" (discussed below).

13. For the thread of its continuation, see Frank Palmeri, "The Autocritique of Fables," in Frank Palmeri, ed., *Humans and Other Animals in Eighteenth-Century British Culture: Representation, Hybridity, Ethics* (Aldershot, UK: Ashgate, 2006), 83–100. Palmeri deftly traces a minority tradition in the ongoing development of the beast fable in which the form voices a critique of the human.

14. Valerie Traub, "The Nature of Norms in Early Modern England: Anatomy, Cartography, *King Lear*," *South Central Review* 26, nos. 1 and 2 (2009): 57, 69 (italics added); see also pp. 66–67 for a discussion of the historiography of this development.

future, the sixteenth-century thinkers considered in this chapter stage a controversy over nothing less than the species coordinates of happiness and misery, freedom and necessity, and creaturely capacity to judge them. These familiar veins of ethical and epistemological concern, of course, shape the long history of inquiry into what it means to be "human" (given the core philosophical interest of this controversy, Greece, Athenian philosophy, and notions of the "good life" will play a role in prosecuting it). Montaigne's effort, for example, raises not only human doubt ("how do I know?") in this terrain but also a potentially leveling question of knowledge across species ("*Who* knowes?"). In a gesture to be considered in chapter 4, Montaigne expostulates: "Who knowes . . . whether divers effects of beasts, which exceed our capacitie, are produced by the facultie of some sense, that we want? And whether some of them, have by that meane a fuller and more perfect life then [*sic*] ours?"[15] His query supposes the existence of diverse creaturely perspectives, a supposition that converts the ethical pursuit of a good life ("fuller and more perfect") and emerging epistemologies of scientific truth alike into political questions that open out across kinds, sometimes with arresting cogency. In ethically compelling interpretations of the ancient Greek injunction to "know thyself," writers including Erasmus, Giovanni Battista Gelli, Montaigne, Donne, and Shakespeare apply it to their own "kind" as a whole and entertain the possibility that it might suffer in comparison to other kinds.

Montaigne may be the most sweeping expositor of the scientific experiment/imaginative act that zoographic critique entails, but he is neither the first nor the last to try it in early modernity. George Boas's *The Happy Beast* (1933) gives a meticulous and ranging account of sixteenth- and seventeenth-century Continental texts that argue for and against animals. To name the animal advocates, Boas coined the term "theriophily." Theriophiles, he describes, "turned their admiring glances below man and found true models in the animals," asserting that they are "more 'natural' than man, and *hence* man's superior." As erudite as Boas's account of the flow of this debate is, his framing conception of theriophily in *The Happy Beast* consistently undermines the intellectual force and cultural impact of the very tradition to which his book gave a name, casting the shadow of doubt on theriophily as passionate partisanship or sentimental weakness. This is not just an etymological effect of the coinage. Boas seems to secure

15. Michel de Montaigne, "The Apologie for Raymond Sebond," in *The Essayes of Montaigne: John Florio's Translation*, ed. J. I. M. Stewart (New York: Modern Library, 1934), 533. Subsequent page references appear in the text.

the tradition in order to declaw it rather than to demonstrate its moral interest or intellectual significance: "It may at times be simply a literary flourish, a smart paradox, a means of social satire; at times it takes on the appearance of serious philosophy and ethics; it enters the fields of theology on the one hand and biology on the other. Nevertheless an historian whose attention it captures should not be misled into exaggerating its importance. It is decidedly one of the minor traditions of European thought."[16] Everything about this extended admonition warns us against taking theriophily too seriously and exudes complacent confidence in the authority and status of human intellectual culture. Boas likens an absorption in questions of animal perspective or exemplarity to an innocence led astray by an animal charlatan or trickster, who deceptively "takes on the appearance" of seriousness and draws us down a dangerous path.

We have reversed course against the presumption that what is "minor" somehow underperforms in terms of signification. On the contrary, if we remain interested in *humanitas* and its histories, accounts of whatever is not human must be regarded as equally instructive. But there is more at stake than a change in our critical frameworks. For example, Montaigne's "Apologie" was a published justification of his own translation and publication in 1569 of a much earlier treatise whose orthodoxy remained ambiguous (it appeared in the Index of Forbidden Books in 1558–59, and its prologue was condemned in the Tridentine Index in 1564); it is an "essay" so substantial it has long appeared as a free-standing book.[17] Yet Boas classifies this effort within the "little" genre of paradoxes: "little essays against the prevailing opinion of mankind [which] were certainly not written for other than conversational purposes" and were only "for literary effect and not for demonstrating truth." Implying that theriophily had less import than a parlor game, Boas opines that "one would have to be peculiarly unimaginative to take all this seriously."[18] So many warnings. The ontological dangers posed by unschooled imagination and the species decorum of serious philosophy are at stake; the ideological infrastructure of the category of man is at stake. In "all this," we are told to keep the animals on

---

16. George Boas, *The Happy Beast in French Thought of the Seventeenth Century* (Baltimore: Johns Hopkins University Press, 1933), 1 (italics in original), v.

17. See, for example, Michel de Montaigne, *An Apology for Raymond Sebond*, ed. and trans. M.A. Screech (London: Penguin Classics, 1987), xii–xv.

18. Boas, *Happy Beast*, 11–13. Taking this material "seriously" is "un-imaginative" (rather than excessively imaginative) because Boas refers to a failure to appreciate the literariness of the tradition's witty flourishes.

a leash as exclusively literary flourishes. Boas's protestations against his own subject, in other words, work to circumscribe the entire logic of the happy beast within an imperturbably human-exceptionalist domain.

Despite these admonitions, the balance of this chapter takes the debate about animals "seriously" to read the happy beast tradition as consequential. It traces its impact beyond theriophily into domains where early modern writers question human estate from a comparative perspective. After addressing the relationship between comparatist doubt about man and Christian perspectives as Donne explores it, the chapter turns to the major classical source for zoographic critique beyond the animal encyclopedias. Plutarch's dialogue "That Brute Beastes Have Reason" expands on an episode from the *Odyssey* concerning Ulysses's sojourn with Circe and the men (many of them Greeks) she has changed into beasts. This dialogue from the *Moralia* is widely known by its subtitle, "Gryllus," the name of the pig who methodically arraigns humanity to an astonished Ulysses on Circe's island. In 1549 Florentine courtier-shoemaker Giovanni Battista Gelli published a robust improvisation on Plutarch's dialogue.[19] Dedicated to Cosimo de Medici, Gelli's *La Circe* presses into this terrain even further, multiplying Ulysses's animal interlocutors to eleven. Together, Oyster (previously a fisherman), Mole (previously a plowman), Snake (previously a physician), Hare, Goat, Hind (previously a woman), Lion, Horse, Dog, Calf, and Elephant (previously a philosopher) argue every point in favor of animals and against man that the conjoint classical, Christian, and natural-historical tradition made available. They even incorporate detailed critiques of "man" from their own past human histories—as laborers or women—into the species controversy. This extraordinary text was quickly translated into English by 1557–58.

Against this backdrop, the chapter returns to *King Lear* to show how much the happy beast tradition saturates the play. Whatever else we may prefer to leave open about Shakespeare's political commitments, ethical positions, and affective investments, we can safely say that theriophily was not one of them. Yet *King Lear*'s account of human estate "takes se-

19. According to Judith Yarnall's account, Gelli was born in 1498 near Florence and self-educated; "in his maturity Gelli was a respected member of the circle of Neo-Platonic thinkers at the Florentine Academy and a valued acquaintance of Cosimo de Medici. He insisted, however, on practicing his shoemaker's trade until the end of his life and refused to become a man of letters solely dependent on patronage." Yarnall, *Transformations of Circe: The History of an Enchantress* (Urbana: University of Illinois Press, 1994), 110.

riously"—and vigorously rearticulates—the happy beast tradition's bleak story about man, demonstrating the range and power of zoographic critique in early modern thought. In *King Lear*, man is no "heavenly animal," as Pico phrased him. Instead, Shakespeare reckons man zoographically as an *unhappy* beast—what Plutarch's Gryllus calls "the most wretched creature in the world" (564), and Gelli's Oyster calls "the most unhappye creature, that is in all the worlde."[20] This reckoning goes beyond skepticism to affirm something worse about man than a likeness to the beasts, whose own claims on and to the world enjoy comprehensive ratification in the happy beast tradition. Lear's man, by contrast, lacks any cosmic place or home. Alone among living things, by birth and by nature, he is born "unaccommodated."

Before turning to the happy beast tradition's arraignment of man as an insufficient animal, attention to Christian theologies of abjection as a related basis for human negative exceptionalism is in order. Among the most ironic passages in Shakespeare is Hamlet's characterization of man (addressed to Rosencrantz and Guildenstern). One of Shakespeare's rare usages of the term "animal" appears there, in sarcastic conjunction with the question of paragons: "What a piece of work is a man! How noble in reason, how infinite in faculties, in form and moving how express and admirable, in action how like an angel, in apprehension how like a god! The beauty of the world, the paragon of animals! And yet, to me, what is this quintessence of dust? Man delights not me—no, nor woman neither, though by your smiling you seem to say so" (2.2.304–11). Miscropped from its context and curtailed of its final turn, the speech often stands in for the orthodox human ideal it satirizes. It cannot easily be performed this way; it unfolds as an exaggerated actor's rant to baffle the slower-witted Rosencrantz and Guildenstern (themselves counterevidence, perhaps, against its lofty vision). Desedimenting centuries of *Hamlet* interpretation, Margreta de Grazia has shown how Hamlet's adoption of the antic's guise has been obscured. Like the clowning and madcap action of the antic role, much of what Hamlet says is "part of his antic repertoire."[21] From the sarcastic melodrama of the "paragon of animals" line, this speech makes a sharp turn to consider man as undelightful "dust" before collapsing into a joke

20. Gelli, "The fyrste Dyaloge: Oister and Moule," *La Circe* (Iden's translation is unpaginated, so Gelli's dialogues are cited by dialogue number and featured animal interlocutor[s]; the first stars the two lowliest creatures in *La Circe*).

21. Margreta de Grazia, *Hamlet without Hamlet* (Cambridge: Cambridge University Press, 2007), 8, 194.

about failures of sexual desire. The antic guise circumscribes the paragon claim, and Hamlet's emphasis on "the quintessence of dust" deflates man in a sobering Christian note.[22]

Christian conceptions of the "vanity" of human knowledge make man incompetent to the dramas of his own salvation. The idea that an insufficient man must depend on the supplement of God's grace appears with varying emphasis throughout Christian thought (as we will see, it indelibly marks Christian representations of ancient material on animal happiness). Thinkers did register the downside risk inherent in the proposition of an immortal soul. Possession of an undying soul that escapes the worldly limit circumscribing the lives of other creatures, of course, represents the key exceptionalist criterion in pre-Cartesian contexts. As a point of comparative anatomy, having such a soul must be a good thing; it provides access to eternity in accord with various theological dispensations. But it also exposes humans to the unique risk of sin and a failure to be redeemed. A concise example of this reflection—from Donne's "Sir, more than kisses"—goes like this:

> In best understandings, sin began,
> Angels sinned first, then devils, and then man.
> Only perchance beasts sin not; wretched we
> Are beasts in all, but white integrity.[23]

Beasts are not vulnerable to sin; they can be seen to possess a certain immunity or "integrity," even a "white" integrity that "wretched we" lack, to our harm.[24]

As Donne exclaims more passionately in the Holy Sonnets, this being-

---

22. For discussion of the scriptural and liturgical coordinates of this dust, see ibid., 31–32.

23. John Donne, "To Sir Henry Wotton," in *The Complete English Poems*, ed. A. J. Smith (London: Penguin, 1986), 215, lines 39–42. See also Rebecca Ann Bach, "'We Are Beasts in All but White Integrity': Animals and Renaissance Sexuality" (paper delivered at the Shakespeare Association of America Conference, Victoria, Canada, April 2005). I am grateful to her for sharing this paper with me.

24. In the human racial contexts of *Titus Andronicus*, whiteness suggests a lack of bodily integrity evidenced in the involuntary blush ("Ye white-limed walls! Ye alehouse painted signs! / Coal black is better than another hue / In that it scorns to bear another hue" [4.2.99–101]), but the brilliantly white-coated ermine provides the referent for this animal "whiteness." In Henry Peacham's emblem on the ermine's purity, it prefers to be devoured by the dogs than to "defile his daintie skinne" in muddy places, shaming those

equipped-with-a-soul makes man vulnerable in ways no other part of the cosmos is:

> If poisonous minerals, and if that tree,
> Whose fruit threw death on else immortal us,
> If lecherous goats, if serpents envious
> Cannot be damned; alas, why should I be?[25]

This lament persisted in a sermon preached at Lincoln's Inn in 1618. Addressing the dilemmas of human estate, Donne writes: "God might have preserved him from sin, by making him better, and so he might by making him worse too; he might have preserved him by making him an angel in a confirmed estate, and he might have preserved him by making him a beast without a reasonable soul, for then he could not have sinned, *and he had been the better for it.*"[26] From the standpoint Donne elaborates, man would be "better" if he were "worse." The soul is an Achilles heel, displacing even the vulnerable body as humanity's weak point by situating us in an *unconfirmed estate* that leaves us exposed to damnation. In a related but less ambivalent gesture, Nietzsche would lament mankind's evolutionary reliance on "consciousness" as a reduction to our "weakest and most fallible organ."[27] Man stands categorically above the beasts for Donne, but his distinction is the vexed one of a capacity to fail one's type and face a judgment worse than death itself. A rational soul is "proper" to man, but it follows inevitably that the risk of catastrophically improper choice is his too.

Human negative exceptionalism based in theological considerations thus yields a troubling risk scenario grounded on the unique vulnerability that the privilege/danger of one kind of soul entails, and period writers display a solemn attention to this vulnerability. But strong limits confront such a doubtful line of thought; regretting the soul (what Macbeth in a more prudent moment terms "mine eternal jewel" [3.1.69]) does not ultimately comport with religious first principles, which necessitate that such

---

who, by comparison to the beast, "care [not] a rush, / With how much filth, their mindes bespotted are." *Minerva Britanna, or a garden of Heroical Devises* (London, 1612), 75.

25. John Donne, "Holy Sonnet 9," in *Complete English Poems*, lines 1–4.

26. John Donne, *A Sermon Preached at Lincoln's Inn by John Donne*, ed. George Potter (Stanford, CA: Stanford University Press, 1946), 36–37 (italics added).

27. Friedrich Nietzsche, *On the Genealogy of Morals*, trans. Walter Kaufmann (New York: Vintage, 1969), 16.

doubt be cut off, overcome, or answered. This is, in fact, what Donne goes on to do. Once he has questioned damnation in "Holy Sonnet 9"—asking "Why me and not goats?"—he cuts short the inquiry with self-critique. "Who am I that dare dispute with thee / O God?" (lines 9–10). Faith cannot sustain a negative or skeptical assessment of the soul's meaning. Obviously the status of faith is under the most extreme question in *King Lear*, and such restoration of it as is proposed in Donne is notoriously absent. This is to concur with accounts of the force of skepticism of the drama. But skeptical grounds cannot fully account for the human negative exceptionalism framing Lear's classification of man.

In terms of the kinship between theological skepticism and zoographic critique, William Elton's *King Lear and the Gods* helpfully describes a "beast-in-man pattern" (the notion of a human capacity to "descend" to "bestiality"), which Elton considers an aspect of Lear's "piety-scepticism configuration."[28] As he elaborates, beast-in-man patterns in "apologetic tracts demonstrate the skeptical affiliations" of Lear's "equation" of the cosmic position of "man and beasts."[29] The function of human bestiality here remains primarily engaged with the idea that humankind can sacrifice its privilege and sink as low as a beast by moral backsliding. Lear does begin by equating human and animal when he seeks to be "a comrade with the wolf and owl" (2.4.211), immediately recasting that comradeship in negative terms and concluding that "man's life is cheap as beast's" (2.4.269). But he then takes humans one critical increment further down. Using a metric of "lack" against man, Lear goes beyond a sense of frayed human fabric relapsing to animal estate to raise the far vaster question of human cosmic belonging itself.

In keeping with his pursuit of a theologically oriented skepticism, Elton suggests that "to appreciate *King Lear*, less a twentieth-century naturalistic view than a more exalted medieval and early Renaissance view of man's hierarchical place . . . is requisite."[30] For zoographic purposes, to set this traditional hierarchy as the horizon of reading is to restrain the range of its critique—then or now. Without advocating a "twentieth-century naturalistic view," we can explore how Lear's discourse on man depends less on a theologically determined skepticism that equates man and beast (by making animals "bestial" and leveling paragonal man to that state)

28. William. R. Elton, *King Lear and the Gods* (San Marino, CA: Huntington Library, 1966), 190–91.
29. Ibid., 192, 190.
30. Ibid., 192.

and more on the comparative critique I am calling zoographic, a critique that elevates an integrity in beasts that it asserts man lacks. Human specification through cross-species reference in *King Lear* enacts this eclectic mode, drawing from the classically derived happy beast tradition, Christian considerations of human weakness, and the vocabularies of a thriving world of natural history writing. In the contexts of *King Lear*, reading zoographically means considering raw exposure to the storm as both a literal problem of weather on skin and a dire elemental question of what it might mean, in the end, to lack a roof over one's head (and God's grace too). It asks what it means, in other words, to be cosmically unaccommodated.

Nudus in Nuda Terra: Unaccommodated Man

"Truely, when I consider man all naked . . . and view his defects, his naturall subjection, and manifold imperfections, I finde we have had much more reason to hide and cover our nakednesse than any creature else," Montaigne writes. "We may be excused for borrowing [from] those which nature had therein favored more than us, with their beauties to adorne us, and under their spoiles of wooll, of haire, of feathers, and of silke to shroud us" (340). Pelt envy, perhaps? "Perfection" is a powerful physiological and moral concept, most familiar from Aristotelian models of male completeness and female incompleteness. In comparing perfections, Montaigne (like the other writers in this tradition) borrows the term authorizing male power over females to describe a superiority of beasts over man, spelling out humanity's deficit in its lack of a coat. Remedying that deficit only "shrouds us" in "their spoiles." Pivotal work on early modern material culture, gender, and performance has shown how characteristics such as sex or social station are effectively layered on through the visible fashionings of cloth, from the trappings of livery to cross-dressing on stage.[31] In the zoographic arraignment of man I trace here, human estate itself comes down to a matter of dress—or, more precisely, of undress. Ann Jones and Peter Stallybrass's comprehensive material history of the social meanings

31. See Ann Rosalind Jones and Peter Stallybrass, *Renaissance Clothing and the Materials of Memory* (Cambridge: Cambridge University Press, 2000). See also Jean Howard, "Crossdressing, the Theatre, and Gender Struggle in Early Modern England," *Shakespeare Quarterly* 39 (1988): 418–40; Stephen Orgel, *Impersonations: The Performance of Gender in Shakespeare's England* (Cambridge: Cambridge University Press, 1996); Bruce Smith, *Homosexual Desire in Shakespeare's England: A Cultural Poetics* (Chicago: University of Chicago Press, 1991); and Valerie Traub, *Desire and Anxiety: Circulations of Sexuality in Shakespearean Drama* (New York: Routledge, 1992).

of clothing prompts the ontological question here of how analysis might extend to animals "dressed" in their own "coats" or whether naked/coated might be as durable a distinction as such familiar criteria as reason, language, tool use, and so on. In the early modern archive, the natural coverings of animals spell out completeness and self-sufficiency, and the integral animal comes armed with a good coat already on its back.

In a cultural context where animal reference is fundamental, we find ready cognizance of the fact that beasts serve as man's literal outfitters, no doubt due to the convergence of traditions all positing human nakedness. The Greek story of Prometheus, the account of the Fall in Genesis, and natural history writing (with diverse emphases) all diminish man as naked— in both literal and cosmic degrees. Human bareness is distinguished from the greater bodily perfection of animals, whose more apt provisioning better suits them for the world. Plato's *Protagoras* narrates one compensatory version of underprovisioned man. Prometheus and his brother Epimetheus were delegated a power of assigning abilities to all living creatures; Epimetheus begged the privilege for himself. After outfitting creatures with "defenses against mutual destruction," he "devised for them protection against the weather . . . thick pelts and tough hides capable of warding off winter storms. . . . He also shod them, some with hooves, some with thick pads of bloodless skin." When, however, he had "absentmindedly used up all the powers and abilities on the non-reasoning animals; he was left with the human race, completely unequipped." Prometheus returns to discover "the other animals well provided with everything, [and] the human race . . . naked, unshod, unbedded, and unarmed," and so he steals practical wisdom and fire from Hephaestus and Athena as compensatory provisions for man (for which he was notoriously punished).[32] Prometheus ekes out an "unequipped . . . naked, unshod, unbedded, and unarmed" humankind with essential prosthetic supplements.

The most broadly disseminated sense of the "naked animal" derives, of course, from Genesis, where the accession to knowledge through sin engenders nakedness as a shameful new estate. Describing Adam and Eve before the Fall, Genesis asserts that "they were bothe naked, . . . and were not ashamed" (Gen. 2:25); after they eat the apple, the next chapter records that "the eyes of them bothe were opened, & they knewe that they were naked"; they use fig leaves to make themselves "breeches" (Gen. 3:7). Does nakedness precede the Fall, since Adam and Eve "were" naked then?

32. Plato, *Protagoras*, trans. Stanley Lombardo and Karen Bell (Indianapolis: Hackett, 1992), 321c, 15–17 (italics added).

Or does the Fall engender nakedness as a morally self-aware state, a state "breeche[d]" in shame? Knowledge and nakedness coincide; if you do not know you are naked, you are not really naked yet.[33] A God dissatisfied with their fig leaves gives Eden's exiles the skins of beasts for traveling coats: "Unto Adam also and to his wife did the Lord God make coates of skinnes, and clothed them" (Gen. 3:21). As Jones and Stallybrass show, animal skins serve as a form of livery for Adam and Eve, indicating their boundness to God.[34] Martin Luther glossed this passage to suggest an analogy between man and the underlying animal whose skin is taken, arguing that its death is a reminder of ours: "Their garments . . . were a reminder to them to give thought to their wretched fall from supreme happiness into the utmost misfortune and trouble. . . . [God] clothed them, not in foliage or cotton but in the skins of slain animals, for a sign that they are mortal and that they are living in certain death." Luther continues, "A pelt was [Adam's] daily garb as a daily reminder of his lost bliss."[35] But the principle of identification in this reminder also runs up against the firm theological limit of humanity's monopoly on eternal life.[36] Either way, the layering on of a second skin from another creature to cover "shame" spells out the radical insufficiency of man. He needs the supplement of divine grace and the pelts of others to address his shortfall in being.

Human bareness, whether classical or Christian in origin, persistently troubled the security of human being in the environs of natural history. There, man's uniquely unequipped condition faces the sharp pangs of physical exposure. Pliny provides the main source on underprovisioned

33. Derrida discusses the role of cognizance/belief in nakedness (see *The Animal That Therefore I Am*, ed. Marie-Louise Mallet, trans. David Wills [New York: Fordham University Press, 2008], 4, 11).

34. Jones and Stallybrass, *Renaissance Clothing*, 269.

35. Martin Luther, *Lectures on Genesis 1–5*, trans. George Schick, in *Luther's Works*, ed. Jaroslav Pelikan (St. Louis: Concordia, 1958), 1:221–22. Using vocabularies of animal happiness discussed below, Luther speaks of how Adam and Eve "ought to have lived *content*" (222; italics added). For an excellent discussion of resonant hides (human skin and inscribed parchments), see Sarah Kay, "Original Skin: Flaying, Reading, and Thinking in the Legend of Saint Bartholomew and Other Works," *Journal of Medieval and Early Modern Studies* 36, no. 1 (2006): 35–74, and Kay, "Legible Skins: Animals and the Ethics of Medieval Reading," *postmedieval: a journal of medieval cultural studies* 2, no. 1 (2011): 13–32.

36. We have already seen Luther equivocate on this monopoly, however, in chapter 1. For the inability of orthodox doctrine to contain this problem, see Karl Steel, "Woofing and Weeping with Animals in the Last Days," *postmedieval: a journal of medieval cultural studies* 1, nos. 1–2 (2010): 187–93.

man for natural historians and Renaissance readers alike. Considering
whether nature has not played the part of "a hard and cruell step-dame,"
he argues: "Of all other living creatures, man she hath brought forth all
naked. . . . To all the rest, given she hath sufficient to clad them everie
one according to their kinde: as namely, shells, cods, hard hides, prickes,
shagge, bristles, haire, downe feathers, quils, skailes, and fleeces of
wooll . . . against the injuries both of heat and cold: man alone, poore
wretch, she hath laid all naked upon the bare earth" (152–53). The descriptive richness of this catalogue of coverings contrasts with the stark characterization of "man alone" as a "poore wretch" left miserably "all naked."
And the world this bare creature finds presents itself to him likewise as an
injurious and "bare earth." A Christian writer such as Du Bartas readily
assimilated this idea to his account of godly creation in *Devine Weekes*:

> Of all the Creatures through the welkin gliding,
> Walking on Earth, or in the Waters sliding,
> Th'hast armed some with poyson, some with pawes,
> Some with sharp antlers, some with griping clawes
> Some with keene tushes, some with crooked Beaks,
> Some with thick Cuirets, some with skaly necks.
> But mad'st man naked, and for weapons fitt,
> Thou gav'st him nothing but a pregnant Witt,
> Which rusts and duls, except it subject find
> Worthy it's worth, whereon it self to grinde.[37]

Du Bartas echoes Pliny's inventorying approach, endorsing a plenitudinous
view of animal provisioning alongside a conception of human rational powers as a potential weakness. The ready adaptability of this language to Christian contexts doubtless strengthened the currency of Pliny's formulation.

The natural histories lavish enormous verbal and visual attention to the
comparative riches of animal hides. With painstaking exactness, Edward
Topsell takes all the time he needs to narrate these details. Here, for ex-

37. Guillaume du Bartas, *Bartas: His Devine Weekes and Workes*, trans. Joshua
Sylvester (London: Humphrey Lownes, 1605), 168–69. In *Dulce bellum inexpertis* (1515),
Erasmus makes original use of the catalogue, arguing that because nature "equipped every one of the other living creatures with weapons of its own" but brought forth "man
alone . . . naked, weak, delicate, and unarmed, with smooth skin and the tenderest of
flesh," warfare must be unnatural for humankind (quoted in Hutton, *Themes of Peace*,
252). For the unkindness of warfare as, instead, a definitional feature of human "kind,"
see below.

ample, is his vivid English distillation of Pliny and Gesner on the hyena's coat: the hyena has a "body like a wolfe, but much rougher haired, for it hath bristles like a horsses mane all along his back, & in the middle of his back it is a litle crooked or dented, the colour yellowish, but bespeckled on the sides with blew spots, which make him looke more terrible as if it had so many eies." In the case of the "deer-goat," Topsell offers an extremely fine-grained description accompanied by speculation about the way the engineering specifications of this animal's body protect its life and activity. He explains:

> The colour [is] in the Winter blacke, and red, set one with another; the beard like a Goat, but more divided and turned backward; his haire very long, even to his knees, a mane full of bristles, stretched out in length through his whole neck, but especially about the top of his shoulder-blades, where it standeth like bunches, being in colour darker then [sic] in other parts of the body; and the hinder legs are covered with longer and harder hairs down to the pastern, (as I think) for no other cause but to defend them from harm in leaping.[38]

These two examples (and countless others like them) show how much comparative reference guides animal specification. The detailed illustrations of animals and their equipage match the precision of Topsell's descriptions. Topsell's images largely appeared first in Gesner's volumes. Gesner had incorporated Dürer's famous martial rendering of the rhinoceros, which interpreted the rhino's body as if it were plated with body armor (fig. 3.1). Gesner's porcupine likewise betrays an almost forensic attention to the dangerous spines that defend the creature against predators, illustrating differences among the types of spines outfitting its body (fig. 3.2). The hedgehog, too (whose image is discussed in chapter 4), bristles with self-protective gear, in its pelt and finely rendered nails. The portrayal of the ram stresses both the defensive natural provisioning of animals (with its elaborate horns) and the foul-weather preparedness made manifest in the creature's shaggy wool, itself the very source of much borrowed warmth for early modern humans (fig. 3.3). (Indeed, Topsell gives sheep thirty-two pages of consideration—not counting separate chapters on the ram, the "weather-sheepe," and the lamb—and gives due appreciation to the utility of wool. "English sheep . . . are neither anoid with the fear of any venemous beast, nor yet troubled with Wolves, and therefore the strength

---

38. Edward Topsell, *The Historie of Foure-Footed Beastes* (London: William Jaggard, 1607), 340, 95. Subsequent page references appear in the text.

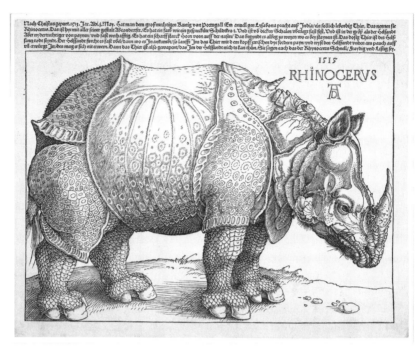

Figure 3.1. Albrecht Dürer, *Rhinoceros* (1515). Image courtesy of British Museum, London, Great Britain. Photograph: © The Trustees of the British Museum / Art Resource, New York.

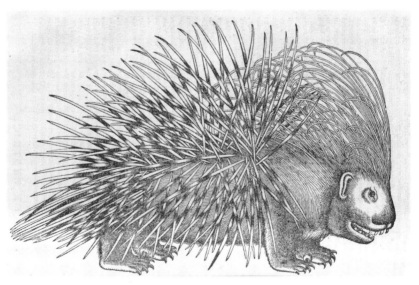

Figure 3.2. Conrad Gesner, *Porcupine*, in *Historiae Animalium, Liber 1 (de Quadrupedibus)* (Zurich, 1551). Image courtesy of the Charles Deering McCormick Library of Special Collections, Northwestern University Library.

Figure 3.3. Edward Topsell, *Ram*, in *Historie of Foure-Footed Beastes* (London, 1607). Image by permission of the Folger Shakespeare Library, Washington, DC.

of their nature and peaceable quiet wherein they live, doth breed in them the better wooll; and besides . . . they quench their thirst with the dew of heaven" [626].) A good natural-historical description—just like the bodies it inventories—would be incomplete without attention to the body's surface in its tactile richness, functional efficacy, and human applications.

The moralizing potential of the integral animal makes its mark, for example, in George Wither's emblem on "vertue" itself, from *A Collection of Emblemes* (1635) (fig. 3.4). It shows a crocodile and carries a long poetic gloss listing the kinds of weapons people hoard (pistols, swords, locks, and bars), but goes on to claim that these supplemental weapons of defense often fail. Instead, he avows,

If, therefore, thou thy *Spoylers*, wilt beguile
Thou must be armed, like this *Crocodile*;
Ev'n with such nat'rall *Armour* (ev'ry day)
As no man can bestowe or take away:
For, spitefull *Malice*, at one time or other,
Will pierce all borrowed *Armours*.[39]

39. George Wither, *A Collection of Emblemes, Ancient and Moderne* (London: Henry Taunton, 1635), bk. 2, 112 (italics in original).

Figure 3.4. George Wither, *Crocodile*, in *A Collection of Emblemes* (London, 1635).
Image by permission of the Folger Shakespeare Library, Washington, DC.

Animal coats thus provide more than clothing for man, who lacks a
"nat'rall Armour" of his own; they also supply the compensatory metaphors that serve to fit out man's lack of integral bodily provision.[40] Either
way, the supplement is "borrowed" and therefore unreliable—exactly as
Lear's exclamation laments.

Montaigne explores this argument that man, alone, is left unequipped

40. Human debt to animals as suppliers of poetic comparison has great effect in
the animal testimonies; Plutarch's Gryllus points out that "if you thinke your selves
to be more hardie and valiant than beasts, how commeth it, that your Poets tearme
those who fight manfully against their enemies . . . wolves for courage; . . . lion-hearted;
and . . . resembling the wild boare in animositie and force: but never doth any of them
call a lion . . . as valiant as a man" (566).

by nature—calling it a "daily" complaint that he hears—and he rehearses the luxuriant details of animal outerwear.[41] These lamenters say, he writes (following Pliny very closely), that

> man is the onely forsaken and out-cast creature, naked on the bare earth, . . . having nothing to cover and arme himselfe withall but the spoile of others; whereas Nature hath clad and mantled all other creatures, some with shels, some with huskes, with rindes, with haire, with wooll, with stings, with bristles, with hides, with mosse, with feathers, with skales, with fleeces, and with silke, according as their quality might need or their condition require. (402)

Despite his equation of human nakedness with the display of "manifold imperfections" and the volume of his prose excoriating man, Montaigne ultimately refutes the fullest reach of the *nudus in nuda terra* complaint. Instead, he reasons equitably, humankind could not have been uniquely left out of nature's general endowment. He proceeds, however, by an anti-exceptionalist argument to contend that nature has *not* been "a most injust and partiall stepdame" (as Pliny had proposed), but rather "hath generally imbraced all her creatures: And there is not any but she hath amply stored with all necessary meanes for the preservation of their being. . . . There is a greater equality, and more uniforme relation in the policy of the world. Our skin is as sufficiently provided with hardnesse against the injuries of the wether, as theirs" (402–3). Theriophily, strictly understood, advances a human negative exceptionalist argument: "the policy of the world" prefers beasts to men. As Gascoigne's hare voices this perspective, "I thanke my Maker, than, / For makying me, a Beast and not a Man."[42] Diverging from theriophily (at least on this point), the literally cosmopolitan Montaigne instead claims due provision for humankind as a part

41. Underscoring human exceptionalism as related to religious orthodoxy, Elton points out that in 1594 Pierre de La Primaudaye attributed this recurrent "complaint" to atheists (*King Lear and the Gods*, 193). Helkiah Crooke has harsh words for this "unbrideled insolencie": "Let Plinie and all the whole rabble of false and counterfet Philosophers, be banished out of the Schoole of Nature, who cease not to wrong . . . her, for casting foorth man naked and unarmed on the bare ground upon his Birthday, to begin the world with crying and lamentation," affirming instead that "unmatcheable Art" and "most heavenly wisdome" framed man's body. *Microcosmographia: A Description of the Body of Man* (London: William Jaggard, 1615), 8.

42. George Gascoigne, trans., "The Hare, to the Hunter" *The Noble Arte of Venerie* (London: Christopher Barker, 1576), 176.

of nature's consistent and general embrace. *King Lear* gives man no such quarter.

The Animals Testify: Plutarch and Gelli

Pliny's stark image of man alone as a "poore wretch" left "all naked on the bare earth" stresses a mismatch between human needs and the world that might supply them (without signaling hope of another world). His *nudus in nuda terra* phrasing calls on the same adjective to gloss man and the world's inhospitality to him, as if the unaccommodating world just mirrored back to man his own unprovisioned state. Despite Montaigne's reassurances, even for him man's wretched bodily nakedness suggests cosmic debility and endangerment. With a body of "manifold imperfections," he stands a "miserable and wreched creature . . . exposed and subject to offenses of all things" (396). These relays from literal nakedness to cosmic vulnerability center on a primal question that writers in the happy beast tradition (and those they influence) consider in species terms and answer "according to kind." For Pliny, every other creature on earth except man knows its own good: "As for all other living creatures, there is not one, but by a secret instinct of nature knoweth his owne good, and whereto he is made able: some make use of their swift feet, others of their flight wings: some are strong of limme; others are apt to swimme, and practise the same: man onely knoweth nothing unlesse hee be taught." Here Pliny even takes on the vaunted brain: "What a while continueth the mould and crowne of our heads to beate and pant, before our braine is well settled; the undoubted marke and token that bewraieth our exceeding great weakenesse above all other creatures?" (152). The foundational question of knowing one's "owne good" and knowing how to thrive concerns happiness itself.

    In current usage, being "happy" mainly conjures a mood or emotion: "Having a feeling of great pleasure or content of mind, arising from satisfaction with one's circumstances or condition; also in weakened sense: Glad, pleased." However, the stronger sense of happiness in early modernity (and certainly in the classically oriented happy beast tradition) emphasizes one's circumstances and conditions themselves: "Having good 'hap' or fortune; lucky, fortunate; favoured by lot, position, or other external circumstance."[43] Happiness here depends on a match, a just proportion, or

---

43. *Oxford English Dictionary*, 2nd ed., s.v. "happy," 4.a., 2.a. For a helpful account of the waning historical force of "happiness" as a public judgment about the conditions of a life, rather than private feelings about it (that is, the happiness indexed in the Solonic

a "happy" convergence between what the world offers and what the creature needs—those needs having been correctly judged. As the animals of
Plutarch and Gelli will assert, they know it and have it, while we neither
have it nor know the means to it. With resonant ancient precedents in Aristotelian ideals of flourishing, as well as sharper Stoic measures of "need"
or necessity, the beasts explode reigning commonplaces about human superiority to assert a fundamental flaw in man: the gross and palpable failure of much-vaunted human reason to have directed humanity either to
the satisfactions of a good life or the just beauties of an eternal truth. The
track record of human reason speaks for itself, as the animals reason it:
in Gelli's Calf's empiricist words, "Every thinge is knowen by his operations" ("The ninth Dialogue, The Calfe").

We have seen in chapter 1 how, for example, Gascoigne's strategy of
thinking from the perspective of hunted animals enabled a political
complaint to be lodged against tyrannical mankind: the testimonies of
the hart, hare, fox, and otter cite chapter and verse to turn man's claims
against animals back against man, indicting his consistently worse, "murderous" conduct. Plutarch and Gelli take animal testimony another direction, moving from the justice arguments in a victim/animal's bitter complaint to representing disinterested animal witnesses who testify against
man about happiness itself.[44] In "Gryllus" and *La Circe*, Ulysses confronts
richly imagined animal points of view. These animals estrange his sense
of those things that normally pass for self-satisfied conventions about reason and happiness among humans. They also deftly constrain Ulysses's
claim to represent all humankind, qualifying him as a Greek and as mar-

---

maxim "Call no man happy until he is dead"), see Vivasvan Soni, *Mourning Happiness:
Narrative and the Politics of Modernity* (Ithaca, NY: Cornell University Press, 2010).

44. Iden and Holland add Christian framing to qualify both dialogues by shifting
the negative implications exclusively onto pagan conditions. Holland glosses Plutarch:
"If reason the guide of the soule have no other helpe than of herselfe, certes, it may well
be truely said; that man is the most miserable creature in the world." His editorializing
would convert Plutarch's dialogue from the comprehensive reduction of "the condition of men to a woorse estate than that of brute beasts" it is into "a forme of processe
against all Pagans and Atheists, to proove that brute beasts excell them, and be in more
happie estate than they," holding Christians exempt from the fate of the pagans (Plutarch, *Philosophie*, "Holland's "Summarie," 562). Iden offers the same corrective, saying
his translation shows "howe lyke the brute beast, and farre from his perfection man is,
without the understanding and folowinge of dyvyne thynges" (Gelli, epistle dedicatory,
La Circe). Such Christian brackets as they adduce to limit the claim that human estate
is miserable, transparent enough in context, make no appearance in *King Lear*.

tial, masculine, privileged, incompletely experienced, and fairly unreflec-
tive. As we will see, Ulysses's speeches prefigure Descartes on these questions, just as Gelli's animals prefigure those who would critique Cartesian
dispensations. In Plutarch and Gelli, imaginings across species enable
cogent, zoographic critiques of humankind—and the possibility of a non-
theological critical distance on humankind is at stake in them.

In contemplating the existence of a point of view that is not our own
(whether human or nonhuman), philosopher Thomas Nagel suggests a role
for the "imagination" as a necessary "aid," rather than just a venue for the
mishaps of anthropomorphic projection: "The distance between oneself
and other persons and other species can fall anywhere on a continuum.
*Even for other persons, the understanding of what it is like to be them is
only partial, and when one moves to species very different from oneself, a
lesser degree of partial understanding may still be available.* The imagination is remarkably flexible."[45] Thus, by Nagel's standard, the inevitable
incompleteness of any imagination of other subjects cannot cancel its partial success; it is not immeasurably harder to refer to "animal testimony"
in these dialogues than it is to call Ulysses's testimony "human." In other
words, the ethical effort to stipulate that another point of view exists (a
gesture that, in animal contexts, we have seen Descartes associate with a
heresy like atheism) affirmatively *requires* the techniques of imagination.[46]
Plutarch's and Gelli's dialogues are routinely cited for the proposition that
"brute beastes have reason" or, less accurately, as debates about it (though
they are also routinely cited as tongue in cheek, mere literary pastimes).
The proposition about reason is perfectly explicit in Plutarch and conso-
nant with his other treatments of animals; it is overwhelmingly indicated
in Gelli. But this idea that animals "have reason" may be the least consequential or controversial feature of these "anti-Cartesian" texts.[47] Instead,

45. Thomas Nagel, "What Is It Like to Be a Bat?" *Philosophical Review* 83, no. 4
(October 1974): 442n8 (italics added).

46. René Descartes, *The Discourse on Method*, trans. Donald Cress (Indianapolis:
Hackett, 1998 [1637]), 33.

47. Plutarch's "Gryllus" holds little debate about reason. In a related dialogue,
though, one speaker (an anti-Cartesian *avant la lettre* in his distrust of binary oppositions) argues for diversity and scaled powers: we do not "inferre and conclude that
man is blinde" just because many creatures "in quicknesse of eie-sight . . . out-goe
all the men in the world"; likewise of beasts "if their discourse and understanding be
more grosse, if their witte be more dull than ours, it followeth not thereupon that they
have neither reason nor naturall witte." "Whether Creatures Be More Wise, They of
the Land, or Those of the Water," 955. This dialogue (a key source for Montaigne) ends

their imaginative affordance of points of view for animals—including critical and deeply ironizing perspectives on man—must be judged their most
arresting achievement. In *Praise of Folly*, Erasmus deployed the Gryllus
episode with relish—"Gryllus was considerably wiser than 'many coun-
selled Odysseus' when he chose to grunt in his sty rather than share the
risks of so many dangerous hazards"—but, from a zoographic perspective, his association of Gryllus's choice with ordinary folly is fairly conventional.[48] Edmund Spenser's engagement with Plutarch's swine is even
more limited in the sense that *The Faerie Queene*'s "Grill" serves within
the confines of human moral allegory to symbolize self-indulgence and
bestial preoccupations (the "hoggish mind") in book 2's consideration of
lust and temperance.[49] The animal testimonies of Plutarch and Gelli, by
contrast, offer thought experiments in dialogism that enable them not
only to voice an estranging account of (animal) happiness but also to lodge
a keen critique of man as the most calamitous of animals. These dialogues
do not in fact debate "animal reason." Instead, they conduct a trial of human *versus* animal estate. Humanity secures no firm verdict in its favor.

After his sojourn on Circe's island, Ulysses desires to return home; he
gets Circe's permission to restore those on the island that she has transformed into animals to human estate and take them back with him to
Greece. But Circe sets one condition. Ulysses must win their consent to this
double restoration. The dialogues baffle Ulysses, opening unexpected discussions of much larger questions. When Plutarch's Circe accuses Ulysses of
"folly" for desiring to "procure damage and calamity" to his friends, Ulysses
initially scoffs, "You should make a very beast of me in deed, if I would suffer my selfe to be perswaded, that it were a detriment or losse to become a
man againe of a brute beast" (562). In the opening of Gelli's fifth dialogue,

---

in a judicial draw between land and water creatures, but its judge reaches a "verdict"
that "mightily confute[s] and put[s] downe those who would deprive bruit beasts of all
understanding and discourse of reason" (980).

48. Erasmus, *Praise of Folly; and, Letter to Martin Dorp*, ed. and trans. Betty Radice
(New York: Penguin Books, 1993), 54.

49. Guyon asks the Palmer to return the animals "unto their former state," at
which restoration "one above the rest . . . / That had a hog beene late, hight *Grille* by
name, / Repined greatly, and did him miscall, / That had from hoggish forme him
brought to naturall." In the Palmer's moralization, "The donghill kind / Delights in
filth and foule incontinence: / Let *Grill* be *Grill*, and have his hoggish mind" (Edmund
Spenser, *The Faerie Queene*, ed. A. C. Hamilton [New York: Longman, 1992], 2.12.85–87
[italics in original].) Plutarch's Gryllus, by ironic contrast, articulates the standard of
temperance book 2 is concerned to establish as human (discussed below).

an increasingly frustrated Ulysses accuses Circe of deceiving him by letting the animals resume speaking but withholding their reason, "for there
is none of th[em] that judgeth it not better, to be a beast then [sic] a man,
the whiche I would never beleve they would saye, yf they coulde use reason
truelye." In each case, Ulysses claims reason as a medium incapable of voicing an anti-human-exceptionalist view. Yet, in arguments both physical and
moral, Plutarch's swine and Gelli's eleven other animals quite methodically
testify to the superior happiness and endowment of beastly life. All but one
refuse to return—to human estate or to Greece. Neatly compressing questions of animal estate, political membership, and the business of thriving,
in Gelli's ninth dialogue the Calf gives this condensed but searing reason
for refusing: "Where one is well[,] there is hys countrye."

Only Gelli's final dialogue equivocates. Until its last pages, the Elephant argues against man, then suddenly yields to Ulysses's final persuasion. Perhaps in a performance of divine furor, Ulysses rehearses a
last-ditch Platonist account of how humankind alone can choose whether
to be plantlike, to be "like the brute beastes," or, if he lifts "his face to-
wardes heaven, playing the philosopher, [to] . . . change himself from an
erthly beast, unto a hevenly animal." The former philosopher-Elephant
then questions why, under such circumstances of freedom, a "hevenly
animal" (echoing Pico) would nevertheless fail to "play the philosopher"
and persistently choose vice and error, as humans notoriously do. At this
point, Ulysses contradicts all the evidence presented to blame bad human
choices on "those partes" man has in common with animals. He proclaims that "all our errours, depende finally, by those partes of nature:
that we have without reason, together and in common with you: and not
by those by the whiche we are men." To err, then, is not human; error is
transposed to an animal origin. Human choice reflects humanness only
sometimes—when men choose right. Ulysses's answer not only opens a
religious turn in the dialogue, as the Elephant in transition chants a hymn
about the "fyrst mover of this whole worlde." It also prefigures Descartes's
dispensation, sounding a strong note of dualism: the entire animal and the
embodied part of man (minus mind or soul) share a common mechanism,
while an alleged supplement of immaterial reason (itself a retreat to invisible criteria that can only be asserted and not tested) grounds the elusive
difference between man and beast.[50]

50. The full philosophical dimensions of *La Circe* and Gelli's relation to Neopla-
tonism exceed the scope of this chapter, and this staggeringly rich text warrants much
more attention in English contexts.

Ulysses's redirection of blame to the animal part in man, of course, does not explain how the add-on of reason palpably fails to lead men to what is true, good, or healthful—a point made repeatedly by the animals across a range of domains. Boas accepts this argumentative non sequitur, suggesting that the philosopher-Elephant "redeems the honor of the Greeks."[51] But we need not wonder long whether the last-minute patch of humanist orthodoxy that the Elephant's consent supplies contains everything that precedes it: Circe herself has already established other parameters for reading Ulysses's single success. Circe's power had transformed the men in the first place, and she enfranchises Ulysses to reconvert such of them he can persuade.[52] Pointedly, he qualifies his own power as delegated when he retransforms the Elephant "by the aucthoritie that she gave me." At an earlier point in *La Circe* (the beginning of the seventh dialogue, with the Horse), Ulysses despairs about his then seven failures of persuasion. But Circe encourages him to keep trying "if this desyre strayne thee so much." After all, she reassuringly suggests, "it can not be, that thou find not some one of those, that is of thine opinion: *for thou knowest howe diverse the wittes of man are*" (italics added). With this stroke, Circe makes Ulysses's chances a statistical matter rather than an ontological question of man. And in archly noting the notorious diversity of men's "wittes," she has largely proved the point that Ulysses's elevated notions of humanity are more a matter of puffery than fact.

These two dialogues, then, let animals testify that they are happy and that mankind is in "a woorse estate." Gryllus lays out the terms of happiness and misery, accusing Ulysses of being afraid to "change from the woorse to the better" and of refusing "to learne those sciences and disciplines, which of sickly, diseased, and foolish, might make them more healthy, sound, and wise" (563). Likewise, in the second dialogue Gelli's Snake emphasizes the same poles: "Nature . . . hath geven you a complexion so weke, and an appetite so unordinate" while "she hath . . . geven unto us a complexion so strong, and a desyre so well ruled." Here I can only suggest some of arguments the animals adduce against man. Animals experience utopian equality within kind (the Goat of the fourth dialogue

51. Boas, *Happy Beast*, 35.
52. In a like-spirited reading, Yarnall reads Gelli as feminist in treating Circe as a reasonable host rather than a deceptive seductress: "Gelli's quite remarkable feminism . . . is not muted by its playful context," she argues, claiming that his use of "humor and indirection" makes his defense of women more effective than the formal polemics of "most of the Renaissance 'defenders' of women" (*Transformations of Circe*, 112).

argues that they live untroubled by the "infelicities" of private property, "possessinge every thing in common" and "havynge amonge us no superioritie at all"). They never accept servitude, but resist it with the valor celebrated in La Boétie: Gryllus stresses the absence of slavery among animals and emphasizes how they "chuse to die . . . rather than to live in servitude" (565). Animals have better scientific method than humans. Gryllus treats animal scent powers as a discernment higher than human taste (567); in the third dialogue, the Hare refutes Ulysses's notion that hares know "not whether [they] be male or female" with the tart "Nay you knowe it not . . . but we knowe it well ynough"; and the Goat argues that animals better judge time "because we[,] not having oure fantasy ful of a thousand toyes, as you always have, fele every little chaunge of tyme." Instead of the anxious anticipation typical of humans, animals discern time—and many other proportionate measures—without the distortion of interfering fears or fantasies.

Questions of gender and diet warrant special interest in the debate because Ulysses actually concedes these two points to the beasts. On diet, Gryllus defines temperance as "a certaine restraint, abridgement, or regularitie of lusts and desires, a restraint . . . of such as are forren, strange, and superfluous, to wit, unnecessarie" in favor of a mean moderating "those that be naturall and necessarie" (567). Gryllus roundly criticizes human omnivorousness (569). Gelli's Snake likewise gives a classic Renaissance critique of diet, based on his knowledge as a physician. He suggests further that nature is man's enemy because she gave him "an appetite of feding so unsaciate, and a desyre so immoderate" that he inevitably engenders "superfluous humors" that lead to the "unperfectnes of the complexion of your nature, subject and bonde . . . unto so many divers sicknesses, the which are not even knowen by us." Superfluities and unperfectness sound the humoral notes of a mismanaged bodily economy.

An entire medical argument arises in this connection, one in which animals have, in the Snake's words, "farre more perfecte phisicke" than man, because "take what kind of beast thou wilt, and thou shalte fynde, that for thinfirmity whereunto the same is subject, nature hath taught him the remedy." As Gryllus puts this, for animals medical knowledge comes "through the force and perfection of natural vertue" and not, as for man, "by way of apprentissage" (569). This reasoning reappears to spectacular effect in Donne's meditations on his own near death and recovery, when he considers that "we shrinke in our proportion, sink in our dignitie, in respect of verie meane creatures, who are *Phisicians* to themselves. The *Hart* that is pursued and wounded, they say, knowes an Herbe, which being eaten, throwes off the arrow. . . . Man . . . is not his owne *Apothecary*, his owne *Phisician*, as they are."[53] To be physician to oneself sets an enviable standard of self-possession and integrity. Clysters (learned of the Egyptian ibis), bloodletting, and a host of herbal remedies and antivenoms all find their original instance in animal knowledge and medical practices. In the very grammars we have just seen Donne echo, Pliny records that "the Bore, when he is sicke, *is his own Physician*, by eating yvie and crab-fishes, such especially as the sea casteth up to shore" (211; italics added).[54] The species with the knowledge gap is man, who not only requires the physical subsidy of another's skin but also must gather knowledge and techniques from beasts when it comes to thriving on earth.[55] All this is standard fare about diet and health in early modernity, and it appears throughout period literature. Thus, to the Snake Ulysses concedes that "surelye in some part thereof thou sayest true."

On questions of gender Ulysses stands similarly defeated. Gryllus argues that "nature swaieth indifferently and equally to either side, as touching courage and boldnesse, neither is the female in that point inferior to the male" (565). In a stunning turn that uses the very platform of Ulysses's singularity (as a roving warrior now returning home to his wife) to undercut human valor itself, Gryllus argues that "men naturally are not endued with prowesse, for if they were, then should women likewise have their part with them in vertue and valor." That women do not (a point to which Ulysses is committed) proves that male valor in humans is "not voluntarie nor naturall, but constreined by force of lawes, subject and servile to . . .

53. John Donne, *Devotions upon Emergent Occasions* (London: Thomas Jones, 1624), 70–72 (italics in original).
54. Pliny assembled many of the recurring medical examples in a single chapter. Its title argues the case: "What Physicall hearbes certain creatures have showed us, to wit, the Harts and Stags, the Lizards, Swallowes, Torteises, the Weasell, the Storke, the Boare, the Snake, Dragon, Panther, Elephant, Beares, stock Doves, house Doves, Cranes, and Ravens" (Pliny, *Historie of the World*, bk. 8, chap. 27).
55. These notions provide a fresh context for understanding *The Tempest*'s Caliban, who provisions Prospero (whose status as an all-powerful knower/magus is thereby ironized) by "show[ing] [him] all the qualities o' th' isle, / The fresh springs, brine-pits, barren place and fertile"; his knowing assurances of the fearful Trinculo and Stephano, "Be not afeard. The isle is full of noises, / Sounds, and sweet airs, that give delight and hurt not" also derives from these conceits of classical natural history writing. The grounds for Caliban's (nonhuman) claim to the island, then, are not only about prior political tenure but also about his natural-historical knowledge. *The Tempest* (1.2.338–40, 3.2.138–39).

customes reprehensions" (565). Bigger fireworks on this subject come in
the fifth's dialogue's exchange with the Hind, who was a Greek woman. In
1933 Boas called the Hind's speech "an oration on feminism which might
have been written by Mrs. Gilman."[56]

The Hind refuses to return to human estate because of the position
of women in Greek culture, noting ancient opinions that gender difference was a question of species difference: "Ther have bene of those wise
men among you, that have bene bold to affirme, that we are not of your
kinde" and (referring to Aristotle's theory of perfection) that women are
failed or imperfect men. While Greek men "kepe women for slaves, and for
servantes and not for companions (as right requireth)," among beasts the
"femal is a companion & no servaunt to the male, aswell in pleasures as
in paines." Gelli also equips the Hind with claims of an escape from Genesis's curse on women: "Neither yet have I so many sorowes in the dely-
veraunce of my younge . . . as I should have . . . being a woman." The Hind
calls man "a most evill and an unjust tyraunt," accusing him of arbitrari-
ness instead of reason: "You make your reason as your selves list." Her arguments on household governance, child rearing, sexual double standards,
freedom of movement, and subsidized masculinity leave Ulysses no room
to conclude anything but that animal estate *really is* better for her. Invoking the political language of "libertie," he muses, "Thus an Hynde, she
lyveth in libertie, a thinge so pleasaunte, as none other thynge is more,
she should beyinge a woman becomme a servaunte: none other thing in all
the worlde more grevous. . . . Let me then seke, yf I can do this benefite, to
suche as it maye do good, since it should do hurt to her."

Having offered this glance at the bracing interest of the dialogues, I
turn to the aspect of this material most consequentially related to *King
Lear*: Gelli's first episode, "Ulysses and Circes, Oister and Moule." Key
threads set here all appear in the play, and each concerns the interface
between creatures and nature. We find an argument for experiential proof
over Athenian philosophy (downgraded and contextualized here as no more
than "human opinion"); shadows of doubt cast on the utility of reason
as a capacity, given its terrible track record; the method or rule by which
to achieve a just measure of true need, given the interference of "unsaciate" appetites in humans; and, most basic, the provoking questions of nakedness, accommodation, and exposure familiar from natural-historical
evaluation. In Du Bartas the poor oyster is "head-lesse, foot-lesse, and
finn-lesse, in a heape confused," while in Descartes, the oyster marks the

56. Boas, *Happy Beast*, 32.

approach of a slippery slope: to deny all animals a soul, he argues that "there is no reason to believe it of some animals without believing it of all, and many of them such as oysters . . . are *too imperfect* for this to be credible."[57] Perhaps the sheer tendentiousness of Gelli's decision to begin *La Circe* with the lowly and ambiguous Oyster—of all the creatures in all the world—appealed to Shakespeare for his story about the demise of a king who stands for a man.

When the Oyster was a Greek and a man, he lived as a fisherman. Ulysses will use this fact against him when it appears the Oyster will choose to remain an Oyster, dismissing him among "vyle persons, and of litle knowledge," ignorant of "the pleasures of the world." But ignorance and experience are exactly the standards the Oyster claims for their debate. Unlike Ulysses, the Oyster explicitly indicates that argumentative method is at stake: "Let us reason frendly a litle togethers, and thou shaltes see yf I[,] that have proved thone life and thother, can shewe thee that, that is trewe that I saye." Proof (experience, testing) supplies proof (dependable evidence). A tension between animals and Athens, between experiential knowledge and Greek speculative philosophy, traverses Gelli's text, and it figures prominently in the Oyster's account. When a "Gretian," he lived in "a place besyde Athens." His livelihood took him to the city, where he observed enough of human philosophy to learn the doctrine that nature—the source of animal reason—"can not erre, as oftenne times I have harde saye of those Philosophers of Athenes, whiles I, to sell the fishe that I toke, stode by the gallaries, where they a great parte of the daye, disputed and reasoned together." The Oyster was no passive spectator to the theater of philosophy, however. Reasoning with Ulysses, he deploys the philosophers' judgment on nature as unerring and concludes from this that "because Nature makynge more accompte of us then she hath done of you" (by supplying animals with a flawless reason instead of the weakness of a "power" to erre), "it foloweth that she loveth us better" and that "we are better and more noble than you." To this logic, a somewhat disarmed Ulysses responds, "What, me thinketh thou arte the best Logitian of Athenes." Disclaiming knowledge of "what Logique meaneth," the Oyster claims to speak only "in such sort as nature hath taught me," suggesting that reason is nature—and vice versa.

Toward the end of their exchange, Ulysses tries out the teleological ar-

57. Du Bartas, *Devine Weekes*, 148; René Descartes, "To the Marquess of Newcastle (23 November 1646)," in *The Philosophical Writings of Descartes*, ed. John Cottingham et al. (Cambridge: Cambridge University Press, 1991), 304 (italics added).

gument that animals are made for human uses and that "we being as your
endes, must be more noble than you." The Oyster goes in for the kill: "Yf
these reasons were true you shoulde have bene also made by [nature] for
the erth, for at the last she eateth you al." But the Oyster also suspects the
turn the debate is taking. He ends the conversation, saying, "Thou begyn-
nest to enter those disputations with me, that I . . . hearde in the galleries
of Athens of those Philosofers, whiles I . . . went about to . . . provyde me
of suche other necessaries as I hadde need of: the whych (I thynke) neyther
they nor others knewe." In this we detect the way that Greece and Athenian philosophy are associated with questions of human estate at the same
time as philosophy takes on a whiff of privilege at best or folly at worst.
Philosophers, the Oyster maintains, are ignorant of the more dispositive
realities of simple self-provisioning. Several of Ulysses's other interlocutors break off conversation over similar turns to a philosophical style of
disputation. While Ulysses dismisses the Oyster as a creature based on
"nede, and not . . . plesure," he misses the Oyster's claim that nature's provision of animal needs yields a firmer and more reliable pleasure than any
that humans experience. In other words, in the Oyster's perspective, need
and pleasure are not opposing modes of being. Rather, "happiness" is the
event when they meet. Gelli gives a bold example of this perfect conjunction. The Oyster feels "that the dewe beginneth to fall, whereof I fede [and]
wherein I have so great delight, and without any trouble or thoughte at all,
that whylst I was man, I never proved the like." He esteems "contentation"—the achieved matching of pleasure and need—the highest value. To
the Oyster, who has actually "proved" both states, human estate cannot
compete with a humble and ephemeral drop of water: "a lytle dewe."

Enter the Mole. He grouchily responds to Ulysses's hailing by asking
what he means "thus to trouble my quietnes," and when he hears Ulysses's proposition he immediately affirms that only folly could lead him to
choose a "worse" estate, whereas "now I live with most great pleasure in
this state . . . where as beying a man . . . I should lyve in continual troubles, and paynes importunate, whereof humaine nature is most abound-
aunte."[58] Like the Oyster, he knows what he is talking about because he
speaks from "experience, maistres [mistress] of all thinges." When Ulysses
tries to qualify his experience as limited (as a plowman), the Mole tes-
tily replies with a powerful categorical assertion: "Doe me none injury,

58. Iden briefly genders the Mole female, likely due to the Italian term (*la talpa*)
because there is no thematization of gender in the exchange, which otherwise calls the
Mole a "plowman" ("The fyrste Dyaloge: Oister and Moule").

Ulisses . . . for every man is a man." When the former laborer Mole points out how the earth readily supplies food for all animal kinds without work on their part, Ulysses suggests that man fed likewise in "thage that was called the golden age." But the Mole scoffs, "Yet belevest thou these tales?" Here the Mole associates Greek fables and Athenian philosophy—classic points of reference for humanity itself—as follies, both equally divorced from experience as the better testing ground for any claim, and especially from happiness. When it comes to a comparative judgment on animal and human estate as "happy" or "miserable," Ulysses's lack of experience of the former contextualizes his confidence in the latter as an assertion of untested opinion.

We have already seen the Oyster open a contest about authority over reason. He claims it for nature (making it available to all), while Ulysses claims that reason is an exclusively human faculty. For the Oyster, the reason supplied by nature "never fayleth to any thynge, of that, *that is necessarye*" (italics added). Whatever is necessary, in this mainly Stoic logic, is not a form of grinding constraint or oppression, but the only "reasonable" guide to the parameters of a good life. Clear cognizance of necessity provides freedom from supervening distractions and superfluities that might derail the rational pursuit of that life. Later in *La Circe*, the Goat puts the problem distinctly. Claiming that the existence of human statutory laws proves "the imperfection and weakenes of your nature," he asserts that man is blind to what is really necessary: "You have so many immoderate desyres, and agaynst your owne wealth and profite, and you are so much ledd by them, that the light of reason is not sufficient to teache you to avoide them." Led astray by himself, man keeps rendering himself, in other words, "imperfite."

In the first dialogue, the harmonious relationship of reason to need provides the road map for creaturely perfection. When this relationship serves as a point of contention between Ulysses and the Mole, their controversy centers on questions of desire and lack. When Ulysses charges lowly creatures with imperfection, the Mole asks, "Why, what doe we lacke?" In typically human style, Ulysses's response (that the Oyster can neither smell nor hear nor move about and that the Mole is blind) substitutes the plenary set of known human faculties for abstract perfection itself. The Mole's analysis, however, points out that "we are not therefore unperfite . . . but we shoulde be imperfit in dede *yf we lacked any of those that belongeth unto oure kynde*" (italics added). Instead of an abstract (here, human) standard, the Mole insists that happiness derives from kind and can only be measured—like perfection itself—according to kind. The Mole argues

that he and the Oyster do not "nede" the senses Ulysses has listed because humans only have them to seek out things humans lack in the first
place, while these lowlier creatures readily find everything they need with
the faculties they have. This triggers Ulysses's most Lear-like line, as we
will explore in a moment: "Although it be not necessarye unto thee, yet
thou shouldest desire to have it." This is the crux of the debate, and it is
a central interest in Renaissance ethical deliberation: whether a good life
entails duly cherishing what is necessary or striving to attain what is not.
In trying happiness across species, what Plutarch and Gelli figure as human contradicts a familiar moral principle from Renaissance *sententiae*,
as compressed in Holofernes's postprandial remark to Nathaniel, "Satis
quod sufficit" (*Love's Labors*, 5.1.1). But in the controversy between beasts
and men, only animals know that enough is (really, exactly, even luxuri-
ously) enough or that, according to the proverb, "Enough is as good as a
feast." This is in part because humans do not follow the guide to reason
that necessariness provides. "Unsaciate" man is dismissive of need and
its measures; he is governed instead by desire in an economy of meaning
where desire returns us again and again to the idea of lack.

   Thus, unsurprisingly, human nakedness and the elemental exposure
that attends it arise as major concerns in Gelli's first dialogue. On this
subject, the lowly Oyster simply takes charge. He begins this thread rehearsing Pliny's epicentral *nudus in nuda terra* passage:

> I will . . . beginne from the fyrst day that [nature] bringeth forthe both
> you and us into the world. . . . What care hath she shewed to have of
> you, syns she causeth you to be borne naked? Wher contrary she hath
> shewed to esteme us muche, causing us to come into the world clothed,
> some with lether, some with heare, some with scales, some with one
> thing, and some with an other, the which is a manifest token that she
> hath greatly in her harte mynded our conservation.

Ulysses partly concedes this point, but he counts it in man's favor. Agree-
ing that nature "hath made us naked, and covered us with so thinne a
skinne, that we are hurte by every lytle thing," Ulysses proposes that this
"wekeness of our complexion" follows humoral principles. He connects
"grosse bluddes" with bodily strength and claims that "they that are of
thinne and quicke fleshe, are lykewyse quicke of witte," arguing that because nature wanted humans to be "reasonable & of most perfit knowledge, [she] was in maner enforced to make us so." The Oyster dismisses
this reasoning as sophistry, and he has good grounds, because Ulysses's

idea that nature was not free to assemble humans however she wanted is quickly exposed as inadmissible and an implausible restraint on nature.

Retreating to different grounds, Ulysses suggests that it may not matter that humans are naked, given that they have figured out how to get coverings from the beasts: "What matter maketh it thoughe nature hath made us naked, since she hath geven us such knowledge and strength, that we can cover us with *your clothes?*" (italics added). But as the Oyster retorts, humans only procure animal coats by exposing themselves to high risk and hard labor, neither of which are required from animals. This leads the Oyster to connect bodily nakedness with an unhoused condition, as he escalates the debate from clothes, to habitation, and all the way to cosmic belonging:

> I will no more become a man againe, and I thinke I have reason, consideringe . . . that nature hath set litle store by you, for besides the bringing forth of you naked, she also hath not made you any house or habitation, of your own, *wher you mought defend you from thinjuries of the wether* as she hath made to us, that which is a plaine token, that *you are as rebelles and banished of this world, having no place here of your owne* (italics added).

These are dire charges. But the Oyster has his grounds to consider the provision of a cased or housed body as an unerring sign of nature's care and love. Showing his shells' operation to Ulysses, he can "open and shutte easely as I have need to fede me, or to repose me, or to defend me from such as would hurt me." He points to tortoises and snails and "howe easely they carye their houses with them." We can see the force of this observation, for example again, in Donne's "Sir, more than kisses." Donne's critique of the human domains of countries, courts, and towns leads him to propose that Wotton regard the snail as a model for integral self-rule and sufficiency:

> Be thou thine owne home, and in thy selfe dwell;
> . . .
> And seeing the snaile, which every where doth rome,
> Carrying his owne house still, still is at home;
> Follow (for he is easy pac'd) this snaile,
> Be thine owne Palace, or the world's thy gaile.[59]

59. Donne, "To Sir Henry Wotton," 159–62, lines 47–52.

Donne's "Be thine owne Palace" doctrine refers Wotton to the school of integrity provided by the snail to protect himself in—and from—the dangerous, even inimical climates of human culture.

Exposure to the "injuries of the wether" serves as a key index in the happy beast tradition's measurement of human estate as, in the Snake's words, "a lodging of miseries." But the Oyster's improvisation on this theme takes naked underprovisioning as more than a sign that nature is a "cruel stepdame" to humankind. He goes further to call humanity, as a kind, both "rebelles" in nature and exiles "banished of this world" in which they live. In other words, the Oyster proposes both cosmic orphanage and nature's enmity as the truth of human estate. And the Mole backs him up: "You have good reason to wepe as ye do when you are borne (the whiche none of us doth) considering the infelicitie and miserye of the state whereunto you come. . . . You begyn to fele *thincomodities of the place*, where you come to inhabite, the whiche . . . *as it is to all other beastes accommodate, it is to you onelye, almoste contrarye,* and therefore wepinge is geven only to you by nature" (italics added). Between them, the Oyster and the Mole elaborate the Plinian idea of humankind as *nudus in nuda terra*, razing that creature's claim to be the "paragon of animals." Throughout Gelli's text, the controversies of happiness set "contentation" (the Oyster's *perfect* fulfillment of honest need by a "lytle dewe") against the sense of lack and trouble always associated with "unsaciate" desire in the period ("nothing els than a continual stryfe, now with one thing, and nowe with an other," according to the Mole). To treat Gelli's dialogue as a tongue-in-cheek exercise or to bracket the horizons of critique it opens by charging it with anthropomorphism is to miss the moral force of its testimonies alleging value in nonhuman lives. There is nothing "merely literary" about the arrestingly self-critical idea that other species might better express these "humanist" values. One thing is clear in this tradition, and the wit of Gelli's play bow is ferocious in giving these arguments to an Oyster: running dramatically against the grain of Heidegger's characteristically modern philosophical proposition that it is the animal who is "poor in world [*weltarm*]," here man is orphaned and alien, the world's most "unaccommodated" creature.[60]

60. Martin Heidegger, *The Fundamental Concepts of Metaphysics: World, Finitude, Solitude*, trans. William McNeill and Nicolas Walker (Indianapolis: University of Indiana Press, 2001), chaps. 3–5.

The Unhappy Beast in *King Lear*

Aristotle asserted that "it must be wrong to say, as some do, that the structure of man is not good, in fact, that it is worse than that of any other animal. Their grounds are: that man is barefoot, unclothed, and void of any weapon of force."[61] Yet just this account of man flourished across sixteenth-century contexts and into the seventeenth. From Gelli and Montaigne, to Gascoigne and Sidney, to Donne and Shakespeare, the vantage that a zoographic critique of humankind made possible appealed to writers interested in looking askance at man and establishing a critical distance not fully assimilable to more familiar theological perspectives on human vanity. *King Lear* relentlessly voices the grim reckoning of human estate that was forged in the happy beast tradition. The play's persistent absorption with unclad bodies and unkind relations raises a transhistorical problem in philosophy and theology—humankind's cosmic place—but its mode of inquiry and its answers express a zoographic critique of man, all the way down.

King Lear offers a rich catalogue of zoographic reference, abridged here in rough order: dragons, monsters, brutish villains, goatish dispositions, the dragon's tail and Ursa Major, mongrels, curs, coxcombs, apish manners, hedge sparrows, cuckoos, asses, horses, sea monsters, detested kites, serpent's teeth, wolvish visages, foxes, oysters, snails, a mongrel bitch, wagtails, halcyon beaks, geese, bears, monkeys, ants, eels, sharp-toothed unkindness, vultures, wolves, owls, creatures, lions, cocks, lice, pelicans, hogs, dolphins, worms, sheep, civet cats, house cats, mastiffs, greyhounds, spaniels, bobtail tikes, swimming frogs, toads, tadpoles, wall newts, mice, deer, vermin, nightingales, herring, boarish fangs, cowish terror, tigers, prey, dog-hearted daughters, crows, choughs, beetles, larks, wrens, furred gowns, swine, adders, butterflies, toad-spotted traitors, a dog, a horse, and a rat. This is not to count repetitions of these names or foul fiends, incubi, centaurs, demons, and spirits, to whatever taxonomic order they belong. If so many animal figures populate *King Lear*, then the presence of a naked man among the *dramatis animalia* of the play—the "naked fellow" (4.1.40, 50) and Lear's "Philosopher" (3.4.152, 171, 175), his "learned Theban," and his "good Athenian" (3.4.155, 179)—only completes the zoographic circle.

After the cascade of social ruptures in the opening scenes, at the end

61. Aristotle, *Parts of Animals, Movement of Animals, Progression of Animals*, trans. A. L. Peck and E. S. Forster (Cambridge, MA: Harvard University Press, 1937), bk. 4, sec. 10, p. 687a.

of act 1 Lear finds himself in the environment where he will live out his remaining time: "out o' door" (3.2.11). It has not begun to storm. But the Fool needles him in a colloquy about bodily exposure drawn directly from the discourses of the happy beast. He quizzes Lear, "Canst thou tell how an oyster makes his shell?" and then continues, "Nor I neither. But I can tell why a snail has a house." Lear plays along with the riddling protocols of cross-examination on stage, and so the Fool rehearses the reason as a sharp lesson for him: "Why, to put's head in, not to give away to his daughters and leave his horns without a case" (1.5.25–31). This early note on uncovering, exposure, and folly sets up the scene of Edgar's disguise. In putting on nakedness to look like a madman, Edgar takes on

> the basest and most poorest shape
> That ever penury, in contempt of man,
> Brought near to beast.
> (2.3.7–9)

Here the indices poorness and bareness appear together as bodily signs of the "contempt of man" attributed to the cosmos. Edgar proposes "with presented nakedness [to] outface / The winds and persecutions of the sky" (2.2.11–12). His act of naked camouflage vividly imagines "Bedlam beggars" with their "numbed and mortifièd arms," who prick and spot their bared skin with "pins, wooden pricks, nails, [and] sprigs of rosemary" (2.3.14–16). Only a numbed madman, the logic goes, could achieve a beast-like immunity to such violence against unprotected skin. The storm that will unfold on the heath constitutes a set of "pins and pricks" to worry a skin inadequate to its assault.

Lear's impending exposure to what Edgar calls "the persecutions of the sky" stems not only from Goneril's "sharp-toothed unkindness" as she attempts to rid her palace of Lear and his followers. When he complains to Regan that Goneril has "oppose[d] the bolt / Against my coming in," and Regan (forewarned) agrees with Goneril's suggestion that Lear "disquantity" his train, Lear rebels:

> Rather I abjure all roofs, and choose
> To wage against the enmity o' th' air,
> To be comrade with the wolf and owl,

a move Lear glosses as a submission to "necessity's sharp pinch" rather than a daughter's hard terms (2.4.134, 177–78, 209–12). The happy beast tradition literally made "a virtue of necessity" (in *Two Gentlemen of Verona*, this phrase specifically describes the life taken up by its "outlaws" as they seek a natural moral code and adapt to living in the "wilderness" [4.1.62–63]). Yet here, Lear wavers in his commitment to outfacing necessity by "abjuring all roofs," and he advances a still-unrevised sense of what it means to be human. When his daughters join forces to winnow down the number of his attendants, Regan finally asks, "What need one?" For the old king, this goes too far. "O," he exclaims, "reason not the need!" To enter into a calculus of necessity, in his view, is to fail to be human. He explains:

> Our basest beggars
> Are in the poorest thing superfluous.
> Allow not nature more than nature needs,
> Man's life is cheap as beast's.
> (2.4.266–69)

By this metric, human estate can only be achieved through "superfluous" possessions; without those (and it does not take very much), a man is no longer a man.[62] He is leveled to the condition of an animal who only needs exactly what it needs. Never mind that the animal's needs are "perfectly" fulfilled: human being "needs" what it does not "need." The storm—escalating "the enmity o' th' air"—begins here.

The play's characters cannot stop referencing the severity of the weather in terms of its force against human skin, stressing its violence even for much better provisioned animals. Gloucester notes that "the bleak winds do sorely ruffle" and highlights the landscape as an especially hostile *nuda terra*: "For many miles about / There's scarce a bush" where Lear might take shelter. And so Cornwall advises him to "shut up [his] doors, . . . 'tis a wild night" (2.4.302–4, 310). The first line of the next scene, on the heath, is Kent's: "Who's there, besides foul weather?" He receives a report on Lear from the Gentleman who has entered, who describes Lear "contending with the fretful elements" and striving "in his little world of man to outstorm / The to-and-fro-conflicting wind and rain." While Lear runs "unbonneted," taking on the storm, by contrast even the hardiest

---

62. As Margreta de Grazia glosses this issue, "A person must have some extra thing beyond subsistence in order to be more than animal" ("The Ideology of Superfluous Things: King Lear as Period Piece," in *Subject and Object in Renaissance Culture*, ed. de Grazia et al. [Philadelphia: University of Pennsylvania Press, 1996], 23).

of animals take shelter. "This night," the reporter laments, is so adverse that

> the cub-drawn bear would couch,
> The lion and the belly-pinchèd wolf
> Keep their fur dry.
> (3.1.1–14)

The coated animals may be born ready for all types of weather, but "this night" they "know their own good" well enough to take shelter. Kent presses this animal measure of the extraordinary storm:

> Things that love night
> Love not such nights as these. The wrathful skies
> Gallow [frighten] the very wanderers of the dark
> And make them keep their caves.
> (3.2.42–45)

Then looking at Lear, he exclaims, "Alack, bareheaded?" (3.2.60). It is at this point that Lear begins to revise his prior judgment about superfluity and necessity. His "wits begin to turn," but it is unclear whether this indicates a single question of sanity as such or, instead, a weakening of his orthodoxies about human status that puts "sanity" at stake (3.2.67).

Lear notices the Fool might be cold. "Art cold? / I am cold myself." Having already heard about the "hovel" they want to take him to, he continues,

> Where is this straw, my fellow?
> The art of our necessities is strange,
> And can make vile things precious.
> (3.2.68–71)

In Lear's first act of "kind-ness" in the play, he reevaluates need and superfluity, finding "art" (if not a "virtue") in necessity. That necessity makes "vile" straw "precious"—just like the Oyster's reckoning of his "little dewe"—directly voices the essential lesson of Gelli's animals. They leave to find the hovel, and a brief intervening scene reveals that Gloucester has lost his house for asking Cornwall and Regan for permission to house Lear in it: "When I desired their leave that I might pity him, they took from me the use of mine own house" (3.3.2–4). When Kent brings Lear and company to the hovel, he urges them in, saying, "The tyranny of the open night's too rough / For nature to endure" (3.4.2–3). Initially the king resists, telling Kent he suffers a "greater malady" than the fact that "this contentious storm / Invades us to the skin" (3.4.6–8). Then Lear agrees to take shelter, but first sends the Fool inside while he contemplates "houseless poverty" 3.4.26).

Lingering "out o' door" to moralize, Lear imagines "poor naked wretches, wheresoe'er you are, / That bide the pelting of this pitiless storm," and he asks,

> How shall your houseless heads and unfed sides,
> Your looped and windowed raggedness, defend you
> From seasons such as these?

Pelted, but pelt-less, "poor wretches" can only cover themselves with "looped and windowed" attire—clothes so full of holes they keep no weather out. The shivering experience on the heath prompts Lear to reconsider human distributions of resources in better accord with need: "Take physic, pomp; . . . [and] shake the superflux to them / And show the heavens more just" (3.4.26–36). Gloucester speaks to like effect when he hands over his purse to the "naked fellow":

> Heavens, . . .
> Let the superfluous and lust-dieted man,
> . . .
> . . . feel your power quickly!
> So distribution should undo excess
> And each man have enough.
> (4.1.65–70)

Gelli's Hare had offered an argument against wealth: "The nature of ryches is, to bring so great feare for the keping thyem, that the possessoures of them, have never one only howre, a quiet mind," and the Goat spoke of animal community of possession and freedom from *meum* and *tuum*: "We known not fortune, and not havyng anye dyfference betwene thine and myne, but possessinge every thing in common, one of us seketh not to robbe an other." But these hortatory visions of Lear and Gloucester, conjuring a greater kind-ness among their own kind based on a better calculus of need and superfluity, remain painfully unfulfilled, as, in a sense, incompletely human ideas.

Meanwhile, the Fool flies out of the hovel, having been startled to find a "spirit" (the naked Edgar) already sheltering in the straw inside. As the king's party contemplates "Poor Tom," Lear wonders whether Tom's daughters did this to him: "Couldst thou save nothing?" The Fool retorts, "Nay, he reserved a blanket, else we had all been shamed" (3.4.63–65). Finally, in the play's most famous lines, the old king reads straight from the zoographic script provided by the natural histories and happy beast dialogues we have been considering. Contemplating poor, naked Edgar, he laments how he "answer[s] with [his] uncovered body this extremity of the skies" (3.4.100–101). Posing what is often construed as an existential question, "Is man no more than this?" Lear answers it zoographically. He calculates man's pathetic condition without the animal subsidies stressed in natural historical accounts of humankind: "Thou ow'st the worm no silk, the beast no hide, the sheep no wool, the cat no perfume. . . . Thou art the thing itself; unaccommodated man is no more but such a poor, bare, forked animal as thou art" (3.4.102–4, 105–7). This intensified use of "unaccommodated" embraces not only houselessness but also a natural failure of bodily integrity.[63] Offering to take off his borrowed coats and reduce himself to a human truth stripped of its animal supplements, he cries, "Off, off you lendings! Come, unbutton here" (3.4.107–8). With his animal indebtedness subtracted from the account, an insufficient humankind hovers not at nothing, but at something short of even that. As discourses of zoographic critique show, a "poor, bare, forked animal," in its flagrant insufficiency, is barely an animal at all.

Pliny's "Proeme" to book 7 ends with an utterly negative-exceptionalist vision of man's place. He falls far short of the animals, who "live orderly and well" among themselves. Even the "verie monsters . . . of the sea" keep peace within kind:

> Man's life is most fraile of all others, and in least securitie he liveth. . . . All other living creatures live orderly and well, after their owne kind: we see them flocke and gather together. . . . The lyons as fell and savage as they be, fight not one with another: serpents sting not serpents, nor bite one another with their venimous teeth: nay the verie monsters and huge fishes of the sea, warre not amongst themselves in their owne kind: but beleeve me, Man at mans hand receiveth most harme and mischiefe. (153)

63. De Grazia notes that "the play's unusual use of 'accommodations' . . . refer[s] to clothing" (ibid., 23).

Like-kindedness should map a firm domain for kindness. The parameters of kindness as a behavior and a category of being are coextensive—for every other kind than humankind. It is a familiar motif across Renaissance letters, that man is a beast to man: *homo hominis lupus*, but *canis caninam non est*.[64] Gelli's Hare develops the argument that freedom from the endless fear and anxiety typical of human life makes animal estate happier, and to explain this freedom from fear, the Hare explains: "I feare not those of myne owne kinde, as you do, the whiche is sufficiente for me." Within *King Lear*, Albany echoes the fulfilled wish of Gascoigne's hart (that man's "murdryng minde" would be set to work among humans, "with many a bloudy Jarre") and voices this moralism: "Humanity must perforce prey on itself" (4.2.51). Among humans, then, unkindness defines kind, not Pico's "great and wonderful happiness."

When Edgar recounts his strategy at the end of the play, he tells how he

> shift[ed]
> Into a madman's rags, t'assume a semblance
> That very dogs disdained.
> (5.3.190–92)

Yet under the extreme pressure of the storm, "the persecutions of the sky," and "the enmity o' th' air," the idea of kind as the limit of kindness is repeatedly tested. When Kent resists Regan's treatment of him, given his status as the king's agent, he complains: "If I were your father's dog / You should not use me so" (2.2.138). Gloucester rebukes Regan, saying, "If wolves had at thy gate howled that dern [dire] time, / Thou shouldst have said, 'Good porter, turn the key'" (3.7.66–67). And finally Cordelia laments her discovery of what has become of her father:

> Mine enemy's dog,
> Though he had bit me, should have stood that night
> Against my fire.
> (4.7.37–39)

As man's coevolutionary partner, dogs are perennially liminal figures, and we see this when the Fool opines, "Truth's a dog that must to kennel. He

---

64. Instances from Erasmus and Luther appeared in chapter 1. For a discussion of this topos in the history of ideas (focused on Continental materials), see Hutton, *Themes of Peace*, 220–64.

must be whipped out, when the Lady Brach [hound bitch, i.e., flattery] may stand by the fire and stink" (1.4.109–11). But a wolf at the door suggests something very different. Normally wolves indexed almost primal enmity, as creatures who saw the battlefield's dead bodies as edible carrion or who circled city walls for food (as in *Titus Andronicus* when Tamora's body is "throw[n] . . . forth to beasts and birds to prey" [5.3.198]).[65] Thus welcoming a wolf at the gate may serve as the most vigorous possible conception of an enlarged scope for cosmopolitan hospitality, a standard designed to highlight its failures closer to home in the play.

In the jurisdictions of *King Lear*, there will be no such extension of kindness; instead there is "a great abatement of kindness" (1.4.59). At the same time, the humanity that might enjoy the protections of clothing or a roof above its head seems not to deserve it. Clothing serves only to cover faults that deserve to be exposed. As Lear puts it, "Through tattered clothes small vices do appear; / Robes and furred gowns hide all" (4.6.164–65). Thus Cordelia's calls for better clothing (to Kent, she urges, "Be better suited," and of Lear she asks, "Is he arrayed?"), along with her renewal of human disdain for life measured at the level of necessity (where Lear had to "hovel [himself] with swine . . . / In short and musty straw"), serve as limping attempts to restore a normality that the play's workings have cast as human self-delusion (4.7.6, 21, 40–41). From the species-comparative perspective outlined here, when Kent insults Oswald with "nature disclaims in thee" and "a tailor made thee," he speaks not just to one class-presumptuous servant, but comprehensively of humankind as a kind framed on the model of Pliny's man, *nudus in nuda terra* (2.2.55–56). Man's nakedness can be patched over by a tailor. But the "bare earth" that presents a cold shoulder to him—a nature that disclaims and disowns him—poses insoluble problems of belonging. *King Lear* thus not only taxonomizes man, literally, and finds him naked and depraved; it goes further to suggest that man's most exceptional and unique attribute is his cosmic orphanage. In this, the play endorses the vision of Gelli's Oyster that "nature hath set litle store by you, for besides the bringing forth of you naked, she also hath not made you any house or habitation, of your own, wher you mought defend you from thinjuries of the wether as she hath made to us, that which is a plaine token, that you are as rebelles and banished of this

65. For more on the wolf and political law, see chapter 5. For a discussion of wolfishness, see Carla Freccero, "Wolf/Man" (paper presented at the Animals and Humans in the Culture of the Middle Ages and Renaissance Conference, Barnard College, New York, December 2010).

world, having no place here of your owne." Those accounts, by contrast, that aggrandize human status may be condemned as frauds: in the play's zoographic frame of reference, when Lear charges, "They told me I was everything. 'Tis a lie; I am not ague-proof," he speaks for mankind as a whole (4.6.104–5).

In this respect, Shakespeare's play draws extensively on the writings of natural history that had shaped the curricula of the sixteenth century as well as the happy beast tradition that developed from it. Despite early modernity's reputation for an invention of humankind in terms of some new omnicompetence, *King Lear* exposes an abject humanity's underprovisioning in the face of the environment and its moral and intellectual incapacity before the great dramas of self-fashioning Pico had celebrated. When Lear disassembles the human edifice erected by exceptionalist thought, however, he does not register the zootopian hopes of a writer such as Montaigne, who held out an ideal of cross-species community with equanimity and cosmopolitan confidence. Instead, Shakespeare's zoographic critique of man pushes humanness past a leveling mark and into the deficit territory reserved for beasts in modern contexts. This man's embarrassment derives from the habits of descriptive attribution established in encyclopedias of living things. Instead of containing all creaturely capacities in a plenary way, Lear's negative-exceptionalist man is a creature without properties—a natural-historical oxymoron.

King Lear relentlessly voices the bleakest thread of the happy beast tradition. In Pliny's sober words, "Man alone, poore wretch, she hath laid all naked upon the bare earth, . . . to cry and wraule presently from the very first houre that he is borne into this world . . . among so many living creatures, there is none subject to shed teares and weepe like him" (152). As Lear considers man in his own final hours he studies birth, not death, and he voices Pliny's words one more time. "We came crying hither . . . the first time that we smell the air / We wawl and cry," he laments; "when we are born, we cry that we are come / To this great stage of fools" (4.6.178–83). Such a vision—at the heart of this major early modern reflection on the cosmic condition of humanity—suggests the force and currency of zoographic critique, even in a writer not prone to flights of theriophilic fancy. The Mole held the world "to all *other* beastes accommodate," and the Oyster saw in man "the most unhappye creature, that is in all the worlde." *King Lear's* man is a solitarily unhappy beast. He not only lacks a coat to keep him warm. His case is "woorse" than that. Left to "wawl and cry" beneath the "extremity of the skies," he lacks a viable claim on the cosmos by which to make himself at home.

Night-Rule:
The Alternative Politics of the Dark;
or, Empires of the Nonhuman

King Lear suffers a further human predicament beyond enduring rough weather on bare skin. He roams outdoors in the dark, a violation of place-and-time species decorum that the play calls a straying "out of season" (2.1.119). The relevant night rules are calibrated by kind: because human faculties face such adversity in the dark, people belong inside. As we know vividly from *Macbeth*, they should also be flat in bed with their eyes shut. Observing the creaturely decorum of night and day, when Banquo must travel late abroad he says he "must become a borrower of night" (3.1.26). Lady Macbeth fears being caught up too late and detected as a night "watcher" (2.2.70). Mistaking night-borrowed time for some special opportunity, Macbeth imagines darkness will "scarf up the tender eye of pitiful day," but instead the fact that he and Lady Macbeth are awake along with the screaming owl, crying crickets, and a crow making "wing to th' rooky wood" indicts them as unnaturally nocturnal (3.2.46–51, 2.2.15). At night, humans enter a risky domain of sensory deficit, their tender eyes "scarfed up" by a blinding and disorienting absence of light. They wander and err; they get lost; their science—wholly contingent on vision—dims, as errancy turns to crime and error. This chapter contends that with the onset of early modern darkness, human authority itself flickers and falls on its knees. Overthrowing more than just vision, nighttime exposes man's vaunted competencies as intermittent and qualifies his claimed sovereignty as merely episodic—"because the night," to vary Patti Smith's anthemic caw of a refrain, "belongs to *others*."[1]

---

1. Bruce Springsteen and Patti Smith, "Because the Night," 1978 (italics added).

Night's Black Agents, Human Night Blindness

Macbeth treats sunset as a transfer of power, a daily alternation that is ominous but also routine. At dusk the "good things of day begin to droop and drowse, / While night's black agents to their preys do rouse" (3.2.53–54). The drowsing of agencies understood as benign cedes dominion to sinister and adverse actors on a quotidian basis. Day creatures literally "droop" from their upright posture to prostrate unconsciousness, while those who are agentive at night rise up, refreshed and ready to act. From a now-vulnerable human perspective, predation entirely defines the life of "night's black agents." Meanwhile, human senses run amok. In *Henry VI, Part 2*, Bolingbroke glosses "deep night, dark night, the silent of the night" as the domain of nonhuman others: "The time when screech-owls cry, and ban-dogs howl" (1.4.15–17). The self-contradiction of calling night "silent" while filling it with cries and howls of creaturely vocalization reflects not simply anthropocentric reading but also the glitchy unreliability of human perception in the dark. Johan Huizinga's classic evocation of the late medieval "tenor of life" stressed a more absolute and palpable contrast between darkness and light, and period literature records its effects.[2] Indeed, for all the daylight traditions of early modern performance (the "sympathizèd one day's error" from noon to five so marked in *The Comedy of Errors* [5.1.398]), one has a persistent sense of night terrors in Shakespeare's drama. Blindfolding what we have seen Ovid praise as man's "stately looke" and reducing human estate to the trembling condition of quarry, the nightly ascendancy of nonhuman agencies draws the line against exceptionalist accounts of humanity—in the period so often said to be incubating a model of sovereign man for the future.

In the world of *King Lear*, a text replete with indexings of "to-night," "this night," and "such nights as these," wandering humans animate the night as "dark-eyed" and "wild" (2.1.121, 2.4.310).[3] Dark-eyedness figures night's predacious discernment and the uncanny accuracy of nocturnal vision for creatures who work by it, undetected; at the same time, it also suggests the waning operations of human vision as the view fades to black (literally, in Gloucester's case). "Wild" is a relative term, only indicating

---

2. Johan Huizinga, *The Waning of the Middle Ages* (New York: Dover, 1999), 1–2.

3. "To-night" appears five times in *King Lear*; the other phrases appear at 3.1.12 and 3.2.43. *Macbeth* refers to "to-night" ten times; *Romeo and Juliet* fifteen; and *Othello* twenty.

nonassimilation to a given perceiver's paradigm of what is domesticated
or civil. *King Lear*'s night oppresses its human subjects: Gloucester refers to "this tyrannous night," and Kent laments "the tyranny of the open
night" (3.4.149, 3.4.2). The regime of night has a dispositive place in defining natural sequence, of course, as Polonius's assurance in *Hamlet* that
"it must follow as the night the day" makes clear (1.3.79). But the daily
return of a nocturnal order also marks an absolutely regular counterpoint
to the daylight regime familiar—and conformable—to the eyes of human
perspective.

Beyond the misrule, then, that describes the temporary states of disorder licensed by human culture in traditional comedy, Shakespeare
evokes a literally alternative domain: a full-blown nocturnal order that
accords human actors, as such, no proper place. Kent stresses the extremity of Lear's situation by saying that even "things that love night / Love
not such nights as these," calling them "the very wanderers of the dark"
(3.2.42–44). But night agencies are not just a matter for the glooming atmo-
sphere of tragedy: in *A Midsummer Night's Dream*, the night-agent Puck
uses the same phrasing to dub himself a "merry wanderer of the night"
(2.1.43). Shakespeare's tragedy and comedy alike populate night with nonhuman actors. From the human standpoint, night indicates not so much
license (taking a breather from the law) but instead a blinded, debilitating
subjection to another law. The nonhuman empire of the night feels like
lawless and chaotic violence to those humans straying there "out of season," but that experience is simply what the night regime has decreed as
just for humans under nocturnal jurisdiction. The gap between felt justice
to those undergoing it and warranted justice to the agent or entity dispens-
ing it is a perfectly traditional political dilemma.

The night gets notoriously darker if you are caught out in the woods.
Henry Peacham's emblem, titled *Nulli penetrabilis* (penetrable by no one),
shows densely clustered trees, "a shadie wood" whose darkened grove lets
no light through from the moon or stars shining above it (fig. 4.1). The
poem describes the wood's "uncouth pathes, and hidden waies unknowne: /
Resembling CHAOS, or the hideous night"; its "thickest boughes, and in-
most entries are / Not peirceable, to power of any starre."[4] In good em-
blem-book style, the poem suggests we should adopt this impenetrability

4. Henry Peacham, *Minerva Britanna* (London: Walter Dight, 1612), 182. This last
line is taken from Spenser's *Faerie Queene* (1.7.6), and the emblem refers to Statius's
Latin verse, *Nulli penetrabilis astro / Lucus iners* (thick grove, penetrable by no star)
("Thebaid X," lines 85–86).

Figure 4.1. Henry Peacham, *Nulli penetrabilis*, in *Minerva Britanna* (London, 1612). Image by permission of the Folger Shakespeare Library, Washington, DC.

as a self-defensive strategy by which to remain "inward close, unsearch'd with outward eies." As we saw in chapter 3 (fig. 3.4), George Wither's crocodile emblem recommended,

> If, therefore, thou thy *Spoylers*, wilt beguile,
> Thou must be armed, like this *Crocodile*;
> Ev'n with such nat'rall *Armour* (ev'ry day)
> As no man can bestowe or take away.

Peacham's remedy for "open-hearted . . . weakenes" likewise urges human self-armament with an integrity borrowed from a nonhuman model that ordinarily terrifies us: the "hideous" night.[5]

Classifying human subjective experience at night as *disturbed* (literally out of its orbit or, in the terms explored in chapter 2, "off course"),

5. Peacham, *Minerva Britanna*, 182.

Thomas Nashe's *Terrors of the Night, Or A Discourse of Apparitions* (1594)
presents itself as an explanation of the humoral distempers underlying
dreams. But it also makes an acerbic contribution to the literary tradition anatomizing human folly. Like Peacham's emblem, its commentary
on the fate of humans at large in a night regime imagines a free fall into
chaos. Nashe invokes the "desolate horrour . . . when Night in her rustie
dungeon hath imprisoned our ey-sight" and calls night "this cursed raven" who "pecks out mens eyes."[6] Assessing the "unconstant glimmering
of our eies" (here the properties of the eyes waver as much as the ambi-
ent light they need), Nashe laments how "our reason . . . yeelds up our
intellective apprehension to be mocked and troden under foote," which
he attributes to "our senses defect and abuse, that those organicall parts
which to the minde are ordained embassadours, doo not their message as
they ought, but by some misdiet or misgovernment being distempered,
faile in their report" (C2r, C3r). Calling even unassisted sight a "glass,"
Nashe compares "the glasses of our sight (in the night)" to "prospective
glasses . . . which represented the images of things farre greater than they
were; each moate in the darke they make a monster, and everie sleight
glimmering a giant" (F4v). (Here "assisted" vision suggests more distortion than enhanced access to truth.) If sight fails, reason stumbles, falls to
the ground, and gets "troden under foote." Consistent with his metaphor
invoking the police power of imprisonment, Nashe's vision of nocturnal

6. Thomas Nashe, *The Terrors of the Night, Or A Discourse of Apparitions* (London:
John Danter, 1594), sigs. B1v, B2r (subsequent references appear in the text). Nashe's
text appears as a parodic counterpart to George Chapman's strained piece of esoterica,
The Shadow of Night—sometimes taken to express the views of a group of intellectuals
surrounding Walter Raleigh, dubbed later "the School of Night" (from Shakespeare's
spoof of such elite preoccupations, *Love's Labours Lost* [4.3.250]). The classic treatment proposing this is M. C. Bradbrook's *The School of Night: A Study in the Literary
Relations of Sir Walter Ralegh* (Cambridge: Cambridge University Press, 1936); the
counterargument appears in Ernst Strathmann, *Sir Walter Ralegh: A Study in Elizabethan Skepticism* (New York: Columbia University Press, 1951). Though this group is
unlikely to have been very formal, Raleigh's associates did include investigators into
abstruse mathematics and new doctrines in astronomy, and period documents include
a motivated Jesuit's allegation that Raleigh headed a "school of atheism" (see Raleigh
Trevelyan, *Sir Walter Raleigh* [New York: Macmillan, 2002], 191). Instead of stressing
the disabling effects of darkness on humans, Chapman's Neoplatonist verse celebrates
human intellectual capacity by embracing a melancholic vision of nocturnal inspi-
ration: "No pen can any thing eternall wright / That is not steept in humour of the
Night." *The Shadow of Night: containing two poeticall hymnes* (London: Richard Field,
1594).

agencies casts night in political terms as a dominion by other kinds. His main night minister is the devil, who enjoys a "nightly kingdome of darknes" as his "peculiar segniorie" (B1v–B2r). He also makes early mention of the "Robbin-good-fellowes, Elfes, Fairies, [and] Hobgoblins of our latter age" who do "most of their merry prankes in the Night" (B2v). In terms of nonhuman animals, a similar order of creatures as those populating *Lear* or *Macbeth* appears, and Nashe accords these nocturnal denizens a power to hold men in awe.

Nashe includes among his tales of "night terrors" a world-upside-down account of people "pursued by wesels and rats, and oftentimes with squirrels and hares" (H1r), harmless creatures terrifying to night-blind man. At night, "a cricket or a raven [can] keepe him fortie times in more awe than God or the Divell" (D1r). Should faith waver, Nashe contends, "me thinkes those dolefull Querristers of the night, the Scritch-owle, the Nightingale and croking Frogs, might over-awe us from anie insolent transgression at that time" (H3r). "Awe" and "overawe" suggest the spectacular coercive force of sovereignty to police "transgression" ("fortie times . . . more . . . than God"). The power of the frog reminds us that "we are but slyme & mud," and the nightingale "puts us in minde of the end and punishment of lust"—both traditionally emblematic warnings. But the screech owl suggests a more intersubjective impact when Nashe refers to "her lavish blabbing of forbidden secrets" (H3r). She operates as a kind of hostile witness. For Shakespeare, who frequently mentions the owl, night's great bird serves as a messenger. *Venus and Adonis* tells how "the owl, night's herald, shrieks, 'Tis very late'" (stanza 87), and Lady Macbeth, associating sleep and death, calls it "the fatal bellman, / Which gives the stern'st goodnight" (2.2.3–4). In each case the owl enforces creaturely decorum and admonishes humankind to withdraw its forces. A song in *Love's Labors Lost* makes a refrain of the "staring owl" (5.2.906, 915), and even Titania commands some of her attendants to

> keep back
> The clamorous owl that nightly hoots and wonders
> At our quaint spirits.
> (*Midsummer*, 2.2.6–7)

The owl watches and wonders, and it sets off a clamorous report; it is an agent, a spy, even a kind of moral arbiter. As we will see, night creatures threaten not only as potential predators but also as witnesses against straying humans by means of superior nocturnal skill. They see Virginia

Woolf's "spot the size of a shilling" on the back of man's head, and the early modern spot is both a technical blind spot and a moral blemish.[7]

Amid the snatching thorns and midnight briars of *A Midsummer Night's Dream*, a host of nonhumans enact and enforce what Oberon heralds as "night-rule," hailing Puck with "how now, mad spirit! / What night-rule now about this haunted grove?" (3.2.4–5).[8] For *Midsummer* (as for early modern texts generally), the census of the night arrays fantastical and actual creatures alike in its constellation of nocturnal agency. Night citizens range from those fairy royals "of no common rate" to Puck, a "lob of spirits," and from Titania's mixed order of servants (Peaseblossom, Mustardseed, Cobweb, and Moth) to whatever "vile thing" she might wake to see, "Be it ounce, or cat, or bear, / Pard, or boar with bristled hair" (3.1.148, 2.1.16, 2.2.40, 36–37). From the "ghosts . . . troop[ing] home to churchyards" before dawn to "spotted snakes," "thorny hedgehogs," "weaving spiders," "beetles black," worms, snails, and the "clamorous owl that nightly hoots," the sheer diversity of the enrolled creatures of the night mark the play's sustained attention to nonhumanity (3.2.381–82, 2.2.6–23 passim). In yet another expression giving the night dark eyes, all of these night agents "consort with black-brow'd night" (3.2.387). Thus the play makes more of nighttime than just the catalyst for identity confusion—among humans—to which an infinity of college essays on moonlight and *Midsummer* attest.

Midsummer's night enacts the acute diminution of human powers as such, both sensory and political. By this comparatist sensibility, the play engages in the zoographic mode of critique outlined in chapter 3, and in this context, as we will see, it actually goes further and enforces human identity *as a constraint*. Even Theseus, the spokesperson of rational authority and civil order in the play, must be reconsidered in this light because *Midsummer*'s night sets sharp jurisdictional limits on the human institutions he represents. When Hermia concedes,

> Never so weary, never so in woe,
> Bedabbled with the dew and torn with briers,
> I can no further crawl, no further go,

---

7. Virginia Woolf, *A Room of One's Own*, ed. Susan Gubar (New York: Houghton Mifflin Harcourt, 2005 [1929]), 89.

8. The first published edition of the play (1600) conjoins the words as "nightrule." The hyphen appears in the second quarto (published in 1619, but dated 1600), which the First Folio follows. *A Midsommer nights dreame* (London: James Roberts, 1600 [1619]), sig. D2v.

she has been reduced from the much-celebrated human privilege of bipedal uprightness to going on "all fours" in an agency crisis in which she then loses the locomotive power of her will. Shorn of self-moving autonomy, she curls up to wait until daylight rule resumes: "My legs can keep no pace with my desires. / Here will I rest me till the break of day" (3.2.442–45). At dawn she can anticipate the withdrawal of night's forces and the restoration of orthodox relations—among humans, that is, and with the firm caveat that they retire to bed on time when night inevitably returns. Too exclusive a focus on the promise of a flourishing human "kind" in Theseus's closing lines obscures his observance of a transition in authority and his acceptance of the ongoing terms that require human confinement or withdrawal on a nightly basis. "Sweet friends, to bed" (5.1.363) gestures not only to sexual reproduction but to the dormancies of sleep.

   Midsummer's night setting thus alters the problem of resort beyond "the *peril* of the Athenian law" (4.1.152; italics added), intensifying it as a literal wandering in the dark without the protections human sovereignty is supposed to provide. To enter "a shadie wood," in Peacham's words, "resembling chaos, or the hideous night," means switching between two perils. As Athenian power extends only to the city limits, so human authority finds the edge of its reach. Instead of a territorial horizon, though, we find a temporal one: human jurisdiction coincides, more or less, with daylight. The fact that Athenians stand for humanity in the play recalls the association of Athens with human pretensions to reason and philosophy evident in Gelli's *La Circe* and in *King Lear*. What I hope to add to the familiar topographies of *Midsummer*, then, is an attention to questions of kind—more specifically, to the diverse capacities distributed across those different kinds. Thus instead of stressing the openly illusionistic, Ovidian transformation of Bottom into an ass and the entire rich field of metamorphosis, *poesis*, and (human) makerly power it suggests, this chapter considers the play's representations of the agentive capacities of nonhuman actors—and the cosmopolitical ramifications of its taking note of them.[9] How does nighttime enfranchise nonhumans? What are the impli-

9. For a superb recent account of this metamorphic generativity across categories of being or kind in the play (and of the play as representative of the challenges posed by theater as a creative engine within Elizabethan culture), see Henry Turner, *Shakespeare's Double Helix* (London: Continuum, 2007). Turner argues that the play likens theater to a laboratory and poesy to experimental science and so provokes "a radical re-questioning of . . . humanism and the categories of life upon which it depended by splicing across as many categories as possible: human and inhuman, natural and artificial, male and female, small and large, organic and inorganic" (98, 102). Within

cations of the daily alternation of night and day not only for human laws
but for cosmic claims about human political tenure itself? If we attend
to the night-and-day jurisdictional implications posed by the play's cast
of nonhuman/nocturnal creatures, how do they qualify "the human" and
the omnicompetence said to be developing for that species in period discourses? Perhaps nighttime in tragic contexts tends to resonate more at-
mospherically and emblematically; as Nashe points out, "When anie Poet
would describe a horrible Tragicall accident[,] to adde the more probabilitie
& credence unto it, he dismally beginneth to tell, how it was darke night
when it was done, and cheerfull daylight had quite abandoned the firmament" (H2v). *Midsummer*'s engagement of night rule, though, specifically
brings it into the orbit of traditional comic concerns about the jurisdictional scope and mandate of (human) civil order.

    Whether as the "rule" accorded to man in Genesis 1, or as Adam's abil-
ity to name the animals, or as the mastery over nature then twinkling in
the assisted eyes of technoscience, human authority depends on claims to
cognitive and political preeminence. This is not a question whether the design of an authoritative man can "withstand the light of day," as our sight-
oriented, very human proverb for testing truth asks. What *Midsummer*
suggests instead is that concepts of humanity and its competencies radically depend on time of day; we might even call them figments of daylight.
Early modern human sovereignty, in other words, unravels in the jurisdictions of the night, when we hold neither cognitive nor political empire.
The enterprises of experimental science and the Enlightenment respond
to perceptions of this specifically human sensory shortfall—a weakness in
whose description scientific and long-standing Christian notions substantially overlap.[10] Because both traditions largely assert human dominion
over creation, both necessarily contend with the dangerous weakness that

---

this larger field of a general or universal hybridity, my situation of the play considers its
capture of a stance from which human "powers" (including poetic, or makerly, power)
are circumscribed *as human*—rather than celebrated *as powers*. In this sense, the play's
zoographic or comparative dimension keeps notions of the specifically human alive
for critique (demonstrating its relation to a larger folly or *vanitas* tradition that looks
askance at human claims).

    10. For an account of early modern understandings of the Fall as the historical
collapse of a prior, perfect form of human cognition and of seventeenth-century science
as an explicit effort to redeem humankind from the cognitive weakness of this fallen
state, see Peter Harrison, *The Fall of Man and the Foundations of Science* (Cambridge:
Cambridge University Press, 2007). This general argument—and a more focused concern for its consequences—first appeared in Carolyn Merchant's groundbreaking *The*

human limits inject into the project. Night subjects human ambitions for rule to the stern disciplines of a circadian rhythm.

This chapter, then, first explores what species considerations have to do with the analyses of cognition and sensation at the heart of two major treatments of doubt and human knowledge in early modernity: Montaigne's "Apologie for Raymond Sebond" and Descartes's *Discourse on Method*.[11] In a larger relay from sixteenth-century skepticism (especially Montaigne's grasp of it as an ethical administration of doubt in light of traditional attributions of "vanity" to human knowledge) to the method-oriented protocols of seventeenth-century science, the workings of cross-species comparison change drastically. For both Montaigne and Descartes, a way of understanding embodied differences among kinds supplies a crucial substrate of analysis. How they handle embodiment, however, sets in motion divergent approaches to nonhuman subjective experience and investment in the world. These opposing treatments of species then underwrite adverse conclusions about human epistemological certainty. Montaigne's "Apologie" deliberatively embraces the distinctness of animal perception and subjectivity as a compelling likelihood that requires us to accept the incompleteness of human perception and so asks us to see claims for human cognitive authority as false. Contrarily, Descartes's *Discourse* dismisses the prospect of nonhuman subjectivity as a kind of heresy against a new orthodoxy that will affirm freestanding human sufficiency to determine truths.

Despite recurring commonplaces about the unreasonableness of "brutes," as we have seen, a variegated spectrum of psychic possibilities readily appeared for beasts, despite the bar later set so forcefully against nonhuman thought in the *Discourse*. Descartes's incoherent trial logic concerning animal capacities (affirming that they can have no thoughts because they have failed to convey them to us) represents not just the ethico-political intervention already considered in the introduction but also a refusal to entertain the classic epistemological problem of "other minds" methodologically. Descartes's antidote to skeptical doubt in general thus also cancels a former power that cross-species comparisons had to qualify human claims, a power vividly on display in Gelli's *La Circe* and wielded

---

Death of Nature: Women, Ecology, and the Scientific Revolution (San Francisco: Harper and Row, 1980).

11. Skepticism takes many shapes; here I explore Montaigne's attempt to derive ethical imperatives responsive to unresolvable doubt. By knowledge, I refer to *scientia*'s historical arc as an *art* of knowing that will become a "method" with Descartes.

also by Montaigne. Although some aspects of this debate are familiar (especially on the Cartesian side), attention to the argumentative details will suggest how pointed the exchange on human fallibility is between these writers—and just how much distinct ideas about species inform it. Returning briefly to the deficiencies of human sensation that night's "rustie dungeon" makes evident, this part of the chapter ends by considering how Descartes and Montaigne handle human blindness and thinking in the dark.

With the species dimensions of the Montaigne/Descartes dispute over knowledge as background, the chapter turns to William Baldwin's nocturnal thriller, *Beware the Cat* (composed around 1553 and published in 1570). *Beware the Cat* describes an epistemological "experiment" played out in the vocabularies of natural history and with the paraphernalia of quasi-medical remedies for human sensory limits. The "experiment" involves the elaborate concoction of mind-altering substances and prosthetic devices that radically enhance limping human faculties. This sensory supplement enables the cognitively assisted user to take in riveting scenes of the nightlife of cats—scenes that, in turn, demonstrate a feline empire extending from London rooftops to Ireland and beyond. The chapter ends by returning to *A Midsummer Night's Dream* (from the nonhuman and nocturnal perspective it conjures) to suggest the stakes of Shakespeare's own qualifying approach to the pretensions of humanity and his imagining of divergent sovereignties when he makes night an alternative, nonhuman empire. Perhaps the most consequential doubt later dispelled by Cartesianism is humankind's ethical and epistemological doubt about itself. But if the Enlightenment sunsets this particular vantage point for the critique of things human, it has only followed "as the night the day" that in a brave new world we would doubt it again, as modern biopower and its erosion of the discourse of rights, on the one hand, and nanotechnology and genetic informatics, on the other, stand a superseded model of "the human" on its once-vaunted head.

Contingencies of Kind: "Who Knowes?"

When Montaigne's "Apologie" and Descartes's *Discourse* take on certitude in human knowledge, they make certain inquiries and assumptions about the proper proceeding in any trial of truth. Embedded in this inquiry we find a far-reaching problem about what and when we are willing to *suppose*. Sixty-odd years separate the two writers, and their differences on the prospect of human certainty index an extraordinary transition in

European cosmography.[12] Montaigne reckons human certitude impossible. Descartes outlines a protocol for validating it, a protocol that he further proposes to be universal among humans: "The power of judging well and of distinguishing the true from the false . . . is naturally equal in all men."[13] Montaigne was known for avowing that the differences among men could be greater than the difference between certain men and certain beasts), and Descartes specifically refutes Montaigne on this point: "Montaigne and Charron have said that there is more difference between man and man than between man and beast."[14] Descartes supports instead a wholly human grid of reference. Of reason, he asserts that because "it alone makes us men and distinguishes us from beasts, I prefer to believe that it exists whole and entire in each of us, and . . . that there are differences of degree only between accidents, but not at all between forms or natures of individuals of the same species" (2). The consequences for the grid of political and cross-creaturely reference are vast: either man and animals can be compared in one capacious table, or they must be divided as irreducibly different. We have already seen Bruno Latour describe this sever-

12. Counterimagining a modernity if Montaigne, rather than Descartes, had set the terms for it, Stephen Toulmin's bracing account considers this historical passage as a decline, a fall from open-mindedness into a regime of rationality he usefully characterizes as rigidly abstract and insistently grid oriented in its visions and desires. See *Cosmopolis: The Hidden Agenda of Modernity* (Chicago: University of Chicago Press, 1990). For a reading that contextualizes and scrutinizes Descartes's thought for its internal resistances and caveats to subjective individualism (while acknowledging the cultural impact of a blunter reading among "people in the western street"), see Timothy Reiss, *Mirages of the Selfe: Patterns of Personhood in Ancient and Early Modern Europe* (Stanford, CA: Stanford University Press, 2003), 469–87. Reiss calls the *cogito* a "passage technique" rather than a doctrine as such (470). I am grateful to Julian Yates for this reference.

13. René Descartes, *The Discourse on Method*, trans. Donald Cress (Indianapolis: Hackett, 1998 [1637]), 1. Subsequent page references appear in the text. See also Valerie Traub, "The Nature of Norms in Early Modern England: Anatomy, Cartography, *King Lear*," *South Central Review* 26, nos. 1 and 2 (2009): 42–81.

14. Michel de Montaigne, "The Apologie for Raymond Sebond," in *The Essayes of Montaigne: John Florio's Translation*, ed. J. I. M. Stewart (New York: Modern Library, 1934), 412; subsequent page references appear in the text. René Descartes, "Letter to the Marquess of Newcastle" (23 November 1646), in *Philosophical Essays and Correspondence*, ed. Roger Ariew (Indianapolis: Hackett, 2000), 276. Pierre Charron was a friend and follower of Montaigne, narrowing the essayist's own Pyrrhonian motto, *Que sçay-je?* (discussed below) into the firmer, quasi-academic skepticism of *Je ne sçay* in his *De la sagesse* [Of wisdom] (Bordeaux, France: Simone Millanges, 1601).

ance at the heart of the modern constitution, with science as the place for
objects and politics as the domain of subjects.[15]

Montaigne condemns how man "selecteth and separateth himselfe
from out the ranke of other creatures . . . his fellow-brethren and compeers" (399), calling it "foolish-hardiness and self-presuming obstinacie"
to "sequester our selves from their condition and societie" (432). As we
have seen in the introduction, he uses spectacularly cosmopolitical language to bring man back among "the generall throng" (406) and imagines
a collaborative community of knowledge. In contrast, Descartes proposes
perhaps the most severely consequential formulation of an ontological barrier between human and animal ever to have been conceived. Comparative examination of the prudence of their arguments raises more questions
than it answers. If strictures against non sequitur reasoning and unargued
assertion hold sway, by standards of persuasive demonstration Montaigne
makes the better case. Yet his essay is barely known, while the Cartesian
motto "I think therefore I am" has proved to be staggeringly durable. In
terms of the pivotal importance of animals to both essays (not to mention
the dramatic consequences of this debate about animal life for animals),
what we can say is that the Cartesian beast-machine doctrine served human convenience and desires for certitude well—though it failed to serve
"science" in the neutral sense of an inquiry into horizons for truth concerning nonhuman mental phenomena.

Montaigne announces his goal ("my purpose is to crush, and trample
. . . this humane pride and fiercenesse under foot, to make them feele the
emptinesse, vacuitie, and no worth of man"), scouring a human perspective from his language by using the third person to refer to it (395). Toward
the end of his long inquiry, he makes it clear he responds to the unwar-
ranted grandiosity of the claims of human knowledge when he concludes
that "the senses . . . are our maisters . . . , [that] science begins by them and
in them is resolved . . . , [that they] are the beginning and end of humane
knowledge," and that therefore "the uncertaintie of our senses yeelds what
ever they produce, also uncertain" (531, 545). In this entirely anti-Cartesian
perspective, the "silly weapons of reason" (395) cannot overcome the sensory vagaries on which they depend. Montaigne instead asserts that there
is no defensible distinction between what we call "senses" and "reason."
Human knowledge is unremittingly corporeal; human reason is a sublu-

15. Bruno Latour, *We Have Never Been Modern* (Cambridge, MA: Harvard University Press, 1993), 27–29.

nary, worldly art, subject to all the infirmities of matter. This Montaigne calls an "extreame difficultie" (534), but he accepts and even relishes this aspect of human estate. There is, in other words, no worldly end run around the mediating force of the particular and limited perceptual set supplied by the human senses.

Descartes lists the very diversities of opinion Montaigne had invoked to prove the limits of human knowledge as a justification to rid himself of all the existing prejudices composed by others and start afresh. He outlines a technique for "conducting one's reason well and . . . seeking truth in the sciences" (1). He argues that whether in contexts of philosophy or human customs "there is nothing . . . about which there is not some dispute, and consequently nothing that is not doubtful"; he concludes that "considering how many opinions there can be about the very same matter . . . without there ever being the possibility of more than one opinion being true, I deemed everything that was merely probable to be well-nigh false" (5). Indeed, the "mere fact of the diversity that exists" among human opinions, customs, and institutions "suffices to assure one" of their "imperfections" (8). Against the backdrop of a radical doubt that holds everything in suspense, Descartes elaborates self-reflexive rules he deems sufficient to govern his proceeding; "the first was never to accept anything as true that I did not plainly know to be such" (11). The demotion of the "merely probable," of course, will have consequences for thinking across kinds, because the subjective experience of others, as such, cannot be "plainly" known without mediation, inference, or imagination.

By the standard of the plainly known, "I think, therefore I am" presents itself, famously, as the limit point for doubt. In this context, what was "well-nigh false" becomes absolutely so: Descartes rejects "as absolutely false everything in which I could imagine the least doubt." He states, "But immediately afterward I noticed that . . . it necessarily had to be the case that I, who was thinking this, was something. And noticing that this truth—*I think, therefore I am*—was so firm and so assured that all the most extravagant suppositions of the skeptics were incapable of shaking it, I judged that I could accept it without scruple" (18; italics in original). By putting the world in doubt, a confirmable self arises: "From the fact that I thought of doubting the truth of other things, it followed *very evidently and very certainly* that I existed" (18; italics added). Against Montaigne, Descartes asserts the radical incorporeality of knowledge: "I could pretend that I had no body and that there was no world nor any place where I was[;] I could not pretend, on that account, that I did not exist at all" (18). Mind-

body dualism flows directly: "I knew that I was a substance the whole essence or nature of which is simply to think, and which, in order to exist,
has no need of any place nor depends on any material thing. Thus this 'I,'
that is to say, the soul through which I am what I am, is entirely distinct
from the body and is *even easier to know* than the body, and even if there
were no body at all, it would not cease to be all that it is" (19; italics added).
Where Montaigne found "extreame difficultie," Descartes suggests a relatively easy path. Leaving the "extravagant suppositions of the skeptics"
behind "without scruple," Descartes's own scheme of suppositions radi-
ates from this literally *ego*-anchored center. From the beachhead on truth
that the self provides, he writes, "I considered in general what is needed for
a proposition to be true and certain, for since I had just found one of them
that I knew to be such, I thought I ought to know in what this certitude
consists" (19). By these suppositional means, Descartes posits a domain of
reason exempt from the vagaries of sense impressions. Those who imagine
"it is difficult to know this" suffer from a failure to "lift their minds above
sensible things," and Descartes specifically includes among these failed
thinkers anyone who subscribes to Montaigne's account of the senses. He
refers to this account as the "maxim in the schools that there is nothing
in the understanding that has not first been in the senses," and he refutes
this maxim by asserting, "It is nevertheless certain that the ideas of God
and the soul have never been" in the senses at all (21). The body and its
sensory limits disposed of, Descartes advances his argument confidently.
As he had previously opined, "Since God has given each of us some light
to distinguish the true from the false, I would not have believed I ought
to rest content for a single moment with the opinions of others" (16). One
knows truth when one apprehends it by the lights of (God-given) reason.

Montaigne draws on ancient and Christian traditions that deemed human knowledge vain in the absence of divine insight or grace, while Descartes charts a method that, though technically orthodox, renders God
vestigial to the scheme. But in addition to this theological distinction, between them we see a further change concerning what makes a fair inference across the epistemological gap of species difference—a change
with both ethical and methodological dimensions. Where considerations
of probability govern in an environment of doubt, Montaigne's sharp an-
tihuman exceptionalism supposes the existence of other minds. In contrast, under the protocols he charts as foundational to human certainty,
Descartes affirms absolutely the nonexistence of nonhuman minds. Both
make animals a critical resource, but for Montaigne beasts give evidence
against man's epistemological presumption, while in Descartes's account,

as we have seen, they appear only to testify against themselves—in a trial procedure that defines them in advance as mute, as we have seen in the introduction.

Descartes's denial of animal subjective states still indelibly marks conventional vocabularies positing "the human/animal divide" in the humanities and philosophy, though its terms lack the same force where scientific research on animals aims to discover *how* to apprehend the array of their nonobvious capacities.[16] When Descartes proceeds to entertain a more elaborate supposition than the earlier claim that he could easily and successfully "pretend" that he "had no body" (18), animals enter the picture. He imagines what would result if God had "formed the body of a man exactly like one of ours . . . *without putting into it, at the start, any rational soul*" (26; italics added). This virtual scientific experiment on hypothetical data transpires inside the mental laboratory of Descartes's thinking "I" (19). He reports that "on examining the functions" of this hypothetical body, his virtual anatomy finds "precisely all those things that can be in us without our thinking about them"—the involuntary impulses to growth, movement, and sensation that had traditionally been allocated to Aristotle's vegetative and sensitive souls (26). Here, Descartes conjures beasts to perform their binary burden as necessary counterpoints to human mindedness and to exemplify what no-mind is (in the Western sense of that idea). He glosses the set of functions found "in" the hypothetical but examinable body as matching "all the same features in which one can say that animals lacking reason resemble us" (26).[17] Embedding the assumption that animals lack reason violates Descartes's stated method of rejecting as false or prejudicial hearsay whatever cannot be known plainly and directly.[18] As we have seen, the cognitive bubble of *cogito ergo sum*

16. A random glance at any Science Times section of the *New York Times* shows that emerging research continually resets the horizon of our suppositions about animal faculties.

17. In *La Circe*, Gelli gives this exact idea some dramatic irony by putting it into the mouth of the unteachably human Ulysses, who answers the elephant's question about why, if human capacities are so superior, there is so much vice and error among them. As discussed in chapter 3, Ulysses's blame shifting allots all human failures to the animal part in us, faulting "those partes of nature: that we have without reason, together and in common with you: and not those by which we are men" ("The tenth Dialogue," in Giovanni Battista Gelli, *Circes of John Baptista Gello, Florentine*, trans. Henry Iden [London, 1557–58]).

18. Descartes calls notions in favor of an animal mind a childhood bias: "To no prejudice are we all more habituated than that which has persuaded us from earliest

by definition can offer no "plain" or "direct" way to know anything about
animal minds. Nor can it provide a hand-, foot-, tooth-, or claw-hold by
which the question of other minds (human or animal) or their capacities
(whether alike or different) might be entertained.[19]

Mind/body dualism, riding in on this assumption about an absolute
difference between man and beast, defines only human estate: the body
that constitutes just half of this uniquely hybrid human equals the un-
mixed entirety of nonhuman animal life. The human bodily vehicle and
the integral animal alike are governed solely by sensory data and instinc-
tual programming or what Descartes repeatedly terms "the disposition of
their organs" (26, 32). By the "addition" of an immortal soul that Descartes
supposes, divine authority backs the attribution of reason to humankind.
Pressed by the Cambridge Platonist Henry More, Descartes would clarify
that he did not deny animals sensation.[20] Rather, his doctrine exiles sensation from the picture of what constitutes mind, cogitation, thought, and
soul and, by making animals all body and no mind, excludes them from
participation in knowledge of the world. Descartes's project instead promotes the radical sufficiency of an exclusively human perspective.

Montaigne rebuts in advance many of the methodological details central to Descartes's proceeding. The refrain of the "Apologie"—"How do I
know?"—adapts its interrogative from the Greek skeptic Sextus Empiricus, whose *Outlines of Pyrrhonism* greatly influenced the *Essais*.[21] But
Montaigne also phrases his question in another way, one that acknowledges and incorporates the epistemological problem of other minds, ask-

---

childhood that living animals think." "Letter to Henry More" (5 February 1649), in Leonora Cohen, "Descartes and Henry More on the Beast-Machine: A Translation of Their
Correspondence," *Annals of Science* 1, no. 1 (1936): 51.

19. Cartesian method exemplifies what Agamben characterizes as a human maneu-
ver: the substitution of one creature's limited *umwelt* (our own) for an objective world
or *umgebung*. Giorgio Agamben, *The Open: Man and Animal* (Stanford, CA: Stanford
University Press, 2004 [2002]), 40 (discussing twentieth-century biologist Jakob von
Uexküll's distinctions).

20. Descartes, "Letter to Henry More," 53.

21. See Ann Hartle, "Montaigne and Skepticism," in *The Cambridge Companion to
Montaigne*, ed. Ullrich Langer (Cambridge: Cambridge University Press, 2005), 183–206,
and Luciano Floridi, *Sextus Empiricus: The Transmission and Recovery of Pyrrhonism*
(Oxford: Oxford University Press, 2002), 48. In a discussion of the politics of skepticism, John Laursen refers to Montaigne's "politics of human fallibility," a phrase that
dovetails with the cosmopolitical frames at issue in this book (John Christian Laursen,
The Politics of Skepticism in the Ancients, Montaigne, Hume, and Kant [Leiden, Netherlands: Brill, 1992], 94).

ing, "*Who* knowes?" This is not simply a matter of deciding among variant human opinions (wise or ignorant, young or old, blind or sighted, awake or dreaming, sick or healthy, French or German—all variables he details). It concerns thinking about thinking across species. Posed across kinds, "Who knowes?" complicates the question "How do I know?" because the idea that other creatures know by different means makes visible the possibility that human means might be inadequate and the probability that human means yield only a partial and even provincial vision of the world. "When I am playing with my Cat," Montaigne muses (in the passage discussed in chapter 2), "*who knowes* whether she have more sport in dallying with me, than I have in gaming with her? . . . If I have my houre to begin or to refuse, so hath she hers" (399; italics added). Montaigne widens the horizon for divergences of subjective experience and investment. Quarreling in advance with the way Descartes draws his conclusions, he asks pointedly methodological questions: "How knoweth [man] by the vertue of his understanding the inward and secret motions of beasts? By what comparison from them to us doth he conclude the brutishnesse, he ascribeth unto them?" (399). Questioning the how of human knowledge and judging its comparative practices, analogical failures, and prejudicial leaps, Montaigne pressures the legitimacy of human reason and its habitual conclusions.

Considering the "excellency beasts have over us" in many of "their workes" (the order of bees, the judgment of swallows, the spider's design— all examples drawn from the natural history tradition), he asks whether human reference of animal abilities to the programmings of instinct is logical or equitable. Because we see that "even in our grosest workes . . . our minde employeth the uttermost of her skill and forces . . . why should we not thinke as much of them? Wherefore doe we attribute the workes, which excell what ever we can performe, either by nature or by art, unto a kinde of unknowne, naturall, and servile inclination?" (402). Montaigne directly challenges the intellectual and methodological warrants for Descartes's proposition that "the fact that [animals] do something better than we do does not prove they have any intelligence . . . but rather it proves that they have no intelligence at all, and that it is nature that acts in them" just like a "clock composed exclusively of wheels and springs" (33).[22] At stake is not only the measure of a fair proof but also the intersub-

---

22. Nashe's earlier vision of clockwork was less sanguine about its perfections. He likens the melancholy brain to "a clocke tyde downe with too heavie weights or plummets; which as it cannot chuse but monstrously goe a square, or not goe at all: so must

jective presumptions we set about it, including who bears its burden in a controversy *between minds.*

Montaigne calls for an ethical administration of interpretation in the contexts of uncertainty. He questions the fundamental rationality of human denials of "deliberation, fore-thought, and conclusion" or "knowledge, consent, or discourse" on behalf of other creatures in the absence of certain knowledge; "why say wee not *likewise* that that is science, and prudence in them?" (402, 415, 409; italics added). Likelihood, he argues, runs in their favor. "There is no *likelyhood* . . . the beasts doe the very same things by a naturall inclination and forced genuitie, which we doe of our owne freewill and industrie." Instead, employing a more reviewable structure of inference and conclusion than Descartes later would use and insisting that our conclusions must heel to the constraints of probability, he urges, "*Of the very same effects we must conclude alike faculties;* and by the richest effects infer the noblest faculties, and consequently acknowledge, that the same discourse and way, we hold of working, the very same, or perhaps some other better, do beasts hold" (406–7; italics added). Indeed, in the expansive revisions of the *Essais,* both "and by the richest effects infer the noblest faculties" and that last rigorous supposition—"or perhaps some other better"—were insertions in the 1595 edition that escalated Montaigne's 1576 point about fair reasoning.[23] His commentary, like Descartes's, concerns a "method of seeking truth" and a protocol for good inferences, but he requires that species be understood as deeply coloring such truths as are perceived.

Montaigne refuses to privilege a human perspective ideologically. But what is also critically important is that Montaigne constantly questions what makes a good inference methodologically. Entering the arena of comparative sensation, he states that his "first consideration" is to question "whether man be provided with all naturall senses, or no" (532). Given his observation (concurring with Plutarch and Gelli) that diverse creatures "live an *entire and perfect* life, some without sight, and some without

---

our braines of necessitie be either monstrously distracted, or utterly destroyed thereby" (*Terrors of the Night,* C3r). While Descartes's image of bodies, and therefore of animals as such, as clocks and robots imagined mechanical functioning as perfect invariability, Nashe's clock-brain suffers "monstrous" disorders—of a perfectly humoral kind.

23. This posthumous edition was edited by Montaigne's *fille d'alliance,* Marie de Gournay, based on the handwritten markup of the *Essais* he left at his death. The additions read, "Et de plus riches effects des facultez plus riches" and "ou quelqu'autre meilleure." *Les essais de Michel de Montaigne: Édition conforme au texte de l'exemplaire de Bordeaux,* ed. Pierre Villey (Lausanne, Switzerland: La Guilde du Livre, 1965 [1924]), 460nn5, 8.

hearing," he asks again, "*Who knoweth* whether we also want either one, two, three, or many senses more? . . . If we want any one, our discourse cannot discover the want or defect thereof" (532; italics added). "Perfection" and completeness normally register the higher developmental attainment attributed to males over "defective" females and humans over lower-order creatures in Aristotelian biology. Montaigne's rhetorical intervention, to give animals the benefit of the force of the concept, scatters the traditional hierarchy, in Puck's words, like "choughs . . . rising and cawing at the gun's report" (3.2.21).

Sight, smell, and taste are not commensurate among humans or consistent over time for one person; from asking what a plenary set of senses might include, Montaigne launches a cross-species consideration of just those senses of which we are aware. Because perception of color was said to vary among humans, especially under circumstances of jaundice or a blood condition said to redden the viewed world, "What know we whether [those humours] are predominant and ordinarie in beasts?" (541). If you squint, he argues, objects "seeme longer and outstretched"—"many beasts have their eye as winking" as this, and that may mean that "this length is then happily the true forme of that [observed] body" (541). Noting that the properties of sound are affected if the normal passages of our hearing are disturbed or blocked, he concludes, "Such beasts as have hairie eares, or that in lieu of an eare have but a little hole, doe not by consequence heare that we heare" (542). Even among shared faculties of sensation, then, we find variability. Whose perception is correct? Who knows? "It is not said," he answers, "that the essence of things, hath reference to man alone. Hardnesse, whitenesse, depth and sharpnesse, . . . concern the knowledge of beasts as well as ours" (541). A pan-species dilemma of judgment arises.

Treating the matter of poisonous bodily fluids between man and snakes (based on the proverbial wisdom that human saliva kills certain snakes), Montaigne poses a further dilemma, asking, "What qualities shall we give unto spettle, either according to us, or according to the Serpent? By which two senses shall we verifie its true essence?" He reports also of Indian fish in Pliny that "to us are poison, and we bane to them; . . . now . . . is man or the Sea-hare poison? Whom shall we beleeve, either the fish of man, or the man of fish?" (541). This view of incommensurate, even adverse sensory determinations triggers the problem already considered concerning what assemblage of subjects might be capable of bringing them into one frame. But Montaigne also goes further, wondering about occult properties such as magnetism that were termed "secret" by Renaissance natural historians. As he speculates, "Is it not likely there should be sensitive

faculties . . . able to judge and perceive them?" (533). Daily observance of
familiar creatures provides some evidence of this likelihood:

> It is happily some particular sense that . . . teacheth a Hen . . . to fear a
> Hawke, and not a Goose or a Peacocke, farre greater birds: That warneth
> yong chickins of this hostile qualitie which the Cat hath against them,
> and not to distrust a Dogge: to strut and arme themselves against the
> mewing of the one (in some sort a flattering and milde voice) and not
> against the barking of the other (a snarling and quarrelous voice). (534)

Something legible to some sense that exceeds our perception may act to
guide these animals; certainly we cannot prove or know that it does not.
While Montaigne's de-perfected mankind patches together truths "by the
consultation and concurrence of our five senses" (542–43), perhaps "there
was required the accord and consent of eight or ten senses" before any
truth may warrant the name (534). Montaigne thus highlights problems
for any truth-seeking method that constrains itself to specifically human
capacities—as Descartes's method wholly and explicitly does.[24]

I stress here comparative matters of cognition and method, having already discussed the political dimensions of this debate in the introduction.
But Montaigne's conjuring of a collective body to engage in collaborative
science makes the range of observed and potential capacities across species
necessary to any ultimate or assured claim; it makes truth the business of
an engaged cosmopolitical negotiation rather than human self-sufficiency.
Diverse embodied perspectives must be conferred in his vision of a conference on truth designed to assemble all the sensory data collected across
kinds. "If the senses be our first Judges, it is not ours that must only be
called to counsell: For, in this facultie, beasts have as much (or more) right
than we" (540). For all man's claims to extraordinary competence as a
paragon, Montaigne's compromised man must welcome beasts as fellow
researchers who sometimes have superior skills.

And whenever night falls, the animals surely do have superior powers—and for the night's duration. As a final point on this controversy between Montaigne and Descartes, I cannot omit brief mention of what use
they make of conventional metaphors connecting light, darkness, vision,
and blindness to a discourse about human knowledge. We have already

---

24. In asserting this last point, I follow the line of thought that takes the second
demonstration of the *Discourse* (concerning the existence of God) as derivative from the
initial claim that an (individual, human) "I" exists.

seen Descartes refer to the "light" of reason. Early in the *Discourse* (before
he begins referring to his insights as easily reached), he speaks of moving
carefully, "like a man who walks alone in the dark," resolving to "go so
slowly and use so much circumspection . . . that, if I advanced only very
slightly, at least I would . . . keep myself from falling" (10). Linking the
danger of limited senses in the dark with that most important criterion of
human exceptionalism, upright posture, Descartes seems to regard night
as a general image for the basic conditions of human inquiry. At night, he
might fall down. By the end of the *Discourse*, though, his imagery shifts
away from the general night blindness of all humans to an image of "actual" blindness. Descartes's blind man represents Aristotelians, school-
men, and "very mediocre" minds—his adversaries.[25] In insisting on specialized vocabularies of the university tradition, he opines, "They seem to
me like a blind man who, in order to fight against someone who is sighted,
had made his opponent go into the depths of some very dark cellar."
Against these adversaries, he imagines his own enterprise "as if I were to
open some windows and make some daylight enter that cellar" (39–40).
For Descartes, darkness and its oppression of human powers stem from
an artificially constrained scenario (the cellar), suggesting a blameworthy,
even bad-faith failure on the part of (some, or most) individuals instead of
representing a universal condition for the inquiring human mind.

   Montaigne handles these metaphors quite differently; for him, we humans are all thrashing around in the dark. Arguing from the proposition
that someone blind from birth cannot know what the sight he lacks is
like, he draws conclusions for the overall human condition from that kind
of blindness: "Therefore ought we not to take assurance that our mind
is contented and satisfied with those [senses] we have, seeing it hath not
wherewith to feele her owne malady, and perceive her imperfection" or to
"discover the . . . defect" (532).[26] The case of blindness is far less exceptional

25. If we consider *La Circe*'s Ulysses as a proto-Descartes who is ironized in dramatic dialogue, we see that his use of the blindness trope likewise tries to disable his
(animal) adversaries. When the Elephant disputes that there is any sustainable difference between sensitive and intellective soul, Ulysses asserts that the Elephant can have
no opinion about intellection: "Thou knowest that it apperteyneth not to the blynde, to
geve judgement of colours" (Elephant's dialogue, *La Circe*).

26. Gelli's animals repeatedly stress this insight, which poses core problems for
Cartesian self-determinings of truth. For example, the Lion argues that "eviles of the
minde" are undetectable to that mind (unlike physical illness to the body): "He who by
them is greved, can make no right judgement of himselfe, the evil being in that parte,
to which the judgement apperteyneth. And for thys cause, folishnes is the gretest evill

than it may seem, especially considering the severity of impaired human vision in the early modern night. In a typically rich anecdote, the essayist describes an example from his experience. "I have seene a Gentleman of a good house, borne blind," he writes, whose use of sighted vocabulary (that a child is "a goodly thing to see" or that the "Sunne shines cleare") strikes Montaigne for the epistemological gap it indicates. He expands, "Give him a ball, he . . . strikes it away with his racket; in a piece he shutes at ran- dome; and is well pleased with what his men tell him, be [the shot] high or wide" (533). The comparative implications for human knowledge are staggering, as Montaigne leverages the image of a gun-happy blind per- son taking aim at random targets to ask, again, "*Who knowes* whether mankind commit as great a folly, for want of some sense, and that by this default, the greater part of the visage of things be concealed from us? *Who knowes* . . . whether the divers effects of beasts, which exceed our capac- ity, are produced by the facultie of some sense that we want? And whether some of them, have by that meane *a fuller and more perfect* life then [*sic*] ours?" (533; italics added). For Montaigne, the case of blindness presents a cautionary tale for humanity about the undetectability of our sensory ignorances; for Descartes it serves as a charge against adversaries self- imprisoned in the "rustie dungeon" of sense impressions.

While Montaigne understands the senses "to be the extreame bounds of our perceiving," Descartes circumscribes their vulnerability by subor- dinating them to the exclusively human governance of reason or the ra- tional soul, which harbors its own protocol concerning what is "plainly" true. Humans, then, have universally available access to the totality of truth in a Cartesian system; animals have no relation to the concept. In the dispute about animal "science" and the stakeholdership of beasts in knowledge of the world, Montaigne's zoographic critique of human suf- ficiency and his claim that "the essence of things . . . hardnesse, white- nesse, depth and sharpnesse . . . concern the knowledge of beasts as well as ours" stand as the precise targets of Cartesian intervention (541). The controversy highlights the interface between political interestedness and status as a subject of knowledge. In the same rising grid by which humans would be compared exclusively to themselves that Traub has described, all humans are deemed to have like access to reason (whether they use it or not), and nonhumans have no relevance to inquiry, nor can they claim

---

that can chaunce to man. For asmuch as he that hath it, never knoeth it: and knowing it not, never seketh . . . any remedy to unburden him selfe thereof" (Lion's dialogue, *La Circe*).

a place at the table where knowledge is to be corrected and conferred, as Montaigne proposes we would need them to do. In asserting the radical sufficiency of humans to truth, then, Descartes also constitutes human-kind's private and monopoly relation to it.

Glancing ahead to the seventeenth-century progress of this enterprise in human self-confidence, we see how advances in lens making—the tele-scope and microscope—appear to prop up the "panoptical man" long theo-rized in exceptionalist accounts of humanity, as discussed in chapter 2. But a major treatise such as Robert Hooke's *Micrographia, or Some Physio-logical Descriptions of Minute Bodies* (1665) indexes almost as much resis-tance by creatures and the material world to human dominion as it sounds any successful human conquest. Although the opening lines of the pref-ace celebrate technology as "the great Prerogative of Mankind above other Creatures" and man's "peculiar priviledge" over them, Hooke's agenda for the Royal Society's work consistently portrays humankind as weak and error prone, a creature rife with infirmities. He speaks of "rectifying the operations of the Sense" and pursuing sensory "defects" in order to "un-derstand how to supply them, and by what assistances we may inlarge their power" so that "our command over things [may] be establisht."[27] He stresses "watchfulness over the failings and an inlargement of the domin-ion, of the Senses" (iii). Concerned mainly with magnification, he laments how "not having a full sensation of the Object, we must be very lame and imperfect in our conceptions about it" (ii). Indeed, prosthetic language abounds: "We" can succeed "by addition of . . . artificial Instruments"; this "we" can "supply . . . [the senses'] infirmities with Instruments, and, as it were, the adding of artificial Organs to the natural" (i, iii). At the heart of a brief for the grand technological knowledge projects of the Royal Society, we still find a lingering vision of man as *unaccommodated*; he is an insufficient animal, an unready species that must be outfitted with prosthetic additions to pursue the animal perfection that eludes him.

Like many other scientists, Hooke conceptualizes this enterprise as a restoration of Edenic knowledge and original cosmic "dominion," remedi-ating the extensive intellectual damage caused by the Fall (i, vii–viii). As a result, his discourse still powerfully reflects the animal comparisons so important to earlier modes of zoographic critique that had tried to measure animal sovereignties and "happiness." In Hooke, though, what was once

---

27. Robert Hooke, *Micrographia, or Some Physiological Descriptions of Minute Bodies made by Magnifying Glasses* (London: John Martin and James Allestry, 1665), preface, i (my pagination; subsequent page references appear in the text).

comparison has evolved into a rivalry or competition. He makes continuing note of how human senses remain in "many particulars much outdone
by those of other Creatures" (ii). Citing an animal ability that had been
widely celebrated across the natural-historical literature, he urges that by
means of "mechanical contrivances" humans might "also judge (as other
Creatures seem to do) what is wholsome, what poison; and in a word . . .
the specific properties of Bodies" (ix). Even for the weaker faculty of smell,
Hooke sets high goals: "Who knowes, but that the Industry of man . . .
may find out wayes of improving this sense to as great a degree of perfection as it is in any Animal, and perhaps yet higher" (xi). How high? Invoking a capacity known only as a property pertaining to other creatures,
Hooke comically calls the human inability to fly a "Defect." Yet he readily imagines that once we supplement "the want of strength in humane
muscles" it will be nothing less than "easie to make twenty contrivances
to perform the office of Wings" (xvi). No thought of Icarus's fate in such an
animal-imitating experiment dampens Hooke's dream of the perfections
ahead for mankind. Hooke's perspective, then, equivocates. On the one
hand, he promotes a vision of humanity as the proud possessor of sovereign, makerly power (to create scientific inventions, to instrumentalize
matter, and to command the planet). But on the other hand, he still reflects
a self-doubting vision that totes up human powers to find them lacking—a
vision of man as imperfect, comparatively deficient, and as much in need
of supplements as *King Lear*'s man had been.

Baldwin's *Beware the Cat*:
Assisted Cognition Reveals Feline Empire!

Hooke's *Micrographia* delivered a series of perspectives that had previously
been not only invisible but also unsupposed. His visual investigation of
the smallest thing (a point) by means of a needle's tip and of the sharpest thing (the straight line of a razor's edge) altered these once miniscule
forms into dense, craggy landscapes. As he puts the effects of this, "By
means of telescopes, there is nothing so far distant but may be represented
to our view; and by the help of Microscopes, there is nothing so small,
as to escape our inquiry; hence, there is a new visible World discovered
to the understanding" (iv). These new world discoveries required only the
supplement of "Optical Glasses," first beginning to be developed in Zeeland the 1590s. But fantasies of assisted cognition and sensory "helps," of
course, predate this. Before there were optical glasses, other aids offered
themselves to the inquiring mind—oil of fox, distillation of hedgehog, and

a mash of animal ears and tongues applied directly to the human head, for example.[28]

William Baldwin's 1570 *A Marvelous Hystory intitulede, Beware the Cat* has mainly interested scholars for its early and innovative place in the history of English prose fiction and for its contributions to religious controversy on the Protestant side. With its vituperous language against "privy masses," its overt complaint about the hearsay dimension of oral communication, and its allegorical attack on aspects of church doctrine that were mere "human" traditions, it offers vivid anti-Catholic diatribe.[29] At times, though, its allegories resist interpretive taming because of the text's large and diverse feline population. When we treat the cats as allegorical figures (as clearly to a good extent it is intended we should), cats and their elaborate rituals represent those traditions of the Catholic Church said to lack a scriptural basis; in this sense, they themselves (and anyone who believes in this account of them too) suggest the credulity toward "hearsay" so reviled by Protestant propagandists. On the other hand, the text's bursting realistic detail invites us to take its cats to indicate cats literally, recalling Derrida's "a real cat [and not] the figure of a cat."[30] As Karen Raber puts it, we find both a deployment of cat figures "to pillory Catholicism" and overwhelming testimony to "the material fact that cats are . . . everywhere."[31] Citing Ovid, Topsell records that the cat was associated with spying and was considered "a watchful and wary beast" in

28. For the perfect ordinariness of conceiving these substances as medicinal, see William Brockbank, "Sovereign Remedies: A Critical Depreciation of the 17th-Century London Pharmacopoeia," *Medical History* 8 (1964): 3.

29. Though the modern edition of *Beware the Cat* calls it "the first English novel," it is notoriously elusive in genre terms. For an account of its anti-Catholic satire, see John N. King, *English Reformation Literature: The Tudor Origins of the Protestant Tradition* (Princeton, NJ: Princeton University Press, 1982). For discussion of Baldwin's treatment of hearsay, oral tradition, gender, and the status of print, see Clair Kinney, "Clamorous Voices, Incontinent Fictions: Orality, Oratory, and Gender in William Baldwin's *Beware the Cat*," in *Oral Traditions and Gender in Early Modern Literary Texts*, ed. Mary Ellen Lamb and Karen Bamford (Aldershot, UK: Ashgate, 2008), 195–207. For a rich argument that Streamer's activities illustrate Baldwin's sense of the "dangers of individuation" (in contexts of communities of reading), see Joshua Phillips, *English Fictions of Communal Identity, 1485–1603* (Aldershot, UK: Ashgate, 2010), 84.

30. Jacques Derrida, *The Animal That Therefore I Am*, ed. Marie-Louise Mallet, trans. David Wills (New York: Fordham University Press, 2008), 6.

31. Karen Raber, "How to Do Things with Animals: Thoughts on the Early Modern Cat," in *Early Modern Ecostudies: From the Florentine Codex to Shakespeare*, ed. Thomas Hallock, Ivo Kamps, and Karen Raber (New York: Palgrave Macmillan, 2008),

Greece and Egypt; he elaborates that "her eyes glister above measure . . .
and in the night they can barely be endured, for their flaming aspect."
At one time, he says, "cats were all wild, but afterward they retired to
houses."[32] Thus the cat's special gaze and its liminality enable it to spy on
humans sneaking around in dark corners—whether recusant Catholics or
bawds and hypocrites of unspecified denomination—to enormous critical
effect. As a result, although cats seem to stand for Catholicism allegorically, what one character will call "natural cats" also make it their nightly
business to police recusancy alongside other human errancies. Baldwin's
cats catch both vice and mice.

Baldwin embeds his story in dizzying layers of reportage. A Baldwin-
like anonymous narrator recounts tales told one night in London by a
showily pedantic and unreliable speaker, Master Streamer, who in turn
reports further matter from more distant contexts. This *tour de force*
in narrative framing grounds the text's importance to developments in
prose fiction.[33] The epistle dedicatory outlines how "Baldwin" has divided Streamer's "Oration" into "three parts, and set the argument before
them and an instruction after them, with such notes as might be gathered
thereof, so making it booklike."[34] With such devices, along with a poem
to the reader, *Beware the Cat* heavily moralizes the oration's contents.
The poem admonishes us that "the Cat gan tell," warning that whoever
might "now boast" needs to "beware" that "the Cat will him disclose"
(1–2). The "Exhortation" proposes that despite the Baldwin-like narrator's
original doubt of the proposition, Streamer's oration has "proved that cats
do understand us and mark our secret doings," incorporating that classic
trope of persuasion, the resistant character successfully convinced. It also
urges us again to "take profit" from the tale and "so live, both openly and
privily that neither our own cat, admitted to all secrets, be able to declare

97–98. Raber's ranging essay provides analysis not only of cats in early modernity but
also of larger questions about their liminality to animal studies to date.

32. Edward Topsell, *Historie of Foure-Footed Beastes* (London: William Jaggard,
1607), 80–81.

33. *Beware the Cat* is also an important precursor for eighteenth-century "it-
narratives," insofar as circulating objects—or animals—travel a route very much like
Mouse-slayer's below, discovering human misconduct everywhere they go. See Mark
Blackwell, ed., *The Secret Life of Things: Animals, Objects, and It-Narratives in
Eighteenth-Century England* (Lewisburg, PA: Bucknell University Press, 2007).

34. William Baldwin, *Beware the Cat: The First English Novel*, ed. William Ringler
and Michael Flachmann (San Marino, CA: Huntington Library, 1988), 3. Subsequent
page references appear in the text.

aught of us to the world save what is laudable and honest; nor the Devil's cat, which will we or nill we seeth . . . all our ill doings, have ought to lay against us afore the face of God" (54). The liminal cat of house and street (a kind of familiar, yet distinctly not "the Devil's cat") operates as a night agent, a spy among, and witness against, humans. Even more than the owl in Shakespeare and Nashe, Baldwin's marginal commentary warns that "cats are admitted to all secrets" (38).

Relations across species prove pivotal to the narrative; questions of kind even provide a somewhat clearer structuring force than the (presumably prioritized) religious allegory does. Baldwin's reference to "Christmas communications" in the epistle dedicatory suggests an interpretive frame of carnival and gives us notice that folly speaks, but the same letter also stresses the "instruction" that can be gleaned from it and advises the reader again to "learn to Beware the Cat" (3–4). As with Erasmus's *Praise of Folly*, sometimes quotation marks mock the speech they enclose, but not always. Opening the story, the Baldwin-like narrator describes how, "at Christmas last," he was at court working with the master of the king's pastimes "about setting forth certain interludes" (5).[35] At night, "it pleased Master Ferrers to make me his bedfellow, and on a pallet cast upon the rushes of his own chamber to lodge Master Willot and Master Streamer, the one his Astronomer, the other his Divine." Under these auspicious circumstances, "we used nightly at our lodging to talk of sundry things." Cutting to the chase, we immediately learn that "on a night (which I think was the twenty-eight of December) . . . there fell a controversy between Master Streamer, who with Master Willot had already slept his first sleep, and me, that was newly come unto bed." The controversy? "Whether birds and beasts had reason" (5). This perennial pre-Cartesian topic—a scene of differentiation to which conversation repeatedly turns—never lacked for a brace of partisans, not only contra, but also pro.

Creaturely decorum in literary and professional contexts precipitates their debate. The king's players were rehearsing "a play of Aesop's Crow."[36] The narrator proposes that while *in a tale* it is "sufferable to imagine and tell of something by [beasts] spoken or reasonably done," he finds it unexampled in performance because it is "uncomely . . . to bring them in lively

35. George Ferrers, master of the king's pastimes in 1551–52 and in 1552–53, later collaborated with Baldwin in writing *A Mirror for Magistrates*; Ringler relays details of Baldwin's time at court, indicating that the night in question was 28 December 1552. The other figures appear to be fictional (Baldwin, *Beware the Cat*, 57–58).

36. There is no record of the existence of such a play (alas).

personages to speak, do, reason, and allege authorities out of authors" (5).
But Streamer, "being more divine in this point than [the narrator] was ware
of, held the contrary part, affirming that beasts and fowls had reason, and
that as much as men, yea, and in some points more" (6). Even the cadence
of Streamer's reported assertion—squeezing in a last supposition about the
prospect of animal superiority in some things—marks his source as the
"happy beast" tradition of Plutarch's dialogues and natural-historical literature generally. The list of particulars duly follows. Streamer, "for proof
of his assertion declared many things," including "elephants that walked
upon cords, hedgehogs that knew always what weather would come, foxes
and dogs that after they had been abroad all night killing geese and sheep
would come home in the morning and put their necks into their collars,
parrots that bewailed their keeper's deaths, swallows that with celandine
open their young ones' eyes, and an hundred things more" (6).[37] The innocent narrator responds with the conventional reply that these things stem
from instinct and represent "natural kindly actions" and not reason, and
he alleges for proof the "authority of most grave and learned philosophers,"
who remain unnamed (6).

In a rich compression of the negotiations between traditional learning
and experiential (or "experimental") approaches that first began in the contexts of fifteenth-century anatomical learning, Streamer—like Descartes
later—asserts that argument by authorities has only the limited value of
hearsay compared to direct knowledge. Of reasoning animals, he says, "I
know what I know, . . . not only . . . by hearsay . . . but by what I myself
have proved." His interlocutors are all ears when he announces that "I
have heard them and understand them . . . as well as I understand you" (6).
This bold assertion sets Ferrers laughing, but the narrator becomes more
circumspect. Recalling having read something "in Albertus' works," he
reflects that there might be more to this subject than meets the eye ("there
might be somewhat more than I did know"), and he presses for details.
Streamer—on the condition his auditors make no interruption—agrees to
tell "a story of one piece of mine own experimenting as should . . . put you
out of doubt concerning this matter" (6). The doubt-resolving "story" of an
"experiment" ensues.

Propped up in bed, Streamer tells of his attentions to certain cats who
gathered outside the window of a room where he once lodged. Having been
kept awake nightly by their noise, when "sitting by the fire with certain of

37. On hedgehogs and the weather, see Montaigne, "Apologie," 415, and Topsell
(noting Aristotle), *Historie*, 219.

the house," he complains of "what a wawling the cats had made there the night before from ten o'clock till one." By this introduction, he continues, "we fell in communication of cats, . . . some affirming as I do now (but I was against it then), that they had understanding" (11). By this fireside, one servant offers his story of having been addressed at night by a cat on the road in Kankwood, who advised him to commend her to his own cat and pass on the news that "Grimalkin is dead." When the servant arrived home and reported the event, likewise "sitting by the fire with his wife and his household," to their surprise their house cat overhears of Grimalkin's fate, speaks to them, and then "went her way and was never seen after." This episode demonstrates how "cats carry news," a topic of later marvel in the conversation (14).

The Kankwood anecdote causes another man to speak up with a tale he never credited before, but which on reflection appeared to be a part of the same Grimalkin story. The men confer about dates and agree that both accounts are about forty years old. The second tale relates events in Ireland (a natural locus for the incredible): one night "we fell in talk (as we have done now) of strange adventures, and of cats" (12). The speaker's elaborate narrative purports to tell of the death of Grimalkin, a sequence including more speaking cats (and one scary cat in particular with a creepily bottomless appetite). Here, "a well-learned" man in the company intervenes to clarify: "There is in cats, as in all other kinds of beasts, a certain reason and language whereby they understand one another. But, as touching this, Grimalkin I take rather to be an hagat or a witch than a cat" (16). This leads to talk of transubstantiation and metamorphosis, with extended speculation about whether they involve an actual material change in the body, movement of souls between bodies, or simply tricks played on deceivable human senses (because ointments and certain candles can easily hoodwink "the right conception of the eye" [17]). Witchcraft also yields a chance to attack the pope: "Natural cats that were not so wise have had [Grimalkin, as witch] and her race in reverence among them . . . like as we silly fools . . . reverenced the Pope" (20). But the still-doubting Streamer seizes on the reference to "natural cats" to return the discussion to them, querying the speaker again about their wit and comprehension.

Here things take a scholarly turn. The "learned" interlocutor gives Streamer a bookish and nuanced answer:

> There is no kind of sensible creatures but have reason and understanding; whereby, in their kind, each understandeth other and do therein in some points so excel that the consideration thereof moved Pythagoras

(as you know) to believe and affirm that after death men's souls went
into beasts and beasts' souls into men, and every one according to his
desert in his former body. And although his opinion be fond and false,
yet that which drew him thereto is evident and true—and that is the
wit and reason of diverse beasts, and again the dull, beastly, brutish
ignorance of diverse men. (21)

Baldwin's marginal gloss to this passage asserts simply that "some beasts
are wiser than men." While distancing himself from Pythagoras, the
speaker distinguishes the doctrine of transmigration from its underlying
basis in species-comparative wit and wisdom, revealing his own reading
in the "happy beast" tradition of Plutarch and others.

This well-read commentator does adduce "daily experience" as evidence for communication among birds and beasts, but he also adds an
anecdote about a bishop of Alexandria who found means to understand
animal speech.[38] What sets Streamer down the path to experimentation is
his reference to "magic natural" as a way "to subtiliate his sensible powers, either by purging his brain by dry drinks and fumes, or else to aug-
ment the brains of his power perceptible by other natural medicines" (21).
Streamer evinces the desire still driving Hooke almost a century later: a
desire for "subtiliated" and remediated or artificially enhanced senses. Instead of outfitting himself with an optical glass, the lore at hand directs
Streamer instead toward self-dosing with "natural medicines."[39] Not yet
an experimental regime that tortures the target object to force it to yield
up its truths (by application of pressure or the vacuum of the air pump, or
heat, or the vivisecting knife), this experiential science instead alters the

38. "Sitting at dinner . . . among his friends, he harkened diligently to a sparrow
that came fleeing and chirping to other that were about the house, and smiled . . . to
hear her. And when one of the company desired to know why he smiled, he said, 'At the
sparrow's tale. For she telleth them . . . that in the highway . . . a sack of wheat is even
now fallen off a horseback . . . and therefore biddeth them to come thither for dinner.'
And when the guests . . . sent to prove the truth, they found it even so as he had told
them" (21).

39. For a discussion of seventeenth-century habits of scientific self-dosing by Hooke
(who detailed these activities extensively in his diaries) and others, where medical
trials involving ingestion of experimental substances and purgation were conducted
on the body of the experimenter himself, see Lisa Jardine, *The Curious Life of Robert
Hooke, the Man Who Measured London* (New York: HarperCollins, 2004), 214–46. See
also Lisa Jardine, "Textual Therapies: Dosing the Ailing Subject" (paper presented at
the English Institute, Harvard University, Cambridge, MA, September 2000).

investigator by medicating him as an observing subject. This science, in other words, strives to repair or enhance the faculties of a dysfunctional *cogito*, taking human subjective weakness as the obstacle to knowledge rather than any particular resistance in the object itself. The first part of his oration ends with Streamer heading to bed, where he "could think of nothing else" (22).

Back in his room, however, he realizes the cats have assembled again outside. Part 2 opens with Streamer's increasing attentiveness, noting first that cats "have sundry voices" and display an order not unlike music, with such a "bass" and "treble" that "it might be counted a double diapason" (23). He approaches the window to observe their gestures, a form of language Montaigne had celebrated: "There is no motion nor jesture that doth not speake, and speakes in a language very easie . . . to be understood: nay which is more, it is a language common and publike to all."[40] Interpreting the "common and publike" language of the scene, Streamer exclaims, "I promise you it was a thing worth the marking to see what countenances, what becks, yea and what order was among them," and the marginal gloss affirms the legibility of gestures, noting that "cats keep order among themselves" and that "cats make courtesy with their tails and necks" (like courtiers) (23). Overwhelmed by curiosity, Streamer "could not sleep of all that night, but lay devising by what means [he] might learn to understand them" (24). Suddenly remembering something he "read in Albertus Magnus' works" about how "to understand birds' voices," he seeks the book. Citing the Latin text of *Liber secretorum de virtutibus herbarum, lapidum, et animalium* (ca. 1486)—a text falsely attributed to Albertus—Streamer records his joy at finding the recipe ("Lord how glad I was" [24]).[41] His night reading leads to a sense of purpose: "When I had thoroughly marked the medicine, . . . I devised thereby how to make a philter for to serve my purpose" (24). Better science through medicine. Streamer's glib unconcern with the origin of the medicine as a recipe for understanding birds will be compounded as he supplements and modifies it freely into more convenient terms. The ripe slapstick of his experiment in mental refinement does not prepare the reader for the consequential account he will give of the alternate, feline jurisdiction his dosings make visible.

The sparse instructions direct Streamer to take two companions on Si-

40. Montaigne argued further that body language is not only legible across kinds but also a more natural human language than speech itself ("Apologie," 401).

41. See Ringler's discussion of sources in Baldwin, *Beware the Cat*, 64.

Figure 4.2. Conrad Gesner, *Hedgehog,* in *Historiae Animalium, Liber 1 (de Quadrupedibus)* (Zurich, 1551). Image courtesy of the Charles Deering McCormick Library of Special Collections, Northwestern University Library.

Figure 4.3. Edward Topsell, *Hedge-hog,* in *Historie of Foure-Footed Beastes* (London, 1607). Image by permission of the Folger Shakespeare Library, Washington, DC.

mon and Jude's Day "with hounds into a certain wood, and the first beast that thou meetest take, and prepare with the heart of a fox." The specified day being too far off and hunting being troublesome, Streamer concludes that the likeliest animal to meet would be a hedgehog ("one of the planetical beasts, and therefore good in magic" (25) (figs. 4.2 and 4.3). Heading for St. Johns Wood, he meets some hunters and procures an already-flayed fox from them—plus a hare for good measure. He himself kills a hedgehog he finds sitting cozily in its den ("in a hole of the earth by the root of an hol-

low tree . . . with a bushel of crabs [apples] about him").[42] Then he hurries
back to his laboratory-abattoir-kitchen, killing a kite by happenstance on
the way and keeping it to supply extra ingredients ("to make up the mess")
for the "medicine" (26). In the cascading series of surplus bodies for this
gallimaufry of kinds, at the last minute a servant shows up with a flayed
cat to boot, and the wildly improvised ritual preparations begin.[43]

After unskinning the "urchin" (hedgehog), Streamer puts its flesh,
along with white wine, rosemary, and neat's tongue, in a vessel to boil,
collecting "the water that distilled from it" (27).[44] Separately he beats together in a mortar segments of the cat's liver, spleen, and kidney; its whole
heart; the fox's heart; the hare's brain; the kite's stomach; and the hedgehog's kidneys—a concoction he bakes on a stone as "a cake." A second set
of diverse parts is "pounded together," and that Streamer places in a cloth
hung over a basin in the sun, "out of which dropped within four hours
after about half a pint of oil very fair and clear" (28). As dinner, Streamer
eats the boiled hedgehog with the "cake" and drinks the "distillation of
the urchin's broth," all of which make him very sleepy. After a nap, he
awakes, and from the mouth and nose he "purged exceedingly such . . .
matters as I never saw before," leaving his head and body "in exceeding
good temper" and his brain "marvelously well-purged" (28). So clarified,
Streamer's perceptual apparatus awaits two contingencies: the preparation
of further sensory aids and the coming of night.

To understand animal language, Streamer next applies concoctions
made of their organs of communication to his own cleansed organs of perception. Their ears and tongues and his head will converge and comingle
in a transfer of properties pertinent to understanding. Grinding the dis-
membered ears of his fodder animals into a jelly and folding in "rue, fen-

42. Topsell describes the hedgehog's habit of "gather[ing] fruit" and "laying it up
against Winter"; when the "Hedge-hog . . . findeth apples or grapes . . . he rowleth himself upon them, untill he have filled all his prickles, and then carryeth the home to his
den" (*Historie*, 217).

43. On roasting and skinning (and on the abuse below when a cat is shod in walnut shells) as part of a larger early modern habit of cat persecution, see Bruce Boehrer,
"*Gammer Gurton*'s Cat of Sorrows," *English Literary Renaissance* 39, no. 2 (2009):
267–89.

44. Topsell recounts similar kinds of diversely medicinal hedgehog concoctions, including a recipe attributed to Albertus Magnus: "If the right eye of a Hedge-hog be fryed
with the oil of Alderne or Linseed" and used as "an eye-salve," it enables one to "see as
well in the dark as the light" (*Historie*, 219–20). See also John Johnston, *A Description
of the Nature of Four-Footed Beasts* (Amsterdam, 1678 [Dutch version, 1652]), 91.

nel, lowache, and leek blades," he stuffs two "pillows" with the mixture, fries them in "good olive oil," and (logically enough) affixes the pillows to his ears (he later ties them with "a kercher about my head" [30]). Taking the tongues of the same group, he soaks them in wine, mortars them with an ounce of "new cat's dung," and adds mustard seed, garlic, and pepper (29). With this brew, he makes certain tablets. Supping on the remainder of his dinner after the afternoon's labors, in a sordid spoof of religious ritual Streamer anoints his head with the wine and oil. Well dosed and toting his "presciencial pills" (one for each nostril and one set above and one set below his tongue), he sets out for his perch overlooking the roof to complete the experiment he has prepared.

The "presciencial pills" work all too well. Streamer finds it almost impossible to parse the noises that flood his ears: "The sound of them altogether was so disordered and monstrous that I could discern no one from the other, save only the harmony of the moving of the spheres" (31). The marginal note points out that "the poetical fury came upon him," and Streamer gives a rumbling inventory of sounds:

> Barking of dogs, grunting of hogs, wawling of cats, rumbling of rats, gaggling of geese, humming of bees, rousing of bucks, crowing of cocks, sewing of socks, cackling of hens, scabbling of pens, peeping of mice, trulling of dice, curling of frogs, and toads in the bogs, chirking of crickets, shutting of wickets, shriking of owls, flittering of fowls, routing of knaves, snorting of slaves, farting of churls, fizzling of girls, with many things else. (32)

When the nearby bells of St. Botolph's then ring in his tenderized ears, Streamer is completely undone. But he gathers himself, adjusts to the volume, and settles in with the moon "to harken to the cats" (36), who reassemble at their appointed hour. Feline orderliness strikes him again, with the assembly doing "their 'beisance as they did the night before" to the large gray cat presiding. But this time, when the gray cat speaks, Streamer understands him "as well as if he had spoken English." The cats' commission reveals an entire feline empire operating across and despite human borders, from London, to Ireland, to Caithness.

Topsell had recorded that "some have thought that [cats] have a peculiar intelligible language among themselves" (83). What Streamer witnesses through the looking glass of his window is a legal inquiry into charges against one "Mouse-slayer," who ably defends herself over several

nights' convenings. He learns a series of details that sketch out a partly
alien, partly parallel cat culture. They have their own oaths (swearing
"by the tail of the Great Bear") and their own time (referring to "the fifth
hour of *our night"*); their monarch rules by both "inheritance and our
free election"; and a perversely feline "law *for* adultery" forbids females
from refusing "any males not exceeding the number of ten in a night"
(though common-law adjudication had established an exception that applied in Mouse-slayer's case) (36, 37, 47; italics added).[45] Similar to the assize courts of Baldwin's England, the feline commission convenes periodi-
cally at different locations, and in this instance they will adjourn till the
next convening in Caithness (51). Baldwin imagines this parallel universe
of political organization, obviously, by extrapolating from human forms
and inverting them—his vision of feline empire recalls the inversive imaginary that frames witchcraft lore, but instead of the gendered reversal of
power evident there, a dispensation between species is at stake.

As we have seen in responses to Pliny's conception of man as *nudus
in nuda terra,* human nakedness marks that species's insufficiency as an
animal, suggesting for man a unique underprovisioning as nature's orphan. In the night world of *Beware the Cat,* humans duly play their parts
in a largely naked condition. Montaigne had charged in his own critical
examination of man that "he must be stripped into his shirt" (436), and
Mouse-slayer's third night of testimony leaves many people in precisely
this condition. While living in the household of a widowed gentlewoman,
Mouse-slayer discovers that she is not only a secret votary of the cult of
Mary but also a destroyer of youth: she "got her living by boarding young
gentlemen, for whom she kept always fair wenches in store," and once
"she had soaked from young gentlemen all they had," they turned to theft,
and she would launder the proceeds (40). In one particular case, the religious widow/brothel keeper goes to extreme lengths to trick an "innocent
woman, otherwise invincible, . . . to commit whoredom" in order to satisfy one lodger. This young (married) woman begs to take Mouse-slayer,
and so the cat circulates to yet another household. While Mouse-slayer
defends herself against the charges from "a law for adultery among cats,"
the young woman persists in secret meetings with the widow's lodger.

45. This is the statute that Mouse-slayer is accused of violating (by refusing the
crude attentions of one Catch-rat), a "transgression" that enhances her credibility in
human terms; the judicial exception to the rule nevertheless disallowed rape. For the
extensive engagement of gender in *Beware the Cat,* see Kinney, "Clamorous Voices."

Events—and nakedness—in this household supply the details of Mouse-slayer's report as a witness as well as her opportunities as a night agent for pouncing on human transgression.

Montaigne had observed that "when I consider man all naked (yea, be it in that sex, which seemeth to have . . . the greatest share of eye-pleasing beautie) and view his defects, his naturall subjection, and manifold imperfections; I finde we have had much more reason to hide and cover our nakedness, than any creature else" (430), and Mouse-slayer's account supplies evidence for this verdict. In the first episode, Mouse-slayer is the victim of a malicious prank: "An ungracious fellow . . . took four walnut shells and filled them full of soft pitch, and put them on my feet" (47). When Mouse-slayer becomes active again "at night when they were all in bed," the clattering of walnut shoes overhead induces pure hysteria downstairs and drives the humans of the house to decide the devil is loose among them. Panicking, the "master and all the rest . . . ran naked as they were into the street" (48). The whole neighborhood is roused in like disarray, watching as an old priest is dispensed to outface the devil with "candle-light . . . and holy-water." Thinking she sees the gear for a "privy mass," Mouse-slayer runs toward the priest and his followers, and this new terror collapses them all backward like dominoes in a tumble of human bodies all dropped on the ground. Mouse-slayer then runs "among them where they lay on heaps (49). With the first priest's burning candle falling into "another priest's breech" (who in the chaos had been busy "conjuring" the maid) and with "the old priest . . . so tumbled among them that his face lay upon a boy's bare arse"—a boy who "for fear had beshit himself" and the priest's face too—this naked, many-legged, and prostrate human pile has little to commend and much to condemn in it. And while the cat auditors all laugh at this tableau of tangled bare limbs and excrement, the human characters extract and upright themselves from the heap, pledge themselves to secrecy, "and for shame departed" (49).

The second installment of human disgrace concerns the ongoing adultery of Mouse-slayer's new mistress. When the husband returns home unexpectedly, and the lover has "no leisure to pluck up his hose, but with them about his legs ran into a corner behind a painted cloth and there stood *as still as a mouse*" (50; italics added), events unfold in their inevitable way. In this cat-and-mouse game, the cat as agent of a retributive justice "all to-pawed him with [her] claws upon his bare legs and buttocks" (through which the lover remains stoically silent). When the mistress tries to induce the cat from behind the arras with a bit of "meat," Mouse-

slayer, "minding another thing, . . . suddenly . . . leaped up and caught
him by the genitals with [her] teeth." When the man finally screamed, in
this early modern script for the very anxiety shadowing Derrida's encounter, the master discovers a "bare-arst gentleman" strangling a cat "with
his stones in [her] mouth" (50–51). In this challenging scene of exposure,
from a species standpoint, we *might* identify with the lover (or one of the
other humans), but from a gender or moral standpoint, we might not. *Who
knowes?*

Two other cats Streamer overhears will shortly characterize this
highly sexualized but nonerotic content from the third night's testimony
as "nothing in comparison" (52) to the nights Streamer heard only as
"wawling." On the first night, one says, Mouse-slayer described her first
years with five different "masters: a priest, a baker, a lawyer, a broker, and
a butcher; all whose privy deceits . . . she declared" (51). The next night
she described her middle years, when "she had seven masters: a bishop,
a knight, a pothecary, a goldsmith, an usurer, an alchemist, and a lord;
whose cruelty, study, craft, cunning, niggishness, folly, waste, and oppression she declared" (52). Mouse-slayer's comprehensive perspective, then,
passes critical judgment on a ranging cross section of humankind, with
each specimen after another displaying some further depravity, hypocrisy,
or hidden meanness of spirit. While Mouse-slayer defeats a charge of sexual misconduct and defends her "loyalty and obedience to all good laws"
(51), the humankind she surveys fares far worse. For all the spleen it directs at Catholicism and all the doubt with which it surrounds Streamer's
account, *Beware the Cat* also delivers a jagged critique of humankind as
depraved, a critique leveraged from the perspective of the cats who roam
among us, watching but unobserved. On the basis of the body of evidence
adduced in the course of this feline investigative commission, it is humankind, not primarily Mouse-slayer, who is on trial. The verdict finds
us, on balance, to be a "bare-arst" bunch.

Streamer's discourse ends with another religious perversion, this time
of the epistemological verses from Paul's Epistles to the Corinthians. The
passage—so familiar from Bottom's garbled variation—sets religious limits on human cognition, distinguishing "the wisedome of this world" from
"spirituall things" known through faith: "As it is written, the thinges
which eye hath not seene, neither eare hath heard, . . . are, which God
hath prepared for them that love him" (1 Cor. 2:9). Parodying this warning
against the human sensory authority so aggrandized by "the princes of
this world" (1 Cor. 2:6, 8), Streamer promises his auditors that—as incredible as his tale has been—"I will tell you other things which these eyes of

mine *have seen* and these ears of mine *have heard*, . . . so far passing this,
that all which I have said now shall in comparison . . . be nothing at all"
(53; italics added). Within the human domains of Christianity, Streamer's
assertion registers as gross impiety, bootstrapping human wisdom and
reason into a quasi-Cartesian authority that Paul's dispensation—or Montaigne's reading—would utterly deny. But one open question lingers, and
it concerns Streamer's "humanity" for these purposes. We have already
seen the sovereign perspectives that Montaigne is prepared to accord nonhumans, most especially his cat. When Streamer joins the rooftop cats in
their laughter at "heaped" human folly, the marginal note informs us of a
further, unnerving detail: "The author laughed in a cat's voice" (49). Perhaps a cat has the last laugh, as human knowledge attends not only to the
limits of "this world" but also to its own limitation by the knowledges of
those others who also lay eyes on it. When Streamer's tale ends, "every
man shut up his shop windows, which the foresaid talk kept open two
hours longer than they should have been" (53). Bedtime, time to close up
(the eyes of) the human shop—it is this creaturely protocol that *Midsummer*'s Athenians transgress to their "peril."

Where the Vile Things Rule: A Midsummer Night

As Peter Quince organizes his players to put on an interlude for Theseus's
"wedding day at night," he exchanges lines with Bottom about his apt-
ness for the suicidal lover's part. Celebrating his power to move an audience in this role, Bottom warns, "If I do it, *let the audience look to their
eyes*" (1.2.19–20; italics added). This is a good cue in a play where—among
humans, at least—the notorious weakness of night vision will exponen-
tialize the general vulnerability of the eyes to desire, misimpression, and
even foul play, engendering a night of sensory and cognitive disarray for
the Athenians who violate jurisdictional principles limiting human sovereignty to daylight hours. Indeed, when Titania hails him as wise, Bottom corrects her: "Not so, neither; but if I had wit enough to get out of
this wood, I'd have enough to serve my own turn" (3.1.135–37). We have
passed from "bare-arst" humanity of Streamer's bold impiety to Bottom,
who with his ass-head experience not only gets the point of Corinthians
right but even develops the theme by means of the garbled synesthesia of
his report: "The eye of man hath not heard, the ear of man hath not seen,
man's hand is not able to taste, his tongue to conceive, nor his heart to report what my dream was" (4.1.208–11). The extensive attention to failures

of human judgment in the play—and the human characters' insufficient "wit to get out of this wood"—sharply contrast the play's tracking of effective agencies for those creatures to whom night belongs and who either hold sway there or operate freely in its domain. In this sense, *Midsummer* persistently sets human shortcomings against a night world replete with sovereign, creaturely life, a world with no rest or leisure to entertain human fantasies of a Cartesian *empire absolu*.

"Night-rule" recurringly transforms existing space for a time by infusing it with new actors. In its domain we find—besides fairies, elves, and spirits—a sprawling census of what Streamer would call "natural" animals and the play calls "live creature[s]" (2.1.172): lions, bears, wolves, bulls, meddling monkeys, busy apes, bats, owls, spotted snakes, thorny hedgehogs, newts, blindworms, weaving spiders, long-legged spinners, beetles black, snails, lynxes, wildcats, leopards, boars with bristled hair, crawling serpents, humble-bees, glowworms, and adders. This is not even to list the host of animal comparisons or emblems in the play. Nor does it include the bird-naming inventory of Bottom's song, sung to prove—of all things—that he is not afraid of the dark when his compatriots scatter at the sight of his shaggy new head (3.1.109–23). If many of these creatures seem dangerous or scary, it only marks a particularly human perspective making its characterizations in the dark. Theseus famously stumps for human reason in act 5 when he professes that such threats are imaginary: "In the night," he suggests (from the relative security of daylight), "how easy is a bush supposed a bear!" (5.1.21–22). Trying to rationalize the night imperially from the daytime safety of human sovereignty, all he manages is to make a claim that does not pertain at night—as the entire midsection of the play has just demonstrated, during which he and Athenian power itself have *slept*. Theseus's rational overconfidence here neglects the caveat night means for sovereign human reason, as the real threat of night creatures is reiterated over and over again in the play. The action of Oberon's love potion incorporates the random developments of whatever "next live creature" comes along (2.1.172); he elaborates how whatever "next thing" Titania sees will overwhelm her with sensations of love, "be it . . . lion, bear, or wolf, or bull, / . . . meddling monkey, or . . . busy ape" (2.1.179–81). These formulations stress the element of surprise encounters with a host of creatures in the woods, night encounters the Athenians fear. Indeed, when the play's "rude mechanicals" (3.2.9) repeatedly return to discussions of how to manage the fearsomeness of the lion's part, we can see it not only as a failure to grasp theatrical suspensions of disbelief but also as the mark of a time when large mammals posed greater threats to humans. The extensive concern with the nonhuman operations of night power index Shakespeare's willingness to notice the temporal and creaturely limits of human authority.

When Lysander and Hermia ring the poetic changes on love's fleetingness, one of their comparisons likens it to the transience of human knowledge; human powers of comprehension set the standard for failure. Even successful loves, they complain, are cut off by circumstances and so rendered as

> brief as the lightning in the collied night
> That in a spleen unfolds both heaven and earth,
> And ere a man hath power to say "Behold!"
> The jaws of darkness do devour it up.
> So quick bright things come to confusion.
> (1.1.145–49)

Here a flash of light overcomes "collied night" to "unfold" or reveal the world, but so fleetingly that human perception lags and fails. The greedy "jaws of darkness" snatch us back from comprehension and deliver us to confusion even before we can say we have seen something. Night makes Athenian senses "weak" (3.2.27). "Dark night," says Hermia, "from the eye his function takes" (3.2.177). Indeed, Puck's core business is to "mislead night wanderers" with false fire (2.1.39). The lovers come up with delightfully absurd compensatory theories of illumination. Helena imagines Demetrius's "eyes are lodestars" (1.1.183), and so she proposes, "It is not night when I do see your face" (2.1.221). Lysander boldly denies Hermia, saying, "Fair Helena . . . more engilds the night / Than all yon fiery oes [stars] and eyes of light" (3.2.187–88). These traditional poetic comparisons typically illustrate lovers' madness, but here they also spoof human reason; they *liken* love and reason in a critique of the powers of the human mind.

Even the lovers' boldest metaphors cannot sustain human powers under the corrosive dark of night. As Demetrius puts it bluntly, for Helena to "trust the opportunity of night" is to misjudge risk (2.1.217). Lysander notices that Hermia has become "faint with wandering in the wood," and because they have lost their way, they must lie down to sleep, as Puck observes, "on the dank and dirty ground" (2.2.41, 81). When Puck reports to Oberon on the mishaps of Bottom's midnight rehearsal, he says that

their sense thus weak . . .
Made senseless things to do them wrong,
For briars and thorns at their apparel snatch.
(3.2.27–30)

Oberon asks Puck to prevent the now-roused Lysander and Demetrius
from fighting by adding another layer of darkness, putting out the moon
and stars:

Robin, overcast the night;
The starry welkin cover thou anon
With drooping fog as black as Acheron,

so that the rivals will be led further "astray" (3.2.355–58). In this pursuit,
first Lysander's agency fails him—"fallen am I in a dark, uneven way"—
and he cedes upright posture to lie down and await daylight's return
(3.2.417). Then Demetrius gives up and adopts a horizontal posture that
looks like death: "Faintness constraineth me / To measure out my length
on this cold bed" (4.1.428–29). Helena too yields to the sovereignty of the
dark, complaining of the "weary . . . long and tedious night" and lying
down to wait for daylight, while Hermia too collapses:

Never so weary, never so in woe,
Bedabbled with the dew, and torn with briers,
I can no further crawl, no further go;
My legs can keep no pace with my desires.
(4.1.431, 442–45)

In every case, upright status gives way to a prone lapse in consciousness in
the play's systematic enforcement of human limits on the Athenian youth.
Deceived by a human sense-apparatus that does not work at night, misled
by creatures who do work at night, and finally stripped of the human privilege of a vertical condition, *Midsummer*'s Athenians make a case study of
human sensory and cognitive weakness—in as pointed a thought experiment as Montaigne's or Descartes's.

Scattered and solitary; faint, flattened, and unconscious on a cold, wet,
forest floor; exposed to all comers—Shakespeare's Athenians, as Demetrius had acknowledged, are left "to the mercy of wild beasts" (2.1.228). In
Oberon's words, "Be it ounce or cat or bear, / Pard, or boar with bristled

hair," whatever fearsome "vile thing" might come upon them will determine their fate (2.2.30–34). Wild beasts, vile things: in a kind of double vision, whatever is vile—in daylight—is base, cheap, despicable, or unworthy of regard. But applied to beasts, "vile" referred to dangerous or destructive animals, and we may think of this as a good nighttime definition.[46] The "vile things" of *Midsummer* are most worthy of regard—in the precise contexts where we cannot see, in a real dilemma of human perception, a dilemma that overreaching confidence in "weapons of reason" cannot address.

The lark sounds, the sun rises, and the lovers are restored, not to truth or Cartesian certitude but only to what Oberon has specified as their "wonted" or accustomed vision (3.2.369). In a compounding of errant human thought (rather than a correction of it), the hoodwinked Athenians will "think no more of this night's accidents / But as the fierce vexation of a dream" (4.1.67–68). The transition between two authorities, though, is choreographed with precision in a tableau of transferred power. When Puck announces, "Fairy King, attend and mark: / I do hear the morning lark," Oberon and Titania take their cue. The stage direction, "Exeunt. Wind horn. Enter Theseus and all his train," describes the stage action as neatly as the proverbial heralding of a transition between sovereigns: "The King is dead; long live the king." As is their wont, the human entourage thinks morning has a special relation to the harmony of the spheres, as they mark the "vaward of the day" with speculation about the music ("one mutual cry") of Theseus's dogs released in the western valley (4.1.102–17). But when the court stumbles on the sleeping lovers, Theseus delivers a rude awakening by summoning the huntsmen's horns to rouse them. As the stage direction remarks, "They all start up"; when they kneel down to him, he raises them back to upright posture with "I pray you all, stand up" (4.1.137.s.d., 140). Demetrius testifies that the night's events have been governed by "I wot not . . . what power / (But by some power it is)" (4.1.163–64). As Bottom's variation on Corinthians explains, it is not for humankind to say. Observing the creaturely decorum of separate spheres and human limitedness, he opines, "Man is but an ass if he go about to expound this dream. Methought I was—there is no man can tell what" (4.1.204–6).

And then, at day's end, regimes change again. Night arrives. Noting that they have stayed up too late and observing proprieties of jurisdictional alternation, Theseus announces, "The iron tongue of midnight hath told twelve. / Lovers, to bed, 'tis almost fairy time" (5.1.339–40). In

---

46. *Oxford English Dictionary*, 2nd ed., s.v. "vile."

this concession, Theseus actually cedes the human authority he has so notoriously represented in our commentaries on the play, acknowledging that there are limits to its jurisdictional scope. "Fairy time" supersedes it, "as the night the day." They all leave the stage. Then Puck returns, singing of the duly periodic restoration of night's black agents:

> Now the hungry lion roars,
> And the wolf behowls the moon;
> Whilst the heavy ploughman snores.
> (5.1.360–62)

Then Oberon and Titania return "with all their train" (5.1.380.s.d.), and their "night-rule" glows with benignity—for now, at least. While Descartes proselytizes for an *empire absolu*, defending human preeminence against Montaigne's charge of "imaginarie sovereignty," Shakespeare imagines a vivid alternative regime of "night-rule" and dramatizes it as a nonhuman empire. Given the temporal limitations on such cognitive powers as undergird human sovereignty, Shakespeare suggests that in the presiding dark of the night we "Athenians" should rest those weak eyes, lie low in our beds—and let the vile things rule.

CHAPTER FIVE

Hang-Dog Looks:
From Subjects at Law to Objects
of Science in Animal Trials

What does it take to have a *look* on one's face? First, one needs to have a face, which is hard to specify in the ordinary sense for Descartes's polemical oysters and sponges, but hard to deny for proximate mammals such as pigs or primates. As Montaigne asked, "What beasts have not their face aloft and before, . . . and . . . descrie not as much of heaven and earth as man doth?"[1] "Face," of course (like "voice"), is a linguistic construct, a name given by some humans to that aspect by which oriented living bodies "front" or "con-front" the cosmos. But it is certainly as a distributed attribute that Darwin's *Expression of the Emotions in Man and Animals* (1872) understands the operations that the word "face" gathers together. Animal faces there do not derive from the human face by projection or watered-down analogy; rather, it is the human face that evolutionary theory casts in derivative terms. J. R. Ackerley's *My Dog Tulip* (1965) instances our practical facility with species contours for faces, describing the intersubjective moral force of a German shepherd's face: "I suddenly espy her . . . motionless at the corner, staring after me with her exclama-tion-mark face. There is no getting away from Tulip's face; with its tall ears constantly focused upon one it demands an attention which it seems unremittingly to give."[2] The dog's face includes emphatically nonhuman

1. Michel de Montaigne, "The Apologie for Raymond Sebond," in *The Essayes of Montaigne: John Florio's Translation*, ed. J. I. M. Stewart (New York: Modern Library, 1934), 430.
2. J. R. Ackerley, *My Dog Tulip* (New York: New York Review of Books, 1999 [1965]), 15. The dog's coevolutionary status with us makes it a special, though not unique, example of how routinely we answer to (some) nonhuman faces. On coevolution, see Donna Haraway, *The Companion Species Manifesto: Dogs, People, and Significant Otherness* (Chicago: Prickly Paradigm Press, 2003), 31–32.

ears that even out-signify her stare. Ackerley does not anthropomorphize her face or exaggerate its legibility. Instead, he imagines the face-to-face in purely ethical terms, as a call. Tulip's literally arresting face "demands" no less than it gives. Ackerley may not know how to answer, but he finds himself answerable.

As we have seen, in Aristotle's biology, "Things which not only live but are also animals have both a front and a back"; frontality is one of the six "dimensions" inhering in living things, humans among the rest.[3] In the modern philosophical tradition, however, we find a more exceptionalist approach to the (implicitly and explicitly human) face and to the status of "the face-to-face" in ethics and epistemology. A specialized sense of the face structures human ethical attention, figuring both accountability and the capacity to be counted. No contemporary thinker invests more in the ethical ideal of "the face-to-face" than Emmanuel Levinas, whose *Totality and Infinity* places it before symbolic language (theoretically sidelining the alleged force of the absence of that language in cross-kind engagements). "The immediate is the face to face," he proposes, continuing that "nothing is more direct than the face to face, which is straightforwardness [*droiture*] itself"; justice appears in "the uprightness [*droiture*] of the welcome made to the face."[4] In John Llewelyn's powerful compression, the "very *droiture* of the face to face, its uprightness or rectitude (*Gerechtigkeit*, justice), is the expression of the other's right over me."[5] The face you are wearing maps another's right; "face" is a misnomer for an interface.

Recent analyses eschew the intimate scale of the face-to-face to develop a political critique of the larger order of "frontality" it subtends.[6] In exposing the racist operations of "faciality" among humans, Gilles De-

3. Aristotle, *The Progression of Animals*, in *Parts of Animals, Movement of Animals, Progression of Animals*, trans. A. L. Peck and E. S. Forster (Cambridge, MA: Harvard University Press, 1937), bk. 4, sec. 4, p. 491.

4. Emmanuel Levinas, *Totality and Infinity: An Essay on Exteriority*, trans. Alphonso Lingis (Pittsburgh: University of Pittsburgh Press, 1969 [1961]), 52, 78, 82. For note on *droiture*, see p. 62.

5. John Llewelyn, *The Middle Voice of Ecological Conscience: A Chiasmic Reading of Responsibility in the Neighbourhood of Levinas, Heidegger and Others* (London: Palgrave Macmillan, 1991), 14, citing Levinas, *Totality and Infinity*, 10 and 40. Chapter 2 of this book stressed the provincial humanity of associating physical and moral uprightness.

6. David Wills turns to what operates "from behind, from, or in back of the human." *Dorsality: Thinking Back through Technology and Politics* (Minneapolis: University of Minnesota Press, 2008), 5. On Levinas, see pp. 42–63.

leuze and Félix Guattari describe a regime of juridical power, "an abstract machine of faciality" that "rejects faces that do not conform"; if "you've been recognized, the abstract machine has you inscribed in its overall grid."[7] A Cartesian legacy undergirds faciality, in which both recognition and nonrecognition have downsides, either as answerability to the grid or as an existence that goes uncredited. Faciality dispenses its selective recognition of subjects, of citizens, of stakeholders—even of those deemed philosophically sufficient to serve as "Others," as we will see. Having a face credentializes the bearer for a subjective interface with power. (In yet another metaphor of bodily orientation, legal discourses cast this sort of recognizability, eligibility, or interfacial capacity as "standing").

In Levinas and after him, a controversy arises over whether animals have faces (apart from a theoretical discussion of whether we can or should explicitly attribute to them what we so often grant in the informalities of the face-to-face). Because Levinasian ethics prioritize a welcoming comportment toward the Other, the nearness of animals should make them compelling candidates for detailed analysis. Cary Wolfe writes that "the question of the animal is . . . not just any difference among others; it is, we might say, the most different difference, and therefore the most instructive," and he presses the importance of the fact that, even so, we find it "consistently repressed even by contemporary thinkers as otherwise profound as Levinas."[8] Indeed, as Steven Connor argues, "It is a mystery that this . . . tradition, which has been preoccupied to the point of mania with alterity—with human others, and the problem of the 'other' for humans— . . . should have managed to remain so singlemindedly uninterested in the proximate

7. Gilles Deleuze and Félix Guattari, *A Thousand Plateaus: Capitalism and Schizophrenia*, trans. Brian Massumi (London: Continuum, 2004), 187, 197. Deleuze and Guattari address these categorical dismissals only among humans. They argue that "the face is produced in humanity"; "the face is not animal"; and "to the point that humans have a destiny, it is rather to escape the face, to dismantle . . . facializations, to become imperceptible, to become clandestine, not by returning to animality . . . but by quite spiritual and special becomings-animal" that "elude the organization of the face" (189). Similar logic appears in Georgio Agamben's later call to destroy the "anthropological machine" (*The Open: Man and Animal*, trans. Kevin Attell [Stanford, CA: Stanford University Press, 2004], 92).

8. Cary Wolfe, "In the Shadow of Wittgenstein's Lion," in Wolfe, ed., *Zoontologies: The Question of the Animal* (Minneapolis: University of Minnesota Press, 2003), 23. For a helpful discussion of the species ideologies of the Levinasian face and of Heidegger's human extremism ("apes . . . have organs that can grasp, but they have no hand"), see pp. 18–22.

otherness represented by the animal."[9] Levinas himself, apparently unin-
tentionally, set the door ajar by describing a biographical episode that involved "Literally a dog!" The essay "The Name of a Dog" recalls Levinas's
time in a Nazi labor camp for French prisoners of war. It recounts how
confinement "stripped us of our human skin," rendering those interned
"subhuman, a gang of apes." Despite this endorsement of subhumanity as
a concept, in the story the prisoners befriend "a wandering dog" who sur-
vived around the camp. They name him Bobby. For Levinas, Bobby's habit
of waiting for their daily return from work and greeting them by "barking
in delight" demonstrates his core philosophical concern: ethical recognition (here manifest at the scale of species and across it): "For him, there
was no doubt that we were men." Levinas adds to Bobby's titles for this heroic act, dramatically calling him "the last Kantian in Nazi Germany."[10]

The recognition proved not to be mutual. Levinas's later denial of the
sightlines he seemed to open falls short of the promise legible, so to speak,
on the face of the essay. Encouraged by the expansive ethical horizons of
"The Name of a Dog," three student interviewers later provided Levinas
a series of questions about whether "there is something distinctive about
the human face which . . . sets it apart from that of an animal." Citing
Levinas's claim that "the commandment 'Thou shalt not kill' is revealed
by the human face," they asked, "[Is it] not also expressed in the face of
an animal?" Using Levinas's own terms, they pressed, "Can an animal be
considered as the other that must be welcomed?"[11] Levinas's somewhat

9. Steven Connor, "Thinking Perhaps Begins There: The Question of the Animal,"
Textual Practice 21 (2007): 578.

10. Emmanuel Levinas, "The Name of a Dog, or Natural Rights," in *Difficult Freedom: Essays on Judaism*, trans. Sean Hand (London: Athlone Press, 1990 [1961/1976]),
152, 153. "The Name of a Dog" separately appeared in 1975 and was added to the second
edition. The language in the quotation regarding confinement intimates the larger
problem of how an ethical rhetoric framed on *"human"* rights necessarily cuts against
the interests of nonhumans (i.e., the implicit acceptability of treating "a gang of apes"
subhumanly or "like animals"). Ralph Acampora calls this "crypto-humanist condescension." *Corporal Compassion: Animal Ethics and Philosophy of Body* (Pittsburgh:
University of Pittsburgh Press, 2006), 88. For the moral tangles triggered by embedding human/animal imagery in ethical standards, see Marjorie Spiegel, *The Dreaded
Comparison: Human and Animal Slavery* (New York: Mirror Books, 1996), and Charles
Patterson, *Eternal Treblinka: Our Treatment of Animals and the Holocaust* (New York:
Lantern Books, 2002).

11. Tamra Wright, Peter Hughes, and Alison Ainley, "The Paradox of Morality: An
Interview with Emmanuel Levinas," in *The Provocation of Levinas: Rethinking the
Other*, ed. Robert Bernasconi and David Woods (London: Routledge, 1988), 171.

wayward initial response suggests he had not given this line of questioning much previous thought. Montaigne had built an ethic around his own
response to an animal's appeal: "I am not ashamed . . . to declare the ten-
dernesse of my childish Nature which is such that I cannot well reject my
Dog if he chance (although out of season) to fawne upone me, or beg of me
to play with him."[12] But though Levinas at first concedes that "one cannot entirely refuse the face of an animal," he goes on to do just that, and
firmly.[13]

How answerable have modern philosophical accounts of man been to
the Darwinian legacy of a "community of descent"? Reversing the chro-
nologies of evolution to claim that whatever face animals have derives
instead from the "priority" of the human face, Levinas contends that he
"cannot say at what moment you have the right to be called 'face.' The human face is completely different and only afterwards do we discover the
face of an animal. I don't know if a snake has a face. I can't answer that
question." After some straying remarks about vitality, biting, and children, he finds his thread. Contravening Darwin's placement of humans as
an advanced development *within* animal estate, he claims instead that "in
relation to the animal . . . the human is a new phenomenon. . . . You ask
at what moment one becomes a face. I do not know at what moment the
human appears . . . but the human breaks from pure being." Here Levinas
makes the face and the human interchangeable; the emergence of a "face"
coincides with the onset of humanness as something "completely different." Recalling Descartes's dualistic leap across a similar logical crisis,
Levinas invokes a somewhat misleading account of Darwin's theory to
classify the entirety of nonhuman life by "a struggle of life, without ethics," while reserving the surplus ethical attribute he posits to make us human.[14] As we have seen with Descartes and Gelli's Ulysses before him—
and will see yet again in this chapter juxtaposing the sixteenth-century
legal trials of animals with seventeenth-century scientific trials—claims

12. Michel de Montaigne, "Of Cruelty," in *Essayes*, 384–85.

13. Wright, Hughes, and Ainley, "Paradox of Morality," 169.

14. Ibid., 171–72. Levinas mischaracterizes Darwin, who placed ethics as the
highest evolutionary attainment (above reason), but rooted it in "the social instinct,"
which itself is "deeply planted" and a question "of degree and not of kind." See Charles
Darwin, *The Descent of Man, and Selection in Relation to Sex* (New York: Penguin,
2004 [1871]), 120, 144, 151, 680–82. Pressing the moral implications, Darwin tells an
anecdote about a monkey and asserts that he would be proud to be "descended from
[that] heroic little monkey, who braved his dreaded enemy in order to save the life of his
keeper" (689).

about humanity remain starkly propositional. "I do not know, . . . *but*" stands as the barest kind of assertion in a discourse committed to the better proofs of demonstration.

When Derrida contemplates his feline encounter to argue (against Levinas, but in his terms) that "it is in this place of the face-to-face that the animal looks at me," his affirmation reaches back through Montaigne to contradict "the other thinkers of the 'I think,' from Descartes to Kant." He stresses how traditions of philosophical disavowal repeatedly deprive "the animal . . . of the power and the right to respond" and "of responsibility (and hence of the law, etc.)" because these faculties are made to depend on a "human face."[15] Derrida's phrase, "the law, etc.," suggests the formal and informal aspects of this interface. The present chapter takes up the problem evidenced in these skirmishes around the animal face, one that contemporary animal studies mainly treats as a general or transcendentally philosophical problem. It tries to bring the "dilemma" to ground historically instead, by rooting it in seventeenth-century challenges to the more cosmopolitical understanding of cross-kind relations described in chapter 1. It is a dated quandary.

This chapter argues that certain extraordinary proceedings—namely, the spectacular animal trials of vivisection and the vacuum tube (also known as the air pump)—operated to normalize for human audiences the more extreme instrumentalization and disenfranchisement of animals in the divisions that would characterize Bruno Latour's "modern constitution."[16] These devices contradict the lingering animal entitlement that sixteenth-century readers found in the Hexameron. Only rarely generating such advances in physiological knowledge as we can now attribute to them, vivisectors repetitively reenacted the same performances, demonstrating already established information with no ongoing prospect of new discovery. Instead of taking a scientific or exploratory rationale for granted, then, we must attend to the larger performative ends that vivisection and vacuum experiments—as recurring performances of standard or set scripts—worked culturally to serve.

Catering to what Darwin would later call "mere damnable and detestable curiosity," the formulaic spectacles of a pulsing heart inside an opened thorax or of bodily collapse due to suffocation under glass endorsed

15. Jacques Derrida, *The Animal That Therefore I Am*, ed. Marie-Louise Mallet, trans. David Wills (New York: Fordham University Press, 2008), 61, 112.

16. Bruno Latour, *We Have Never Been Modern*, trans. Catharine Porter (Cambridge, MA: Harvard University Press, 1993), 13–15.

human "dominion," confidence in which was apparently insufficient to render these restagings unnecessary or redundant.[17] Though the theatrics of vivisection and the vacuum tube backfired to a degree (spawning some passionate moral opposition), this fact did not curtail live-animal experimentation. Instead, it retreated from seventeenth-century spaces of semipublic demonstration to concealment behind the institutional walls of proprietary and disciplinary secrecy—until nineteenth-century reform forced it into some minimal regulatory scrutiny. Seventeenth-century experience showed that experimental violence on living animals under public view entailed some risk; mechanism's abstractions about animal insensitivity to pain proved unsustainable in face-to-face conditions. As a result, live-animal experiments would become a gross exception to the vaunted transparency so fundamental to the self-representations of modern science, and experimental animal subjects would be interned inside the regime of fortified invisibility so crucial to their modern condition.[18]

In the modern dispensation Latour described, as we have seen in chapter 1, "the scientific power [is] charged with representing things and the political power charged with representing subjects."[19] To some extent, this act of division constitutes things and subjects for modernity, separating "nature" from "society." But animate creatures raise special problems

17. Darwin held vivisection "justifiable for real investigations on physiology; but not for mere damnable and detestable curiosity. It is a subject which makes me sick with horror." Letter to Ray Lankester, 22 March 1871, in Francis Darwin, ed., *The Life and Letters of Charles Darwin* (London: John Murray, 1887), 3:200. Called before the Royal Commission in 1875, Darwin supported passage of the 1876 Cruelty to Animals Act (which, with broad exceptions, required that anesthesia be used in the experiments and that an animal be used only once and put down). He was asked, "You have never, I think, yourself, either directly or indirectly been connected with the practice of trying experiments on living animals?" He replied, simply, "Never." When asked about the infliction of "any pain that was not absolutely necessary on any animal," he ended his testimony by saying, "It deserves detestation and abhorrence." *Report of the Royal Commission on the Practice of Subjecting Live Animals to Experiments for Scientific Purposes; with the Minutes of Evidence and Appendix* (London: Her Majesty's Stationery Office, 1876), 233–34 (facsimile accessed at http://darwin-online.org.uk/, 15 March 2011). On Darwin and reform, see David Feller, "Dog Fight: Darwin as Animal Advocate in the Antivivisection Controversy of 1875," *Studies in History and Philosophy of Science Part C: Biological and Biomedical Sciences* 40, no. 4 (December 2009): 265–71.

18. For critical coordinates of animal visibility and confinement, see the introduction.

19. Latour, *We Have Never Been Modern*, 29.

within any general treatment of "nature" at the hands of seventeenth-century technoscience.[20] Animals were not fully *reducible to* "nature"; rather, as we have seen, they were widely understood to have a special *relationship with* "nature," as favored progeny or worthy ambassadors. The new indistinction between things and animals in the modern constitution effaced a prior line, one drawn between creatures and the things that accommodated them. Genesis 1 made "everie grene herbe" (Gen. 1:30) a thing by entitling animal and human subjects alike to eat it. Early modern readers understood the alteration of that Edenic arrangement as part of their dark inheritance of a fallen condition. Persisting notions of animal stakeholdership (with subordinate but cognizable interests and in conditions straitened by human sin, to our shame) gave way to the emerging limits inscribed in the Hobbesian contractarian politics of modernity, where the idea of an animal claim would become an absurd or impossible contradiction. The former cosmopolitical scope of the premodern constitution shrinks as modernity comes to countenance only laws of a human origin and the human "state."

Herding animals across the gap between subjects and nonsubjects and negating their creaturely relation to "the law, etc." was no simple task. To jettison the older framework of cosmopolitical relationship across species and constrain animal difference to a "human/animal divide" instead—to deprive animals, in other words, of their "faces"—was a sufficient historical and cultural adjustment to require technical support. Borrowing a term from Thomas Browne's mid-seventeenth-century *Pseudodoxia Epidemica*, I refer to a larger process of "disanimation," a techno-euphemism for death that evokes a surgical removal of soul.[21] The double sense of anima as both soul/spirit and physical breath is nowhere more vexed than in these contexts. For in the same timelines in which Aristotelian and other notions

20. Before Latour, Carolyn Merchant's landmark contribution to ecocritical historiography in *The Death of Nature* concisely names the larger process. *The Death of Nature: Women, Ecology, and the Scientific Revolution* (New York: HarperCollins, 1989 [1980]). Merchant also cites Horkeimer and Adorno (from *Dialectic of Enlightenment*), who argue that "the program of the Enlightenment was the disenchantment of the world" ("The Violence of Impediments: Francis Bacon and the Origins of Experimentation," *Isis* 99 [2008]: 736). The term I use, "disanimation," specifies this "death" and "disenchantment" in the animal case.

21. Thomas Browne, *Pseudodoxia Epidemica: Or, Enquiries into Very many Received Tenents, And commonly presumed Truths* (London: Nathaniel Ekins, 1658 [1646]), 104 (of the kingfisher's alleged occult ability to judge the wind after death) and 150 (of the computation of death in a glowworm).

of animal "soul" were being discounted, vivisections and vacuum tube
experiments targeted *respiration* to probe the curious necessity of what
Royal Society member Robert Hooke (in his "Account of an Experiment
made . . . of Preserving Animals alive by Blowing through their Lungs
with Bellows") repeatedly terms the *"supply of fresh Air."*[22]

In the spectacles of vivisection and the air pump, creatures were endlessly cast for seventeenth-century audiences as the "machines" they al-
legedly already were. By means of theatricality and repetition (otherwise
enshrined in scientific method as the objective values of witnesses and
verifiability), the performative enterprise of disanimation staged scenes
that either chained quadrupeds on their backs to vivisection boards with
their splayed limbs strapped down, depriving them of the locomotion so
central to their prior status as *animated* or instead deprived smaller animals (birds, mice, snakes, kittens, and puppies, for example) of air, likewise stilling first the alertness and then the movement that had defined
their mystery since Aristotle. Vivisection and the evacuated cylinder
constrained animals to look like things, and then these scripted formu-
las were reenacted on countless new candidates, methodically following
the steps of prior performances. The most vivid element from accounts of
these ordeals is a fascination with how what Hooke calls "the life of an
Animal" could be artificially sustained—or turned off, on, and off again—
for spectators in an almost dissociated way that evokes children toying
with a light switch.[23]

Exploring changes to the larger interface between animals and "the
law, etc.," then, this chapter charts the rise of technoscientific trials of
disanimation against the decline of a fascinating legal phenomenon in pre-
and early modernity: the criminal and civil trials of animal defendants.
The arcs of these two trial modes cross in the sixteenth century. In the
waning (and largely Continental) modality of the legal trial, animals had
a certain standing as subjects of law; in the new practices technologizing
knowledge through demonstrations, animals are recast as objects of science. The legal trials of animal defendants—about two hundred recorded
cases in Europe, occurring mainly from the fourteenth through the sixteenth centuries—transpired as formal proceedings in ecclesiastical and
secular jurisdictions, complete with due process, discovery, a verdict, and

22. Robert Hooke, "An Account of an Experiment made by M. Hook, of Preserving
Animals alive by Blowing through their Lungs with Bellows," *Philosophical Transactions of the Royal Society* (London, 1667), 2:540 (italics in the original).

23. Ibid.

a hanging in criminal cases; there was even the standard fee for the hangman. Modern scholarship on these trials tends to pose one fundamental
query: should we consider these episodes "real" legal trials, or should we
understand them more anthropologically as a cultural ritual? Shapin and
Shaffer's work on the role of witnesses and the sociology of the laboratory
opened the way for science studies to posit similar interpretive ambiguities for scientific trials and the Royal Society.[24] Animal defendants in the
legal trials were usually found guilty—but not invariably so. Certainly the
far larger number of creatures undergoing the theatricalized traumas of
vivisection and the evacuated cylinder fared no better. If we read these
legal and scientific trials together, however, we see the larger-scale renego-
tiation of status in which animals are transformed from subjects at law to
objects of science.

The balance of this chapter considers the stakes of the legal trials,
analyzing the reasoning in a French case where creaturely defendants
prevail on the merits in 1545 and assessing the careful proceduralism regarding defendants' rights in these cases overall. It next suggests how the
cosmopolitical frame of the animal cases informs two further scenes of
law beyond Shylock's notorious examination in Shakespeare's play about
cosmopolitanism and its limits, *The Merchant of Venice* (1596), and demonstrates Shakespeare's uncanny familiarity with animal executions, formal and informal. Against this legal backdrop, the chapter maps the rise
of vivisection and other live-animal experiments, from Vesalius and the
Renaissance reception of Galen to the seventeenth-century animal trials
of Hooke, Robert Boyle, and others in England. To what extent did legal
trial formats shape the scientific trial? More specifically, how should we
understand the quasi-judicial/extrajudicial language of torture that stains
even the vivisectors' accounts? In *The Advancement of Learning* (1605),
Bacon proposed that "as a man's disposition is never well known till he be
crossed, nor Proteus ever changed shapes till he was straitened and held
fast; so the passages and variations of nature cannot appear so fully in the
liberty of nature as in the trials and vexations of art."[25] Language like this
inevitably disfavors nature's "liberty." When a chained nature undergoes
trial *as vexation*, it yields up secrets to be instrumentalized by human
reason. Bacon later says, furthermore, that nature should be met "by main

24. Steven Shapin and Simon Schaffer, *Leviathan and the Air Pump: Hobbes,
Boyle, and the Experimental Life* (Princeton, NJ: Princeton University Press, 1986).
25. Francis Bacon, *The Advancement of Learning* (New York: Modern Library,
2001), 77.

force" and "laid on by manacles."[26] Literalizations of this imagery will
be analyzed below. My treatment of the disanimating process and its corrosive effect on ideas of animal stakeholdership ends with a brief look at
reflections on this "science" in seventeenth-century literature itself. Exchanges across Latour's emergent divisions were still very active, but we
see the beginnings of a disciplinary distance. In Robert Burton's *Anatomy
of Melancholy* (1621) and in Browne's 1646 *Pseudodoxia*, too, literary perspectives on this cutting up of creatures in the name of human knowledge
send us back to human folly instead. But at that point the animals have
already been reduced to parts.

Answerable Animals in a Justiciable Cosmos

A "hang-dog look" is a deflated look, conscious of guilt and anticipating
punishment or shame. The term "hang-dog look" now largely describes
human defendants in courtrooms and ordinary (not guilty) canine physi-
ognomy in about equal measure; then follow references to baseball players and male character actors such as Walter Matthau and Marcello
Mastroianni. How, in the contexts in which the expression arose, did an
animal's face—the "look" on an animal's face—come to visualize such
complex social relays as guilt and shame? As an English figure of speech,
"hang-dog look" does not derive from formal likeness between the deflated countenance of a guilty person and the drooping eyes, jowls, and
ears of an ordinary hound. To the contrary, a far less poetic sense lurks in
its pedigree, which goes back to a practice of killing individual "bad dogs"
by hanging; canine and other quadruped malefactors swung and choked
on a rope (or, in Shakespeare's pun on the leash discussed below, "a halter"). The phrase "hang-dog look" contemplates a condemned dog, not a
dewlapped one.

According to the *Oxford English Dictionary*, the word "hang-dog"
indicates the shamefacedness of "a despicable or degraded fellow fit only
to hang a dog, or to be hanged like a dog"; another source defines "hang-
dog" more sharply as "a low, mean, base fellow, fit only to be a hangman
of curs."[27] Both definitions incorporate dog hanging as historical fact.
The number of English proverbs invoking dog hanging suggests the prac-

26. Francis Bacon, *The Works of Francis Bacon*, vol. 3, *The Wisdom of the Ancients*
(1619), ed. Basil Montagu (Philadelphia: Parry and McMillan, 1859), 297.

27. *Oxford English Dictionary*, 2nd ed., s.v. "hang-dog"; *The Encyclopaedic Dictionary*, ed. Robert Hunter, vol. 4, pt. 1 (London: Cassell, 1884), 119.

tice was widespread and memorable. Tilley's dictionary of sixteenth- and seventeenth-century proverbs gives several examples: "Many a dog is hanged for his skin"; "He that would hang his dog gives out first that he is mad"; and "[He was] cozened as the dog was, who thought to go to breakfast and went to hanging" instead.[28] Other sources add the following: "A dog once hanged is past loving or hating"; "There are more ways of killing a dog than hanging it"; "Give a dog a bad name, and soon he'll be hanged"; He "sit[s] where the dog was hanged" (an ill omen); and, last, an American variant defers finality "until the last dog is hung."[29]

The gallows work absorbed into these proverbialisms and retailed to posterity apparently served to eliminate dogs who were dangerous, disruptive, resistant to training, or just too spirited. Lodovick Bryskett's *Discourse of Civill Life* (1606) tells of a mastiff who "had a qualitie to worry sheepe by night"; once caught, his master accuses him, "Thou sheepbiter, thou sheepbiter, thou must be hanged; and so indeed had purposed . . . *to have him executed*," but (taking good heed of the warning) the mastiff was able to "runne away to escape hanging."[30] Local forces beyond the household were also brought to bear on unruly English dogs. Bruce Boehrer notes that "impromptu executions of dogs, some with and some without legal adjudication, remained a common means of punishing game poachers in England well into the eighteenth century."[31] The minor but ancient ecclesiastical post of "dog-whipper" also served "not to expel from the church all dogs, but to remove such as did not behave themselves well," either

28. Morris Palmer Tilley, *A Dictionary of the Proverbs in England in the Sixteenth and Seventeenth Centuries* (Ann Arbor: University of Michigan Press, 1950), 165–67.

29. *English Proverbs and Proverbial Phrases: A Historical Dictionary*, ed. G. L. Apperson (London: Dent, 1929), 159–61; *Oxford Dictionary of Proverbs*, ed. Jennifer Speake (Oxford: Oxford University Press, 2003), 78; *Early American Proverbs and Proverbial Phrases*, ed. Bartlett Whiting (Cambridge, MA: Belknap Press, 1977), 116–71; and *Morris Dictionary of Word and Phrase Origins*, ed. William Morris and Mary Morris (New York: HarperCollins, 1988), 273.

30. Lodovick Bryskett, *A Discourse of Civill Life: Containing the Ethike Part of Morall Philosophie* (London: Edward Blount, 1606), Hh1v–Hh2r (italics added). I thank Jean Feerick for this reference.

31. Bruce Boehrer, "Shylock and the Rise of the Household Pet: Thinking Social Exclusion in *The Merchant of Venice*," *Shakespeare Quarterly* 50, no. 2 (Summer 1999): 164, citing Douglas Hay, "Poaching and the Game Laws on Connock Chase," in *Albion's Fatal Tree: Crime and Society in Eighteenth-Century England*, ed. Douglas Hay et al. (New York: Pantheon, 1975), 195–96. See also Keith Thomas, *Man and the Natural World: Changing Attitudes in England, 1500–1800* (Oxford: Oxford University Press, 1983), 98.

with a special whip or wooden "dog tongs."[32] Thomas Nashe's *Pierce Penilesse* (1592) refers to "the dog whipper in Paules."[33] The scrums of hunting and other dogs, kept in and around larger houses and freely foraging around human tables, suggest similar scenes of minor chaos. Crab, of *Two Gentlemen of Verona*, leaps to mind, as he enters "the company of three or four gentlemanlike dogs under the table," and an uproar ensues (4.4.16–18). Perhaps hanging offered a larger-animal alternative to the drowning of unwanted litters (suggesting an unexpected spin on the proverb "He who is born to be hanged will never be drowned"). But death *by hanging* does more than dispatch unwanted animals; it enforces justice, however informal, through the spectacular publicity of an execution staged high on a gallows tree.

The gibbeting of dogs and other animals was not just a feature of popular, rural, or domestic life in late medieval and early modern Europe; it also occurred in significantly more formal cultural registers and venues, on the Continent in particular.[34] While rough justice has been done on

---

32. William Tate, *The Parish Chest: A Study of the Records of Parochial Administration in England* (Cambridge: Cambridge University Press, 1969), 108; see also Susan McHugh, *Dog* (London: Reaktion, 2004), 130. Dog-Whipping Day (October 18) marked an old episode from "Catholic days," when a priest dropped a consecrated wafer in York Minster, and a dog snatched it and paid the price. William Walsh, *Curiosities of Popular Customs and of Rites, Ceremonies, Observances, and Miscellaneous Antiquities* (Philadelphia: J. B. Lippincott, 1897), 341.

33. Thomas Nashe, *Pierce Penilesse, His Supplication to the Divell* (London: Abel Jeffes, 1592), I2v.

34. My discussion does not address animal executions in bestiality cases (familiar in England) because the animals had no standing as trial parties. The 1533 Parliament made the "abhomynable vice of buggery . . . commyttid with mankynde or beaste" a felony punishable by death for the human participant; the statute set no sentence for the animal (*25 Henry VIII. c. 6*, cited in Jonathan Goldberg, *Sodometries: Renaissance Texts, Modern Sexualities* [Stanford, CA: Stanford University Press, 1992], 3). The animal's execution ensued without attribution of responsibility. As Keith Thomas argues, these executions were "not as a punishment, but as a symbolic way of expressing abhorrence" (*Man and the Natural World*, 97–98). Bruce Boehrer likewise argues that "the main work performed by Renaissance English attacks on buggery was discursive, rather than material." Bruce Boehrer, *Shakespeare among the Animals: Nature and Society in the Drama of Early Modern England* (New York: Palgrave, 2002), 50. On the rationales for moving livestock outdoors to avoid an intimacy interfering with the property status of animals and the concomitant rise of (eroticized) pet keeping, see Erica Fudge, *Perceiving Animals: Humans and Beasts in Early Modern Culture* (Urbana: University of Illinois Press, 2002), 132–36.

animals since time immemorial (the biblical ox that gored was killed, not tried), in a subtle and ranging account, Esther Cohen suggests that it "took the medieval legal mentality to assume that one could no more punish an animal than a human being without a proper trial." This stems from a sense of the cosmos as justiciable—what Cohen calls "a universe of justice that transcended the human community."[35] Scholarship on these trials has largely deliberated protocols for reading them. Are they extreme evidence of human cruelty that we should liken to the ordeals of blood sport?[36] Do they enact human ritual symbolizations through the pressed stage work of animal actors? Or are we to entertain the idea that the trials were "serious" legal processes?

To some extent, these oppositions depend on modern ideas about law that define it as a human-authored artifact applicable only to humans, a conception centered on contract and consent, intent and conscience, and notice and legibility. In other words, these adverse interpretive frames tend to assume the divisions of the "modern constitution" before their time. As chapter 1 described, by contrast, more heterogeneous late medieval and early modern notions of law situated human positive law as a lowly imitator within a larger system of laws they called natural and divine; they also sometimes elevated the relation animals had to natural law in particular, as we have seen in chapters 2 and 3. And so, in addressing the modern conundrum these trials represent, Cohen carefully distinguishes between medieval animals who are made substitutes for humans and used symbolically in public rituals (scenes to be read anthropologically or allegorically) and those animals standing trial in their own capacity, "enduring punishment for their own misdeeds" if they lost their case, which "was by no means a foregone conclusion."[37] Animal legal trials, then, do not necessarily call for a different protocol or a more symbolic or ritual interpretation than any other historical lawsuit. Instead, they evidence the historical traction of fundamentally different conceptions about animal participation in a constitutional commixture of politics, theology, and law—a mixture that was not monoculturally human.

E. P. Evans's 1906 *The Criminal Prosecution and Capital Punishment*

---

35. Esther Cohen, *The Crossroads of Justice: Law and Culture in Late Medieval France* (Leiden, Netherlands: Brill, 1993), 124, 100.

36. On the grim dynamics of bear baiting, see Rebecca Ann Bach, "Bearbaiting, Dominion, and Colonialism," in *Race, Ethnicity and Power in the Renaissance*, ed. Joyce MacDonald (Teaneck, NJ: Fairleigh Dickinson University Press, 1997), 19–35.

37. Cohen, *Crossroads of Justice*, 110, 123.

of Animals is the sole monograph in English on the trials, and subsequent
anglophone commentaries tend to rely on its ranging archival work, tabulations of data, and appended documents.[38] Evans records 191 cases of animal prosecution and a head-spinning inventory of creatures: dogs, wolves,
roosters, locusts, grasshoppers, pigs, cows, donkeys, termites, rats, goats,
doves, horses, worms, weevils, sheep, slugs, gadflies, snails, dolphins,
bloodsuckers, field mice, beetles, bulls, oxen, eels, serpents, moles, and
"unspecified vermin" (appendix F, 313–34). The majority occur in the fif-
teenth and sixteenth centuries, although cases appear from the ninth to
the twentieth. Most arose in the regions of France, Germany, Italy, and
Switzerland; Cohen stresses a French origin.[39] The processes are of two
kinds, and forms of animal accountability differ between them. The first
involves suits waged against vermin or pests, who live in large groups and
whose transgression combines trespass with the destruction of crops or
food stocks. That such swarms are impossible for a sheriff to seize deter-
mines the noncriminal form of their prosecution.[40] These cases occurred
in a jointly civic and ecclesiastical format, and punishment ranged from
eviction and relocation to excommunication (or, more technically, anathematization). The second type of process involves secular and criminal
violations and so was prosecuted by civil magistrates. For homicidal quadrupeds, the punishment was hanging.

In vermin cases, despite obvious logistical challenges, there is little
evidence of doubt about jurisdiction as such.[41] The case with the most de-

38. E. P. Evans, *The Criminal Prosecution and Capital Punishment of Animals*
(Union, NJ: Lawbook Exchange, 1998 [1906]) (subsequent page references appear in the
text). Evans engages three earlier works: Karl von Amira, *Thierstrafen und thierpro-
cesse* (Innsbruck, Austria: Verlag der Wagner'schen Universitäts-Buchhandlung, 1891);
Carlo d'Addosio, *Bestie delinquenti* (Naples, Italy: Luigi Pierro, 1892); and especially
Léon Ménabréa, *De l'origine de la forme et de l'esprit des jugements rendus au moyen-
âge contre les animaux* (Chambéry, France: Puthod, 1846). Of subsequent anglophone
scholarship, only Cohen forages substantially beyond Evans.

39. Cohen, *Crossroads of Justice*, 110.

40. "Specimens" were sometimes captured and killed as part of the process (Evans,
Criminal Prosecution, 3).

41. Evans notes "occasional" protests about jurisdiction claims over animals, citing
a 1591 quarto that argues that corpses, the ashes, and memory of the dead, brute beasts,
and inanimate things "are not legal persons (*legales homines*) and therefore do not
come within the jurisdiction of a court" (Evans, *Criminal Prosecution*, 109); see Pierre
Ayrault, *Des procez faicts au aadaver, aux cendres, à la mémoire, aux bestes brutes,
aux choses inanimées et aux contumax* (Angers, France, 1591).

tailed surviving record commenced in 1545.[42] In St. Julien (with its famous
vintages at the heart of the controversy), swarms of greenish weevils had
infested the vineyards. Vineyard stakeholders made an official complaint
against the bugs, a procurator and advocate were duly appointed for them,
and a hearing date was set. Instead of a verdict against the weevils, this
first hearing resulted in an official determination on 8 May 1546 as follows: "Inasmuch as God, the supreme author of all that exists, hath ordained that the earth should bring forth fruits and herbs . . . not solely for
the sustenance of rational human beings, but likewise for the preservation and support of insects . . . it would be unbecoming to proceed with
rashness and precipitance against the animals now actually accused and
indicted" (38).[43] In other words, as entitled creatures—cognizable citizens
of creation—the bugs were not only party to a trial; they prevailed at the
first hearing. Genesis 1:30, which chapter 1 described more broadly as
the basis for the disseminated sense of a cosmic charter before the seventeenth century, here functioned as a dispositive statute in a formal case
where humans proceeded against insects. In contrast to many other cases,
here the human request for injunctive relief against the defendant weevils
was *denied*. Instead, the plaintiffs were urged to fulfill a series of religious
observations to appease God. A *procès-verbal* (an official descriptive account) signed by a curate attested that these rites had been performed and
that the insects "soon afterwards" left (39).

Forty-two years later, however (in a neat attribution of corporate perpe-
tuity), the weevils returned. The inhabitants of St. Julien petitioned again,
represented by the town syndics and procurators. On 13 April 1587, they
asked for new counsel for the weevils to be appointed because the previous
ones had died, and they petitioned the court to visit the grounds to observe

42. My summary follows Evans's detailing of the 1545–46 process and the resumption of proceedings in 1587 (*Criminal Prosecution*, 37–50). For the latter, Evans
transcribes twenty-nine original folio pages titled *De actis scindicorum communitatis
Sancti Julliani agentium contra animalia bruta ad formam muscarum volantia coloris
viridis communi voce appellata verpillions seu amblevins* [Of the action of the syndics
of the community of St Julien, plaintiffs, against brute animals in the form of winged
flies of a green color, commonly called *Verpillions* or *Amblevins* (weevils)] as appendix A (*Criminal Prosecution*, 259–85).

43. This is Evans's translation. Evans does not give the original Latin proclamation;
the gist of it reappears in 1587: "Cum a principio ipse summus Deus qui cuncta creavit
fructus terre et anime vegetative produci permiserit tam substentatione vite hominum
rationabilium et volatilium super terram viventium quamobrem non sic repente proce-
dendum est contra prefata Animalia" (*Criminal Prosecution*, 266).

234

the renewed damage and to begin a process. Almost two months later, Evans reports, a distinguished procurator and new advocate appeared, and the advocate, Pierre Rembaud, made an answer for the weevils. Rembaud argued that his clients were acting within their entitlement to inhabit the vines and so had not trespassed in a way warranting excommunication. He based this claim, again, on Genesis and quotes the relevant passages.

Rembaud stressed that "Deus ante hominis creationem ipsa Animalia creavit" (God created these very animals before the creation of man); priority in time has traditionally enjoyed a privilege in any question of land and the rights to occupy it. Rembaud's argument cited scripture explicitly, and he linked Genesis 1:24 (each created in their kind) with 1:22 (the blessing and exhortation to multiply) from the Vulgate: "Producat terra animam viventem in genere suo jumenta et reptilia et bestias terre secondum species suas benedixitque eis dicens crescite et multiplicamini et replete aquas maris avesque multiplicentur super terram." This conjunction of verses gave force to the claim that the weevils were only enjoying their due rights according to the charter of creation; their creation and the exhortation to be fruitful occur before the arrival of man on the Edenic scene. The advocate then stressed the biblical provision of plants expressly to all living creatures whether rational or brute ("omnium Animalium tam rationabilium quam irrationabilium") for sustenance (270). The weevils, he concluded, were only exercising their hexameral rights when relocating to the plaintiffs' vines.

Four procedural adjournments later, the plaintiffs' counsel replied, arguing that the prior creation of the animals constituted, instead, evidence of their subordination to man and that they had no purpose beyond man's use—counsel thus stressed the biblical language of domination and argued one verse of Genesis against another.[44] The weevils' advocate methodically replied that because he had not been provided the required copy of this response, the case should be adjourned again, and it was. A final verdict was delayed still further due to new evidence. During the course of the suit, negotiations had been under way to settle out of court. The plaintiff hu-

44. Evans paraphrases the argument (44) and provides the full transcript of the original document: "Etiamsi cuncta ante hominem sint creata ex Genesi non sequitur laxas habenas concessas fore immo contra ut ibidem colligitur et apud . . . in . . . psal. 8 Corin. 5 hominem fore creatum ac constitutum ut coeteris creaturis dominaretur ac orbem terrarum in aequitate et justitia disponeret. Non enim homo contemplatione aliarum creaturarum habet esse sed contra. Nec reperitur illam dominationem circa bruta animantia ac eorum respectu suscipere limitationem verum in divinis cavetur omne genuflecti in nomine Jesu" (274).

mans were preparing a deed of perpetual conveyance to offer a land area to the defendant weevils for them to inhabit instead of the vineyards. Debate ensued over whether said lands were sterile or adequate to sustain weevils (as Genesis requires). These negotiations were presented to the court, and one of the last entries provides for experts to evaluate the proffered land. At this point, 20 December 1587, the record ends. The bottom of the last folio page "has been destroyed," Evans reports, not by fire, flood, or time, but by the sharp-toothed gnawings of "rats or bugs of some sort"—who, with poetic justice at least, managed to have the last word (49).

Even though theoretical jurisdiction over nonhuman animals can be asserted without too much difficulty, the challenge of establishing physical authority over animal groups that cannot be captured remained. As a result, vermin trials were noted for the development of procedural devices (in the best sense). Bartholomew Chassenée, later a distinguished jurist, established his reputation by representing the rats of Autun. Rats were destroying the province's barley crop, and Chassenée was appointed to defend them. Chassenée scored a number of procedural victories in the action. He challenged normal summons procedure, arguing that the dispersed situation of the rats rendered a lone reading of their court call in a single location insufficient. A second citation then had to be "published from the pulpits of all the parishes inhabited by the said rats" (19). When this was done and the rats remained in apparent contempt, Chassenée successfully argued that coming to court would unreasonably endanger them: they were threatened by the "unwearied vigilance of their mortal enemies, the cats, who watched all their movements, and with fell intent, lay in wait for them at every corner and passage" (19). On the one hand, these sound like the wittiest of proceduralisms. But they also set a precedent for equitable review to ensure that a procedural entitlement such as notice was being effectively achieved (indeed, the ruling had later bearing on rights to notice and a hearing in a case involving heresy charges that Chassenée would eventually hear as a justice) (20).

Three things stand out about the vermin cases. First is the scripturally based argument entitling all creatures, even troublesome insects and rats, to certain rights of existence and mobility that can contend with and even prevail over human property rights. Defendants appealed to Genesis 1, and the citation had a direct effect. Second is the rigorous endorsement of rights to due notice, highlighting strict procedural fairness for (animal) defendants.[45] And third, despite some technical debate over whether the

45. Evans, *Criminal Prosecution*, 24; Cohen, *Crossroads of Justice*, 110–12.

desired verdict is excommunication (ejection from ecclesiastical community) or anathematization (which has a general exilic effect without assuming church community), these inquiries posit a measure of animal membership in the community of creation that is at least minimally adjudicable.[46] As we have seen in chapter 1, the establishment of a broad creaturely canopy in Genesis 1 exerts considerable constitutional force. Even in a cosmic deliberation over the particular application of hexameral entitlements, bugs are afforded rights of representation and notice matching those of a sixteenth-century human defendant.

The same meticulous proceduralism characterizes the second kind of case: the criminal prosecution of quadrupeds. Here, no excommunicative decree or injunctive relief is sought; instead, a gallows scene ends the drama. Many cases concern pigs and child victims. Swine often roamed freely in towns, leading inevitably to collisions when the larger animal charges, crushes, or otherwise injures the smaller (and sometimes instigating) creature. As Cohen describes, these "secular trials followed the inquisitorial procedure strictly," with civic authorities imprisoning the animal, prosecuting the case, and summoning witnesses.[47] The most famous instance involves a sow in Falaise who killed an infant. Evans reports that a fresco of the scene decorated a wall in the Church of the Holy Trinity at Falaise, but was sadly whitewashed in 1820 (141). The sow was hanged, with the town hangman receiving a customary gift of gloves. On the basis of records in Falaise that include a receipt for this labor, Evans stresses that this was no butcher "but a public functionary, a 'master of high works' (maître des hautes oevres)" (140; appendix G, 335). In another instance, a sow was convicted of "murder flagrantly committed" on a five-year-old and sentenced to be "hanged by the hind feet to a gallows-tree"— her six offspring had also been found stained with blood and were included in the indictment as accomplices, but they were exonerated on evidence provided by six (human) witnesses.[48]

In the anglophone tradition, research since Evans—historical accounts, cultural studies, and law reviews—fundamentally repeats the same question: what did medieval and early modern human actors have in mind

46. Some writers "do not recognize this distinction between anathema and excommunication on the authority of many passages of Holy Writ, affirming that, as the whole creation was corrupted by the fall, so the atonement extends to all living creatures" (Evans, Criminal Prosecution, 51–52).

47. Cohen, Crossroads of Justice, 111.

48. See also ibid.

when they tried animals at law, while in other contexts they denied them the rational capacity on which a meaningful trial depends?[49] As Erica Fudge puts the problem, humanness is often defined "by the capacity for intention" now so central to liability.[50] Evans himself, though a meticulous chronicler of the trials, calls them a "travesty of the administration of justice" and a "parody and perversion of a sacred and fundamental institute of civil society" (41). With these words, however, he was negating an alternative possibility raised in 1846 by his French predecessor, Léon Ménabréa. As the first modern historian to research the trials, Ménabréa warns his reader to resist the impulse to "charge this custom with superstition and barbarism" and points out that "when one sees a custom rooted in a people and maintained for centuries, it is necessary to listen carefully . . . before charging it with absurdity or ridicule."[51] Instead, he engaged in a brief thought experiment considering the trials another way: "There was something strikingly beautiful in the thought that assimilated the insect of the field to the masterwork of creation and made the one the equal of the other. If man should in effect respect the retreat and domain of the worm, how much stronger reason is there for man to respect man, and for each to restrain himself according to equity!"[52] As Ménabréa's reflections suggest, "travesty" might not be the most apt term for the animal cases. Chassenée himself had addressed cosmopolitical themes related to the elevated variant expressed in Ménabréa's cross-species vision of *égalité*. He argued that animal communities themselves have laws and punish violations and that domestic animals can commit crimes against man consciously (34–35). Indeed, his arguments favoring judicial proceedings were based on a criticism of man's tendency to punish animals summarily and auto-

49. See, for example, Piers Beirne, "'The Law Is an Ass': Reading E. P. Evans' *The Medieval Prosecution and Capital Punishment of Animals*," *Society and Animals Journal* 2, no. 1 (1994): 27–46; William Ewald, "Comparative Jurisprudence (I): What Was It Like to Try a Rat?" *University of Pennsylvania Law Review* 143, no. 6 (1995): 1905; Fudge, *Perceiving Animals*, 121–25; and Jen Girgen, "The Historical and Contemporary Prosecution and Punishment of Animals," *Animal Law* 9 (2003): 97–133.

50. Fudge, *Perceiving Animals*, 139.

51. Ménabréa, *De l'origine de la forme*, 3–4 (my translation).

52. Ibid., 4 (my translation). The passage reads: "Il y avait je ne sais quoi de beau dans la pensée qui assimilait l'insecte des champs au chef-d'oeuvre de la création, et qui rendait l'un l'égal de l'autre. Si l'on devait en effet respecter la retraite du vermisseau, combien à plus forte raison ne fallait-il pas que l'homme respectât l'homme, et que chacun se gouvernât selon l'équité!" For a decidedly anglophone reaction to this idea, see Evans, *Criminal Prosecution*, 40–41.

cratically: Evans describes Chassenée's insistence that "under no circumstances is a penalty to be imposed except by judicial decision—*nam poena
nunquam imponitur, nisi lex expresse dicat*—and in support of this principle [he] refers to the apostle Paul, who declares that 'sin is not imputed
where there is no law'" (35). Animal liability was of sufficient seriousness
that Chassenée, eventually chief justice of the Parliament of Provence,
published a treatise on it. His *Consilium Primum . . . De excommunica-
tione animalium insectorum* (a tract on the excommunication or formal
condemnation of animals and insects) was first published in Lyon in 1531
and reprinted in 1581 and 1588. The publication dates of Chassenée's volume substantially overlap with the timelines for Montaigne's translation
of and apology for Raymond Sebond, with its constitutional vision of a
"generall throng,"[53] and it is tempting to connect Chassenée, Montaigne,
and Ménabréa (and perhaps Derrida) in a Gallic tradition of cosmopolitical
egalitarianism.

Evans describes Chassenée's *Consilium primum* as scouring the written record for proceedings against insects and other vermin to provide an
account for the precedents and proper procedures for it. The work ranges
broadly from Moses to Justinian, from medieval hagiography to Pico della
Mirandola, and from Aristotle to Ovid, and, of course, cites diverse scriptural sources (23). The *Consilium*, however, was not the only sixteenth-
century work addressing causes of action against creatures under the law.
Another influential and more widely disseminated legal treatise likewise
gives a chapter to animal prosecution. Joost de Damhouder, a jurist born
in Brugge and trained at Leuven, first published his *Praxis rerum criminalium* in Antwerp in 1554. The comprehensive 1562 edition of this much-
reprinted volume reflects the rich publishing culture of that city: each
crime has a chapter, and each chapter includes a woodcut illustrating the
crime it describes.[54] Chapter 142 categorizes crimes by quadrupeds, variant owner responsibilities under a range of circumstances, and the liabilities pertaining to humans and animals.

Titled "*De damno pecuario*" (Of livestock injuries), the chapter considers a range of harms committed by a *bestia laedens* (offending animal), including not only sheep and cattle but also dogs, swine, boars, foxes, bears,

53. Montaigne, "Apologie," 406.

54. Joost de Damhouder, *Praxis rerum criminalium* (a treatise on criminal law
practice) (Antwerp, Belgium: Ioannem Bellerum, 1562). This edition can be viewed at
http://www.bvh.univ-tours.fr/index.htm.

lions, wolves, and other similar wild animals (*aut similem fera[m]*), breaking down distinct forms of responsibility. In addition to familiar treatments of third-party liability (where other persons or animals were insti-
gators or where the intervening negligence of servants or other custodians
insulated the animal's owner from liability), we also find direct quadruped
liability in cases of malice (*malitia*). A beast harming a person out of its
own malice is to be punished personally, not the owner or the servants
(*bestia laedens ex interna malitia, ipsa punienda est, non dominus, non
famulus*). Likewise, if an animal commits violence on another animal out
of its own malice (*ex propria malitia*), it is to be condemned (*damnanda*).
Here we see quadrupeds credited with something akin to the notorious
criminal concept "malice aforethought."[55]

    The woodcut illustrating this chapter within a general treatise on
criminal practice vividly illustrates the malice crimes, bypassing the detailed considerations of owner or servant liability and problems of instiga-
tion parsed in the chapter (fig. 5.1). In the foreground, a bristling boar with
a dastardly criminal expression ravages a screaming child swaddled in a
cradle. In the middle ground, a charging ox or bull leaps on a man he has
knocked to the ground and is about to gore him with well-aimed horns.
And just behind the hoofed gorer, we see a "sheep-biter": a dog poised to
kill sheep among the flock he should protect. From the sheep to the prostrate man to the swaddled infant, the homicidal quadrupeds have selected
their victims scandalously. The vulnerability of the child and the sheep
is echoed by the adult tossed down from his upright stature to a defense-
less position on the ground. In traditional iconographic style, we see the
future on the horizon but within the frame. On a distant hill, a stark gallows "gape[s] for dog" (in Shakespeare's words from *Henry V*), and circling
crows anticipate a meal of four-footed felons on a gibbet. In late medieval
and early modern culture, as now, a range of assumptions about animal
capacities were held by different people; even at an individual level, then
as now, beliefs about animals were likely to contain contradictions. But
what two hundred cases and these conventional legal treatises about trial
procedure show is that even in established and formal domains, a cosmopolitical perspective pertained in which animals could be considered as
answerable as man before the law—where they sometimes even prevailed
against him.

---

55. Ibid., 404–6. Damhouder contemplates wild animals held or domesticated in
human custody ("Ales domi").

Figure 5.1. Joost de Damhouder, *Praxis rerum criminalium* (1570 [1562]).
Image by permission of the Folger Shakespeare Library, Washington, DC.

Whip Him Out; Hang Him Up!
Cosmopolity in *The Merchant of Venice*

According to the historical record, these formal trials were an exclusively
Continental phenomenon. It is unlikely that some English proceeding has
been lost, despite the plethora of English references to dog hanging. The
separate development of English common law, particularly in terms of
property, supplies the main reason for this difference. An older doctrine
of deodand evolved in English courts of assize to define the agent in such

cases as an "instrument, animate or inanimate," requiring the owner to pay a sum to the sovereign.[56] This regime establishes a system of third-party liability for animal acts (as Damhouder's elaborations did too, after the cases based on *malitia*); owners pay damages as a fine. And so, in Keith Thomas's words, England had "no real counterpart to that curiosity of continental legal history, the trial and execution of homicidal animals."[57] Some commentators insist on the impossibility of animal trials in England, because the property principle and animal prosecution seem mutually exclusive. Others note that archival evidence may be incomplete, with one early twentieth-century legal historian speculating that such trials may have been common in Elizabethan contexts.[58] This seems unlikely, but, as Thomas continues, there were "plenty of informal trials."[59] Shakespeare himself makes a very special appearance in the scholarly tradition on this obscure aspect of formal and informal citizenship. As historian of criminology George Ives observed (against the claim that such trials were unknown in England), "Shakespeare, 'who knew everything,' alludes to the practice."[60]

A search for proximate terms in Shakespeare flushes a wealth of references to the whipping, beating, and hanging of dogs in particular. This not only suggests that Shakespeare was no dog person but also indicates the degree to which "man's best friend" serves as his likeliest figure for revulsion and violent ejection from human company—paralleling the formal anathemas and excommunications sought in Continental trials. *Richard III* ends when "the bloody dog is dead" (5.5.2); Iago is redundantly called an "inhuman dog" (*Othello*, 5.1.65); *Henry VI, Part 2* cites "the ancient proverb . . . 'A staff is quickly found to beat a dog'" (3.1.170–71); Falstaff imagines that if the prince "were here, I would cudgel him like a dog" (*Henry IV, Part 1*, 3.3.87–88); and the fool observes Kent's fate and concludes that "truth's a dog that must to kennel. He must be whipped out, when the Lady Brach may stand by the fire" (*King Lear*, 1.4.109–11). These

56. Fudge, *Perceiving Animals*, 123–24; see also Beirne, "'Law Is an Ass,'" 34.

57. Thomas, *Man and the Natural World*, 97–98.

58. See Beirne, "'Law Is an Ass,'" 34; for the view that there were no English animal trials, see also J. J. Finkelstein, "The Ox That Gored," *Transactions of the American Philosophical Society* 71, no. 2 (1981): 3–89. Compare W. W. Hyde, "The Prosecution and Punishment of Animals and Lifeless Things in the Middle Ages and Modern Times," *University of Pennsylvania Law Review* 64, no. 7 (1916): 709.

59. Thomas, *Man and the Natural World*, 98.

60. George Ives, *A History of Penal Methods: Criminals, Witches, Lunatics* (Montclair, NJ: Patterson Smith, 1914), 256n4.

phrasings reflect the liminality of dogs, then and now. Inclusion is subject to sudden potential for offending. As with any kind of membership, conditions apply.

The hanging of animals also pervades Shakespeare's language. When Lear says

> my poor fool is hanged! . . .
> Why should a dog, horse, or rat have life,
> And thou no breath at all,

we hear the connection (5.3.311–13). In *Much Ado*, Benedick laments a singer's bad voice and exclaims, "An he had been a dog that should have howled thus, they would have hanged him," while the bumbling law officer, Dogberry, professes, "I would not hang a dog by my will, much more a man who hath any honesty in him" (2.3.81–82, 3.3.62–63). Pistol observes Bardolph's fate:

> He hath stol'n a pax,
> And hangèd must a' be—a damnèd death!
> Let gallows gape for dog; let man go free.
> (*Henry V*, 3.6.40–42)

And then there is Crab in *Two Gentlemen of Verona*, whom we left misbehaving under the duke's table. Launce reports: "If I had not had more wit than he, I think verily he had been hanged for't; sure as I live he had suffered for't; you shall judge. . . . 'Out with the dog!' says one: 'What cur is that?' Says another; 'Whip him out' says the third: 'Hang him up' says the Duke" (4.4.13–22). Launce regales the dog whipper ("the fellow that whips the dogs") with a list of occasions when he has endured judicial penalties as his dog's substitute ("I have sat in the stocks for puddings he hath stolen, otherwise he had been executed; I have stood on the pillory for geese he hath killed, otherwise he had suffered for it" [4.4.24, 29–33]), and he explains that the little gift dog he replaced with Crab "was stolen from me by the hangman boys in the marketplace" (4.4.53–54). In all these references, we see repeated notes of quasi-legal retribution cheek by jowl with practical familiarity and the ubiquitous presence of animals. A curse from *Romeo and Juliet* compresses this double gesture of exclusion and inclusion, where the sharpest insult calls an adversary "a dog of the house of Montague" (1.1.7). To be a dog is to suffer imminent condemnation or precipi-

tous ejection from a community ("Out with the dog! . . . Whip him out . . .
Hang him up"), even as being "of [a] house" names a place of precarious
membership, a space at (or under) the table. The informal or quasi-citizen
has some of the liabilities and some of the benefits of "belonging."

The citizenship dilemma of the dog returns us to Shylock, the self-
denominated "stranger cur" (1.3.116). *The Merchant of Venice* stresses the
capaciousness of Venetian law, emphasizing that its cosmopolitanism
must be maintained in order to preserve what Salerio calls "the freedom of
the state" and Shylock calls the "charter" and the "city's freedom" (3.2.278,
4.1.39). Antonio elucidates the uncontroversial idea:

> The Duke cannot deny the course of law;
> For the commodity that strangers have
> With us in Venice, if it be denied,
> Will much impeach the justice of the state,
> Since that the trade and profit of the city
> Consisteth of all nations.
> (3.3.26–32)

"The commodity that strangers have / With us" indicates the renowned
openness of the city, its provision of a customary privilege or freedom to
go about one's business. Under Venetian law, in other words, "strangers"
are *accommodated*. The city's "justice" equips them with legal protections to support their enterprises; it tolerates each according to his kind;
and (occasionally) offers further accommodation, such as an invitation
to supper. Strangers are not "out-laws" like the "banished men" in *Two
Gentlemen of Verona* who seek a governor who then restores them to the
freedoms of citizenship in Milan (5.4.153–60). Rather, strangers in Venice
are present under the law, a law that officially deems them accountable
but also creditable and even protectable—until something changes. Foreign status and the overt anti-Semitism of the entire cultural situation are
not sufficient in themselves to generate the play's case and controversy,
for the crisis around Shylock stems not from his status as a *stranger* but
from his conduct as a "stranger *cur*." This is not to say that Shylock is
bestialized and diminished thereby, but somewhat contrarily to say that,
like a "malicious" animal, the measure of Shylock's marginal social inclusion registers in his ability to make himself vulnerable to process, like
Damhouder's *bestia laedens ex interna malitia*, whose currish conduct
triggered liability under the criminal law.

No neutral designation, the English noun "cur" seems to derive from the Germanic verb *kurren*, to growl.[61] Currishness rejects courtesy. A cur turns; a cur snarls and bares its teeth; it threatens to bite—it might even snatch "a pound of man's flesh" (1.3.164). When asked to explain his demand for this infamous in-kind payment from Antonio, Shylock proposes that his irrational insistence on the terms of his bond need not be justified. He answers:

> As there is no firm reason to be rendered
> Why he cannot abide a gaping pig,
> Why he a harmless necessary cat,
>
> . . .
>
> So can I give no reason, nor I will not,
> More than a lodged hate and certain loathing
> I bear Antonio.
> (4.1.53–55, 59–61)

Revealing at once the terms of his Venetian accommodation (like house-cats, strangers are accommodated on condition of being "harmless" and "necessary") as well as his refusal to remain "harmless," Shylock's bold hostility and confession of a "lodged hate" foreclose any need for question on the legal element of malice.

Boehrer provides helpful analysis concerning how dogs were largely understood as servants with useful functions when notions of pet keeping first began to emerge; he points out the ancient ambivalence in canine symbolics between the "identification of dogs with slaves and other abjected individuals [i.e., creatures who serve] and the association of dogs with predatory outsiders."[62] The discourse of currishness in *Merchant* splits this difference to figure a hostile *insider*, a quasi-citizen and familiar who turns predator within the community. When Shylock confronts Antonio, saying, "Thou calledst me dog before thou hadst a cause, / But since I am a dog, beware my fangs," he seems to agree that a "cause" has arisen and that he has given cause for complaint, being no longer "harmless" and

---

61. The *Oxford English Dictionary* (2nd ed.) associates the noun "cur" with onomatopoetic verbs from northern European and Scandinavian languages for growl and snarl (etymology for "cur").

62. Bruce Boehrer, "Shylock and the Rise of the Household Pet: Thinking Social Exclusion in *The Merchant of Venice*," *Shakespeare Quarterly* 50, no. 2 (Summer 1999): 154, 163.

"necessary" (3.3.6–7). This currishness makes him not just any dog, but a
malicious one, and therefore no ordinary dog, but one to be prosecuted by
the state: a "damned . . . dog" or *bestia damnanda* (4.1.128).

Shylock is called a dog as often as Richard III is—and more suggestively
so, in terms of the questions of legal membership and jurisdiction we have
considered animal trials to raise. He is a "cutthroat dog," "a stranger cur,"
"the dog Jew," a "creature that did bear the shape of man," an "impenetra-
ble cur," an "inhuman wretch," a "damned, inexecrable dog," and a "currish Jew" (1.3.109, 116; 2.8.14; 3.2.275; 3.3.18; 4.1.4, 128, 290). In the trial
scene where Shylock demands his bond, Antonio figures the impossibility of negotiating with him as a species problem: "You may as well use
question with the wolf" (4.1.73). As the Continental trials show, this trope
indicates less technical impossibility than at first it may seem, because a
practice of "using question with a wolf" was a matter of some familiarity.
It is the wolf's enmity, not its rational incapacity, that makes "question"
futile.

Shakespeare's most explicit reference to the criminal prosecution and
capital punishment of animals appears in Gratiano's speech, as he contemplates Shylock's intransigent "fangs":

> Oh, be thou damn'd, inexecrable dog!
> And for thy life let justice be accus'd.
> Thou almost makes me waver in my faith
> To hold opinion with Pythagoras,
> That souls of animals infuse themselves
> Into the trunks of men. Thy currish spirit
> Governed a wolf who, hanged for human slaughter,
> Even from the gallows did his fell soul fleet,
> And, whilst thou layest in thy unhallowed dam,
> Infused itself in thee.
> (4.1.128–37)

There are no recorded formal executions of animals in English archives—
but in Shakespeare's time there were no wolves in England either.[63] As

63. Boehrer describes a central European practice of hanging condemned Jews
"between or alongside dogs," where dogs "stand in for the thieves executed with Jesus,"
hung upside down in keeping with the typologization of Jews as anti-Christs ("Shylock," 165–66). He examines an astonishing German woodcut (ca. 1510) illustrating this
practice and reads the image to indicate degradation through a "reversed Crucifixion"

Boehrer concisely describes this sequence, the "invective refigures Shylock not as a domestic slave but rather as interloping carnivore; hence the smooth transformation of 'dog' into 'cur' into 'wolf.'"[64] While currishness manifests in the serviceable dog turned hostile, wolves figure simpler enmity toward the human community as a rival top predator (as England's long program of extermination for wolves registers). Early moderns loved to mock the Pythagorean argument for a transmigration of souls up and down the scale of being, according to a judgment or verdict on the morality of one's life. But like Gratiano, and despite their scandal or merriment, they could not shake the metaphorical power of Pythagoreanism to describe the animated universe they observed. Its apt imagery expressed a cosmos in which the dynamic operations of justice reach well beyond the confines of a human community.

For Shylock, then, the many jokes about the gift of a "halter"—with its pun on the animal leash and the hangman's noose—not only inscribe his fate as a hostile stranger who makes himself vulnerable to a death sentence but also indicate an animal's fate as a justiciable quasi-citizen. Launcelot cuts short his father's intention to give Shylock, Launcelot's master, a gift: "Give him a present? Give him a halter!" (2.2.100–101). And when Portia urges, "*Down*, therefore, and *beg* mercy of the Duke," Gratiano exults in Shylock's final condition: "Thou hast not left the value of a cord; / Therefore thou must be hanged at the state's charge" (4.1.361, 364–65; italics added). When Portia asks Antonio what mercy he might render Shylock, Gratiano interjects to limit Antonio to the gift of "a halter, gratis!" (4.1.377). Here, in Shakespeare's play about the reach and the limits of cosmopolitanism—where the legal system is repeatedly marked as hospitable to diversity—we find an extended metaphor likening Shylock to the defendants in animal trials. His insistence on exacting a payment that would kill converts him from a "harmless necessary" neighbor to an enemy of the state, just as murder *ex propria malitia* could for animals. Does the proximity of Shylock and the *bestia laedens* mean that animal trials afford a paradigm for reading Shylock as excluded through bestialization? Or does the discursive system used to create Shylock traffic in the quasi-citizenship status of animals in the early modern imagination of justice?

(165, citing R. Po-Chia Hsia, *The Myth of Ritual Murder: Jews and Magic in Reformation Germany* [New Haven, CT: Yale University Press, 1988]). This practice hangs dogs symbolically rather than for their "own misdeeds" (Cohen, *Crossroads of Justice*, 110).

64. Boehrer, "Shylock," 163.

Does the cross-species likening here distance Shylock from humanity, or does it undermine the gap between humanity and animals? The notion of Shylock as simply dehumanized by the play depends partly on a modern sense of animals as wholly outside the law or political community rather than as the subjects of law they could be in the early modern imagination. My immediate claim is that the proximity between answerable animals and this "stranger cur" in Venice places them all *inside* the multikinded, justiciable cosmos to which it testifies.

Shylock's soul seems to Gratiano like one derived from a wolf. This is not just any wolf, or the idea of wolf; nor is it "The Wolf" in the emblematic sense that the bestiary tradition might provide. Instead, it is a particular wolf (possibly the wrong one, of course) formally brought to public accountability for killing a human being, a wolf executed by the process that precedes any creature's arrival and death on "*the* gallows," itself the formal and public domain of a town or jurisdiction. As Thomas emphasizes, "In the towns of the early modern period, animals were everywhere. . . . For centuries, wandering pigs were a notorious hazard of urban life."[65] Likewise, Evans points out that swine roamed free in medieval and early modern contexts; he even uses the legal concept of the "freedom of the city" to describe the urban accommodation "enjoyed by medieval swine" (158–59). Thus while Agamben theorizes that "animal nature" lacks "any relation to law and the city," the late medieval and early modern situation contradicts the claim.[66] Animals were not only at large in cities but also habitually cognizable to the law in its formal and informal expressions. In many ways, Thomas continues, domestic beasts in particular "were subsidiary members of the human community."[67] In a social context where all membership was inevitably inflected by rank, "subsidiary" membership counts as membership.

Like Shylock, early modern animals for the most part did not find the law to be written to their particular advantage. Then, as now, most trials end with a guilty verdict. What interests me most, however, is the sense of possibility in the act of putting beasts in a rough equality with man *before the law*. In the case of animal trials, attestations of subject status can extend even to the horizon of judicial practice, where membership and pol-

65. Thomas, *Man and the Natural World*, 95.
66. Giorgio Agamben, *Homo Sacer: Sovereign Power and Bare Life*, trans. Daniel Heller-Roazen (Stanford, CA: Stanford University Press, 1998), 105.
67. Thomas, *Man and the Natural World*, 98.

ity are formally defined. Judicial and cultural notice of animal claims to stakeholdership—the possession of legitimate, subjective investments in the world as fellow creatures of the single cosmic fashioning in Genesis— simply manifests this cosmopolitical perspective. The same multikinded demography characterizes almost any townscape or domestic scene from the period. Unleashed animal actors stray in the margins, forage under the table, or roam the street on their own free recognizance.

Laid on by Manacles: Disanimation, Vivisection, and the Vacuum Tube

In his glance at the relationship between hanging and scientific trials for animals, Shakespeare offers *Cymbeline*'s queen as a figure for the live-animal experimentalist. When she asks her tutor/doctor for a fresh supply of "drugs" ("poisonous compounds"), she claims her training justifies this next course in fatal substances:

> Having thus far proceeded—
> Unless thou think'st me devilish—is't not meet
> That I did amplify my judgment in
> Other conclusions? I will try the forces
> Of these thy compounds on *such creatures as*
> *We count not worth the hanging*—but none human—
> To try the vigor of them.
> (1.5.4, 8, 15–21; italics added)

From the perspective of 1765, Samuel Johnson opines that there is "in this passage nothing that much requires note" but confesses that he cannot "forbear to push it forward into observation"; he speculates that its "thought would probably have been more amplified, had our author lived to be shocked with such experiments as have been published in later times, by a race of men that have practised tortures without pity, and related them without shame, and are yet suffered to erect their heads among human beings."[68] The passage shows that the legal language of trials and

---

68. *The Plays of William Shakespeare in Eight Volumes*, ed. Samuel Johnson (London: J. and R. Tonson et al., 1765), 7:279. This exchange from *Cymbeline* was commonly cited in the antivivisection movement. See, for example, an arraignment of the shortcomings of the 1876 Cruelty to Animals Act that ends forcefully with the authority

conclusions did not depend on Bacon to introduce it to experimental contexts. The queen's reckoning of her small-animal victims juxtaposes those
"not worth the hanging" with those that are. Though she excepts humans from her list, the doctor suspects her and provides substitute compounds rather than fatal ones. He voices the traditional moral critique of
animal cruelty: "You Highness / Shall from this practice but make hard
your heart" (1.5.23–24). Of the queen's expression that "such creatures as /
We count not worth the hanging," the doctor speculates aside that she
will first "prove" the compounds on "cats and dogs, / Then afterward up
higher" (1.5.38–39). But Shakespeare's language and popular culture both
obviously reckoned cats and dogs "worthy" enough to hang. Those "not
worth the hanging" suggests birds, mice, frogs, snakes, and perhaps kittens and puppies—more manageable creatures who would later fit easily
in the confines of the vacuum tube.

Larger-animal experimentation, however, entailed a physical struggle.
In Bacon's figure for natural things under scientific review, Proteus and his
flock "at liberty" or "free and unrestrained" represent the "ordinary structures and compositions of species." But more than "ordinary" information was sought. To get at the secrets that nature tries to hold back, Bacon
outlines, an *"expert minister of nature* shall encounter matter *by main
force*, vexing and urging her with intent and purpose to reduce her to nothing, she . . . being thus caught in the straits of necessity, doth change and
turn herself. . . . Constraint or binding will be more facile and expedite,
if matter be *laid on by manacles, that is, by extremities."*[69] If the highly
gendered object of science withholds her testimony, "expert ministers of
nature" have ways to force out a confession. Merchant shows that increasing secrecy and use of torture in Star Chamber practice under the Stu-
arts likely influenced Bacon's language and thought.[70] Torture and other
"extremities" of technique tempt investigators across time; the critique
of such methods as unreliable and likely to yield bad information also ap-

of *Cymbeline* (J. F. Purcell Fitz-Gerald, "The New Cruelty to Animals, or Vivisection
Bill," in *The British Friend: A Monthly Journal, Chiefly Devoted to the Interest of the
Society of Friends* 34, no. 11 [1876]: 4). Frances Power Cobbe, a leading antivivisectionist
and Darwin's correspondent, commented on a performance of *Cymbeline* to the *Daily
News* (19 September 1896), directing readers' attention to Johnson's note (reprinted
in *Zoophilist* 16, no. 6 [1 October 1896]: 101). For a professional rebuttal, see "Shakespeare's Doctors," in *Lancet* 1, no. 17 (23 April 1864): 477.
    69. Bacon, *Wisdom of the Ancients*, 297 (italics added).
    70. Merchant, "Violence of Impediments," 750–51.

pears in diverse historical contexts.[71] Torture techniques contradict the careful emphasis on procedural rights and representation seen in the legal trials of animal defendants—where the presumption of godly review registers more vividly. Investigators in a torturing regime are perfectly prepared to reduce their object, in Bacon's words, "to nothing." In a regime of law, a party defendant's existence, possession of legitimate subjective investments, and concomitant rights, however minimal, are stipulated. In this sense, technoscientific trials of obliteration borrow less from legal models than they do from the law's perversion.

The episodic history of vivisection begins in ancient Alexandria and its renowned library and medical school. Perhaps due to overlapping cultural influences, proscriptions against human vivisection proved possible to evade, and circa 280 BCE the Greek physicians Herophilus and Erasistratus subjected human criminals to vivisection there.[72] The Alexandrians made lasting discoveries in anatomy and physiology, including Erasistratus's observations on the heart and its valves, later replicated by William Harvey. But taboos against human vivisection were sufficiently strong to prevent further institutional instances. (Aristotle, for example, did not even vivisect animals, though he dissected dead animals and sometimes killed them for the purpose.) After Alexandria, formal dissection and vivisection of humans and animals largely disappeared until Galen, roughly four hundred years later.

In Roman contexts, Galen was again able to vivisect animals. Noting the comparable displays of cruelty to humans and animals then considered normal enough (also a feature of early modernity), Anita Guerrini describes the importance of publicity for Roman dissections and vivisections, especially when a challenge had been made between two anatomists. In one such demonstration Galen proved that arteries contain blood rather than air (a lingering question in their differentiation from veins); he performed the vivisection as a public entertainment.[73] Galen opened a range of unanesthetized animal bodies, mentioning pigs, goats, sheep, apes, horses, asses, mules, cows, lynxes, stags, bears, weasels, mice, ser-

71. On ancient resistance to vivisection on these grounds, see Anita Guerrini, *Experimenting with Humans and Animals: From Galen to Animal Rights* (Baltimore: Johns Hopkins University Press, 2003), 6–9. Later critics of Harvey revived the idea that "vivisection caused pathological changes . . . that invalidated the data" (ibid., 37).

72. Ibid., 9, citing Celsus, *De medicina*, trans. W. G. Spencer (Cambridge, MA: Harvard University Press, 1960), lines 23–27, 40–43.

73. Guerrini, *Experimenting with Humans*, 13.

pents, fish, birds, and one elephant; one commentator compares this range with Harvey's.[74] Investigating the nervous system, he cut the spinal cords of live dogs, pigs, goats, and apes at various points along the backbone to measure the extent of bodily paralysis entailed at each; he also vivisected the brain of an ape, stimulating sections to see what body parts were affected. Then, for roughly a thousand years after Galen, no formal, public, or university-based performances of dissection or vivisection are recorded.

The rise of the dissection of human cadavers in the anatomy theaters of the Renaissance has received detailed attention.[75] A quest for comprehensive mapping of the human body represents the earliest mark of an emerging "experimental" approach to systematic knowledge for modernity, although according to one historian of medicine, it can also be seen as a return to ancient practice.[76] Such a "return" was the framing strategy chosen by Andreas Vesalius, the Flemish anatomist whose *De humani*

74. K. D. Steele, "Three Early Masters of Experimental Medicine: Erasistratus, Galen and Leonardo da Vinci," *Proceedings of the Royal Society of Medicine: Section of the History of Medicine* 54 (July 1961): 579. Celebrating Galen's capacity to design experiments, Steele describes a pig vivisection that ended debate about the interface of bladder and kidneys. For Galen's gruesome but jubilant account, see *On the Natural Faculties*, trans. A. J. Brock (Cambridge, MA: Harvard University Press, 1916), 1::xiii, 57–61. Galen almost broke the heart's secret, but it was too hard to see "in the quick-moving heart of a pig," and so it "was not until Harvey selected snakes for vivisection due to the slow action of their hearts that systole and diastole . . . were successfully analyzed," proving "the importance in experimental medicine of choosing the right animal" (Steele, "Three Early Masters," 580).

75. Roger French makes a detailed case for the claim that these historically and culturally anomalous activities had a negligible relation to either clinical practice or research and discovery, emphasizing instead their role in negotiations of institutional power and professional authority in medicine. See French, *Dissection and Vivisection in the European Renaissance* (Aldershot, UK: Ashgate, 1999). Jonathan Sawday argues for the influence of anatomical investigation in establishing a broader intellectual "culture of dissection" in *The Body Emblazoned: Dissection and the Human Body in Renaissance Culture* (London: Routledge, 1996). Katherine Park shows that the conduct of anatomies, *as such*, did not represent a total revolution in practice about "opening the body," as is often alleged; instead, she describes changes in the conditions under which they occur (i.e., the publicity of the anatomy theater contrasts the domestic spaces Park describes). Park, "The Criminal and the Saintly Body: Autopsy and Dissection in Renaissance Italy," *Renaissance Quarterly* 47 (1994): 1–33.

76. Andrew Cunningham argues that the Renaissance anatomical project should be viewed less as a program of modern, self-authorizing observation and more as a return to ancient values. *The Anatomical Renaissance: The Resurrection of the Anatomical Projects of the Ancients* (Aldershot, UK: Scolar Press, 1997).

corporis fabrica (1543) took western Europe by storm. Vesalius justified
his empirical investigations by stressing that he *"joined Galen* in urging
medical students . . . to take on dissections with their own hands."[77] But
whether we focus on Vesalius's new discoveries and break from tradition,
or accept his claims that dissection and vivisection were methodologically
traditional, it was on the turf of comparative anatomy that he challenged
Galen's authority by inventorying his transpositions from animal to human bodies.[78] Vesalius argued that "it is just now known to us from the
reborn art of dissection, from a careful reading of Galen's books, and from
the welcome restoration of many portions thereof, that he himself never
dissected a human body, but was in fact *deceived by his monkeys."*[79] Vesalius charged Galen with aping the human instead of anatomizing it. But
despite the terrain of the controversy, Vesalius too remained dependent on
animal bodies. For dissective purposes, he obtained dead animals in an
imitation of the way in which human bodies were often procured for these
ends—and in a hollower echo of the formal execution of quadruped defendants. As one historiated capital in the lavishly illustrated *Fabrica* shows,
dead dogs could readily be produced by hanging and cudgeling (fig. 5.2). In
terms of vivisection, Vesalius remained dependent not only on animals
but also on Galen's vivisective scripts.

Galen's most celebrated demonstration had concerned proving the
brain as the driver of the nervous system. Proof arose when he accidentally
severed the recurrent laryngeal nerve in a live pig's throat; the nerve is
now known as "Galen's nerve."[80] The twinned nerves run from the brain,

77. Andreas Vesalius, preface, *On the Fabric of the Human Body, An Annotated
Translation of the 1543 and 1555 Editions of Andreas Vesalius' De Humani Corporis
Fabrica*, ed. and trans. Daniel Garrison and Malcolm Hast, http://vesalius.northwestern
.edu/ (italics added; passage on original page 4r).

78. His challenge was widely perceived. Detailing disparities between men and
apes, Topsell names his source: "Vesalius sheweth . . . that [the apes'] proportion dif-
fereth from man's in more things than Galen observed" (Edward Topsell, *The Historie
of Foure-Footed Beastes* [London: William Jaggard, 1607], 3). See also Daniel Garrison,
"Animal Anatomy" (2003), http://vesalius.northwestern.edu/essays/animalanatomy
.html (accessed 15 March 2011), and Kenneth Gouwens, "Human Exceptionalism," in
The Renaissance World, ed. John Jeffries Martin (London: Routledge, 2007), 415–34. For
contextualization of Vesalius's approach, see my "Invisible Parts: Renaissance Anatomies of Human Exceptionalism," in *Animal Encounters*, ed. Manuela Rossini and Tom
Tyler (Leiden, Netherlands: Brill, 2008), 137–57.

79. Vesalius, *On the Fabric* [online version], 3r (italics added).

80. Adel Afifi and Ronald Bergman, *Functional Neuroanatomy: Text and Atlas*
(New York: McGraw-Hill Professional, 2005), 89.

lum, & alterum ipſiu

propria circumſcript

Figure 5.2. Andreas Vesalius, historiated capital *T*, in *De humani corporis fabrica* (Basel, 1543). Image courtesy of the Wellcome Library, London.

toward the heart, and back again to the larynx, where they control vo-calization; when either nerve is cut or ligated at the throat, the animal continues struggling and trying to voice a protesting squeal, but no sound except the whistling passage of air through the esophagus issues from its effort. This showing firmly displaced Greek ideas about the heart in favor of a governing brain, and a full public staging was therefore arranged by

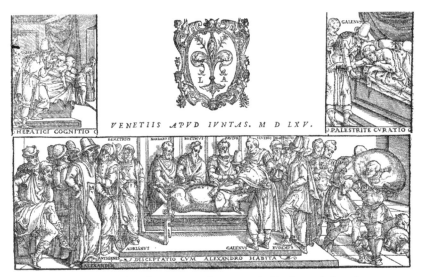

Figure 5.3. Galen, frontispiece, *Opera omnia* (Venice, 1565 [1541]).
Image courtesy of the Wellcome Library, London.

Galen's patrons. This performance, "the first *experimental and publicly
repeatable evidence* that the brain controls behavior," became a classic exercise in physiological demonstration.[81]

The landmark experimental scene circulated as an icon for Galenic
skill and knowledge. Beginning with the first Junta edition of 1541 and repeatedly used in later editions, Galen's signature public vivisection adorns
the frontispiece of his collected works (fig. 5.3).[82] The assembled politicians
and intellectuals of that first Roman performance appear, gathered around
an enormous pig secured by bindings. A figure marked "Galenus" leans
over the pig's throat. On the right side of the image, another pig and some
sheep are carried in, bound for the eventualities of the demonstration. This
tableau of a classic vivisection—not only showing the role of the brain but

    81. Charles Gross, "Galen and the Squealing Pig," *Neuroscientist* 4, no. 3 (1998):
220 (italics added). See also Steele, "Three Early Masters," 581, and Edwin Kaplan et al.,
"History of the Recurrent Laryngeal Nerve: From Galen to Lahey," *World Journal of
Surgery* 33, no. 3 (2009): 386–93.
    82. Galen, *Opera omnia latine in septem classes digesta* (Venice: Junta, 1565 [1541]).
See also Jan Gérard de Lint, *Atlas of the History of Medicine: Anatomy* (New York: Paul
Hoeber, 1926), 22; Gross, "Galen and the Squealing Pig," 219; Guerrini, *Experimenting
with Humans*, 17; and Steele, "Three Early Masters," 581.

VA
nis p
ría,h
auto
do ſ[
ttionis
princi
pia.
uere
ſeme
ille c
ad q
Con
men
tuò t
ne pl
quea

& calidum frigido, & humidum ſicco. Eoῷ fi
meritò dicatur. At ſemen ſanguine quidem ſic

Figure 5.4. Andreas Vesalius, historiated capital Q, in *De humani corporis fabrica* (Basel, 1543). Image courtesy of the Wellcome Library, London.

also more dramatically staging the suppression of an animal's power of vocalization—also marks Vesalius's *Fabrica*, where it appears as a leitmotif and a credential for the brash young professor at the University of Padua.

Opening Vesalius's dedication to Charles V, a striking historiated Q replays the Galenic scene of the silenced pig. Some dangerous-looking *putti* reenact the set steps of the ancient demonstration (fig. 5.4).[83] A vivisection board appears clearly, along with a heavy chain used to tie the pig's head back, as a knife-wielding cherub prepares to make the cut that will reveal "Galen's nerve." We see one of the *putti* holding a book, which can

83. Vesalius, *On the Fabric* [online version], [iii].

only be Galen's instructions for replicating the exercise.[84] At the end of the *Fabrica*'s last book, Vesalius dedicates a final chapter to assessing which anatomical questions require vivisection, following sequentially through zones of the body. He tells how to replicate Galen's live experiments on the spinal chord. To see for oneself the scope of resulting paralysis, "you should tie a dog to a plank . . . in such a way that it presents its backbone and neck to you; then take a large knife and cut off a number of vertebral spines until you lay bare the spinal marrow. . . . *Nothing is easier than to observe* the loss of sensation and movement in the parts below the incision."[85] These recommended "experiments" were more like school figures, rehearsed and perfected in the course of medical training. They did not seek new discoveries. Vesalius defers the classic recurrent laryngeal nerve exercise (key to "the more drastic vivisection that I normally present in the schools") for the final discussion, subtitled "Vivisection That Is Normally Performed at Padua and Bologna as the Last Part of an Anatomical Investigation."[86]

For this demonstration, Vesalius advises, a "sow is better because of its voice; for after a dog has been tied down for some time it will often not bark or growl no matter what you do to it, so you cannot investigate whether its voice has been lost." As a point of human knowledge, Galen's demonstration had long ago settled this detail with celebrated finality, but Vesalius emphasizes that each person can experientially re-prove it for himself, with a virtually Cartesian suspicion of hearsay knowledge.[87] He continues:

Lay the animal down on its back so that the front of its neck and . . . trunk . . . are facing upward. . . . Tie it down to the board as strongly as you can. . . . You must take particular care that the upper jaw is tied firmly to the board; for this you should use a chain or strong rope in front of the canine teeth . . . making sure the animal's neck is stretched

84. Likewise, in Rembrandt's *Anatomy Lesson of Dr. Tulp* (1632), in front of a human cadaver we see a propped book that must be the *Fabrica*, given its enormous size and the fact that Rembrandt shows a hand and wrist dissection (Vesalius's own professional signature). See Vesalius's portrait (*On the Fabric* [online version], [xii]).

85. Andreas Vesalius, *On the Fabric of the Human Body*, bk. 6, *The Heart and Associated Organs*, and bk. 7, *The Brain*, ed. and trans. William Richardson and John Carman (Novato, CA: Norman Publishing, 2009), 265 (italics added).

86. Vesalius, *On the Fabric* [print version], bk. 6, 269, 271–74.

87. See René Descartes, *Discourse on Method*, trans. Donald Cress (Indianapolis: Hackett, 1998 [1637]), 16.

Figure 5.5. Andreas Vesalius, pig on vivisection board, in *De humani corporis fabrica* (Basel, 1543). Image courtesy of the Wellcome Library, London.

out and its head . . . immoveable and yet that the animal can breath freely and make a noise.

As Vesalius's description proceeds ("Now I take a sharp razor . . ."), he exposes the recurrent nerves. "Sometimes," he writes, "I tie these off and sometimes cut through them . . . to demonstrate clearly how, when this nerve is tied or cut . . . half of the voice is destroyed, how it vanishes entirely if both nerves are interfered with, *and how it comes back again if I undo the ties*" (italics added). The voice can be silenced; it can be revived. Concluding this segment of the "normal" demonstration in the schools, he duly notes the climactic, showpiece detail: "One can readily hear how strongly the animal breathes out although it has lost its voice."[88] Vesalius's image of a straining pig on a vivisection board literally enacts Bacon's later "image" of nature "laid on by manacles" (fig. 5.5). These "trial" scenes—where a controlling human actor turns an animal's voice off and on for a crowd of spectators, surgically silencing its vocalizations of protest and complaint—stage mankind's appropriation of a disanimating power.

Another spectacular set piece in the vivisective repertoire features the pregnant quadruped, usually a pig or dog. Vesalius ideally sought a pregnant animal for the vivisection he "normally performed" in schools in order to be able demonstrate the dramatic instincts of newborn breathing.[89]

88. Vesalius, *On the Fabric* [print version], bk. 6, 271–74.

89. Ibid., 272–73. For Vesalius's gloss on this instinct ("How beautiful!"), see French, *Dissection and Vivisection*, 196.

Figure 5.6. Andreas Vesalius, historiated capital Q, in *De humani corporis fabrica*
(Basel, 1543). Image courtesy of the Wellcome Library, London.

The *Fabrica* memorializes this practice in another historiated capital illustrating the removal of a puppy from a dog's uterus during a live-animal experiment (fig. 5.6). Vesalius's most famous student, Realdo Colombo, would develop a vivid improvisation on this already dramatic performance. In Colombo's version of the vivisection of the pregnant dog, he added a flourish we can only call a "trial within a trial." When he would remove a puppy from the opened uterus, he would present it to the mother to allow his audience to marvel at her solicitude for it. Dying herself, the mother will howl if the puppy is harmed before her eyes and lick it "with

great piety" if it is brought toward her face.[90] This particular "administration," as Colombo termed each vivisective script, became his signature, a
demonstration of what he called (apparently without stopping to reflect on
the vivisector's implicit role) the "charity and piety" of the "crucified and
unhappy dog."[91] As French emphasizes, a sense of religious marvel and
even animal expressions of "piety" supported a habit of repeating these
shows to audiences who would request to see particular favorite scenes of
this kind performed.[92]

By the seventeenth century, such set pieces of vivisection had been in
long use. Yet the best-known seventeenth-century English vivisectors—
Hooke, Boyle, and their successors—continued to conduct trials on similar formats at the Royal Society for audiences of learned and lay spectators.[93] As Lisa Jardine recounts, "Hooke and Boyle *vigorously promoted
Harvey's model of endlessly repeated dissection . . .* to understand . . .

90. French, *Dissection and Vivisection*, 204, 209. See also Nicolaas Rupke, *Vivisection in Historical Perspective* (London: Croom Helm, 1987), 18.

91. French, *Dissection and Vivisection*, 206, 209.

92. Ibid., 208 (Colombo recounts audience demand for the laryngeal nerve
performance).

93. William Harvey vivisected an enormous number of animals (for a description
of a rabbit case, see Guerrini, *Experimenting with Humans*, 23; she also notes how
little Harvey has been criticized, compared to Descartes [33]). No gleeful showman like
Galen, Vesalius, or Colombo, Harvey presents an exception to the rule that these procedures achieved little or no new knowledge. Though some contest his "discovery" of
circulation, it would seem to be the sort of research purpose that enabled even Darwin
to approve some use of vivisection. *Exercitatio anatomica de motu cordis et sanguinis
in animalibus* (An anatomical exercise on the motion of the heart and blood in living
beings) (Latin, 1628; English, 1653) resolved the mystery of systole and diastole and
affirmed—for modernity at least, though Galen had speculated likewise—that blood
circulated rather than ebbed and flowed. Harvey's method was strictly comparative. He
considered animals direct evidence, and he also performed a (nonthoracic) vivisection
on a man. The solely human anatomy for which Vesalius strove struck him as provincial. "They are to be blamed in this," he writes, "who whilst they desire to give their
verdict . . . look but into man only." They "do no more to the purpose than those who,
seeing the manner of Government in one Commonwealth, frame [a notion of] Politics,
or they who, knowing the nature of one piece of land, believe they understand agriculture, . . . as if from one Particular proposition they should go about to frame Universal
arguments." Here, the normally generalized abstraction of the human has been diminished to a figure for the particular and defrocked of its claims to universality. William
Harvey, *The Anatomical Exercises: De Motu Cordis and De Circulatione Sanguinis in
English Translation*, ed. Geoffrey Keynes (New York: Dover Publications, 1995 [1953]),
41. For Harvey's intervention, see Harold Cook, "Medicine," in *The Cambridge History*

the mechanics of respiration."[94] Their dog experiments (including blood infusions and transfusions) gained special notoriety—despite the extraordinary historical detail that both men recorded some discomfort with aspects of the procedures.[95] In 1664 Hooke performed a vivisection on a dog, which he described three days later to his friend and fellow member of the Royal Society, Robert Boyle, who had missed the demonstration:

> The . . . experiment (which I shall hardly, I confess, make again, because it was cruel) was with a dog, which, by means of a pair of bellows, wherewith I filled his lungs, and suffered them to empty again, I was able to preserve alive as long as I could desire, after I had wholly opened the thorax, and cut off all the ribs, and opened the belly. Nay, I kept him alive above an hour after I had cut off the pericardium and the mediastinum, and had handled and turned his lungs and heart and all the other parts of its body, as I pleased. . . . But though I made some considerable discovery of the necessity of fresh air, and the motion of the lungs for the continuance of the animal life, yet I could not make the least discovery in this of what I longed for, which was, to see, if I could by any means discover a passage of the air of the lungs into either the vessels or the heart; and I shall hardly be induced to make any further trials of this kind, because of the torture of this creature.[96]

Even for Hooke as "minister of nature," the spectacle of the trial not only suggested excessive cruelty but also prompted the stronger term, "torture." (Note that Vesalius had already achieved artificial respiration and

---

of Science, vol. 3, *Early Modern Science*, ed. Katharine Park and Lorraine Daston (Cambridge: Cambridge University Press, 2006), 425–27.

94. Lisa Jardine, *Ingenious Pursuits: Building the Scientific Revolution* (New York: Anchor Books, 2000), 114 (italics added).

95. For a subtle analysis of the gap between Boyle's early anticruelty writings and his later experimental practice, see J. J. MacIntosh, "Animals, Morality, and Robert Boyle," *Dialogue* 35 (1996): 435–72.

96. Robert Hooke, "Letter from Robert Hooke to Robert Boyle (10 Nov 1664)," in Michael Hunter, Antonio Clericuzio, and Lawrence Principe, ed., *The Correspondence of Robert Boyle* (London: Pickering and Chatto, 2001), 2:399. Jardine highlights the comparative "deadpan" of the official trial report: "A Dog was dissected, and by means of a pair of bellows, and a certain Pipe thrust into the Wind-pipe of the Creature, the heart continued beating for a very long while after all the Thorax . . . had been opened" (*Ingenious Pursuits*, 116).

resuscitation before 1543.[97]) Despite Hooke's avowed reluctance to under-
take the performance again, he proceeded to do so. Because the society's
next two attempts at "the dog and bellows demonstration" were so "thoroughly botched by less skilled" vivisectors, Hooke "again took over the
public performance of this experiment."[98]

Professional challenges also spurred Hooke's return to the vivisection theater; "Eminent Physitians" had asserted against his original experiment that "the Animal would immediately be suffocated as soon as
the Lungs should cease to be moved."[99] Hooke's resumption of the bellows demonstration attempted to prove that "the *bare* Motion of the Lungs
without fresh Air contributes nothing to the life of the Animal" and that
death was caused not by immobility of the lungs or the failure of blood to
move, but instead by "the *want* of a sufficient *supply of fresh Air*" (540;
italics in the original). The living dog's severed trachea was "bound upon
the nose of the Bellows," and the bellows controlled the air supply. The dog
was "kept alive . . . for above an houre, in which time the Tryal had been
often repeated, in suffering the Dog to fall into *Convulsive* motions by
ceasing to blow the Bellows, and permitting the Lungs to subside and lye
still, and of suddenly reviving him again by renewing the blast" (539; italics in the original). Hooke's description emphasizes brinksmanship with
life and death in a pageant of human control over repetition and reversal
in the trial drama.

By swerving back and forth between a controlled death spiral and a
controlled revival, Hooke convinces his "Judicious Spectators," whom
he describes as "fully satisfied of the reallity of the former Experiment."
Then Hooke contrives a second bellows to be attached to the first so that
a continuous air supply with no lung movement might be tried. By "prick-
ing all the outer coat of the Lungs with the slender point of a very sharp
pen-knife," Hooke makes the animal "breathe" *without any corresponding bodily movement*, estranging spectators' own embodied sense of what
breathing is (539; italics in the original). The even flow of air "being continued for a pretty while, the Dog . . . lay still . . . his eyes being all the

97. "As I do all this I am careful to keep inflating the lung every now and then
[with air blown through a reed] so that the movement of the heart and arteries does not
cease but the animal is kept alive" (Vesalius, *On the Fabric* [print version], bk. 6, 274).

98. Jardine, *Ingenious Pursuits*, 118.

99. Hooke, "Account of an Experiment made by M. Hooke," 539. Subsequent page
references appear in the text.

time very quick, and his Heart beating very regularly." But "ceasing this
blast, and suffering the Lungs to fall . . . the Dogg would immediately
fall into Dying convulsive fits; but be as soon reviv'd again by the renewing . . . of his Lungs with the constant blast of fresh Air" (540). Against
the orderly heartbeat sustainable by technoscience, the dog left to its own
broken devices bursts into a chaos of convulsive, terminal activity. The
demonstration repeatedly "suffers" the dog to fall into a death spiral and
stage-manages sudden revivals for him, all through the overtly mechanical controls of a *deus ex machina* who is a man. This imperial dynamic
performs the dissociative cultural work of vivisection's disanimating
theater.

Meanwhile, vacuum-tube experiments also explored the dynamics of
respiration on intact animals placed inside evacuated cylinders, enabling
related observations on traumatized ordeals of breath for smaller animals. In "Experiment XLI" of his *New Experiments Physico-Mechanical,
Touching the Spring of the Air* (1660), Boyle outlined numerous iterations
of the vacuum-tube experiment as applied to animate creatures. "Experiment XLI" pursues an inquiry "to satisfy our selves . . . about the account
upon which respiration is so necessary to the animals that nature hath
furnished with lungs."[100] The first animal treated is—of all the possible
candidates—a lark, the persistent representative not only of vocalization
and song, but of anima itself. In Shakespeare's Sonnet 29, a lark embod-
ies the human soul, reviving from despair to rise "at break of day . . . /
From sullen earth" and sing "hymns at heaven's gate" (lines 11–12). This
awkward selection provokes Boyle parenthetically to mention his "being
then unable to procure any other lively bird, small enough to put in the
receiver." He stresses the lark's liveliness and how able it is to "spring
up . . . to a good height" (if not heaven's gate) inside the receiver—despite
one of its wings having been broken by the shot "of a man we had sent
to provide us some birds for our experiment." The vessel closed and the
pump "diligently plied," the bird appeared "lively enough" for a while, until "she began manifestly to droop . . . and very soon after was taken with
as violent and irregular convulsions, as are wont to be observed in poultry,
when their heads are wrung off." With the onset of her convulsions, they
"turned the stop-cock, and let in the air upon her, yet it came too late."
The "whole tragedy," he writes without any trace of irony, was "concluded

100. Robert Boyle, *Works of the Honorable Robert Boyle*, vol. 1, *New Experiments
Physico-Mechanical, Touching the Spring of the Air* (1660), ed. Thomas Birch (Whitefish, MT: Kessinger Reprints, 2003), 63. Subsequent page references appear in the text.

within ten minutes of an hour" (63). The failed revival sets the stage for attempts at better timing in the interim revivals to follow.

Next they try a "hen-sparrow" not wounded by her captors. Just like the lark, the sparrow "would briskly raise her self" to the top of the receiver. While "she seemed to be dead within seven minutes . . . , upon the speedy turning of the key, the fresh air flowing in, began slowly to revive her, so that . . . she opened her eyes." When she had sufficiently recovered and shortly "threatned to make an escape at the top of the glass," they stopped the receiver a second time, and "she was killed with violent convulsions, within five minutes." The next candidate is a mouse "newly taken." He makes the same effort, "leaping up very high" to escape through the top of the cylinder—proving, like the lark and sparrow had, that breathing creatures quite accurately detect the source of fresh air (a point of no apparent interest to the investigators). Soon the mouse "began to appear sick and giddy, and to stagger: after which he fell down as dead." At this point they "hastily" let in fresh air "by which he recovered, after a while, his senses and his feet" and then was "able to skip as formerly." They begin pumping the air out again (fouling up their time-keeping by a "mischance . . . at the stop-cock"), and the once "skipping" mouse "fell down quite dead," with the observers marveling at his "alacrity so little before his death" (63). A variant procedure on another mouse "kept him alive full twelve hours, or better," and then the experimenters, "by sucking out part of the air," made him "droop," until "by letting in the air again, *we soon reduced him to his former liveliness*" (64; italics added). Only a blurring of categories in the to-ing and fro-ing with death could translate an interim restoration to "liveliness" as a reduction.

"Experiment XVI" includes a long section titled "Digression Containing Some Doubts Concerning Respiration." Boyle concedes that his experiments have "made respiration appear . . . rather a more than a less mysterious thing," but he still defends the utility of the vacuum tube in hopes that "the trials made in our engine will at least assist us to discover wherein the deficiency lies" (64). This account of the barren research effort enumerates quite a range of other trials that were conducted. The stories begin to suggest that the publicity so central to the demonstrations had some interfering impact. Having "divers times tried the experiment of killing birds in a small receiver, we commonly found, that . . . the bird would be surprised by mortal convulsions, and within about a minute more would be stark dead, beyond the recovery of the air, though never so hastily let in." Accumulated observations of this apparently surprising scenario make the experiment "seem so strange" that Boyle feels an obligation to repeat it more publicly, "which gained it the advantage of having persons of differing qualities, professions, and sexes (as not only ladies and lords, but doctors and mathematicians) to witness it" (68). These more public displays demonstrate the usual interest in dramas of suffering, spiral, and revival, but they also introduce occasional interference with scientific "progress" due to sudden sympathies across species. In one instance, the investigators' attempt to compute the speed of suffocation is foreclosed by a spectator. A bird "so little sensible of his imprisonment that he eat very chearfully certain seeds that were conveyed in with him" (who thus might have lasted an unusually long time before convulsing) is saved by "a great person, that was a spectator of some of these experiments" who "rescued him from the prosecution of the trial." In the case of "another bird . . . reduced into a sprawling condition, upon the exsuction of air," the intervention results from "the pity of some fair ladies . . . who made me hastily let in some air" so that "the gasping animal was presently recovered, and in a condition to enjoy the benefit of the ladies compassion" (69). With the rescue of these birds from "the prosecution of the trial" by the intervention of observers motivated by "compassion," we see the start of the modern anticruelty movement—and the roots of its strong feminist component are suggested as well. On the basis of "humane" judgments of suffering and compassion (more than a notion of constitutional justice or entitlement), modern ideas of animal *abuse* were first forged in the theatrics of seventeenth-century technoscience.

In a grim moment where hanging and vivisection converge, Boyle reports his hope to convey "into our receiver young ones, ripped out of the womb of their dams, with their involving coats intire," in order to see what dramas of respiration might unfold in the special case of fetuses who have not yet begun to breathe. In partial response to this challenge, "we took a bitch that was . . . almost ready to whelp, and having caused her to be hanged, we presently opened her abdomen, and found four puppies . . . one of these we took out, and . . . freed . . . from the integuments that involved him. . . . He quickly opened his mouth very wide, moved his tongue, and exercised respiration." But it does not stop here. They then open "his abdomen and his chest, and cut asunder the diaphragm, notwithstanding which, he seemed often to endeavor respiring." During this puppy's vivisection, all the other puppies died. Overabsorbed by his own method, Boyle reaches for dissection to prove it: "We took them also out of the womb, and *having opened them, found none of them so much alive,* as to have any perceptible motion in his heart." Meanwhile, the exposed heart of the puppy who "had once enjoyed the benefit of respira-

tion" continued to beat. "We ourselves observed the auricle to beat, after
five or six hours; and a servant that staid up and watched it after we were
gone to bed, affirmed that he saw the pulsation continue about two hours
longer" (70). Perhaps the "fair ladies" and "great person" spectators of the
vacuum trials were kept well clear of this puppy enterprise, but Boyle and
his collaborators register no hesitation about what might be condemned as
obscene in the experiment. As Johnson lamented a century later, no fear
of censure dilutes the report. This midcentury state of things—a scene
of relatively public, live-animal experiments with certain compassion-
ate interveners on one side and unabashed, mechanistic vivisectors on
the other—suggests the split jurisdictions of the modern constitution, but
with a twist. For some, the conceptual line drawn against animal subjectivity cannot withstand the evidence that their own eyewitnessing
provides.

John Evelyn had witnessed Hooke's 1667 open-thorax trial of the dog.
He wrote in his diary that he had watched "a dissection of a dog, *the poore
curr*, kept long alive after the Thorax was open, by blowing with bellows
into his lungs, & that long after his heart was out, & the lungs both gashed
and pierced, *his eyes quick all the while*: This was an experiment of more
cruelty than pleased me."[101] Perhaps there was some comment on "the
poore curr's" quick eyes in the course of that performance because Hooke
also recorded notice of them. In causing the dog to "breathe" without
movement, Hooke described how the even airflow from the double bellows
made "the Dog . . . lay still . . . *his eyes being all the time very quick*, and
his Heart beating very regularly" (540; emphasis added). For Evelyn, the
"poore" dog's eyes command a shred of address, some force of the face-to-
face. For Hooke, the dog's "quick" eyes instead index his own scientific
success at the breathing experiment. One observer sees a face; the other
does not—a gaping divide separates these two seventeenth-century human observers and the cosmographies that inform them.

Darwin's theory did not utilize live interventions on the body or torture scientific objects. Rather, it employed forms of observation and narra-
tion more akin to the traditions of natural history reaching back to Aristotle. In this sense, Darwin has, in Latourian terms, "never been modern."
The modern confinement of animals used in live experiments (and in the
far vaster proprietary spaces of industrial food production) disables the operations of the face-to-face that seventeenth-century demonstrations had

101. John Evelyn, 10 October 1667, in *The Diary of John Evelyn*, ed. Guy de la Bédo-
yère (Suffolk, UK: Boydell Press, 2004), 165 (italics added).

revealed as problematic for a "modern constitution" in which animals are assimilated to the "thing" column. In the strange itineraries of the phrase "hang-dog look," its contemporary appearance in official tabulations of suffering in laboratory animals is only fitting. According to 2008 guidelines from the National Research Council of the National Academy of Sciences, a distressed dog shows not only the *quick eyes* of an "anxious glance." The "poore curr" will further display a "hangdog look." An appendix gives a host of markers by which lab workers can judge the suffering of lab animals (not counting the fact of confinement). Yet it undercuts the very idea of cross-species legibility with the obfuscatory caveat that *"little is known* about behavioral changes directly attributable to stress and even less about distress."[102] Darwin had considered the relevant knowledge already obvious. "Every one has heard of the dog suffering under vivisection, who licked the hand of the operator; this man," Darwin asserted counterfactually in 1871, "must have felt remorse to the last hour of his life."[103] If, in the disappeared condition of its modern confinement, a hang-dog *looks*, which of these two human kinds will be institutionally placed to return its gaze? Boyle or Evelyn? A uniformed interpreter of self-contradicting national guidelines or a Darwin?

A Scotch Verdict on Humanity

Robert Burton's *Anatomy of Melancholy* scores humanity by means of melancholy's close relation to (classical and Christian) "folly," itself the great alternative to reason as humanity's signature feature. As Foucault memorably put this counterdiscourse, "The head that will become a skull is already empty."[104] Jonathan Sawday has shown how the concept of anatomization came to indicate a comprehensive or even exhaustive intellec-

---

102. Committee on Recognition and Alleviation of Distress in Laboratory Animals, National Research Council, *Recognition and Alleviation of Distress in Laboratory Animals* (Washington, DC: National Academies Press, 2008), table A-5, 103, adopted from D. B. Morton and P. H. M. Griffiths, "Guidelines on the Recognition of Pain, Distress, and Discomfort in Experimental Animals," *Veterinary Record* 116 (1985): 433. The title of the twenty-seven-page appendix, "Tools to Monitor and Assess Health Status and Well Being in Stress and Distress," proposes that there can be "well being" in both "stress and distress" (95).

103. Darwin, *Descent of Man*, 90.

104. Michael Foucault, *Madness and Civilization: A History of Insanity in the Age of Reason* (New York: Vintage Books, 1973 [1961]), 16.

tual accounting in the period.[105] But a striking anecdote in Burton's long preface challenges the sectioner's partitive technique, rating the anatomist stymied or frustrated rather than triumphantly or globally successful. Explaining the nom de plume "Democritus Junior," Burton invokes the rascally sage Democritus of Abdera (the "laughing philosopher"), who took human folly's measure and mocked it.[106] His satirical, antisocial behavior and irreverent laughter cause Democritus's neighbors to think him a madman, and they call in no less a figure than Hippocrates for a diagnosis. When Hippocrates and the villagers go to see Democritus, they find him "without hose or shoes, with a book on his knees, cutting up several beasts."[107] Like Vesalius's *putti*, Democritus proceeds—knife in hand—by the book.

But after colorfully itemizing human follies and "ridiculous contrariety," Democritus concludes that people are "like children, in whom is no judgment or counsel, and resemble beasts, saving that beasts are better than they, . . . being contented with nature" (50–51). Here Democritus voices the natural-historical discourse of human negative exceptionalism that we examined in chapter 3. When "a boar is thirsty, he drinks what will serve him, and no more," but "immoderate" humankind brings itself to ruin and shame (49). Given this observation about animal comparative perfection or happiness, why seek to find the grounds of a folly designated human within the bodies of beasts, as Democritus is doing? Scattered around him lie the dissected bodies of animals reduced to parts, as he seeks an anatomical locus for (human) folly. As he himself admits— echoing Pliny, Plutarch, Gelli, and *King Lear*—"I do anatomize and cut up these poor beasts, to see these distempers, vanities, and follies, yet such proof were better made on man's body . . . who from the hour of his birth is most miserable" (51).

If animals lack whatever organ puts one in need of moral or satiric correction, we might ask further, why would one want such an organ? Here we see that what Democritus calls "folly" coincides with the Christian

105. Sawday, *Body Emblazoned*.

106. Period accounts of Democritus of Abdera (460–370 BCE) were based on Diogenes Laertius.

107. *The Anatomy of Melancholy* saw five lifetime editions (1621, 1624, 1628, 1632, and 1638) and one posthumous edition containing corrections by Burton in 1651. Robert Burton, *The Anatomy of Melancholy* (New York: New York Review Books, 2001), 48. Subsequent page references appear in the text and refer to this edition.

soul that must err to be redeemed. Notions of what it means to be human have variously depended on these immaterial propositions. What Burton's vignette shows is that suddenly the human monopoly or signature feature, the "part" that sets us apart from all others, can be neither located nor demonstrated. It comes as no surprise, now, that a core tenet of belief cannot be independently verified. But in the emerging epistemic contexts of a science that enshrines verifiability and ocular proof, what once passed more simply as an article of faith must be reclassified in a new category made inevitable by scientific procedures. Along with the immortal soul, humanity finds itself in this new category: the embarrassed category of the *not proven*. Though the revenge is surely inadequate, the creatures disanimated in the new forum of the experimental trials testify as major witnesses in a virtual trial of humanness itself. And this trial ends in a Scotch verdict on "the human" as an unverifiable proposition.

In the *Religio medici*—published in 1643, exactly one hundred years after Vesalius's book—Thomas Browne opines, "In our study of Anatomy . . . , amongst all those rare discoveries . . . I finde in the fabricke of man, I doe not so much content my selfe, as in that I finde not, that is, no Organ or instrument for the rationall soule; for in the braine, which we tearme the seate of reason, there is not any thing of moment more than I can discover in the cranie of a beast. . . . *Thus we are men, and we know not how.*"[108] The soul is still alleged to be integral, but in a powerful new way it cannot be found or seen. Looking into the very "cranie of a beast," experimental research cannot specify a "human/animal divide," verify a signature animal deficit, or point to any human signature. We can call the continued affirmation of human exceptionalism a kind of ongoing theology or faith. But we also see that the cross-species anatomical and physiological investigations of "the new science" force claims for "the human" more overtly into the realm of the unproven. In the new world of demonstration, the naked assertion becomes more evidently (and more defensively) just that.

"Thus we are men," Browne alleges, but the avowal wavers in a new tension with his concession that "we know not how." Levinas echoes: "I do not know at what moment the human appears, *but*," he asserts just the same, "the human breaks from pure being." As Gelli has Circe observe, such are the "oppinion[s] of the greater part of men," who insufficiently "credite" the experience of other forms of life, whether because of self-

108. Thomas Browne, *Religio medici*, in *The Works of Sir Thomas Browne*, ed. Geoffrey Keynes (Chicago: University of Chicago Press, 1964), 1:47 (italics added).

absorbed preening or because other animals are overwhelmingly screened from view. Gelli's Ulysses proposes to the Goat, "I have ever hard [*sic*] say by your wise men of Gretia, that man is the most perfecte & most noble creature that is in all the world." Knowing otherwise by direct experience—and thus weary with such Greek philosophical hearsay—the goat responds to this persistent human taste for self-praise with indulgently sarcastic condescension: "They did like wyse men to say so, for one should ever prayse his own." After all, this accommodated animal continues (growling his warning at Descartes's back *avant la lettre*), "If I should recken the commodities to the[e] that we beastes have, thou woldest not thinke them commodities, nor yet ever sholdest thou be able to understande them."[109]

109. Giovanni Battista Gelli, "The fourth Dialoge, the Goat," in *Circes of John Baptista Gello, Florentine*, trans. Henry Iden (London, 1557–58).

Raleigh's Ark:
The Early Modern Arithmetic of Livestock

The story of Noah's ark taxed the early modern imagination. Calvin
shuddered at the details of close quartering cheek by jowl with "everie thing that crepeth": Noah "was commanded to descend, as into the
grave, for the sake of preserving his life, and voluntarily to deprive himself of air and vital spirit" where "the smell of dung alone pent up . . . in
a closely filled place, might, at the expiration of three days, have stifled
all the living creatures in the ark."[1] For many observers, a less visceral
reaction to the logistical challenges posed a host of problems for biblical
interpretation. Was literal belief in the story necessary to faith? How did
it relate to New World evidence of creatures unattested in Europe's traditions? Had animal carnivorousness arisen at this point in biblical time? If
so, did it require masses of sheep to be huddled in a bleak steerage, or did
predacious beasts revert to docility and an Edenic diet, consuming only
"fruit, vegetables, and chestnuts" for the duration?[2] Technical uncertain-
ties about the magnitude of the historical cubit triggered a whole sequence
of further difficulties.

Fundamental doubt about how Noah could have built a craft sufficient
to hold all the earthly kinds (plus their necessary provisions) induced early
modern commentators into the cold waters of mathematical calculation.

---

1. John Calvin, *Commentaries on the Book of Genesis*, trans. John King (Edinburgh: Calvin Translation Society, 1847), 1:261. Calvin also clearly dreads being pent
up at sea.

2. Johannes Buteo, *The Shape and Capacity of Noah's Ark* [Arca Noë, cuius formae,
capacitatisque fuerit, libellus], trans. Timothy Griffith and Natali Monnette (Eugene,
OR: Wipf and Stock, 2008 [1554]), 27. Subsequent page references to English and Latin
quotations appear in the text.

Although we associate the reproductive language of "multiplication" with the animals in the first chapter of Genesis and with their representatives entering the ark "two by two," the early modern arithmetic of embarkation had nothing to do with multiplication or exponents. Under the pressure of a desire to secure literal belief, the blue pencil of this math stresses subtraction instead, marshaling numbers to bolster the literal plausibility of Noah's story. In the process, arithmetical deliberations on the ark's capacity presented opportunities to forge a metric to represent flesh by the dram. Among earlier treatments, Augustine's *De civitate Dei* set a high-water mark in the exegetical tradition; his rich unfolding addresses technical logistics right alongside a reading of the ark as "a figure of the Citie of God, travailing in this world as a stranger."[3] Animals had already long served as quasi-currency, a bank deposit on legs—counted not by the face, but by the head. (That a "pecuniary" interest derives from *pecu*, or "flock," shows the trace of this service.) But compared to Augustine's way of reading, the turn to a more exclusively mathematical approach suggests a quest for the common denominators around which the modern commodity could be built.

Silent on the traditional allegories associated with the ark, French mathematician Johannes Buteo defended faith and literal reading by addressing the technical challenges the story posed. The calculations of his *Arca Noë, cuius formae, capacitatisque fuerit, libellus* (1554) were so detailed that subsequent treatments—by Walter Raleigh in 1614; John Wilkins, cofounder of the Royal Society, in 1668; and the German Jesuit polymath Athanasias Kircher in 1675—cite them as authoritative. Buteo opined on hull design, insisting that the Latin *arca* and the Hebrew words it translated refer to a "chest" so that the form of the ark was neither a ship nor a pyramid (Origen's model), but the long blunt box soon adopted in the Geneva Bible (15) (fig. 6.1). Regretting that confusion about "the units of measurement" (the historical cubit) had provided heretics with an "opportunity to deride the Scriptures," Buteo unexpectedly affirms that similar confusions beset the well intentioned. He seeks to justify Noah's project by the numbers, in the face of both incredulity and faithful overcompensation. He does not argue that divine power resolves all difficulties or that such matters are properly mysteries. Surprisingly enough, he claims instead that unbelievers and justifiers *alike* have "grossly exaggerated the

---

3. Walter Raleigh, *The History of the World* (London: Walter Burre, 1614), 110, citing Augustine, *De civitate Dei*, bk. 5, chap. 26 (Raleigh's translation). Subsequent page references appear in the text.

Figure 6.1. *The Ark*, in *The Bible and Holy Scriptures* (Geneva, 1560). Image by permission of the Folger Shakespeare Library, Washington, DC.

size of the ark" ("laxitate nimia opus extendant") (3, 45). And so Buteo aims to explicate the math and reduce the ark to a scale for ready belief.

After reviewing contenders for the proper measure of the cubit and defending the smallest ("the one-and-one-half-foot cubit"), Buteo proceeds to "the important measurements" of the ark (28). Including the triangular "prism" of area under the roof, he calculates the ark's volume at 457,500 cubic cubits. From this he subtracts the volume of the atticlike top (7,500 cubic cubits) to compensate for the space "occupied by various impediments, such as columns and their supports, the thickness of the floors, and the boards forming stalls and storerooms"; the remainder will abundantly suffice ("largiter sufficere") to house all the animals (29, 58). The biggest challenge has two aspects. How many kinds of animals existed for the ark to hold? And by what method should the space needs of these diversely sized creatures, plus their food for the full interval of the Deluge, be calculated? These are the points that "heretics ridicule most" (29). Buteo makes a show of repeatedly rounding his (low enough) estimates *up*, instituting what modern calculations routinely call a margin of error.

Genesis gives no help on the exact number of the created kinds. For this, Buteo—like so many others—turns straight to Pliny without any hesitation or remark. He makes a "careful investigation of those writers who took care to record such things for posterity" and, following Pliny, lists the elephant first among animals that include the familiar (oxen, camels, bison, horses, cows, deer, donkeys, bears, monkeys, rabbits, hares, squirrels, mice, hedgehogs, tigers, lynxes, hyenas, otters, and weasels, for example) and the fabulous (winged horses, manticores, hellhounds, and even satyrs) (29–31). His ensuing inventory totals eighty-nine different "quadrupeds"; he places larger reptiles among them and lets smaller ones (vipers, asps, basilisks, "lizards otherwise green and tiny," and so forth) find their own spaces in the interstices of the ark's design (35). He does not itemize birds because "they can hardly be said . . . to be a fiftieth part of the creatures that walk the earth," but ironically he includes them with Noah and company on the top floor—*as bipeds* (35). Buteo's innovation, however, centers less on the art of tallying created kinds than on crafting a formula that elides their bodily diversity (in which natural-historical thought had been so deeply invested) to generate workable common denominators for the calculus at hand.

For these purposes, Buteo reduces "all these species of animals . . . by comparing them to three well-known species ["ipsas in tria maxime genera nota, comparatione distribuam"]: the cow, the sheep and the wolf" (29, 58). Because Aristotle had described an elephant as four times larger than the familiar cow, for example, Buteo counts the ark's two elephants as "equivalent to eight cows in terms of space and food required" (30). The large, noncarnivorous quadrupeds tote up to "forty-five and one half" pairs of cows, which he rounds up to sixty to compensate for any errors of omission (30). For smaller quadrupeds, "the sum . . . comes to forty pairs of sheep." His estimations of the carnivorous animals lead to a sum of "thirty-two pairs of wolves," but again he will "assume some extra so that the total comes to forty pairs" (32). Buteo details the theological warrant for including sheep as both passengers in their own right and as food for those denominated in "wolves," and he adds 3,650 sheep to the tally (measured and stowed in the ark's animal quarters as sheep, but marked as fodder for the carnivores) (32). Having reduced animal bodies into equivalency ("corpora . . . peraequata redegimus") and so converted diverse animals into their value in a metric of cows, sheep, or wolves ("i.e. 120 cows, 3730 sheep, and 80 wolves"), he details a floor plan of stalls for an entire quadruped story in the ark, calibrated on the bodily measurements of the common denominator kinds (62, 34, 32–33).

Although Buteo turned to Pliny to enumerate the kinds requiring a place in the ark, no trace of the signature natural-historical commitment to open-ended particulars remains, as the kinds are "reduced" to their cow, sheep, or wolf equivalents. The technique elides animal properties and peculiarities, their "signatures," to create a biomass of flesh measurable— and divisible—by conventional preset units in a fairly simple format of commodification. In an early application of "empirical" method, Buteo turns away from exegesis and registers faith in the kind of numerical representation Mary Poovey argues will later form the basis of "the modern fact."[4] Certainly his treatise foreshadows the passage that James Bono describes as a move "from symbolic exegesis to deinscriptive hermeneutics" and that Peter Harrison characterizes as a transition from "interpretive" to "mathematical science."[5] Interest shifts from collecting animal "names and natures" to assessing a technical capacity to hold (and manage) their numbers.

In the hands of a writer such as Walter Raleigh, the affordances of a numerist approach register clearly when he uses it—with perfectly transparent motivations regarding navigation and colonization—to secure feasibility for the ark story. In *The History of the World*, Raleigh brings his entrepreneurial mariner's attention to the problem, remarking that the ark needed no mast or sails since it did "no otherwise move then the Hulke or body of a ship doth in a calm sea," this because "it is not probable, that during these continuall and downe-right raines there were any windes at all." He observes that the ark was flat bottomed (since it needed no bow "to cut the waves"), noting appreciatively that the rudderless box was "directed . . . without the helpe of a Compasse or the North starre" (109–10).[6] Raleigh calls Buteo's treatise learned and cites the computations already described, but he adds further reductions in his can-do approach to the ark problem (112). Citing Augustine, he points out that "it was not needfull to take any kindes of fishes into the Arke" (not something Buteo had

4. Mary Poovey, *A History of the Modern Fact: Problems of Knowledge in the Sciences of Wealth and Society* (Chicago: University of Chicago Press, 2004).

5. James Bono, *The Word of God and the Languages of Man: Interpreting Nature in Early Modern Science and Medicine* (Madison: University of Wisconsin Press, 1995), 168; Peter Harrison, *The Bible, Protestantism, and the Rise of Natural Science* (Cambridge: Cambridge University Press, 1998), 2–4 (discussed above in chapter 1).

6. Raleigh reviews the debate on the historical cubit's magnitude, supporting a declension narrative in which because human stature has shrunk, the cubit has too (since it measures "from the sharpe of the elbow to the point of the middle finger"), but he assumes this is moot, speculating that animals have shrunk in the same proportions (110–12).

addressed), *nor* "those creatures . . . which could live in the waters," *nor*
"those fowls which sit and swim on them" (111). The stakes heighten when
Raleigh exploits Buteo's musing that mules might be excludable because
they did not manifest a "kind" (31). With this opening, Raleigh addresses
the collision between literal readings of the ark, on the one hand, and the
traditional view of an unlimited, even prodigal, nature for which animal
variety served as a prime synecdoche, on the other.

In the time of Noah, Raleigh proposes, "it is manifest, and undoubt-
edly true, that many of the Species, which now seeme differing and of severall kindes, were not then *in rerum natura* [among the things of nature]."
These creatures need no space on the ark: "For those beasts which are of
mixt natures; either they were not in that age, or else it was not needfull to praeserve them: seeing they might be generated againe by others,
as the Mules, and the Hyaena's and the like: the one begotten by Asses
and Mares, the other by Foxes and Wolves" (111). Given the harsh biblical imperative of extinguishing a current population while preserving the
minimum stock from which to restore it, weeding out such creatures as
could easily be reconstructed rationally conserves available space. At the
same time, an explosive profusion of new creatures revealed by expedi-
tions of trade and colonization intrudes to complicate the math. It is here
that Raleigh's undercutting of difference as such contributes most to the
shift from a proliferating list model (marked by the wagging tail of John
Caius's usual multiplier, "&c," we have seen in natural history) to the in-
tegers of a more contained numerist grid.[7]

When Montaigne contemplated the beasts in "that new Corner of the
World, which our fathers have lately discovered," he marveled at the "infinite difference and varietie in this world."[8] But Raleigh rebuts this sense
of wonder, arguing instead that any notion of the fundamental difference
of the new worlds and exotic creatures revealed to early modern European
travelers stems from an error: "Whereas by discovering of strange landes,
wherein there are found divers beastes and birdes differing in color or stature from those of these Northerne partes, it may be supposed by a super-
ficiall consideration, that all those which weare red and pyed skinnes, or

7. John Caius, *Of Englishe Dogges, the diversities, the names, the natures, and the
properties*, trans Abraham Fleming (London: Richard Johnes, 1576), 4.

8. Michel de Montaigne, "The Apologie for Raymond Sebond," in *The Essayes of
Montaigne: John Florio's Translation*, ed. J. I. M. Stewart (New York: Modern Library,
1934), 470.

feathers, are differing from those that are lesse painted, and weare plaine russet or blacke: they are much mistaken that so thinke" (111). To believe in observed and embodied difference is to be duped by superficial reading. Casting the surfaces of animal bodies as worn costumes, Raleigh echoes the gender anxieties that marked responses to the English stage and warns that unsuspecting or inexpert readers mistake the clothes for the body. Renaissance juxtapositions of the "painted" and the "plain" normally expressed strong views about meaningful moral difference. But here, whether dressed in red feathers, or pied, or wearing plain black, an animal is an animal is an animal.

Raleigh avows, "*I finde no difference,* but only in magnitude, between the Cat of Europe, and the Ounce of India." A difference "only in magnitude" makes "no difference" in substance. The "common Crowe and Rooke" is "full of red feathers in the drown'd and low islands of Caribana," and the "Blacke-Bird and Thrush hath his feathers mixt with blacke and carnation" when found "in the North parts of Virginia" (111; italics added).[9] Ending the discussion by returning to Buteo's mathematical scheme of representation, Raleigh asserts: "There are three sortes of beasts, whose bodies are of a quantity best knowne; the Beefe, the Sheepe; and the Wolfe: *to which the rest may be reduced*" (113; italics added). Note Raleigh's use of the name of a commodity, "Beefe," for the name of a kind, "cow." No matter that actual wolves had not been seen in England for ages: to these three kinds, all the rest can be "reduced." By "taking the kindes precisely of all creatures," Raleigh concludes that "the Arke, after the measure of the common Cubit, was sufficiently capacious to contain of all, according to the number by God appointed" (111). "Taking the kindes *precisely*" means tallying them restrictively by the deamplifying force of common denomination. Such a tally pauses for no natural-historical exposition of "the di-

9. This thinking takes Raleigh in an interesting direction: "If colour or magnitude made a difference of Species, then were the Negro's, which wee call the blacke-mores, *non animalia rationalia*, not men, . . . and so the Giants of the South America should be of another kinde, than the people of this part of the world" (*History of the World,* 111–12). Even though this universalizing humanness seems surprising, it comports with what Valerie Traub describes as an emerging "concept of a universal human nature by which one can compare 'humanity' *to itself*" (Traub, "The Nature of Norms in Early Modern England: Anatomy, Cartography, *King Lear,*" *South Central Review* 26, nos. 1–2 [2009]: 57, 69 [italics added]). Human universals, read alongside the developing modern coordinates of animal commodification, lose some of the utopian glow of political "equality."

versities, the names, the natures, and the properties" of creatures (as the subtitle of *Of English Dogges* so prodigally varied this older investment).

Buteo adopted a reductive approach to kinds in order to support a literal reading of Noah's story; Raleigh makes further reductions to meaningful difference in the course of defending the plausibility of sea traffic. But the impulse to reduction reaches new levels in John Wilkins's *Essay Towards a Real Character, and a Philosophical Language* (1668). Wilkins himself was among the original founders of the Royal Society.[10] His *Essay*, a quixotic attempt to forge a universal language for science and diplomacy, succinctly announces Wilkins's belief that the *Essay* is "sufficient for the business to which it pretends, namely the distinct expression of all things and notions that fall under discourse."[11] Familiar perhaps from Borges's likening of its "ambiguities, redundancies, and deficiencies" to a fictitious "Chinese encyclopedia"—or from Foucault's burst of laughter in response to Borges in the first sentence of *The Order of Things*—Wilkins's *Essay* divides the entire expressible world into forty genera.[12] Privileging animal classification, Wilkins illustrates the stakes of his method by exploiting the Noah's ark story as an ideal example.

At the end of his enumeration of "the several species of Animals," Wilkins makes room for "a short digression" on the difference between opinions "occasioned by a more general and confused view of things" and those based on "a more distinct consideration of them as they are *reduced into order*" (162; italics added). This reductive technique reveals that there

10. The first royal charter of the society (1662) enshrines the "promoting by the authority of experiments the sciences of natural things" (1). For original Latin and English translations of the evolving charters, see http://royalsociety.org/about-us/history/royal-charters/.

11. John Wilkins, epistle dedicatory to the president of the Royal Society, in *An Essay Towards a Real Character, and a Philosophical Language* (London: Samuel Gellibrand and John Martin, 1668), [ii]. Subsequent page references appear in the text.

12. Borges concocts an encyclopedia called the *Heavenly Emporium of Benevolent Knowledge*; "In its distant pages it is written that animals are divided into (a) those that belong to the emperor; (b) embalmed ones; (c) those that are trained; (d) suckling pigs; (e) mermaids; (f) fabulous ones; (g) stray dogs; (h) those that are included in this classification; (i) those that tremble as if they were mad; (j) innumerable ones; (k) those drawn with a very fine camel's-hair brush; (l) etcetera; (m) those that have just broken the flower vase; (n) those that at a distance resemble flies." Jorge Luis Borges, "John Wilkins' Analytical Language," in *Selected Non-Fictions*, ed. and trans. Eliot Weinberger (New York: Viking, 1999), 231; Michel Foucault, *The Order of Things: An Archaeology of the Human Sciences* (New York: Routledge, 2002 [1966]), xv.

are actually not "more things" but *fewer* "things in heaven and earth" than Horatio dreamed of in his philosophy (*Hamlet*, 1.5.175–76). For example, someone looking at "the Starrs, as they are confusedly scattered up and down in the Firmament, will think them to be . . . innumerable, [and] of so vast a multitude, as not to be determined by any set number." But once they are "reduced into particular constellations . . . it appears . . . there are but few more then [*sic*] a thousand in the whole Firmament" (162). In just the same way, he continues, if one puts the question, "how many sorts of beasts, or birds, &c. there are in the world," even the learned imagine that "there are so many hundreds of them, as could not be enumerated." To the contrary, against these waning et ceteras, on due investigation we find that "they are much fewer then [*sic*] is commonly imagined, not a hundred sorts of Beasts, nor two hundred of Birds" (162). The translator of Caius's *Of English Dogges* had marveled at creaturely variety ("an ignoraunt man would never have been drawne into this opinion to thincke that there had bene in England such variety & choise of dogges, in all respectes . . . so divers and unlike"), and Caius himself found that even dogs "cannot all be reduced and brought under one sorte."[13] Wilkins answers the natural historian's baffled delight—in a wholly antipoetical way. A Mr. Gradgrind *avant la lettre*, he celebrates the finitude that reducing the world to the order of a universal language for "the distinct expression of all things" would afford.

The ark digression takes aim at the "Atheistical scoffers" who raise objections to "the truth and authority of Scripture"; such scoffers argue from a "prejudice" in favor of natural plenitude that "it was utterly impossible for this Ark to hold so vast a multitude." Like Buteo (whom he cites a great deal), Wilkins laments the "miserable shifts" earlier writers were put to, citing their needless travails over the historical cubit and unhelpful suppositions that the human stature on which the cubit depended had diminished (163). Wilkins considers these problems fully resolved in Buteo's treatise, which "proves Mathematically that there was sufficient capacity in the Ark." Yet Wilkins takes exception to one aspect of Buteo's work, namely, "his enumeration of the species of Animals, several of which are fabulous, some not distinct species, [and] others that are true species being left out" (163). Wilkins will "offer another account" to correct any lingering miscalculations his admired predecessor made concerning the ark. No additions are involved.

13. Caius, *Of Englishe Dogges*, 3.

Disqualifying mules as "a mungrel production, and not to be rekoned as a distinct species," and excluding seals, turtles, sea tortoises, crocodiles, and other animals "as can abide in the water" ("tho if . . . necessary . . . there would be room enough for them"), Wilkins subtracts the overtly fabulous animals that Buteo's recourse to natural history allowed. And in order "to prevent . . . Cavils," Wilkins follows Buteo in "suppos[ing] that those Animals which are now Praedatory were so from the beginning" (165). As before, this requires a substantial addition of sheep (but only half of the numbered "3,650 meat-sheep" that Buteo had assumed [33]). The eligibilities determined, Wilkins neatly tabulates a passenger list pared down from eighty-nine to fifty-eight quadruped kinds, cross-referencing not only their dietary needs but also their equivalences in Buteo's common denominators, "beeves," sheep, or wolves (fig. 6.2). "Upon these suppositions," Wilkins concludes, like Buteo and Raleigh before him, in favor of "convenient room in . . . the Ark to contein the forementioned sorts of beasts" (165–66).

There is, however, one other consideration not clarified by the conversion of animals into equivalents: what constitutes "sufficient" or "convenient room"? This question brings Wilkins to juxtapose the imagined living conditions of the ark's animals with those of the livestock animals being shipped on sea voyages in his own time.[14] He remarks that "there might seem no just ground of exception if these beasts should be stow'd close together, as is now usual in Ships, when they are to be transported for any long voyage," but he opts not to crowd the ark's creatures. "Yet I shall not take any such advantage, but afford them such fair Stalls or Cabins as may be abundantly sufficient for them in any kind of posture,

---

14. The history of a global traffic in animals presents further issues, but it may suffice to note that the expanding population of "English" livestock in colonial contexts quickly outstripped the number of English human settlers. Of the Massachusetts Bay Colony, for example, one commentator wondered in 1634, "Can they be very poor where for four thousand souls there are fifteen hundred head of cattle, besides four thousand goats and swine innumerable?" See William Cronon, *Changes in the Land: Indians, Colonists, and the Ecology of New England* (New York: Hill and Wang, 2003 [1983]), 128. For the role of English livestock as vectors of colonization in the unfolding relationship with native peoples, see Virginia Anderson, *Creatures of Empire: How Domestic Animals Transformed Early America* (New York: Oxford University Press, 2004), and especially Anderson, "King Philip's Herds: Indians, Colonists, and the Problem of Livestock in Early New England," *William and Mary Quarterly*, 3rd ser., 51, no. 4 (1994): 601–24.

Beafts feeding on Hay.				Beafts feeding on Fruits, Roots and Infects.				Carnivorous Beafts			
Number.	Name.	Proportion to Beeves.	Breadth of Stalls feet	Number.	Name	Proportion to Sheep.	Breadth of the Stalls. feet	Number.	Name	Proportion to Wolves.	Breadth of their Stalls. feet
2	Horfe	3	20	2	Hog	4		2	Lion	4	10
2	Affe	2	12	2	Baboon	2		2	Beare	4	10
2	Camel	4	20	2	Ape	2		2	Tigre	3	8
2	Elephant	8	36	2	Monky			2	Pard	3	8
7	Bull	7	40	2	Sloth			2	Ounce	2	6
7	Urus	7	40	2	Porcupine	7	20	2	Cat	2	6
7	Bifons	7	40	2	Hedghog			2	Civet-cat		
7	Bonafus	7	40	2	Squirril			2	Ferret		
7	Buffalo	7	40	2	Ginny pig			2	Polecat		
7	Sheep	1	30	2	Ant-bear	2		2	Martin		
7	Stepciferos	1		2	Armadilla	2		2	Stoat	3	6
7	Broad-tail	1		2	Tortoife	2		2	Weefle		
7	Goat	1	30			21	20	2	Caftor		
7	Stone-buck	1						2	Otter		
7	Shamois	1						2	Dog	2	6
7	Antilope	1						2	Wolf	2	6
7	Elke	7	30					2	Fox		
7	Hart	4	30					2	Badger		
7	Buck	3	20					2	Jackall	2	6
7	Rein-deer	3	20					2	Caraguya		
7	Roe	2	36							27	72
2	Rhinocerot	8									
2	Camelopard	6	30								
2	Hare										
2	Rabbet	Sheep									
2	Marmotto										
		92	514								

Figure 6.2. John Wilkins, inventory for Noah's ark, in *An Essay Towards a Real Character* (London, 1668). Image by permission of the Folger Shakespeare Library, Washington, DC.

either standing, or lying, or turning themselves" (166). The imagined ark, with its divine specifications justified by the human science of mathematics, uncannily reflects the exact demands made in contemporary calls for minimum standards concerning livestock confinement—suggesting there was as little real mystery about creature comforts then as there is now.[15] But the real traffic in livestock that Wilkins describes looks totally different, with immobilized "beasts . . . stow'd" as stock inventory and pressed "close together." Though he sees no "just ground" to argue against supposing such realist conditions for his calculations on the ark, he piously allows for "fair . . . Cabins" instead, perhaps in some lingering trace of the cosmopolitical accommodation this book has described.

The math is entirely concocted, either way, but Wilkins's uncanny illustrations show the stakes of choosing between "fair" accommodation and immiserating confinement (fig. 6.3). In his floor plan of the ark's hold, we cannot now fail to see the imminent expansion of a transatlantic trade in human chattel—a contradictory phrase, as "livestock" is. Wilkins's equivocation between accommodation and confinement prefigures the obscene debate about calculations that would arise among ship captains and investors in the eighteenth century: whether "tight-pack" or "loose-pack" methods better maximized slave ship profitability in light of staggering mortality rates in the Middle Passage.[16] In this respect, the manipulations of the status of animals described in chapter 5 make up one episode in a much longer history of the procedures that aim to disanimate bodies—a history that we can afford to read across kinds.

In the elevation of the ark as it was visualized for the Royal Society, we see an opaque gridded box (one window, one door) that eerily evokes the freight containers now transporting domestic animals in grim commerce every day or the no-frills minimalism of modern storage facilities—warehousings that screen our consciousness from the oxymoronic quality of "livestock" as a conceit. In the imagined holds of Noah's ark, early mod-

15. As noted in the introduction, California Proposition 2 (2008), Standards for Confining Farm Animals, prohibits "the confinement of farm animals in a manner that does not allow them to turn around freely, lie down, stand up, and fully extend their limbs" (standard features of life in veal crates, pig gestation crates, or, for hens, battery cages). See "California Proposition 2 (2008)," http://ballotpedia.org/wiki/index .php/California_Proposition_2_%282008%29. See also Amy Hatkoff, *The Inner World of Farm Animals* (New York: Stewart, Tabori, and Chang, 2009). The approach taken by Temple Grandin, by contrast, recalls Cartesian binarism by sequestering "the way animals think" as a mystery that nonneurotypical humans can "decode" and "translate into English." This understanding does not much disturb the Cartesian paradigm—or Grandin's "meat-packing industry" employers either. Temple Grandin and Catherine Johnson, *Animals in Translation: Using the Mysteries of Autism to Decode Animal Behavior* (New York: Scribner, 2005), 6–7, 12.

16. See Hillary Beckles and Verene Shepherd, *Trading Souls: Europe's Transatlantic Trade in Africans* (Kingston, Jamaica: Ian Randall, 2007), 66–67.

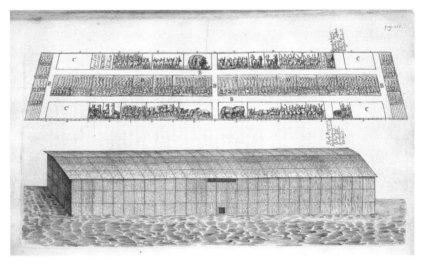

Figure 6.3. John Wilkins, floor plan/elevation of the ark, in *An Essay Towards a Real Character* (London, 1668). Image by permission of the Folger Shakespeare Library, Washington, DC.

ern calculations disanimate creatures more abstractly than the theatrics of vivisection or suffocation did. But together these methods did more than strengthen barriers against any ethical and epistemological accountability to the subjective investments animals might have. Appreciation of the prodigal diversity of nature's forms had long endured as a central cultural and religious value in its own right. As we saw in the context of traditional imaginings of the embarkation (plate 2), the sheer diversity of animal embodiment held pride of place in manifesting that value. In foreclosing our consideration of animals as even liminally legitimate stakeholders, all these seventeenth-century techniques helped to erode what Boyle saw as an inconvenient "veneration" of natural variety as such; his innovation was to cast this admiration as retrograde because it operated as "a discouraging impediment to the empire of man over the inferior creatures of God."[17] If Noah's ark embarked as a ship of cosmopolitical state, where the array of animal representatives entered of their "owne accord" in a great pageant of kinds, the terms and conditions of its modern landings suggest their sinister conversion to chattel instead. Implementing a program of *empire absolu* over docile bodies, these disanimating human

17. Robert Boyle, *A Free Enquiry into the Vulgarly Received Notion of Nature*, ed. Edward Davis and Michael Hunter (Cambridge: Cambridge University Press, 1996 [1686]), 15.

schemes "reduce" the claims of nonhuman creatures, in Bacon's words, "to nothing."[18]

In the elevation of humanity that attended this reduction, little remains of the self-deprecating species critique that was so compelling to Montaigne. He had ended "Of Experience" (the last essay in the *Essais*) with the decidedly un-Cartesian musing that "it were an absolute perfection, and as it were divine for a man to know how to *enjoy his being loyally*"; though humankind longs to "get upon stilts," he counsels, "yet must we goe with our owne legges."[19] Humility, which Montaigne paradoxically understands here as loyalty to our embodied particularity, disappears from the language used by advocates for prosthetic or technoscientific human mastery—Descartes's "empire absolu sur tous les autres animaux"; Hooke's "Prerogative of Mankind above other creatures"; Boyle's "empire of man over the inferior creatures."[20] But even these phrasings still sound the echo of a dispensation that conceived human power over their nonhuman subjects in fundamentally political terms. Insofar as interspecies relations were framed as political or constitutional ones, they intimated some scrutiny over the legitimacy of (human) authority and the just exercise of (human) power. Thus Montaigne's book winds down to a waggish end with a deflating caution about how human sovereignty fares under such scrutiny. "Sit we upon the highest throne of the World," he points out drolly, "yet sit we upon our owne taile."[21]

18. Francis Bacon, *The Works of Francis Bacon*, vol. 3, *The Wisdom of the Ancients*, ed. Basil Montagu (Philadelphia: Parry and McMillan, 1859), 297.

19. Michele de Montaigne, "Of Experience," in *Essayes*, 1013 (italics added).

20. René Descartes, *Oeuvres et lettres*, ed. André Bridoux (Paris: La Pléiade, 1953), 1254; Robert Hooke, *Micrographia, or Some Physiological Descriptions of Minute Bodies made by Magnifying Glasses* (London: John Martin and James Allestry, 1665), i.

21. Montaigne, "Of Experience," 1013. The French refers (less metaphorically than Florio's translation) to what William Baldwin's *Beware the Cat* called our "bare arse": "Et au plus eslevé throne du monde si ne sommes assis que sus nostre cul." "De L'Experience," in *Les essais de Michel de Montaigne: Édition conforme au texte de l'exemplaire de Bordeaux*, ed. Pierre Villey (Lausanne, Switzerland: La Guilde du Livre, 1965 [1924]), 1115.

INDEX

accommodated (definition), 11–12, 141–73, 279–81
Ackerley, J. R., 218–19
Adam, 40, 43, 48, 51, 57–64, 76, 80, 142–43, 182
Aelian, 86
Aesop, 73–74, 201
Agamben, Giorgio, 3, 34–35, 53–54, 81, 129, 131n8, 190n19, 220n7, 247
Albertus Magnus, 205
Alstijns, Steen, 100–101
Ambrose, 86
Anderson, Virginia, 279n14
anima, 26, 88, 99, 225–26. *See also* disanimation
animal (as English noun), 2, 6–11, 53, 80–81, 129, 137
animal complaint, 19, 53, 61, 64, 76, 116n78, 118n81, 151, 257
animal imagery, 5–6, 31, 35–36, 49, 199
animal reason, 152–53
animal rights, 32, 38, 221n11
ant, 17, 71
ape, 1, 71, 91–92, 96, 213, 250
Aquinas, Thomas, 55
Aristophanes, 91
Aristotle: on animal classification, 48, 92, 99, 202, 265, 273; on animal development, 141, 158; on human negative exceptionalism, 165; on motion, 26, 84, 91, 94n35, 107, 116, 219, 226; on parts, 82n1, 84, 219, 250; on political life, 3, 54, 56; on speech, 54, 71; on uprightness, 82n1, 88; on vision, 97n38

ark, Noah's, 11, 21–22, 48, 59–64, 99, 270–82
asp, 273
ass, 8, 29, 216, 250
Atwood, Margaret, 75n110
Augustine, 271, 274

Bach, Rebecca Ann, 67n23, 138n23, 231n36
Bacon, Francis, 86, 104, 227–28, 249–50, 283
Baldwin, William, 184, 199–212
baselisk, 273
bear, 8, 67, 113, 131, 168, 180, 213, 250, 273
beast (as English noun), 7, 9n20
beast fable, 69, 73–74
beast-machine doctrine, 1, 14–15, 17n32, 18, 186–90. *See also* clock; machine; robot
Bentham, Jeremy, 3
Berger, John, 22, 50
Berry, Edward, 67n98, 114n76
bestiality, 230n34
bestiary, 8, 71
bison, 273
blackbird, 64, 276
blindness, 194–96. *See also* humans
boar, 9, 62, 100–101, 112, 157, 180, 239
Boas, George, 134–36, 155
Boehrer, Bruce, 18, 129, 207n43, 229, 230n34, 244
Bono, James, 48, 94, 274
Book of Creatures, 4n7, 6, 46–49
Borges, Jorge Luis, 110, 277
Boyle, Robert, 27, 259–60, 262–65, 282, 283
Breton, Nicholas, 76
Bryskett, Lodovick, 229
Brockbank, William, 108n64, 199n28

finch, 64
Fleming, Abraham, 111
flight (volitation), 95, 198, 262–63
Floridi, Lucian, 86
fly, 17, 40, 64, 79
Fontaine, Nicholas, 48
Foucault, Michel, 34–35, 98, 118–20, 266, 277
fox, 8, 71, 112, 202, 207
Freccero, Carla, 172n65
Freedberg, David, 110
French, Roger, 251n75
Freud, Sigmund, 97n38, 126n92
frog, 73, 94, 179
Fudge, Erica, xv, 1n2, 18, 52n63, 60n79, 71, 86n12, 129, 230n34, 237

Galen, 95, 227, 250–57
Galileo, 48
Gascoigne, George, 19, 76–78, 105–6, 108n64, 115–18, 149, 171
Gelli, Giovanni Battista, 131, 136, 151–64, 169, 171–72, 268–69
Genesis: on animal entitlements, 11, 12, 19, 41–42, 64, 75–79, 81, 100, 107, 225, 233–36; on animal innocence, 51, 57, 81; as a constitutional document, 2, 19, 35–42, 68; creaturely idiom of, 10, 11, 40; on the dispensation after the Ark, 59–64, 76, 270, 271–72; Edenic human stewardship, 13, 56, 98, 182; on the Fall of man, 56, 59–66, 79, 80; on nakedness, 142–43; as natural history, 35–42, 53, 68, 74, 272; on plants, 100; on the order of creation, 57, 59, 78–79, 248; sixteenth-century readings of, 37, 49–53, 56–66
Gesner, Conrad, 33, 48, 92, 109, 145
giraffe, 21
goat, 25, 136, 139, 155, 156, 250, 269
Goldberg, Jonathan, 10n23
Golding, Arthur, 88
goose, 7, 194, 202
Gouwens, Kenneth, 92n30
Gradgrind, Thomas, 278
Grandin, Temple, 281n15
Gratian, 45
Greenblatt, Stephen, 130
greyhound, 84
Guerrini, Anita, 250

hang-dog look, 228–30, 266
happiness, 150–51
happy beast tradition, 134–36, 173, 202, 204

Haraway, Donna, 5, 49–50, 130, 218n2
hare, 112, 115–18, 136, 149, 156, 169, 171, 207, 273
Harrison, Peter, 47, 108–9, 182n10, 274
hart, 8, 78
Harvey, William, 9n20, 250, 251, 259n93
hawk, 194
Hearne, Vicki, 97n38
hedgehog, 145, 180, 202, 206–7, 273
Heidegger, Martin, 164
hellhound, 9, 273
hen, 194
Herophilus, 250
Herrup, Cynthia, 45
hind, 8, 70, 136, 158
Hobbes, Thomas, 55, 108, 225
Höfele, Andreas, 18, 132n11
Hoffmann, Hans, 100
Homily on Obedience, Edwardine, 43, 102
Hooke, Robert, 26–27, 197–99, 226, 259–62, 283
Hooker, Richard, 44, 103
horse, 7, 8, 22, 40, 62, 68, 95, 136, 155, 250, 273
Howard, Henry, 105, 106
Huizinga, Johan, 175
human exceptionalism, 12–13, 17, 20, 34, 53, 56, 91, 91n30, 107, 128–32, 135–41, 149n41, 154, 173, 195, 197, 219, 268
human negative exceptionalism, 7, 20, 82, 132–33, 135–41, 149, 170, 173, 267
humans: bad diet of, 156–57; blind spots, 27–28; bloody-mindedness of, 77–78, 81; children, 236, 239; constitutional cruelty of, 76; creation of, 50–51; Fall of, 51–52, 182n10, 197; folly of, 20, 79, 153, 166, 178, 181n9, 196, 211–12, 228, 266–67; as naked, 19–20, 125–26, 127–73; nearsightedness of, 36, 96, 98, 193; night blindness, 178–79; panoptical aspirations of, 19–20, 98, 118, 197; slavery among, 156, 221, 281; as upright biped, 19–20, 83–85, 88–98, 124–26, 127–28, 180–81, 214–16; women/gender, 57n75, 93n31, 141, 156, 157–58, 193
hyena, 145, 273, 275

Ives, George, 241

James I, 46, 56, 86, 121–22
Jansen, Theo, 26
Jardine, Lisa, 204n39, 259
Jardine, Nicholas, 36